AMERICAN CYCLE

AMERICAN CYCLE

Larry Beckett

Running Wild Press

Published in North America and Europe by Running Wild Press. Visit
Running Wild Press at www.runningwildpress.com
ISBN (pbk) 978-1-947041-65-3
ISBN (hdbk) 978-1-947041-71-4
ISBN (ebook) 978-1-947041-66-0

Contents

U. S. Rivers

Highway 1

Key West: *Oh the cuckoo*
the ship, missing
stays and drifting
in the Gulf Stream, gone down
on the mermaid reefs
is a pretty bird
where hurricanes rake,
and it's, Wreck ashore!
where the first man
to it has rights of salvage.

I dance all night
At the rickety pier,
the chains in rust,
vague shacks in the first light,
and out
of the old-time Palm Tree Saloon,
with a bottle in my hand
with a stop
to gas up at the Chevron station,
no map,

the only traffic, this early,
oncoming
pickups, with fishermen,
the morning prayer
on the buzz radio,
and she warbles
I gun it
and shifting, into high
as she flies
I'm rolling, only one way:

turn onto A-bomb Avenue,
into
New Deal Boulevard,
I'm looking for a woman

the Overseas
toward Islamorada
ain't got no man
on the ghost railroad line,
over the manatees,
one hundred miles.

Salt wind, high wave:
no meaning *and I see yes
I see*:
in the Chevrolet Impala,
the V-8 engine sings
like the birds of
America, in this key:
*on the fourth day
of July*: skyrockets,
and our rainbow.

Off the king's road,
in the scrub oaks,
low palmettoes,
the pine barrens,

he wades into
black mud, on this
indian horse,
to the mangroves:

at last, it's caught
in Audubon's
eye, the first white-
crowned pigeon.

Look, sandpipers: and a green rush,
Columbus:

a stick, with marks,
cane, grass, *Children go*
and a candle, lifted:
the Indies, on
internal power with
the launch vehicle,
aim at the naked men:
obey or die.

T minus 12 *apostles*
seconds and counting,
the conquistador,
and his chaplain, 11
who went to heaven
What longitude, *go where*
see miracle, a light
9 *bright shiners*
ignition sequence starts,
where I thunder,

in the alien sky
oh long enough
to say two Credos: 8
April rainers
downrange, launch vector east
near the equator,
as the earth whirls:
7 *stars* Capture Seloy,
I send rename it 6
proud walkers after

the day, St. Augustine:
5 *symbols at*
your door: de Leon, man
in the moon, walks
all waters, looking for
the fountain, easter,

finding this island, flowery,
Florida, fire,
before
the Caloosahatchee arrow,

3 *rivals* here,
at Cape Canaveral,
in the canebrakes,
2 *lily-white boys*
the Saturn V *in green*
1 *one and all*
alone zero, liftoff
on Apollo 11,
tower cleared: *Children*
go where I send thee.

      Long night, St. Pete,
      Kerouac can't
      drift off, in his
      lawn chair, empty

      bottle, listens
      to the wind blow
      off Long Bayou,
      talking to him

      in the branches,
      Shimmy, show, shhh,
      the Georgia pine
      tangled in stars.

The sanctuary *Hushabye*
on the backwater
don't you cry Ebenezer,
the rock of help,

is a haven: I got no bitch,
says Davis,
with the black pioneers:
for the white ibis,
in the tupelo and cypress,
the heron:

cutting the March
to the Sea, for our wagons
go to sleepy
of corn, all plunder off
the Georgia plantations
little baby where
our bummers shot ever last
pig: let em starve:
it's them slow followers
we freed, always hungry.

Okefenokee: walk
on the blowups,
and the earth quivers:
from deep in, paradise,
the sun daughters
save hunters, and then, Pole
off, on the blackwater,
When you wake or our men
will do you in: *you shall have*
that island, lost.

Once over: the creek
in winter: take up
the pontoons, and strand them
all the pretty.
But at the rear, the rebels
shoot contrabands,
coming to slash
boys, girls to death, and haul

the women back
little horses to masters:

nowhere to go, the old man's drowning,
No more
hundred lash and the wife's under,
for me the son
washes away: *Many thousands*
gone: he'll
make brevet major general.
In the rear view
mirror, it's burning:
oh headlights, light up grace.

      Back from the late
      turpentine camp
      juke joint, down home,
      the mother, Ma

      Rainey lays down
      her ostrich plume,
      necklace of coins:
      she blues, *Rider,*

      her audience
      the tethered rain
      and her soul, *See*
      what you have done.

Outside Columbia,
in the low country,
she boils the black-eyed peas
tender 2 cups,
across from the pine ridge,
The hills shall fly

8

exiled to the old farm house
by the redcoats
from her home, Buckhead,
fries six thick bacon,

Light Horse:—This siege
may fail, *my turtle dove*:
more come, we see their lights,
and the Swamp Fox,
cooks onion clear, celery stalks, half
bay leaf,
regrets to burn your mansion.
Rebecca Motte:
—Don't hesitate. You may
use these fire arrows;

and the loud billows burn
3 from the long
bamboo quiver,
half teaspoon red pepper,
simmers, set flame
to the shingles;
before my heart
scared of their own powder,
the British climb
out into bullets, stirs in

2 cups brown rice,
shall ever fail their colors
fall, and the white flag rises,
and foes pitch in
to save the house: she serves
up Hoppin John,
or I a traitor turn
to Carolina.
—You were heroic.
—Any American woman. . .

At Snow's Island,
laurel shadow,
where nobody
can ever follow,

Marion rakes
sweet potatoes
out of the ashes:
Unblindfold him.

The officer:
Your uniform?
Is my old rags.
You live on roots?

And swamp water.
You draw good pay?
Not a cent, sir.
I don't follow.

For liberty.
He shakes his head:
What chance have we?
I'm quitting war.

Governor White, gone for supplies,
Oh bide,
no time, no Angels, spent
against the damned
Armada,
sailing, years after, crosses
the treachery waters
to the barrier islands,
anchoring at the colony

lady, bide:

the old red man, starting
the milk white doe
in the shaky land,
box kite dragging, on high,
White sees fire, has them
trumpet old tunes,
he always tells her, no
answer: grass burned,
and savage prints, *bide*,
increase wingspan

over chord, for lift:
he hunts her up
the Island, to the Sound,
White finds no crosses,
testimonies, cut
in the bark, danger,
front rudder, against pitch,
at Roanoke,
the medicine man had
will be your love

the sea nymphs change her
Then she becomes
Where is Virginia Dare? First child:
down houses,
high palisade, lost colony:
she crosses
the Ridge, wing warping,
against roll,
a turtle dove
and one young maid escaped

the slaughter, *to fly*
up in the air

back rudder, against yaw:
books torn, maps spoiled
with rain, White looks
south to Cape Hatteras,
no sign, and north,
across Shallowbag Bay
to Kill
Devil Hills, the life saving station,

as Wright feathers
the vertical wing, he
shoots the silver tipped arrow
and he becomes
through her *an old cock pigeon*
into the freezing
headwind, at Kitty Hawk,
over the dunes,
and sees Virginia,
and they *fly pair and pair*.

On a fire hunt
out at Deep Creek,
lifting the light,
behind the hazel

and plum bushes,
he shines its eyes:
Boone, his rifle
up, flinches, why,

and the deer bolts:
he chases her
back to her covert
at Bryan's farm:

she has become,

in her rose skin,
a girl, sixteen,
and shined his eyes.

Six days upriver *Oh*
Shenandoah,
this tidewater will
be farms, they haul Smith:
in the York estuary,
Washington's fires
after six years, because
the count, his frigates
and his ships of the line,
hold Chesapeake,

I long to hear you
and the young marquis,
over the peninsula,
holds Carolina,
against retreat:
a captive, and across
the double ditches:
he digs siege lines
in dirt easy from rain,
the cannons open

at Yorktown: they take two
redoubts *away*
you rolling river
to the sacred ground:
American winds
turn back last hope
ferries from Gloucester Point:
at the long house,
in coonskin robe, before
the fire, before

Powhatan, in bravery:
supply line cut,
old meat, biscuits with worms:
water to wash,
feathers to dry, feast and powwow
we're bound
away: lay hands on him,
lay down, lift clubs:
the wanton, Pocahontas:
the works crumble:

white flag: the drum
parley: dear daughter, crying
in vain, cradles
his head, lays hers on his,
what is she? twelve
returns of the leaf old:
the lord surrenders
his sword: eight thousand
prisoners: and her
bare breast on his: *I love*

your daughter and
saves him: in the green field
they lay down arms:
the king: Hatchets for me,
and bells of copper
for her *I crossed*
and Jamestown will
hang on, her cartwheeling
your rolling water ring,
and the war's won.

The winter slams
against the coast,

and ice is on
the reeds: there go

the blackbirds and
my love into
the common clouds.
Ah, Chesapeake!

the sun is low,
the water's black
and blue, what she
had said, blowing

away. I rock
to sleep, but for
my heart there is
no lullaby.

Grace walks out of
the cherry trees, the roaring
Hurrah! hurrah, boys,
after the election:
twenties, into the oval
office: so tired:
in that swinging glass
Lincoln sees *we bring*
the jubilee two faces.
At the White House,

south portico,
the Marine Band playing
the anthem *O say can*
you and she sees
his spirit, his hands
behind his back: the generals
and aides, ladies in hoop

skirts, Cabinet,
hats off: get up, it's gone,
lie down, it's there.

The President hauls on
the cord *the flag*
that makes you free; it sticks;
harder: nine stars
rip off: pale double;
his wife: a sign you won't
see life through your
next term: his ghost looks over
the Potomac *from*
Atlanta to the sea.

Open fire, Tom
Jefferson, he
sighed, in the snow
of revolution,

oh and lay
the redcoat low:
I had no heart
for violence

and let him go.
I woke up to
the morning news
on the radio.

Out at the Highway 17
bridge, over
the Combahee *River*
Jordan's deep, the engineers,
under the marsh, uncover

rice fields, unearth
They call her Araminta
these shards, all burned:
and hire her out to masters
site of the raid

in sixty-three: for dozing
at the cradle,
whipscar, her face:
the ferry crossing *and*
wide: these Union gunboats:
She says she's Harriet
in command *Tell*
old Pharoah and she walks
up the Eastern Shore,
out of Maryland,

morning, early *When the sun*
come back
blast horns, lift flags
to the slave huts *the first*
quail calls:
no arms open to her: she lays
the underground
railroad *Follow* They crowd
the launches *Let my*
people, and won't let go

till she sings *Milk and honey*
to peace them *on*
the other side Black soldiers
burn down the bridge,
fire the plantations:
seven hundred fifty-six
go free, hitch rides, the big
rigs rolling on
the widened highway: Call her

go down Moses.

> In Mobtown, with
> red eye shot glass,
> the Sun deadline
> before morning,
>
> Mencken, at his
> old exalted
> typewriter, cock-
> eyed on blue pig,
>
> is marking out
> for us, the long
> American white
> lightning language.

In the November frost,
the opening
All paths, the doors
of the calumet, *and*
the wigwam rattles,
songs: the Declaration
Jefferson had lain
on the table: *We*
will live on the shore,
sloping down to

the Delaware *while*
the creeks and rivers run
at Shackamaxon,
summer fishing, where
chiefs come: Independence
from the king *captivating*
them, into slavery

struck out by Georgia:
without a firearm, Penn
says *love* under

the Treaty elm:
to keep open a market
in a half moon,
Tammanend, for the down river
people: by Carolina
where MEN should be
bought & sold council,
each hand *one flesh, one blood*:
Ah, Philadelphia:
they shout, *Amen*.

> Never, says Ben
> Franklin, again
> stand by while she's
> burning, never,
>
> Quaker City,
> at the first cry
> thither we will
> repair, with our
>
> buckets, our bags,
> and our fire hooks,
> with salvation,
> pumping water.

Washington crossing,
his blue army walks
in snow, barefoot, bleeding:
Dance to the Kill
King? Power! *music*

assassinates the window:
Joseph, divinity
student, rounds up
East State, make peace
All we need is a drummer.

The rebels take
King, and aim the cannons:
So that the dancers Diamonds
fly off, apples,
easy chairs steal away,
golf balls stinging the pigs
on Perry *just won't hide*:
this officer, cracking
off a warning, is jammed,
guns Joseph down.

Under the Battle
Monument, firebombs
kill Trenton, bricks
hail on the firefighters
the horns blowing: only
abandoned lots,
hotels: the governor holds
an ice cream cone:
Go home! over the river,
crossing Washington.

    Impossible.
    Not in series,
    in multiple
    arc, and the wire:

    not platinum.
    Not silicon.
    Not I forget,

says Edison.

In a vacuum,
thread of carbon:
it burns so long.
Incandescent.

Come on and hear The river
that flows both ways:
Beilin, on bags and samovar,
and featherbed:
Gull Island,
where the Lenape catch fish:
his last name, melting:
Baline, ship's manifest,
dipping to starboard,
Israel at the rail:

Alexander's Ragtime Band
in the sound
of the mystery Hudson,
Oyster Island,
where the Dutch salt herring:
Come on along
On the Lower East Side,
the sidewalk rhymes:
take you in New York Harbor,
Ellis Island,

where he listens to them
dreaming in twelve
languages, under the four
bronze cupolas:
green Liberty: first song,
for the Chinatown
cafe and Marie,

thirty-seven cents;
on the sheet music, the misprint:
Irving Berlin.

In your last days,
unknown, burning
with rum and all
the losing,

in a back room,
you picked out tunes
on a broke down
piano.

Fly down, oh minstrel,
for just a day,
in the American
air:

any old kid
on the long sidewalk
can sing you Oh!
Susanna.

The oldest municipal rose,
Hartford,
and where the river once,
the highway goes,
to Accident & Indemnity,
and terms
that limit coverage:
the lesser of:
your interest in *sea surface
full of clouds.*

The silver current runs into
New Haven
Harbor, around the Green,
the grid, to Ives
& Myrick: in determining
the cost,
do not include: excavations,
foundations,
piers, shores, or *Central Park
in the dark.*

      —Come on in, to
      the billiard room,
      take a swallow
      of this raw corn,

      and call me Sam.
      Plenty of light:
      out that window,
      Connecticut,

      out this, deck of
      a sidewheeler,
      the Mississippi:
      this manuscript

      is voices in
      the air, hero
      a refugee
      of pain, floating

      down with his now
      free companion:
      I can brag; my
      quill was lightning.

After the *we left behind*
lullaby,
from the so muddy road,
the sleep before
flying, waking
to listen *look ye there*:
who is it, ah, she lifts the latch,
Anne, banished
from the Colony
for defending Eve

and the redskins,
the steeple blown away
gone east of Eden, down
into Rhode Island;
—Open the *look ye there*:
she sips our cider
as the rain falls, sits at
the stranger's fire,
and whispers, —It's
a blessing to be a woman.

     Out of the grey
     estuary,
     the damnation
     triangle: rum,

     to Africa, slaves,
     like crayfish in
     tins, to the Indies,
     molasses, to

     Newport: old salt
     hangs out, sign of
     sanctuary,

a pineapple.

Old Solitaire,
that gull, on the Long Wharf
Why come ye hither, long years,
signs bad weather:
the April night: October morning:
the king's
redcoats photo reconnaissance,
crossing
the river: launch site
your heart what madness

at San Cristobal:
Kennedy:—Air strike—but then. . .
In the North Church steeple
show two lanterns
if out by water,
if by land, one:
Joint Chiefs *danger*
on our hills: all out invasion,
if it bring holocaust:
and the Sons of

Liberty send
Revere, riding to Lexington,
warn Hancock, warn
Oh hear ye not: stop Soviet
ships bound for Cuba *but*
ye'll learn to back:
the rebel's arrested,
and the deacon's horse:
Strategic Air Command
goes DEFCON 2:

one slip, and the last fire:

shots, they abandon
him *wild and free*
as the day breaks. In secret
we withdraw Jupiters
from Turkey: cold warriors
govern by fear. The gull
lands: Boston answers:
against the easterly blow,
this vigilance.

Ah, why leaf through
it, that blue book,
the empty sky,
the clouds the white

absurd, in winds
no syllables,
but noise, and on
the throne, no being?

Sailor, not faith,
that froth, for us,
white on white on
the old surface:

like god, you are
nowhere; for now,
I look down, to
words redeeming

the ivory page:
heaven's your art.
In the beginning
was Ishmael.

At the raising,
the sailors come in from
New Hampshire miles
and dare *A Yankee* sloop:
the master builder —*Blow,*
boys, blow: into
the sun, to lift
the frame *her masts*, and pin
the ribs *and spars*,
and set the ridgepole, sails.

At noon, kids run
and wrestle, as old timers
smoke and gossip
over cider: What shall
we christen her? The Ranger:
name on the barn:
Her colors? Silk, girls cut
from gowns; the Stars
and Stripes, for the first time,
float out behind her.

      He, to windward,
      is giving chase
      in the light air,
      and advancing.

      She, coming up
      on the larboard
      quarter, abreast:
      commence broadside.

      In fire: making
      headway, he rams
      her stern: and she:
      —Has your ship struck?

The rogue, alias
Jones, smiling:
—I have not yet
begun to fight.

You get a line the Chevy
shaking over
the two-lane highway flowing
north, *for beauty*
in the dark, like
the Allagash, old trail,
in Maine: she shows me briar,
and blueberry,
fireweed: *I'll get a pole*
white pine, rare birches

honey: this mist, these ghosts:
the power, what's
unseen: desire
is south. *I'm looking for*
I downshift
past Caribou, as U. S. 1
runs out, I turn
toward *a woman* the Windy
City: slide otherways,
follow the moon.

Thoreau, floating,
with his old flute,
charming the moon
in the shallows,

remembers dark
summer, the fire

by the edge, sky-
rockets, sailing,

dear brother, on
his lonesome, at
home, on the wild
American shore.

Old California

Sobre el balcon, la luna,
de las noches blancas:
a ella, le arrojo mis besos,
y alzo una cancion.

Sobre la tierra, estoy,
para las frontreras
cortada; y la batahola
esta sin fin.

Embarcadero

I hear them horses coming, ah! in the dull
thunder, ain't going to let them catch me,
cut loose from the Old Bay, and now the bark
the Iris, around the Horn, out of the blue
bag of waters, jump ship, go walking Spanish,
as I touch shore, I'm an outlaw: so this
is California! I won't suffer the old man,
his lash, for one more hour, sick of gawking
at mermaids: how can you screw if they're
all fish below? It's the first mate and his
sailmaker, hunting me: should I have hid
in the sea mist, in that pine grove? I hunker,
in a low creek, inside a willow; a ranchero,
it's all over, on a dream horse, and silver-
figured saddle, sees me, and steps on past,
intercepts them: "Americanos, what do you
look for out here in the wiregrass?" "Oh,
one more runaway sailor: you seen him?"
"Quien, senor? Not on this rancho." "It's
fifty U. S. dollars if you turn him in."
"Lo siento; I've run into no stranger on
my morning ride." His colt's tail, switching.
They whirl off, on grays on loan, and he
swings lightly to the earth, gold studs
in his sun spurs. "You didn't finger me:
it's good money." His shoulders go back,
all honor: "Ah, a thousand hills, a woman
with charms, and the old fandango tonight:
I don't need dollars; but if I had only one
pale adobe, you are my guest, I would not
betray you." "But I crawled on to your land
by chance." "Or were dropped by a stork:
ride back with me, senor, on the half moon
anquera behind the saddle; I'll welcome you
with firewater." "I've nothing but the salt of
the seven seas to thank you for my freedom."
"Call it even," he says. All this babbling,

I want a suck. Hey Swan, another round;
that free?
        The blue-eyed bartender, saying,
Oh sure, whiskey for naething, and I'll buy
me oatmeal wi' a smile, you bastart,
                banged
a bottle down, by the can of oysters, box
of crackers; the fugitive sailor, John Light,
opened his hand toward his companion at
the table, saying,
          All right, amigo, how'd you
get here?
        Donde es su tierra? My country
is where I live, and not where I was born.
Touch glasses.
         A su salud, compadre! Well,
who is your mother?
          She is the green hills.
Your father?
      He's here, not visible.
               Why
do I talk to you? I get nothing out of you.
Green hills. I swear, from now on I'm going
to call you Misterioso.
          You're dreaming me,
amigo.
     They listened, waves like horses.
Captain Light,
         day-dark in the entry, this
indian, in sea otter skin, said. Light stood,
and nodding toward him:
           Ship's in, vamoose!
to work. What does it come to, Mister Swan?

Out of the rainbow of bottles in the first
saloon, down the street to the pine canyon,
the beach where the Spanish merchant looked,

in vain, for pearls and empire, later claimed
by the captain, slinging pebbles, pulling
up grass, possession, while the sharp padre
said mass and dreamed of northern missions,
nothing there now but white sand, old oak,
the dug out calaboose for sleeping it off,
down shore from the adobe Custom House,
where the U. S. commodore and marines,
not finding any troops, officials in town
to overcome, hoisted the Stars and Stripes
and conquered California, last year, after
skirmishes, and the Los Angeles surrender,
Light, who they called captain but who
was not, walked, with a red bandanna on
his gypsy head, pure shirt, blue pantaloons,
fisherman's shoes, at his side, faithfully,
his mystery partner, dark, in white, tall
but slouching, born to the vulgar tongue,
and in back, the indian, leading the way,
his robe flapping open on his naked body.
He took a breath of the year of grace '47,
and whistled three times, gazing out over
the bay of Monterey, into the grey offing,
the local horizon, where earth touches heaven:
this was before the revolution stars faded,
before the gold rush, and the southern wound,
in the days before paradise turned invisible.
Out of his rough shanty, on the white hill,
old sails, around redwood poles, for walls,
sight of the water, landfalls and departures,
red men with nothing on were shouldering
stacks of skins and baskets on down into
the launch: the lashings were undone from
the pier of stones quarried by deserters,
prisoners, indians, as he sat in the stern:

Moon Snail, what ship?
                              Columbia.
                                        She
was riding at anchor, with her sails reefed.
Ah, Hudson's Bay Company.
                              Misterioso sang
ahoy, out to its empty deck:
                              Hail Columbia,
the dove, who sailed over the lifting waves:
to this green island.
                              You and your double
talk: it's another job, and heads or tails.
Indians rowed through easy water, Light
at the rudder:
                              Fine haul this morning, boys.
His dark amigo, out of nowhere:
                                        I worked
for this old cock: first day: "You're new,
I got to learn you my ways. I'm a man of
few words: when I whistle, I don't mean lag
or ask why: you just come running." I said,
"I'm just like you, few words; now, when
you whistle, and I shake my head like this,
it means, I ain't coming."
                              Misterioso, now
I feel bad for commanding.
                              It's a good bad.
Oh whistle, and I'll come to ye, my lad.
At the rope ladder, Light:
                              Where's Burns?
The mate above:
                              Long story. I'm supercargo
this run. What skins you bring?
                                        Ah, blacktail
deer, wildcat, otter: seen their baskets?
                                        For
the love of

Yeah: it's iris, cattail, bulrush,
willow, in coils, and all these little shells
sewn in, to shapes.
        The best I ever
             They're
watertight, go mother to daughter.
                Why are
your red men trading for red cinnabar?
                  Skin
painting.
        I'll haul their consignment up. . .
Light said to lift the sail on the one mast
of his quick cutter, no name, looking out
over the bowsprit to Lovers Point, catching
the wind that blows off the land at sundown,
holding to shore, by Pinos, canting south,
the lonesome cypress, coiling out of time,
white surf booming into the cliffs, giving
sea room to the green shoals, oh running in,
violet waves, and in the mist, Point Lobos,
his partner leaning on the pole, and singing
under his breath.

        Low hills, like a woman
on her side, lying by the slow San Jose
Creek, sliding into the ocean, the danger
waters, and a village to last only through
summer, built over and over for centuries,
on land that glory, Dona Abrego, sold
por nada to soldiers, to General Castro,
who reckoned all who lived on it as his.
Lion Howling, the chief, thin silver beard,
walked naked to his willow house, its walls
of tule reeds, where his wife sat wrapping
up balls of acorn meal in alder leaves;
he asked her if there was more than plenty
of the manzanita wine Captain Light loved,

and said in seeing him come up the beach:

Bienvenido to all that's left of Ichxenta,
el capitan!
        No need to hold festival when
it's only me.
          Feast first, and business after:
we love to dance, for the lightest reason,
for days. Our ceremony house is only
a circle of raised earth and a brush fence.
We have pine seeds, blackberries, fresh
mussels, trout, cider, acorn bread.
            I give
you thanks, or is that trading?
           Ah, senor,
white men only talk past me; you listen,
we heart to heart.
        To be honest, you were
a market I had to myself, but now I value
your prayer sticks and your peace.
           I'm saying
what I say like our brief prayers, carried
in smoke up to the sun. We're in the swim,
these days, uncertain waters, and under-
currents. But this, our commerce, our give
and take, may only last more circles of
that sun if you marry my girl, Salt Wave.
You'd get a woman, and a home, season
by season, kin, a circle of hands to work
for you. For a bride price, all I'm asking,
one stone, red obsidian: our grace to you,
for by your graces we hang on.
          I know
riptides, off shore, and in these times.
What is rippling in her green heart?
          Oh we
can't let her wed just anybody: marriage,

more than desire, is connection, a river
of hope. We've chosen him for her since
Coyote and the first woman.
                              Stars are in
my eyes! I hadn't cast off to dream of man
and wife. And what if she
                              Looks outside
your bed of grass? You overlook it.
                              Who
owns this country?
                    Quien sabe? You're all
questions and no contract: sleep over it.

Seeds in cocoons, in hoofs, rattling,
sticks, hand claps, log drumming, reed,
bone whistle, blowing, voices moaning,
dancers lifting: Salt Wave, her hair
free, her lily earrings, blue tattoos,
scallop necklace, on her bare breasts,
low riding skirt, of lark and raven,
on her tilting hips, on her bare feet,
she swayed, above her, a shower of
the downfall stars.
                    His partner lifted wine:
It's so: lo bailado. The dance, once danced:
they can't take it away.

                    In the quiet of
the stars, Pacific, history, over the big
adobe, no bull or bear out back, whores
all done and gone, the men at sea, in their
dream waters, this supply depot and long
time hotel, one light was burning, against
open questions, and the dark, the newsman
drawling away at Light:
                    Our little rag's
first in the territory, but the all fired

and sky west press they give me! So old,
Adam must've let roll the book of names
and scrapped it: I ain't a typesetter, I'm
a damn archaeologist! Holes in the balls;
no rules, no leads: I cut em with a jack-
knife; type all rusty: I took and scoured
the letters; ink in a keg; and nothing but
cigarito paper to print on; my lord! Out
of this chaos comes the one sheet gazette:
it sure ain't how we done them almanacs
back home.
   And what's the news?
         Loose hogs
are banned in San Francisco.
        Simple, out
of Kentucky, tall as a horse, in buckskin
and fringes, and a foxskin hat never off
his flashing head:
       Yeah, and the war with
whoever, mail from the south, brush fire:
the usual.
   Foolscap,
      Misterioso murmured:
the newsman gave him a look.
        Well, I'm in
cahoots with Mayor Colton. And what else?
Oh, by order of the governor
       Who, Fremont?
You're funny.
    And where is the Pathfinder?
Under arrest, in the capitol.
      How come?
He had floated his hand-painted Bear Flag
Republic over California, but when he had
himself appointed to it, the real governor
said mutiny.
    His liquor is power, and

41

his hangover, disgrace,
                          the shadowy man
put in. Light paused:
                          But don't the gringos
love him?
               That horse thief? Oh yeah, for
his winter crossing of the high Sierras,
and hauling the battalion down to battle
and carrying back the Peace of Cahuenga
instead.
               You don't?
                               I recollect him on
reconnaissance in the Blue Ridge, to take
out the Cherokee.
                       Oh Simple, you won't
believe, but this Ohlone chief wants me
to wed his daughter.
                          Squaw man? Ah, you'd
be lost, marrying into a tribe of ghosts,
dispossessed of their own names. I seen
it happen.
               I'm sleeping on it: I watched
her dancing, naked, and the stars shooting
from the pale heaven—no thought of love:
unsteady, but what is missing? That touch,
oh that tender give and take!
                                    Pipe down,
John, you'll wake the sailors.
                                    Sorry, I'm all
worked up.
               Over what all?
                                  Simple asked,
and sighed:
               What is marriage? Ah, a contract
between shadows, the bride to be, and her
old promises, to her man tomorrow, and we
who vow and waver day to day.

But look,
you get a son, a daughter, and in love,
live, blossoming.
After the honeymoon, is
it love, or only custom?
Love is strange,
said Misterioso:
Out of the yellow roses
on the mission altar, so much was born,
when Maria Gutierrez, single, long ago,
in the first expedition, with her whirling
songs, cigarillos, and her Sonora laughter,
in her black hair, Spanish ribbons, married
Juan Lopez, and the old bells rang: the last
gobernador, Pio Pico, and oh their grand-
daughters, Ramona, Francisca, Trinidad
the loveliest, la Primavera, any has seen,
and strong Josefa, in her black hair, pearls
of Loreto. At chocolate hour, her father
lowers his violin; the governor's come
to court her, and she casts the tortoise
shell comb, gold bands, away: it comes
back in the hand of the blue sailor with
a serape, first Yankee, with all for sale,
Henry Fitch. "No one in California but you
can wear. . ." "Only kin can. . ." "I come
with it. . ." "Not of my church, my country?"
"I will cross over." And in his violet eyes,
she slips that cloudy comb into her hair.
Padres, the governor's eye on their missions,
won't baptize him; the adjutant blows out
the ceremony: before daylight, they sing
Yankee Doodle, like on the hurdy gurdy
that first morning on the trading brig,
at the governor's window, sail Valparaiso
to marry, and home to jail. The tribunal:
hold sacraments, candles, tell the rosary,

give music to the Plaza Church. Oh love,
you have ten buds on the latest branch,
and in Los Angeles, the new bell rings.
At that, Simple took off his foxskin hat
to rub his forehead:
                    It happens ever day.
She waited in John Cooper's adobe, there
up Alvarado; who'd he done get hitched
to? Encarnacion.
                    The window was early;
over the wild lilac bushes, it was coming
on morning. Light jumped up:
                                    I can't go
straight home to the shanty.
                              Misterioso,
smiling:
        Go by a crooked way.
                              They shook
adios, and his partner strolled off humming,
while Light walked up into the sandhills.

Over the plaza, in the rickety barracks,
of adobe and redwood, for long gone
soldiers, through the window bars, cold
daylight, the one-year mayor, Colton,
dipped his pen to lay yesterday to rest
in his black journal: the captain leaving
for the United States; land theories out
of their element on a man-of-war at sea;
tonight, in the cypresses, bear hunting;
when the door knocked, and the big-bellied
constable, saying,
                    Drunk in public, Alcalde,
muscled his man in, and without a squint
at the dim prisoner, Colton was scrawling:
Your name?
            Mystery.

                    I see nothing prior
on you: ah, you're charged with breaching
the peace. How do you plead?
                              You go down on
one knee, and lift your arms for mercy.
                                        No:
guilty or not guilty?
                    Oh, senor, innocence
is in the eye of the beholder.
                            Ah, constable,
what evidence?
                    He's outside Pacific House,
singing, at break of day.
                        At break of law,
you mean:
            the prisoner.
                        Where do you live?
I am driftwood.
                    Get two horses, constable.
I get so tired, all you lushes, skylarking
till dawn; I swear I'm going to shut down
grog shops. Well, anything to say before
I pass sentence?
                    Your honor—what is honor?
I call to witness the cocks of Monterey,
watching by the first light, the law-
abiding sun, the cockle shells repeating
what the sea said, the blue-eyed grass
on the lookout, the white walls joining
in that flirting song, I'm a fool, if to
love you is folly, I was sober, for once.
Oh I confess, my morning's morning is
a kiss and tell albada, bottles ballads,
I, flush with shanties, tight with hymns,
go rolling from bar to bar, to the last
cadence, when I fall into melody's arms
and dream, old catches going in my head.

If all your sentences lack music, then
whistle this, low and lowly: Judge not,
that ye, etcetera.
     Hush! I rest your case.
I'll just sign and seal this, to make it legal.
Where's the damn wax? Here, hey, where did
you go?
   He had looked up, at last: no one
was there; banged out the door, and brushing
past the peon sweeping the hall, he broke
outside:
    The prisoner is loose! Where is
the constable? Did anyone come out?
          Not
a soul, sir. What's his description?
          Ah hell,
I don't know.
     He shook his head, hunched
back to his office. Laying down the broom
and the sombrero, Misterioso strolled out
into the liberty sun.

      The dark vaquero,
slow riding, not galloping? in the brown
grass, on a palomino of light, sings
Que yo soy el necio, as the crazy rain
comes down, heading for the first house,
oh all a dream. She folded back the flag
of Mexico she slept under, not the star-
spangled rag of the blue conquistadors,
in the old Custom House, its wings open
to the east, the tender waves; stepping
to the window, grey hour after cockcrow,
barefoot, she was sashaying, doing el
caballo, to what's that song, her waist
dipping, el nombre encantador, and her
slip hitching, her delicate hand at her

46

collarbone, el candor, and her wild hair
black clouds, coiling around her face:
Como una ensonacion, la la. . .
                              In English,
Miss Martinez,
                    said the girl, awake on
her cot, in the empty classroom.
                                    Por que?
Yo no soy Americano.
                          It's the room's rule;
la maestra will make me say. It's a, como
se dice, grace, in a new tongue, Rosalia.
She, gazing:
                Como una ensonacion: like a. . .
Daydream.
                Un rayo de luz: and like. . .
Daylight.
                Como un amenecer: like a. . .
Daybreak.
                It's coming. Ah padre, why
lock me in here? Go back to sleep, Maria.
I promise not to talk in the old tongue
till I'm back home. I'll be out the window
on the balcony, looking out for the light.
Oh, que hombre tan hermoso the stranger!

Out of the chaparral, that tangle, greening,
day coming, the mist was walking out to sea,
Light sloping down the white sand street,
uneasy, and no halting till he's at peace,
what did the mystery man say, marriage is
colonial, the conquest, then the dream of
independence, kicking by the wild weeds,
poor yard, kid in rebellion will outlaw,
end up across the road, in the new jail,
and he, at liberty, unkissed, by the long
garden, can the old world trader sail over

ruts cut by rains, from where to where,
the hammer asleep, and the anvil waiting,
slipped down the hill, combers slapping,
fool singing, off there, by the blue gate,
and up a little rise, the lilies in charge of
the presidio till morning, the first saloon,
the ships whirling, the rifles of manifest
destiny at ease, the backwoods dreaming,
oh to cross the plaza, cradle in the boat,
rocked by that green arm, restless water,
the harbor, no longer the port of entry
to the old Custom House, on its faded
roof, gulls, and on the balcony, leaning,
in a white shift, and looking down, into
his upward eyes, a girl.

For this the hours are counted, burning,
in the sanctuary bells, night slips off
her mantilla, daylight, stars roll away,
to rise in back: for this, a wave, unknown
to her before, him following, steals
across bewildering waters, to break into
music, foam, fall, shoot white scripture
over the flat sand of the, after so long,
the longed for shore, of the country of one
angel, like nobody, to adore: for this,
their eyes encounter and the dove flies,
the summer, he dreams his hands the rain,
her waist the dirt, the heaven of seed,
oh love's alluvials, and the green answer.

Pueblo

Light, ignoring the old garden, invisible,
and striding by our lady praying inside
blue, and the presidio chapel, unvisited,
shook his head at his vague sidekick:
No kidding, you, arrested for singing?
How did you get loose?
                Justice is blind.
What can I say? You, dazzled by a girl?
How did you get caught?
                Love is blind.
As well.
      But a balcony? Come on: What light
through yonder window. . . You are hopeless.
No word from her, no sign, no name, is why
we're sliding toward the estuary, instead
of sleep.
      Well, it's good you're free, because
you're innocent.
           And you're captive, because
you're innocent.
           Why can't we just go to
the Custom House?
             Ah no, you'd face a wall
of questions with a ladder of sand. Look
at yourself; you look like a pirate.
                  I'm
not a pirate.
      The red bandanna and
the burning eyes: amigo, in their eyes
you're a freebooter from the high seas, out
to ravish her.
        When I was ravished.
                Truth
is water; it comes up from under. You
won't find it in the false official clouds,
speeches of air, but in the ditches, down
where it gathers, from sailor's rumors and

servant's whispers: you can hear it spill
on the low banks of this green lagoon,
from the washerwomen. Listen.
                              . . . back to
the rancho. So, Mariquita, if she's not there,
what are those drops of love on the old man's
white sheets?
                   Ay, Faquita, there was only—
it must have been. . .
                         Her name! Ah, spit it out,
old woman!
              I will, if you tell what will
happen to Fremont: my senor has made
a wager.
           In the court martial?
                                    I know
what neither of you knows: I was wavering
in the Boston Store, and overheard a trapper
say he'll be found guilty and pardoned but
won't go back into the army because of
his moustache and his pride.
                               Misterioso,
it's just like the weird sisters, only without
the thunder.
               Ask your question.
                                    If I may,
senoras, can you tell me who is the girl
I saw at daybreak out on the balcony
of the old Custom House?
                          La nina? Maria,
or, —did she speak?
                      Spanish, under her breath.
The first washerwoman slapped linen on
the stones, and laughed:
                         Ah si: the tender rebel,
Rosalia de la Luz, born of the old commander,
Senor Martinez.

She lives there? How can I
court her?
The second eyed him, and he reddened:
If I could only—
And the third said,
Go where
lovers have gone before, do what was done.
Ask Juan de la Manca.
What can I give you
in thanks?
News that we haven't heard! Our words
are water, and for free.
Gracias, madres. Ah,
Misterioso, who is that Juan?
John Cripple,
with the bad arm; you know, Yankee skipper,
who looted the Star of the West on the Point
Lobos rocks last year; he whirled the flotsam
as damaged through customs, and has retired
from sailing.
John Cooper. Let's go see him.
Oh, if only I had three wishes, like a hero in
the Thousand and One Nights.
His companion
whistled at him, and said:
One just came true.

Out of the sun and business, in the adobe,
the brick so deep, around the little sala,
that peace can be, days cool, chairs back
to the white walls, guitar and tambourine,
brandy and water, dark beams, dark floor:
the stubby captain came down the stairs,
in sallow slouch hat, blue sailor's jacket,
grey sleek pants, cowhide shoes, his good
hand fingering a mother of pearl coin
in the mahogany stair post:

How can
I help you lads, this morning?
                                        I was sent
by the local sibyls.
                    The who?
                                        Out at
the gulch: the oracles of laundry.
                                        Of what?
The washtub soothsayers.
                                        Ah, quite. What do
they say out here? When the river
                                        His amigo
finished:
            When the river sounds, it's carrying
water.
            Light took off his bandanna:
                                        I want
to spark, I am on fire, to back and forth
with a California girl, a captain's daughter,
I saw this morning at the Custom House.
I'm here because the soap and water seers
said you would know the way.
                                        You look
like a pirate.
                What did I say?
                                        said his
true friend.
                    Answer me this: what citizen
are you?
            American.
                        Alien. What faith?
Protestant.
            Heretic. What occupation?
Indian trader.
                Unemployed. You're quite
a catch, Mister—seaweeds! I didn't catch
your name.

John Light.
                I was once John,
and now I'm Juan.
                And I fail all
                        You are
in a hurrah's nest, and won't get out till
you can answer that old man's catechism
like so: Mexican, Catholic, in the money.
She goes to Isbell's school; let me see, no
invitations to my half brother Larkin's
fandango, on the full moon: all come. Ask
her duena for your lover's bearings, while
the girl is dancing.
                What can I give you
in thanks?
                If you can navigate, come scud
with me one day.
                You're not retired?
                        I'll never
stop sailing. Oh, and learn to ride a horse.

All cantinas closed by the mayor's order,
these army boys, volunteers from a late
disbanded regiment, talked Mister Swan
into scrawling posters with boot polish,
lining up whale oil lamps for footlights,
and opening red, white, and blue blankets
on the first theater, the Union, music
by the military band, the minstrel show,
that night, scenes out of Romeo:
                        I am
no pilot; yet wert thou as far as that
vast shore, wash'd with the farthest sea,
I would adventure. . .
                And Juliet:
                        My bounty
is as boundless as the sea; my love

as deep; the more I give to thee, the more
I have; for both are infinite.
                                   Out back,
after the woo pitching, the blue-eyed
bartender poured whiskey for nothing
to all comers, high-flying, and here's
to the local Juliet. Light's sidekick said,
Station that brass band out in the plaza
at sundown, to blow marches for the kids
peeking around a corner, and slow airs till
the old timers circle the tunes and Viva:
where all of the rifles fail, California
will fall to music.
                          Light tugged him aside:
Fall to music! Oh man, I played Romeo
in the orchard, tonight! I lugged your old
guitar, past other lovers with their lutes
and serenades, to the house where she is,
and like a fool, I sang up to the building,
to the barred window, this old-time prayer,
in her dark tongue, touching it with mine:

El cielo inspiracion tienes el nombre encantador;
En tu alma puso Dios toda la gracia y el candor;
Tu risa de angel que alegra mi vida
Que me olvida que existe el dolor.

Como una ensonacion en me existir llegaste tu,
Como un rayo de luz llegaste a mi radiando amor,
Como un amenecer al despertar hermosa aurora,
Como un rayo de luz llegaste a mi, mi dulce bien.

In heaven's fire, the name, enchanting;
into your soul, grace, innocence;
you laugh like angels: it delights
my life, and it oblivions pain.

Daydream, into my days you come,
daylight, to me, love and radiance,
daybreak, rousing the sky, aurora,
and light, to me, oh my ideal.

El cielo inspiracion tienes el nombre encantador;
En tu alma puso Dios toda la gracia y el candor;
Tu risa de angel que alegra mi vida
Que me olvida que existe el dolor.

Como una ensonacion en me existir llegaste tu,
Como un rayo de luz llegaste a mi radiando amor,
Como un amenecer al despertar hermosa aurora,
Como un rayo de luz llegaste a mi, mi dulce bien.

I sang, out of the low indifferent street,
to her immaculate balcony, to break
down verticals, to bring us eye-to-eye
in a human music. The increasing moon
was cocked over the roof, and I was dizzy;
the stars were coming out of hiding, but
not the woman: I saw her at the window,
in her delicate hand, a candle, burning.
What does it mean?
                    In the silence, he
was praying; his friend, who knew the signs,
said,
        Yes.
            In the seesawing launch, tied to
the pier, in the heat of the day, Light, his
amigo, trading fried tortillas and this
pale cheese coming out of Encarnacion's
kitchen, old mission recipe, and taken to
perfection:
            Well, it's luscious. Speaking
of women, how should I go about it at
the fandango?

Out west, we say, woman
is fire, and the man kindling; in comes
the devil and blows up sparks. Why do girls
get chaperones morning to night? Touch her,
and she surrenders.
       Down east, the doctors
call it sin, when the factory girls make
money, and then talk back: the true woman
is frail and skittish; she lays to conceive,
and lives to mother, to sanctuary the home
for her hay-making man.
        But you, you look
with eastern eyes in western light, what is
woman to you?
      Ah, Rosalia! On the street
only on Mondays, going to mass, in black,
her shadow with her, carrying cloth mats
to kneel on. She lifted her lace veil back:
in her look, summer heat; psychology
was smoke, and I was out of words.
         Why
not court your own, without all this trouble;
why go against the current?
       I'm a salmon,
born to buck it. Her duena crossed over
and handed me this spray, of daylilies,
in a white ribbon.
      She's talking to you
in the alphabet of flowers.
      In the what
of what?
   Oh: words that would shake
our houses go unsaid, but must be said,
and so we tie ideas to the wildflowers:
white rose, you're pure in heart, red rose,
a queen, johnny jump-up, you are so shy,
red cress, the heart is bleeding, white cress,

I'll be a nun, star jasmine, you're a flirt,
sweet william, I should be jealous, blue
crown, I hate you, sunflower, I can't bear
to see you, gillyflower, I sigh for you,
dahlia, I love you in the world, geranium,
for always, evergreen, love without end,
hydrangea, let's marry, daylily, I wait
for you.

      At the fandango. I'll go! Ah,
hold on; you see how hard it is with you?
I ask you how to go about it with her;
you say, woman is fire.

              His amigo brushed
his hands off, laughing:

              Love her upright,
then lying down. At the last dance, last word,
the custom is, embrace the girl you desire.

Light, jumping the slop left by the rain
in Principal, thought, Hey, I'm already
dancing! as he passed by the Four Winds,
the hall of records blowing out to nowhere.
The house, a marriage of colonial rooms
and a southern veranda, local adobe in
a redwood frame, up to a second story,
home to the old consul, Larkin, and head-
quarters of American law and pleasure,
was full of Monterey, the true fandango
spilling into the patio, with sperm candles,
with its asking guitars, answering violins,
at cross music with the band in the parlor.
With a silk handkerchief tied on his head,
and a white cambric scarf, green jacket,
blue damask vest, embroidered shirt,
pale sash, red velvet breeches, and deer-
skin shoes, he looked like a Californio.
The fiddler:

Jose, why play the burro
so slow? I got to whack you to get you
going.

Joaquin, I didn't want to run
ahead and lose you. Ah, el tecolero
is calling for the jota.

I'll count it off;
andale!

The men and women, lining up
under the stars, singing, To the country,
go back, little dove, did the old reel,
and hand in hand, the chorus: Manana
me voy para Vera Cruz a ver a mi chata
Maria de la Luz; and he saw her, the light
on her thick braids, silver pearls at her ears
and throat, lace trim chemise, bare arms,
under a white mantilla she shifted so well,
silk belt and muslin petticoat, rose flounces,
blue satin shoes, in motion, on the dirt floor:
he looked with love. The music, alighting
on a long note, before it took wing again,
the men retreated to horseback, whooping
at nothing, the women, to the sheets hung
for walls, and Light joined Misterioso at
the wine bottle, who said:

That's her, in white,
eh, amigo?

How did you know?

I followed
your eyes. Oh, listen, it's the sweet potato;
this is your chance: when the stanza is over,
salute, fall back.

Light opened his hand to
her hand, canting with her in the slow grace:
Ah, senorita, where I come from, they say
dancers have better heels than heads; but I
didn't believe, and sailed away.

Well, senor,
in this country we say, como, el mundo,
ah: the world is a fandango; only a fool
won't dance.

She smiled: the sun. The time
come, he stepped back bowing, and another
man, sombrero in hand, took her as partner:
he winced and swung around, the idea of
a rival, burning. Misterioso had an eggshell
and laid it on his palm:

Save it for later;
it's your cascaron.

At that, he was cracked
on the head from in back, gold spangles,
cologne, showering over him; when he
turned it was Rosalia running, squealing.
He stepped over to her duena, the daylilies
woman, saying,

I'm John Light. And you?
Old, but her hair still black, she answered,
I am El pim pam pum, but my name is
Maria de la Gracia de Dios Antonia
Arellanes y Carillo, but you can call
me Tia.

Buenas noches.

How can I
stop you? Help you?

How can I court her,
senora?

Write a letter to her old man;
be patient, let the full moon run to full,
and let him have time to consider how
he will say no. Tonight, the flower is
dahlia: anyone can dance with anyone.
Buenaventura, senor.

What can I give
you, Tia?

Rose mallows.
                              Out of the unresting
music, the dances rose and broke, dissolving
on the tender shore: la bamba, the woman
balancing a glass of water on her head,
kicking a handkerchief up to her hand;
la sota, the jack of hearts, men mirroring
the words; el son, hombre to the mujer,
clapping, to the center, whirls, and another,
till his favorite is dancing under his hat;
la zorrita, the fox, for couples, and quick;
el burro, odd man out in the center, at
one word, corazon, take a new partner;
el borrego, man fights the woman bull
with a red sash, and woman the bull man;
el caballo, the horse, they balance to
the other, and she rides her skirt in fists
in front and back; el fandango, walking,
waving, at bomba, make up poetry;
la contradanza, the old, weaving, slow;
till at last, is it daylight? la canastita,
the garland, in a ring, all singing, and
at the last word, love's arms. Light moved
to Rosalia de la Luz, and lay his palm
in the small of her back, her eyes downcast,
when he leaned under, she wrestled away;
he chased her, breaking his eggshell over
her, showering her hair like night with silver
stars, lavender. No eggs, she whipped at him
with a wet sash, but he caught it and reeled
her in; before she could let go, he kissed
her dark beauty; for a moment, she stilled,
and said under her breath,
                              You're a pirate.

In the plaza, at the long white El Cuartel,
at the threshold, morning, of the mayor's

office, American girl, clear-eyed and straight,
the stars and stripes dangling behind her
on the flagpole, in the salty air, with black
bonnet and shawl, her arms hidden inside
her blouse, all buttoned up, and her body
in a corset, and her feet invisible below
a coarse blue skirt. Light nodded goodbye
to her and her ways, and opened the door.
Colton, daydreaming,
                                    You have business here?
Yeah, I want to surrender America, and win
Mexico.
                You mean switch citizens? When
it's all flowing the other way? You are
aware the United States in a brief war
has conquered California and annexed
it?
      You mean stole it.
                                    It was independent
of Mexico anyway.
                                    It don't matter. I
don't run with thieves.
                                    And by the treaty
of Hidalgo, if a citizen doesn't declare
as Mexican, he slides into American
after a year. Most do: no overthrows,
more liberties, in the U. S. So what
is your true reason?
                                    Light thought, After
that kiss, I crossed into another country:
It's invisible lines for lawyers and soldiers.
I am John Light. This war is over.
                                    All right,
I'll get this up to the military governor.

That night after Adam, and Eve in a skirt
of spangles, at the Union, he wrote a letter

to the Pinole hacienda, to her hard father.

I am no rider, of your wild palominos,
like you, loping across the burning grass:
my seed's a stranger, my voice infidel,
and my hands vagrants, and I have only
this language, no translation, to sway you
like the wind in the live oaks, and shake
out hope. If I can't mean, I can music:
oh California, I love your daughter, and
my country is her eyes at the last dance,
my faith is that first kiss, my wealth the round
hills of her, and the flat hollows, the circles
of shade. And I recant: I ride green horses,
with white manes flying, and as I make land,
I say a prayer, for one more day in her light.

Presidio

Rain in winter, but easy, blown up from
the sun-flush south, on a morning with
no frost, rippled down on the evergreens
in the shrine of the hills. Light was led by
his amigo to the old capitol, one gunshot
from the ocean, its stone walls gone into
Monterey, pillars and galleries, a memory,
only low buildings and the chapel left,
and cannons sinking into the new mud.
Misterioso ripped down a page nailed
to the flagstaff, saying:
                              You have a rival.
Out here, when we duel over romance,
it's not with pistols, but with poetry.
Light took the paper, without seeing it:
What in the world? Good lord. You mean,
I down my gauntlet at your iambic feet;
we meet when day stipples the east with red;
choose the weapon: sonnets at forty paces.
Like that?
            Ah, no: this man, Pedro Higuera,
at the fandango, with her, in los camotes,
has tacked this up in challenge.
                              You think she
has read it?
            We all have.
                        Light recited:

They say two's company, but three
is none; your moon's fading away
before my morning: it's time to say
adios, and to let the woman be.
Her padre's promised her to me:
you danced, she'll wear my ring, oh
because she'll never talk your lingo:
it's best for her to wed the man
next door with all his failings than

to live a stranger with a gringo.

And how do I answer?
                                    You turn it over
and scrawl out your own espinela; follow
the rhyme.
                    What do I say?
                                            Write wildflowers.
The rain had blown over the dark sandhills;
Light knelt by the ruin of the presidio gate,
and waited through the morning, till he wrote:

They say from love and love we see
only love; only look in her eyes
when the moon walks into the skies,
and answer, is it for you or me?
Her father's spoken, but she is free;
we danced, she dipped her sandal;
at school, my words are hers to handle;
love has no borders: it marries pure
spirit to spirit, and this is sure:
I sang to her, she lit the candle.

In the only restaurant, across the plaza
from El Cuartel, old, smoky, the owner
drawled in Spanish to the indian cook,
officers played billiards in the next room,
when Light and his compadre loitered in,
sat looking out at the mother-of-pearl
day, and the muchacho waited on them,
while Misterioso talked:
                                    Here is the bill
of fare: olla, with beef, asado, of beef,
guisado, with beef, bad coffee, one dollar.
What's your pleasure?
                            Can't eat.
                                            Can't eat?

69

I can't; my gut's whirling with love. I can't
sleep, sick over the rival; I lay my head
down, and tears.

Love, eh? Sounds inviting.
You are water for chocolate. Eat something:
got to keep your strength up for the pining.
I'm sorry.

No joke. You look at her, what
is she, sixteen? ordinary girl, and I see
the angel of her.

And what rival? You
always compete so hard.

What? I do not
compete.

Ha! What about loteria?

It's not
the same. You do what in a game? You try
to win.

You go wild if you lose a game
of chance.

Ah, no: I'm meek.

Meek?

Yeah,
you know: we're going to inherit the earth.
And I'm going to be the first line in line
when they're handing out earth. All right,
I'll have tortillas and vino blanco.

And I'll
go with the beef and the coffee. What's your
next move?

Convert.

Man doesn't live by
tortillas alone. What is your church?

New
Presbyterian, down on Estrada.

Next to
the carpenter's house.

Yeah; you know how
the Sunday school teacher gets kids out of
the Catholic chapel?
No, how?
Pays them
a nickel. After catechism, they run over
to him.
Well, Don Juan, before you get
all hallowed and reborn, I want to show
you religion in this world, on horseback,
and ride out to the Mision San Carlos
Borromeo del Rio Carmelo, down south.

The road from Monterey was Via Crucis,
over the steeps, into the pine hollows,
old broken down crosses, Light listening
to his companion:
Ah, priests were flying
from a world where the laws of motion had
melted god down, the constitution kicked
faith to the side. Out in this wild, in indians
sharing the seeds and honeycomb, they saw
paradise, and open country for this last
outpost of dogma. On the Camino Real,
they lifted domes to conversion, bell towers,
locked sick women away from sex and air,
whipped rebels back to the slavery fields,
all this for xtian love. But when Spain
let go Mexico, and Mexico the faith, oh
sixty years on, the holy lands were sold,
to anyone, and San Miguel is a saloon,
San Luis Rey a barracks, La Purisima
a hole for bandits.
Where the river runs
into the shallow bay, was Carmel Mission,
in the day's dead angelus and still litany,
its outbuildings down, its corrals deserted.

They walked into the hollow square, and by
the twisted cemetery, the abandoned olive
trees, under the belfry, to the blank windows
and the weathered door, into the lost house.
On one side, the chapel, cracks in the walls,
hundreds of birds, on the other, the sacristy,
below the font, dead pig, in the choir loft,
the crooked star, up, black and white saints,
what's left, torn lettering, and past the cow,
the high altar, falling, and the gold, flaking,
white owl, startled out of its nest, beating
over the padre's tomb.
                    They auctioned it
off,
    said his amigo:
                    No takers. We say
Creense del aire: Believe in the air.
Backtracking to the drowsy ocean town
in the country of oranges, so welcoming,
no need for hotels, only open adobes,
Light breathed:
                    I think of Jesus walking
by the calm waters, the sea of Galilee,
Consider the lilies, and no miracle but
blossoming, of the field, and no bible
but a white dove lifting, how they grow,
no priest but the foam on the little waves,
they toil not, and no chapel but his words,
neither do they spin, and the only easter
in what we do.

                    Between the dead, in pain,
in heaven, a pyramid, and the dragon's jaws,
in hell, hit by pitchforks, in the bare chapel,
the stations of the cross, Spanish madonna,
old Padre Ramirez was leading the marines
through the gospel pages, by the parlor

organ, and its sheet music, a polka. Light
opened and closed the dusty door, looking
a question.

        At ease, men.

                To the sailor:
What can I do?

           I'm here to turn Catholic.
And what's your church?

              It's Presbyterian,
but I

    Ah, but you left your conscience at
Cape Horn.

        Ah, that's not it.

              I'll baptize you,
but first you have to deny your old faith
as heresy.

      I won't, but I have no creed
to lose.

    So you just drift with the stronger
eddy?

    If you say so.

           But that's too easy:
what's the true reason?

            Light thought, I
adore a maiden, and in her dark eyes find
deliverance:

        It's a mystery. And name me
Juan.

    Come this way. After, you will confess.
Light shook his head, offed his bandanna.

Ignacio Martinez, the one-time comandante
of Yerba Buena, rechristened San Francisco,
in a brown sugarloaf sombrero, dark serape,
short jacket, and wide trousers, was cocking
his head, in Jos. Boston's store, at the chalk
lines, spirit levels, iron dividers, knob locks,

spring bolts, union scales, hooks, hinges,
nails, hasps, staples, rivets, and wondering.
Light, told he was here, picked him out:
Senor, I am Juan Light, and sent you my
prayer for your daughter Rosalia, and I,
I, I wait your answer.
     The old man turned,
his big spurs jangling:
       Good morning, you
pale-face son of a bitch; long time no see.
Encantado; ah the devil, I no can speak—
how's every little thing, you god-forsaken
bastard? And what in hell brings you
in here, you damn lowlife?
      Light blinked
at the smiling old man, till a caballero
took him aside:
    He learned your language
from this joker who gave him insults for
greetings.
   All right, and gracias.
       He said:
Oh, nothing much, you jackass. I sent you
a letter.
   Si, I remember: the round hills
of her, eh? You desire to marry all my
sun-blessed acres, thousand wild horses,
many thousand cattle, my vineyard, and
orchard, heavy with pears. And what do I
get in return? You can't be a go between,
with no indians left up at Carquinez Strait,
senor.
   I'll do anything
     Si, for one more
day, and I take you at your word: the day
is this sabado; meet us at the presidio;
bring hunger, for the merienda.

Gracias,
for the invitation. But I desire no acres
or animals, and nothing from your earth
or autumn, padre, only her light hand.

Old Tia dragged up the Custom House stairs,
knocked and opened:
Hola! Rosalia, you
are waking?
Awake and dreaming. You
speak American?
Yes, I am in school.
You are robed now? So early? Ah, yo se,
this day your sailor is coming: ay chica,
no love like the first love.
Rosalia took
her white mantilla by its corners, whirled
it above and back, and gathered and crossed
it over her breasts, and tightened it around
her hips. Her duena led her down stairs,
but in the dark plaza, she looked back to
the ocean:
I see the fish quicksilvering
by the old wharf, like always, but so full
of light I dazzle, and the porpoise break
water as if in joy, and the whale spout
as my heart pounds: after that kiss, I walk
on the same shore, but I swim in beauty.

At break of day, through orange blooms,
in the wet air, blackbirds circling over
dark roofs, away from the vague fort,
no history and so free, slow cavalcade
rolling, in carts with ox-tall wheels,
axles squealing up into tawny hills,
and the wild oats: nine sisters, as in
days gone, Antonia, Juana, Encarnacion,

Luisa, Susana, Francisca, Rafael, Dolores,
Rosalia, with her slender legs hanging,
kids too many to count, and counted,
under a green cloth heaven, climbing
out, at the coyotes' bark, back in, men
and women, and carne, tamales, dulces,
and the old riders, down no road, out to
the laguna blanca, its circle, wider from
the rains, wildflowers, the ring of oaks,
the California sun. White shawls on mats
laid out, all lounged: the bread and wine
of this sallow world were offered, and
for every gracias, May it do you good.
Light, on his side, in the same grass,
in the same air, as Rosalia, after a free
and easy kiss, giving back and forth
rare murmurs, through the day:

                            You're
from the east?

                    I came west to forget. I'm
from the harsh shores, by always slanting
seas—I'll tell you; but under this sun,
on this fandango dirt, I am born over,
in a new name. But you tell me.

                            She was
tying a garland, of flowers in reach,
in a grass thread, and held it up:

                            My day,
out on the rancho, is this little: I wake
up under mama's lock and papa's key,
to birds' singsong, recite the alba prayer,
hymn at the open window, gracias for
the morning; my hours are fruit, bread,
soap, candles, needlework; after supper
and sugar in water, I play the guitar,
the only book the family history, kiss
buenas noches, bow low.

He loved her talk,
skimming by consonants, to linger over
a vowel. Smoke from the live oak coals
under the iron spit was tingeing the air,
the old man in siesta, the aunt playing
cards, in little circles, guitars and low
songs, boys teasing a bull, who got away
to the pool's center; Rosalia leaned in
and whispered:
                They won't go back till
it's dusk, and Tia's room is open to us.
Head down, he smiled:
                    Won't your padre
miss us?
        She will cover us.
                  He walked
to his horse, and swung to the anquera,
and after a breath of air, she followed.
She wore his hat, and steadied by his hand
at her sweet waist, his left holding reins,
they traced on back to simple Monterey;
in that ecstatic ride, his only thought,
That she curves in, how she curves out. . .

Low light from candles burning by the blue
madonna, in the altar, on the white wall,
Rosalia, turning to him:
                 I see your history
in your blue eyes.
              For Light, words weakened
at sight of evergreen sprigs, wildflowers,
coiled in her hair: he slipped the shell comb
out of the crown, and tugged the silver pin
by its globe from in back, as all poured down
like luxury, unloosed her white mantilla
from around her graceful hips, uncrossed
and ungathered it from over her breasts,

and on his knees, rolled down her stockings,
oh slowly, to bare her. She lay back on
the bed, thin mattress on a bull's hide,
her hands open over her head. In this
lying down dance, his vows of pressure
were kisses, and thick as love, all language
from skin to skin, all certainties at her
split lips.

        It was soon dusk, the waves
now plain: silences between, then slaps,
like blood crashing, in over and over
caresses. She was sliding her ring off and
on her finger, touched fingers to his mouth:
I have to go.

            He kissed her hand:

                          What will
you tell your padre?

                Que? Nada.

                      I mean
about the marriage.

              I am his daughter and
will marry who he chooses.

                  What are you
saying?

        I'm saying

              And what was all this
we've done?

          It was love. Amor mio.

                      I feel
light as a feather.

            I'm in a family. I
must follow

            He's chosen him for silver
dollars.

        It doesn't matter.

                And for his
pure blood. Oh steal away, with me, tonight!

Into freedom.

                  Ah no; you love the heart
in me that makes me do this.

                              How can
you know?

              You love old California in me.
And I

        I'm in the prison of my ribs.
Love isn't strong

                  No, mi querido! Don't
say it!

        What are you losing? Ah, don't cry.
Ah, hush.

             Out the window, white skyrockets
in the darkening street, but not for Saint
Guadalupe: a man running past, what was
he barking?

            Gold! On the American River!

On your ivory shore, where the last drama
coils, downfalls, issues in sighs, in kisses,
this wavering border, all's shimmering as I
touch the surface, between you alive and
only stardust. On this frontier, I won't
look long at who I was, but cross into
your inland, to that pine grove, rooted in
your histories, and with my red hosannas,
make it sacred. And if in the bare morning,
the world that wearies, its laws that crack
liberty's bell, no sanctuary for its lovers,
exile me from your arms, I'll go back to
this stolen hour, to see, as countries melt,
our skins, one color, in the tender light.

Oro

Our horses were stolen, last night.

                             His amigo
shaking his head.

              By who?

                    Ah, volunteers:
only men left. Moon Snail saw them, flying
away.

        What can we do?

                    I've heard bad signs
from the red men, omens of the discovery:
the moon so close, only a cable's length,
and a white raven lighting by a baby, and
owls ringing chapel bells.

                  I'm not going to
cross my fingers.

            Oh, we can borrow some
old swaybacks, winded and slow, hope they
hold out.

        Out of Monterey, all the men
gone, to the gold fields, rivers, diggings,
they rode north over the Salinas flats,
swapped horses with a mail rider, night
with no stars, no food or water, with one
watching, sleeping, as the wolves barked,
under thunder:

            a cold morning sky, over
the abandoned mission, San Juan, they hit
a shanty, with hard bread, salt pork, hills,
the barrens, with surviving grass, only
a coat for cover, a saddle for pillow, in
the wet:

        at day they doubled the spur,
long cove, wild oats, and a fat stream,
sun going down, camp here; invited to
a rancho, they kept by the horses, cliffs
in firelight, and watched, in dark, a wolf
watch them:

break and away, they went
to ground the grasshoppers had stripped,
no grazing, to a waterhole, a shack, with
beef and potatoes, no sleep, fleas drove
them out:
       poor plow, and waving fields,
Santa Clara, no bells, his horse spooked,
and snapped his girth; river between hills,
at dusk, the grass scanty, burning willows,
on a bad slope, a stone at side, to keep
from sliding:
        woke near the water, rolling
country, oak, pine, green prairie, farm,
snag fence for fire, meat, salt, is all,
to travel: blind shot at a thought wolf,
waking fear red men:
         they rode across
the Tulare open, to steep hills, looming
stone, the San Joaquin, wild horses in
a muscular flood, and the faraway trees,
wild geese, too tough:
        rowboat in river,
mounts in the wake, swimming; dry arroyo
and grave, man drowned, in flash waters,
tangled in tackle, and going to the mines:
on the level, horns, of elk, light timber,
the green grass escaping the fire drifting
the hills, to a creek, trail faint:
         no fish
biting, a crow rattling, on a dead limb,
path coiling, into the Sierras; sad men
coming out on foot, in rag shoes, clubs
banging skeleton mules, asking for bread,
paying in gold: at night, buzzards covering
the stars:
       into bluffs and chasms, down
in the valley, they crossed a stretch, into

a grove of shadows, over the rock heights,
and twisting into a canyon, a line of tents,
white sun.

       This bummer, led by his shadow,
saying he's Ragshack Bill: in a broad-brim
hat, red flannel shirt, and blue jeans inside
his boots:

       Hell, yes; I can show you the ropes.
This ditch, with the wind blowing hail down
on the frail tents, men from the world's four
corners, to their knees in the mud, in hope,
failing, the chills and fever that congregate
on this cold river, this rumor, digging in pits,
is eldorado. You camp, and you prospect
in the iron earth, till you see the color,
pan out a few, and if it pays, you stake
a claim, forty foot square, pick and shovel
hold it ten days, and then you nail a sign,
of where you're from, live in a shanty, and
work it, to the bedrock, renew the sign,
it'll be jumped, get word, and always go
look for better, and you may hit a strike
or go dead broke.

       Light wrestled out
a black frying pan, clawing dirt into it:
Oh that'll do. Now dip it under water,
and ah,

       Like this?

       Dissolve it with fingers,
and now,

       It's muddy.

       Shake out pebbles,
and rake it with

       Here's shingle.

       It's a shore:
look, and cast off.

No gold.
                    You stir
it hard, now collect all at one
                    Out of
the water?
                    Yeah, tilt it, steep, good.
Let little waves
                    By wrist.
                              break and
drag mud away.
                    I see.
                              Let the water do
the work.
              That it?
                         Ah, two more times.
Till less than a handful
                         Is left. All right;
I don't
         Now level and circle it.
                                    What
will
    Wash away all but gold.
                              I see flash-in-
the-pan sunlight. Oh, flakes!
                              You stub them
with a dry finger.
                    To where?
                              Drop them
in a flask of water. It's worth one dollar:
a pinch of dust.

              After a yellow day,
    Light asked,
              Where are we?
                              and Ragshack Bill:
It's Wood's Creek bank, and it's paydirt.
Light nodded:

85

Any other camps?
                                    The miner
dragged his hat off:
                          You ain't see nothing.
You can go to Ground Hog's Glory, Red Dog,
Whiskey Bar, Rawhide, Coyote Hill, Dead
Mule Canyon, Loafer's Ravine, Jackass Gulch,
Wild Goose Flat, Love Letter Camp, Mud Springs,
Boomerang, Rough and Ready, Slap Jack Bar,
Hog's Diggings, Liberty Hill, Greenhorn Canyon,
Seven Up Ravine, Brandy Gulch, Poker Flat,
Greaser's Camp, One Eye, Toenail Lake,
Last Chance, Rattlesnake Bar, Yankee Doodle,
Sugarloaf Hill, Stud Horse Canyon, Lousy Ravine,
Skunk Gulch, Chicken Thief Flat, Hungry Camp,
Bogus Thunder, Dead Wood, Coon Hollow,
Wildcat Bar, Rat Trap Slide, Poverty Hill,
Humbug Canyon, Pancake Ravine, Plug Head
Gulch, Christian Flat, Hell's Delight, Skinflint,
Sluice Fork, Humpback Slide, Dead Man's Bar,
Swellhead's Diggings, Quack Hill, Graveyard
Canyon, Puke Ravine, Gospel Gulch, Grizzly Flat,
Hen Roost Camp, Poor Man's Creek, Snow
Point, Paradise. And while I's listing off those,
these sprung up: Shirttail Bend, Shanghai Hill,
Bluebelly Ravine, American Hollow, Ragtown,
Shinbone Peak, Petticoat Slide, Barefoot Diggings,
and Brandy Flat.

                    On this low or high water
creek named for a salesman hawking eggs
and bread at jacked up prices who laid out
the forty-niners' good money on bad ideas
and lost it, flying by night, now named for
this prospector, out of the north, jammed
with men from the dry diggings, Light sat
cross-legged at a manzanita fire:

This
is earthquake country.
                          Under the close moon,
black hills, blue distance, only hoofbeats,
and quail and coyote. He saw, in a brush
shanty next to their white canvas tent,
this old hombre, by his bull lantern, make
signs and circles in the muck, draw cards
out of a greasy pack, and stare up into
the constellations.
                          Senor, what's it all for?
Misterioso asked.
                          Ah, this here's petering
out; I'm trying to divine a better vein.
In the beginning, it was a shore boulder,
quartz, thick with gold, and the red man,
looking for obsidian, slipped back into
the wild, as we come in. Well, you go to
Se compra oro, walk in, weigh out your dust,
fourteen dollars the ounce, and twenty-two
percent to the buyer. And then pickpockets,
now swindlers, and hard to pan two grains.
Ah, before you can spit, away they'll go,
and it's wind blowing into a ghost town.
I know: where is Hornitos? It's bullet holes
in the weathered door, the dead saloon,
and the forsaken plaza. Hey, I'm old
Tom Moore; they call me the traveling sign.
I crossed the Great Divide, the American
Desert; I's coming into California, east
of the sharp ranges; we're down to a pair
of oxen, killed the one, and dried the meat,
in the morning, climbed, up the north bank
of the we thought Walker River, up there
in Disaster Peak country. We made a gorge,
it branched off into a canyon: I's sent
to see if it would let us down; following

indian trails, ten miles in, I guessed I'd
go north to hit them going west, and come
to a dry gulch, oh prodigal with gold, big
as my fist, all through. I couldn't stay
to mine it, the snows were coming, hell,
so I loaded all my trouser pockets, and
on the next peak, I set up sticks, with my
old coat and hat, twig finger, that way.
Oh I been back, the god-damn scarecrow,
I ain't found it; I never heard tell of any
strike in them mountains; that gold is still
up there, where I'm going, as best I can
memory, into the high Sierras.

                         Light let
his eyelids down, and seeing stars. . .

                            I turn
the pages, my account, our wedding ring,
on a white table, by the sea, green, clear,
long sweetening like the breasts of Rosalia,
flash breaker washes over, the book is dry,
and the ring gone, and she is here, hoisting
her skirt, Look, honey, it's the one dance
we didn't do, she tilts her head, and heel-
and-toes, and I, Here is one of the legends
of our ring, I lift my hand, it's there, in my
finger and thumb.

                    Morning, the old hombre,
no trace, gone for the Scarecrow, nobody
in the ice water, the sabbath, no digging,
only prospecting, or play, so Light and his
double, after beans and salt pork, shortcake
in the gold pan, went walking down the line,
deep pits, poor shanties:

                    Wen shi jian qui
wei he wu

          yuu-k hummis waakse amakma,
piinaway, pirie his YsYesYte

                    Ich bin heute
ein fruehaufsteherin
                    to seh, Learn fi dance
before yuh go
                Che giorno della settimana
Dio ha creatore la donna?
                        Elle se sent bien
dans sa peau
                Ik moet eerst de Kat uit de
boom kijken
                    a draft of whiskey, and then
one of river water
                    Para beber, quero
vino tinto
            says, Ah'm so tired Ah don't
know whut tuh do
                    Is glas iad na cnoic
i bhfad wainn
                    and most all of the gals
turned out and had a fine frolic that day,
sliding
            pae aku I ka 'aina
                        Amor, amor,
nada hay peor, ni mejor:
                        all runaways,
the celestials, indians, yankees, slaves,
mexicans, kanakas, gypsies, blowing in
from the whole globe, sailors, farmers,
mechanics, merchants, steamboat pilots,
privates, shysters, sawbones, one-time
gospel pitchers, listening to the thimble
riggers, card dealers, string game men,
jokers, bartenders, outlaws, auctioneers:

High boots! I got 'em spitnew, waterproof,
of the best rawhide, two soles: you can lace
'em on your mudhooks, one hundred dollars!

Pour out your dust.

That's high, but give me

a pair.

Hey, penny-pincher!

Ah, fool's gold

for boots and seven shots.

What'll it be?

Straight fire.

Red eye for me.

One flash

of lightning.

Any cocktails?

The wild riders,

who could sling a knife and lean at a gallop
to snatch it, war whooping along the clay
of the street, hauled up at Winter's hotel,
shoving into the saloon, on one wall,
short flasks, long bottles, in that hell,
a b c, poker, twenty-one, faro, monte:

The jack of diamonds, the jack's a winner,
your money back!

. . . the mystic science. Ride
the wheel, a number, red or black, the eagle
bird. . .

Six ounces, boys, nobody can say
where's the joker. . .

Knock off? Like hell!
I'll find it or I'll dig ten thousand miles
to the other side!

I won all stakes on
the ace; one more like that. . .

Your cut:
the card. It's queen and deuce! Your bets,
gentlemen.

I'll ante up.

Come down with

your dust.
       It's twenty-four on the deuce,
mister.
     Don't tempt your luck.
                 I'll break
the bank, or get broken.
               Another shuffle,
another layout. King, queen. . . The game
is ended, and you lose.
           Oh, I don't care.
And he sang, strutting out:

> I come from Salem City with
> My washbowl on my knee,
> I'm going to California,
> The paydirt for to see.
>
> I jumped aboard the Liza ship
> And rocked upon the sea,
> And ever time I thought of home
> I wished it wasn't me.
>
> Oh! California,
> That's the land for me!
> I'm going to Sacramento with
> My washbowl on my knee.
>
> The pilot bread was in my mouth,
> The gold dust in my eye,
> And I thought, sailing far away,
> Dear brothers, don't you cry.
>
> I'll scrape the mountains clean, my boys,
> I'll drain the rivers dry,
> Bring home a pocket full of rocks,
> So brothers, don't you cry.

Oh! California,
That's the land for me!
I'm going to Sacramento with
My washbowl on my knee.

Hey, pipe up all you want, but do you have
money to come and go?
                          Well, let's keep it
on the quiet; know what was in that bag?
Nothing; a pound and a half of buckshot.
They'll be cussing when they open it! Ha,
don't that beat all?

                    Dusk smeared the street;
the gong banged at the dining hall across
the water, skin and bones man staggering:

Hey, bears! Ain't no food here! Back off!
This mine is mine.
                        Ah ha. Must be the booze
talking.
          Oh yeah? When my gold rolls in,
I'm nobody's yes man; judges can shine
my boots for money.
                          And I'm equal to you,
thanks to the universe!
                              Hey, you know what?
My country tis of thee.
                            Damn right, we'll be
a state come fall.
                      Shit yes, with old Fremont
for our senator.
                        This week, the 4th of July,
I say we walk all outsiders over the hill.
You, stop!
              He saw Misterioso leaning out
of a low hole:

          Ah Light, don't ever go
in with the whores!
                 Hey, greaser! This is
American Camp! All ours. And you're gone
Thursday, savvy?
             We were here first.
                     Oh
yeah? Well, I'll be the first to kick your ass,
you stinking
          Light raised his hand:
                       Hey,
man, it's late; you're stiff. Let's let it slide
to morning.
          What the—this is between me
and California. Who in hell are you?
                     I'm
Juan. Let's go. Amigo, what was so wrong
in that cathouse?
          Ah God, the first I saw,
in there: Salt Wave.

             On the next night,
late, Misterioso jumped into the tent;
that morning, bored with panning, he'd
lit out, all day, now overflowing:
                  Lo!
And, it goes without saying, behold!
                    Eh?
Que pasa?
          Well, I got to—I'll tell you
a story. This old forty-niner, who's always
out of luck, died and went to heaven. But
at the pearl gates, St. Peter said, Full up,
no room, try me later. The old guy kicked
around limbo, said hello to unbaptized
Adam, and hustled back to kingdom come;
he waved a seraph over, and whispered

that they'd struck gold in hell. Well, that
set off a rush of angels down to the fire
and brimstone, and heaven opened up. But
the old galoot hung back, watching them go;
St. Peter gives him a look and says, Are
you coming in, or not? He answers, I's
just wondering if there was any truth
to that rumor.

     All right! What's it about?
Misterioso opened his shirt, and poured
out thousands of dollars in gold.

          Christ!
Where is it from?

      Not far. Buscaras y
hallaras: seek and find. I squeezed in by
these mountain junipers, out of the rock,
into a lost hollow, dry creek, cut gold
with my butcher knife, out of the cracks
in the quartz walls.

      Anyone see you go
or come?

    Alone, this morning, invisible
this evening.

     Let's bury this loot under
your bedroll, and manana, I'll go with you.

After thick sleep, no dreams, Light lifted
up on one arm: his companion was gone,
the sack of gold, blood all over his blanket.
Sick in his guts, he walked the camp, talking
to nobody, looking, and finding him down
this abandoned hole, living, and hauled
him out. The so-called doctor patched him,
but fever rose, and over his protests, no
money, no marriage, Light bought them
a mule, hoisted him shaking on its back,
and led them down, by the sliding waters,

the wind whining, out of the Sierras, by
women arriving from the Plains, their faces
sunburnt, their hair dried by alkali, and two
men, skeletons, still hanging from a branch,
the wounded man, nothing would stop him,
naming the indians by their old tongues:

Pomo. Miwok. Wintun. Maidu. Yana.
Yuki. Ohlone. Essalen. Salinan. Monache.
Yokuts. Chumash. Gabrielino. Luiseno.
Kumeyaay. Serrano. Cupeno. Cahuilla.
Kamia. Hupa. Yurok. Karok. Wigot.
Modoc. Achomawi. Atsutgewi. Paiute.
Washo. Mono. Chemehuevi. Yuma.
Mohave. Halchidhoma.
                              They sloped
in the white pines, on the down grade.

I glory in the sun-dull chaparral her hair,
the Siskiyous clear brow, and in her lakes
those eyes ah Shasta, Tahoe, and her tongue
the surf at Eureka, her Sacramento throat,
her back wild horses on the Mariposa plains,
bare shoulders Sonoma, her Sierra breasts,
her belly San Francisco, San Joaquin veins,
the wines of San Fernando, the oranges
San Gabriel, the olives San Diego, Mojave
hips on fire, and her loins Los Angeles,
her San Bernardino thighs, Imperial calves,
her feet the border, her hands the tidal flats
and the dune grass, with a Monterey heart
go back to her mosaic lips, kiss California.

Rancho

Old Monterey, once the capital, but now
cut loose from history, in a backwater,
trade routes gone north, blue bay, faithful
sea breath, Estrada, Principal, Alvarado
its only calles, and its white casas, bygone,
but let stand, where time idles, adobe
won't burn, and custom lives, was welcome
to the men dragging in from the gold fields.
Misterioso lay on his healing bed:
         I slept
it off; it's broken now.
       It's good to hear;
see what el medico says.
         I should have kept
one eye open, I'm sorry.
         I should never
have dragged you up into that chaos; look
what happened.
      Behind, so clear; before,
so hazy.
    Ah, and so the vein of dichos
wasn't cut.
      And when I'm up and around,
we'll go back in.
      To the Sierra Nevada?
            Si,
as gold diggers.
      No: I've seen the elephant.
It ain't worth it.
      But Juan, you're Mexican,
Catholic; you have to get in the money, to
marry—
    You're stabbing me. I won't go.
If I'd lost you
      If you love me, you must
do three things to win me: be a citizen
of dream, have faith in doubt, and buy

time with me for a song.
                                Amen to that.
Ah, where to now? Quien sabe.
                                        Oh you
are going, somewheres.
                                And how?
                                        Migration.
The swallows come back to Capistrano,
on the exact day, every March.
                                        What, to
the mission?
                        They leave on the exact day,
every October, and white-throated swifts
move into their haunts.
                                Into those nests
of mud.
                        That hang, in shelter, in the eaves
of the sold mission. Well, the winter comes
on and drives the cliff swallows, in flocks,
to the north, arriving
                                On the same day.
It's hard to believe.
                                Believe. In a cloud,
from the Pacific, on the down sanctuary
between two rivers, a flight of swallows
falls like evening, over the bells, into
the arches.
                        And how?
                                Miracle.
                                        El capitan,
said Moon Snail, in the door, handing in
a sheet of paper.
                        It's from Aunt Tia: oh!
the old man's six feet under, in San Jose;
she says the son, Jose Jesus, is now the don
at Rancho Pinole.
                        Dios mio! Well, go on,

man, ride out there.
                        What good is it? If I
see her—
            See him. What if the old man's
judgement, and the son mercy?

                                First sight,
through an apple grove, by rose mallows,
the adobe, crosswise to the compass, sun
shining in each window as the day goes,
the veranda, north, and summer, the patio,
south, and winter. At the door, the caballero
who saved him in the general store, saying,
Ah. Bienvenido. And in the parlor, oh love
alive! Her madre, saying:
                                La casa es suya.
And Light, blushing:
                        What is this room?
He gazed at opening, the chairs shying,
the tables bowing, back from this axis
to the white walls, all rooms give on it,
and all else is side to this heart, spring
in the wood as he walked:
                                It's where
we dance.
            Eyes swimming, he imagined
women and men living for the fandango.
His voice was low:
                        I do lament your loss,
senora, and wish you and all yours well.
To Rosalia
            Jose waved:
                                Senor, what
can I say against my invisible padre,
or this don, who honors us, his blood
where Coyote Creek slides by destiny
into the tidewater, who asks her hand?

I'm in the saddle with the morning star,
to see the rancho, daybreak, and back
for chocolate, pinole and sugar, and out.
We're easy here, as the horses run free,
no grass is cut, the cattle rove, the wind
blows off the grain, and seeds next year.
What do we do? We live, with few desires,
no cares, and dance for bounty, beauty,
love and children. The world, its wrangles,
over the horizon—what are they looking
for? This. And what will sift it all away?
Marrying
          Rosalia slipped through the door,
with her betrothed, Pedro, her hand in his,
Light electric,
             vagabonds, out for balls,
and gambling, on bulls and bears, racing,
wine, and sailor's delights, till it's all sold,
ah league by league, to the last mantilla,
and pawned to memory. It is the end
of ceremony, of opulence, and of what
we loved. Do not ask us to marry into
this downfall.
          I will tell you what I told
your padre: I desire, nada! Go disinherit
her, uninvite me from your old rancho:
I'd give it up, one kiss, and my poor shack,
her there, is heaven.
            She reddened, and
with broken syllables, in undertone, tore
her fingers free, lifting her skirt, escaping
up stairs. Her madre called after,
               Rosalia!
Jose said, hot:
         Senor, I invite you to her
wedding, the first of May.
            Light bowed:

I won't trouble you, or your long family,
this room of grace, longer. Mis recuerdos.

Misterioso was stripped down, with no
sombrero, only his linen shirt, his soft
blue jeans, no spurs on his bare heels,
no whip, no saddle, only a horsehair rope
around the girth of El Rayo, his eyes
fiery, his neck arching, his mane, silver,
his long body shining, his legs, slender,
true palomino, high-stepping in grace
down the field, by serapes and mantillas,
to the starting post. His rival, the black
mustang, El Vengador, was so long, from
shoulder to hip, deep belly, bones cannons,
sullen, and hungry. Misterioso had bet
money he didn't have against any loose
doubloons, pieces of eight, silver dollars,
American gold. Alcalde Colton, whose
heart had opened in the Monterey air,
let his black hat fall, and the two racers
slapped horse, jumped on the sliding back
and high-tailed it, like lightning, to the yells
of Viva, and the dark stallion loped ahead,
at one quarter, by inches, edging, by feet,
blowing, but not ever shaking his rival off,
till half way over, the sun showed between
the horses, their heart's thunder, bolting,
at three quarters, El Vengador in front
a length, Misterioso in hands and heels,
and rowing, let El Rayo have his head,
and like a skiff quickening in the current,
was catching up, when the other man used
his latigo, and lashed at the black flesh,
the hurt animal shying, out of balance,
and the dream horse sailed across the line.
His rider shone, thinking, Caballo que

vuela, no quiere espuela: A horse that flies,
no need of spurs.

              In the silk morning,
May first, Light stood in the black mud
of the road to the mission, looking out
for her cavalcade, by Carquinez Strait,
peninsula, rack over Cougar Mountain,
and the salt marsh, thick with cordgrass
and weeds, alive with sea otters in, out,
and herons wading. He saw her horses,
a ways off, and said, to nobody:

                      Ah love,
in the five springs since the dove fluttered
out of your eyes and into mine, what have
I given up? The letters of fire, my name,
breathed at the baptism by another bride,
the mercy in her voice. What faith I kept
out of the spray in my whirls and voyages,
god, unknown, at sea, out beyond prayer.
Seasons, begging the heartless waters for
gold, in the cold Sierras, where my brother
in dreams was knifed. My ragged courting
is over, nothing left to sacrifice, but I
stand wishing your union, this day, and all
to come, be full of light. Adios, my only.

The line was closer, calicos and dapples,
and the new don, ahead, palm up:

                    Senor,
no rider on the groom's horse; we walked
it to you here, where love has hauled you up:
where else, but on this shore? We like to say
the more you give, the more a man you are.
Salud, hombre. And I give her, liberty. Ay!

Against love and chance. . . surrender. I had
to say his lines for the new ghost, but now
I can at last look in our madre's eyes. And
I saw yours! You love, not only her, but
where she dances. Vamos! to the chapel.

Light saw her coming, ah! on a red roan,
bay wedded to white, leading a palomino,
with mane of sunlight, and back of water,
in caparison, stealing his dark bandanna
for her own hair, handing him a sombrero
graced with wildflowers; with compadre
behind her and comadre in front of him,
his hollyhocks, and her pale roses, rode
to the last mission, after independence,
without approval, and with its own spring,
where the river muscles days and nights
to the open ocean; she was on a silver star,
her stirrups of cloth and embroidery, he
on a half moon, circle of pendants jingling,
through the blue-eyed grass, and owl clover.
At the door, morning, she, in yellow satin
with green ribbons below, flesh stockings,
white shoes, and he, in ordinary clothes,
but a red sash, tassels, joining their hands,
with girl for poppies and boy for ring,
after the priest strung the lasso of silk,
fringes of gold, over her nape, his neck,
and thirteen coins, oh wife, were raining
out of his fingers, oh husband, into hers,
the padre sighing, I am only a witness,
your voices the ministers, in your hands
the sacrament, will you, I will, quivers
till he touched her slight shoulder, his
and her names twining, you, I take you,
I unite you, under holy water, and as
the groom was sliding the gold blessing

on the bride's finger, the versicle married
the response, and the benediction lifted
its arms; at the altar, he gave glories
to the saint of where they are, she lit
the candle with fire from her baptism.
Outside, kissing, and the brass exploding,
to shots of music, in a hail of pinole,
they rode, on the one horse, to the rancho,
under a pale rainbow, promenading through
larkspurs, hyacinths, irises, white lilies,
as his companero, his saddlebags full
of vivas, was reciting his outlaw song:

To the country, the hunters,
go back, little dove,
and tell them not to shoot
at the queen of my love.

The crow is in the air,
flying open-eyed,
flying back and far,
flying up and wide.
If stone is hard, then you
are diamond; in the end
my song to you is not
able to make you bend.
I give you a caress,
you give me melancholy,
say I'm a fool: I am,
if to love you is folly.
So you go on, ungrateful,
but one day you will sting
and in a dream remember
that I was your king.

Among the lily flowers
no one can recognize

you, not only woman,
but angel from the skies.

Tomorrow I'll go by
the willows, like a lark,
and I will see that maid,
Rosa of the dark.
Tomorrow I'll go by
the harbor, like a kite,
and I will see that darling,
Maria of the light.
But in the end, the cuckoo
always sings off-key,
and though a vivid bird,
the cardinal's not for me.
Little dove, so white,
in your beak of coral,
carry to my queen
this, my sprig of laurel.

Rockets, bells, music, at the rancho, with
unbroken mares, wild, but faithful to
the stallion, not for riding but breeding,
flying, his shoes were stolen and redeemed
with aguardiente, as he and the bride, side
by side, at the long table, welcomed in
the fiesta de boda, out of the hornilla,
puchero, enchiladas, bunuelos, pastelitos,
three days and nights, no invitations, all,
Pico, Estudillo, Peralta, Yorba,
Sepulveda, Olvera, Dominguez, Valle,
Antonio, Olivera, Arellanes, de la
Guerra, Latallade, Estrada, Aguirre,
Pastor, Negrete, Castro, Soberanes,
Alvarado, Arguello, Galinda, Martinez,
Mesa, Carrillo, Vallejo, Juarez,
under green boughs, inside the cloth,

on dirt wet down, with fiddles leading
guitars following, with madres humming
and padres throwing silver dollars, his
mystery other, light, dancing with any,
the rival eyeing her sister Maria Dolores,
and now, la marcha, in long lines, women
upright, eyes down, hands down, sliding
invisibly, men circling, spirited, holding
motion in, and inside the casa, kin, eyes
glimmering, as she changed they unveiled
her first long looking glass, and coming
down, she said, Who is that lovely girl?
After carne asada, tortillas, frijoles,
queso, pozole, azucarillo, she's dancing
the magnetic waltz with him, to local
melodies, and the boys and girls at blind
man's buff under the moon, till daylight,
sleep three hours, merienda in the pear
orchard, women swimming, men riding,
at last, the groom and bride are released
by poetry, you're roses, you're blessed,
the angels long for this, the married life,
the stories I can tell, and adios, padre,
madre, man live in her, woman in him,
and breast to breast, the Californio way.

In bed, toward the third morning, birds
were singing:
                            I dreamed days back, after
I heard of the swallows, long wait, only
you and me, and I'm missing this chance
to kiss, you smile at me to say so, I read,
I kiss, you, oh the kiss!
                                        I love that: when
I smile, you do; what is the word? intimacy.
In my first dream, this casa, with your rival,
and out, to offer bread to the shore birds,

and in, you're on the floor, for me, I turn,
I say, I'm ah with him, he goes, we hug,
it's so, and it's so right.

               Before daybreak,
you're flickering in and out, you can't get
away, are leaving him, but in a while,
had left with him, come back, together
with me tonight, or tomorrow, you two
had plans, I can't hold you, my arms,
one place, only friends, I ask your sister
why's all she says come true and I can't
ever foretell? You are half-naked, I see,
small of your back, its arch, and dimples,
all this desire, go on, even if you're
not free.

         And so I dream I find us places
on a big carreta, and who is in between?
you say, let me decide, and we'll be side-
by side, we're holding hands, I see your
I love you smile.

             You made your mind
up in a dream, like a red woman, after
a vigil, as the world of spirit in sleep
talks to matter.

           You're everywhere, in
my life, that poem, my dreams,

                  Oh and
in the Sierras, I dreamed our wedding
ring, on

       I saw this palomino

             You first.

Day slants, into the blue rim, as we enjoy
the sun, in our apostasy, our son pacing
on a mustang through foam and history,
and daughter playing with her stick lady,
till we turn from the windwarp cypresses
to the hacienda, and holy night. I know
the long fandango comes to the canastita,
last dance, last word: I'll see land grants
dissolving, lawyers paid in country, but
no decline, with Rosalia's kisses, the waltz
with her. The future is louder. But you
may come on a lost cove, canyon; it will
remember, as in that peace, you catch,
if only a vestige, our innocent music.

On the balcony, the moon
in the white nights:
to her, I kiss my fingers,
I raise a song.

On the earth, I stand,
cut by borders,
where the hurly-burly
is unending.

Paul Bunyan

1

Out of the wild North woods, in the thick of the timber
And through the twirling of the winter of the blue snow,
Within an inch of sunup, with the dream shift ending,
A man mountain, all hustle, all muscle and bull bones,
An easy winner, full of swagger, a walking earthquake,
A skyscraper, looking over the tallest American tree,
A smart apple, a wonder inventor, the sun's historian,
A cock-a-doodle hero, a hobo, loud, shrewd, brawling,
Rowdy, brash as the earth, stomping, big-hearted, raw,
Paul Bunyan lumbered and belly-laughed back at the stars.
He was rigged out in a slouch hat, a red work shirt
Under his faithful mackinaw with its hickory buttons,
Suspenders and high-water stag pants, which were tucked
Into his brass-hooked and buckskin-laced black boots,
And this foot-loose blue ox was sashaying at his side:
Babe, who was combed with a garden rake, who measured
Exactly forty-two ax handles and a plug of Star tobacco
Between the eyes, who was crazy for parsnips, who ate
And just bellowed for joy, his bray rocking the country,
And who romped off the deer path, skylarking, and leaving
The thousand and one hoof prints which are now Maine lakes.
Out of the scud covering up the dusty morning stars,
The baby-blue snowflakes of the first blue snowfall
Were scurrying down sky-blue, all over, like butterflies,
In flurries, blue as Monday, blue as the moon, as heaven,
Decorating the pines, blue as a ribbon, blue as bluegrass,
As blue songs and blue laws, and glittering on the boughs
Like jays and berries: it was icing up the evergreens,
Sticking to itself, and stacking up in balls and drifts
Like fury, and the seconds were as tight as the icicles;
It was quiet like it's quiet before the sour beginning
Of the redbreast's la-de-dah, and in that minute there
All of a sudden Paul Bunyan itched for big-time work.
He uprooted a tree, combed the frost out of his beard,

Rolling fifty-two notions around his burning head
Till it all flashed on him, and he invented logging!
He whistled and walked over to the local iron range,
Fixed up a blade, fit on a white pine for a handle,
And jogged back with his ax: he carved himself a gabriel
Out of a cedar, lifted up the horn and let out a honk
Whinnying from the Rockies all around to the Rockies
Like day breaking; and when the wide yellow sun rose,
Old Paul braced and, taking a colossal breath, he roared,
"Roll out or roll up, boys; there's daylight in the swamp!"
All this ruckus was to bounce lumberjacks everywhere
Out of bed, and between the horn and the ballyhoo
His boys woke up. While the man power was on the way,
He sized up the eastern timber, and scribbled a claim:
He spit into his broad palms and circled his ax back,
Leaned like a natural into his swing, and every whack
He grunted like he was happy, chopping into this tree
So thick a man might sprint round it in a day, so tall
It'd take a week to see its top up in the clouds;
When the big stick was whittled on down to a whistle,
It crackled, it swished, it got the shivers in its limbs,
And when it snapped, it tilted, timber splintered, twigs
All tore off, and it rip-roared down in green confusion.
Babe tagged behind Paul, chawing off the little branches
And hauling out the logs; and to level out the country,
Bunyan strung up the stumps in chains, to an iron spool,
And hitched it to Babe, who jerked them free and lugged
The breaking plow, which had a huge furrow, and filled in
The hollows, and they cleared hundreds of acres, easy.
Old Paul scrawled the plans for the shanties on the air
And plunked the logs crisscross for walls, jacking roof poles
And trueing them, checking out his plans, slapping up shingles
In dovetailing and overlapping style against the rain
In fog so heavy he nailed six feet of shingles on it,
And for his big finish to this bang-up job, he squatted
On the roofs and welded the timber as tight as anything.
Now all the burly, joking, gallivanting lumberjacks

Showed up and rolled in, sailing, thumbing, and hiking,
Foreigners out of the old countries, and talking funny,
Like Limeys, Micks, Frogs, Canucks, and Scandihoovians,
And Yankee Doodle boys hailing from the four corners
Of the United States, Fly-up-the-creeks from Florida,
Evergreen men from Washington, Pine tree men from Maine,
California Golden Bears, with Corn Crackers, Knickerbockers,
Granite Boys, Green Mountain Boys, Old Liners, Old Colonials,
Buckeyes, Muskrats, Panhandlers, Mudcats, Yellowhammers,
Hardheads, Sandhillers, Tarheels, from down East and Dixie,
An all-star team, and the ruggedest crew ever crowed:
Wrestlers, wreckers, boozers, barnstormers, roustabouts,
Breadwinners, ramblers, fiddlers, roughnecks, runaways,
Penpushers, windjammers, daredevils, and crackhunters,
And no galoot in the whole gang under eight feet tall,
Come in with a caterwaul to join Paul Bunyan's camp
On the river and kick off the original lumber drive.
The camp sprawled from the Smiling River to Honey Creek
Sunning and curling around the Big Rock Candy Mountain,
Where the strawberry bushes, where the raspberry trees
All ran wild on the slopes with berries as big as plums
By the plash and swizzle of the rock-and-rye springs,
Under the gillygaloo, which brooded up on the steep
Of Pyramid Forty, with its stand of one million pines,
And laid square eggs which wouldn't roll down the hill
And when collected and hard-boiled were good for dice,
And way over behind beyond, the whangdoodle whistled.
Down in the bottom lands below Honey Creek, in soil
As smooth as butter, old Paul's dairy farm spread out
Like paradise, where the wheat was growing in fields
So thick the geography just creaked under the weight,
The corn so quick a crack logger couldn't hit it twice
In the same for heaven's sake spot, and where sting bees
The size of doves went whizzing into the tall dandelions,
Where the red clover cows gave milk that didn't sour
And the devil grass cows gave straight cough medicine,
Where the green vegetables were rooted so god-awful deep

It took an inventor to pick them, and where a redneck
One day chanced to see sparrowgrass sprout up so hard
It went roots and all into the air, and lived on nothing
But the climate, and he saw vines dragging punkins along,
And when he got tangled up, he went for his jackknife
And found a big cowcumber that had ripened in his pocket.
When Pea Soup Shorty clattered the triangle for breakfast,
The boys stampeded for the cookshack and grabbed up forks
At a pine table so long a story started up at one end
Was so tall at the other end they had to hire a flunky
To shovel it out the door. Now first off, and for starters,
There was oatmeal mush, logging berries, hasty pudding,
Eggs fried over easy, over hard, sourdough biscuits,
Klondike spuds, pilgrim marbles, apple grunt, sowbelly,
With all the trimmings, and a gallon of bullshit a man:
When they rolled sugar cookies down the table the boys
At the foot got gypped, and so Big Ole the blacksmith
Dreamed up the hole and toted the doughnuts on a stick.
All this was only horse ovaries before the main dish:
Hotcakes! They had a choice between pancakes, flatcakes,
Slapjacks, griddlecakes, stovelids, battercakes, flapjacks,
In piles, topped with skid grease, floating in maple slick.
The iron griddle, one hundred yards wide, over a fire
Kindled out of an acre of scrub and two of timber,
Was oiled up by kids who strapped on slabs of bacon
And skated across: out of sugar boxes, flour barrels,
Crates of rooster's eggs and a fancy dairy the cook
Conjured up the batter in a bucket big as a steamboat,
Which was hoisted up and tipped over, creating puddles
On the stove, and he used popcorn to flip the flapcakes
To the waiters, who were on roller skates to go faster.
The boys dove into the breakfast like wildcats, chomping
And slurping with a noise like Niagara, and they busted
Out the door into the frosty camp, with the raw sun
In the east sky, all rosy on the froth of the river,
And the waking up pines stinking up the air real pretty,
And Paul Bunyan standing out on American mud, ready

To big-talk to his bunch of drifters, and brag up logging:
"It's an okay morning, boys, and it's good to breathe:
This country's lucky, and so splendiferous you want
Oh, to cartwheel and kick your initials in the sky,
Spread-eagle, hug the whole territory for dear love,
Whoop hallelujah just to hear your god-damn voice,
And reel off here and yonder with a square dance heart!
I swear only a yellowbelly or a lazybones could go
And let this morning slide, and keep from sinking steel
Into white pine, but it's obvious as a mockingbird
We can't scatter like a mess of kids out of school
Or we'll wind up with nothing but a little sawdust;
All right, so slack up a minute and promise with me
On the river, your bible, to go by the logger's rules.
One, always talk straight; be bald-faced, stick to it
Like it was old whiskey: I hear of a man dealing
In a double-talking lie, I'll hang up his ax myself.
I don't mean you can't story, now; I've been fishing
And I like to stretch it for fun, but it's the fakes
And the horse traders, the two timers I'm against.
Two, there's no brawling and no boozing in the woods:
I might see a little back-of-the-shanty roughhousing,
Or a short nip on a cold Sunday, and turn my head,
But when your drunk or free-for-all holds up the drive
By a wink, say goodbye to your pals, because you're gone.
Three, if you drag yourself to the city come spring
I want you to be all slow fingers and sweet talk
With the fillies. I imagine your idea is belly bumping,
Which is wonderful, but I catch you beating on a woman,
Look out: whatever you give her I'm going to give you.
Okay, boys, speak up; you're on your own say-so, here:
I need upwards of half of you as sawyers, to fall
The trees, whirling an ax sharp as sunlight around you
Till you steam, and ache all over, till your veins bulge;
I need plenty of swampers, to bust up the scenery,
And slash and rut the trails, and to lop off the limbs
From the down pine, which calls for backbone and stay;

And I need ox-strong skidders, to tug the logs to sleighs
And snake the load across the ice, over the toteroad
On down to the rollway, on the slopes of the branch;
And at the spring breakup I need the top lumberjacks
As the water rats, who'll ride the logs down the river
Into the snags and jams, just for the glory of it.
Now take a breath of this almighty Appalachian air,
Grin like an old pioneer, and pitch into the timber!"

Winter broke out in the up country with a big bang
And a big wind, blowing all morning without a letup,
Wheezing like a harmonium, whooping through the boughs
Of the stiff pines, squabbling with itself, puffing so hard
It tossed rocks like kisses, ripped holes out of the ground,
It hit an old black bear in the mouth and it whisked him
Inside out, it squashed the clouds, it snatched the feathers
Off the chickens and stuck them on the ever-loving hogs,
It leaned everything east, and tried to bully the sun.
There was a log chain hanging from the roof of a shanty
For a wind gauge: if it rattled it meant it was breezy,
If it was swinging, it was real windy, if it laid out flat,
It was a gale, and it was floating off into the blue.
This wind was cuckoo; it'd blow up, blow down, and
Then it'd stand still and blow six ways from Sunday;
It was kind of like the weather in the big timber days,
And the balled up seasons when the calendar got knocked
Out of whack: a haywire spring, oh maybe a winter,
A screwball fall, a buffalo summer rolled in at random,
Nothing took turns, and after, say a couple of summers
And no spring, or a month with four seasons squeezed in,
The almanacs took up comedy, and the weather prophets
Went south. This foolishness was foxing Paul Bunyan,
Who was up to here in his ledgers, logging the logging,
Who, with such-and-such receivables, so-and-so payables,
His red invoices, his black bills, his ice cream payroll, was
Writing his chronicles, and book-balancing like an acrobat.
He got blisters on all of his fingers counting up like so:
One horse, two bits, three cheers, four stars, five fingers,
Six shooter, seven natural, eight ball, nine day wonder,
Ten gallon hat, start over. He set his green fountain pen
Down on his desk, rubbing his face to wake up, snarling:
"Oh man, I'm tired of this god-almighty paper work!
I'm liable to squat and bust if I can't hit my old woods;

My boys are breathing hard, falling the ponderosa, yeah
And I sit here doodling, tuckered out by the numbers.
I'll bet they're goofing up without a straw boss there,
But how can I be the man when I'm totally swamped
By accounts? I'm missing the whole hoot owl morning!
I add up the figures, but all I get is one more figure,
And it's not like I don't look for short cuts, but hell,
I calculated with both hands, and I just got woozy;
I gave the boys a pop quiz to see who might spell me
And graded it on a curve, but ha! everybody flunked;
I called up a gang to carve my arithmetic on trees,
I'd holler out three numbers at once, they'd screw up,
And when I lost track of them, I scrapped the idea;
I invented logarithms, which was natural, but it seems
My characteristic was always fouled up in my mantissa,
And I'd monkey with it so long I wasn't saving time;
I don't know, I guess I'm just bound to let a foreman
Go and crack the whip, while I wrestle with the math."
The original push Paul signed on was Shot Gunderson,
The iron eater, the bear tamer, the all-creation hunter,
The rip-snorting snuff chewer, who could knock a cougar
Spang out of a bull pine with one good tobacco squirt.
He was a big noise on account of his mouth thunder,
And he was a slam-down jack-up bawl-out old bastard
Who might reel it off for days, like a one-man riot,
And it's said he could cuss the quills off a porcupine.
One time all his curses were written down in a book
Called The Ox-Skinner's Dictionary, but it burned up,
And the story goes it was by spontaneous combustion.
Shot Gunderson was breaking in his highball system
On the Tadpole River, up in the Bullfrog Lake country,
And he was croaking so loud into this absurd wind
His voice cracked up into nothing, into a squeak,
And without his old thunder it was goodbye job, but
Shot's back talk had caught on real glorious with the boys,
And from that day on lumberjacks used flowery lingo.
The new foreman was punch-drunk Chris Crosshaul, who

Was a white water maniac and loved to ride the logs
With a hundred-damn-verse song, and a fanatic smile,
And who hustled the timber down White River, rolling
By the unreal badlands, and right on past the town,
Which obliged the river pigs to drive it back upstream
In an upstream drive, an immortal rough grind
Which winded them, when Paul fed Babe a sack of salt
And had the blue ox slurp water till the river reversed.
Old Paul sent this bad character back to the swamp
Without a farewell party, and kept his ear on his boys:
"Hey tenderfoot, look out!" "You talking to me, fool?"
"I don't see nobody else." "I didn't hear you say sir."
"I was wondering if you saw the black hodag go by you."
"What on earth's a black hodag?" "Oh, it's a thing that feeds
On mud turtles, water snakes, muskrats, and human beans;
It's like a rooster with steel feathers which it can throw
With dead aim; it was right behind you, and you missed it."
"I was too busy watching the luferlang in your tree."
"Now don't you josh me, kid." "Oh yeah, it's triple-jointed
And dark-striped, and it's got a fox tail. I understand
It'll attack you for nothing, and if it bites you, bang!
You're on ice. It eats you and it's harmless all year."
"I guess it ain't hungry. Hey, what's this about a pilgrim?"
"The word is a Swedish mountain man, big as Bunyan,
And with a razzle-dazzle style, is coming to the camp."
"Oh mama, what was that, an earthquake or something?"
"I believe it's walking!" "I'll be—" "Hey, hold on, man!"
Big Swede, the bull of the woods, was swaggering up
Out of nowhere, sure as Shenandoah, yellow-haired,
Sky-tall and red-faced, grinning his great buck teeth,
His eyes blue fight, and his big paws jammed in his pockets.
Old Paul looked, but he didn't need a barber to tell him
This was his foreman: he walked over to say howdy
And it felt funny, because it was his first handshake.
His new old friend greeted everybody with a yawp:
"Welcome! Hello, boys. Good morning, I'm Big Swede!
I come from Sweden. I'm over here in America now.

I was walking on the mountains. I heard of logging.
This is the job for me, I said. This is a lot of fun.
This beats walking on the mountains. Oh, I sailed away!
I crossed the puddle in between us, I mean the Atlantic.
I work like a mule, but I'm better. I don't wear out.
I'm with you guys, if it's all right. There is one hitch:
I don't take baths. I don't like water. I'll wash up
On January one. Okay? Happy new year! Thanks."
Old Paul got thick with Big Swede, and after a little
Back slapping and joke swapping, he rallied the camp:
"Way out yonder in the grand frontier Dakota country
And somewhere from the Souris to the Cheyenne River
Is the mountain that stands on its head, like an upside
Down miracle, steep as a winter moon, and miles high.
Its peak's stuck in the ground, and on its green slopes
The timber grows down, all the creeks run backwards,
And flittericks, the flying squirrels, go zooming, quick
As cannon balls, in barrel rolls, lazy eights, loop the loops:
Its foot's a flat I don't exactly know how wide, and
Up there the springs are burbling, and the phillyloo bird,
With a big beak like a stork and no feathers to spare,
Sails with its belly up to the sun to ward off colds.
Buck up, you hayseeds, I want you to log this mountain:
It's an out-and-out dare to a real lumberjack, boys,
And on top of that it'll make my chronicles look good.
Whether you walk turvy-topsy or up on your hands
Is Big Swede's business, I'm signing him as your push.
Okay now, everybody scream hurray, and go to work!"
Big Swede and the boys waded into the green trees,
Hooting like indians, and high-stepping over the weeds,
While Paul kicked a pine cone, and slunk into his office.
First off, they logged in the lowlands, whopping so fast
They took time outs to cool their broadaxes in the river,
And the hurricane work went just as nice as whiskey,
Outside of the trouble of keeping all the axes sharp:
The old method was to kick a boulder off a hill
And run like hell beside it while holding out the ax

And letting it scrape till it was all honed and true,
And so Bunyan invented the grindstone out of mercy.
Big Swede hustled lumberjacks between woods and camp,
And after hollering for the get-up-and-go shift
He took them on the quiet to tackle the mountain,
Without a word, let alone a huddle, with old Paul,
Who was left behind with his approaches on paper,
And who shook his head over it, but let the slap go.
By and by the first men trudged back, all washed out,
And Big Swede, a little frazzled, with a blank eye,
Rousted another crew and headed out to the mountain.
The lumber output dwindled down to splinters and chips,
And so Paul dropped everything to go out for a looksee:
Big Swede had lashed these cables from trunk to trunk,
From which, upside down and by tight timber hitches,
All of the swampers and sawyers were hanging, hooked,
Dizzy and red, with the dirt and sawdust in their eyes,
And their caps, pipes and flasks tumbling away for miles,
While Big Swede honked and yammered, wheedling the men:
"Yikes! We've got a goose egg, here! Why won't you, now?
Look, if you chop the trees I'll give you a big surprise;
If you don't chop I'll knock all your heads together!
Why don't you chop the trees? This is Big Swede talking:
Oh come on, you can do it, I say you can! You can't.
Hold on, boys! We've got axes and ropes, what's wrong?
We've got a bum mountain. Mister Bunyan's loony. Aw!"
Paul rambled back for his old double-barrel shotgun,
Which was so big that when it was busted and he used
Its barrels for the smokestacks of the first sawmill,
They were so tall they were hinged to let the clouds go by:
He had Big Ole the blacksmith make outlandish bullets
Out of brass-bound and sheet iron-capped cedar logs,
While the boys walked in, bitched, buggered, and bewildered,
Winking their eyes, too blown to go back to the mountain;
And when Big Swede shrugged his broad-beam shoulders and
Said the mountain was too many for him and move on,
Old Paul spit and reddened, stamped on his heel and roared.

Now he had three voices: first, his snort, inside a room,
Was gracious, like a sea breeze, just a curl in the air;
Second, in the great outdoors, his yell was a living gale;
And third, his roar was so loud it would light a fire
In the woods and snuff it, like he boomed this morning:
"Damn you good-for-nothing saps, where in hell are your balls,
You dumb jackass dimwit thickskull lunkhead greenhorn
All thumbs chicken-heart weak-knee baby-face oafs?
What kind of wag-tail sissies are you, you milkmaids?
Mom's calling, you bums, go home: you're so lackadaisical,
Hey! you couldn't cut down a daffodil with a ripsaw!
Do you imagine a sea dog quits it just because he's
Sailing in the wind's eye? No, man: he trims his canvas
And scuds close-hauled, and that old head wind's in his sails.
Can you see a dirt farmer just kissing his fields off
To the flood when a fence-lifting rain falls? No, man!
He slaps a dam up and wham, there's his July water.
It's just horse sense, I mean, trouble ain't trouble, see,
You big palookas, if you've got the lumberjack's eye.
Come on, Big Swede, you windbag, you all follow me;
Why, logging this upside down mountain will be easy
As blinking at the sun: you just watch a good worker."
Out at the mountain old Paul cocked and skied his popgun,
And, jerking the trigger, shot fire out of both barrels:
It rained all kinds of rubble, and when the smoke spun off
All of the dazzled men sang whoop-de-doo to their stars,
Because the two shells had sheared off a thousand trees,
Which had dove down and become an upside down woods.
Paul Bunyan banged the trees, quick-loading, sharpshooting,
And his jacks bumped them over in a flash, in a snap,
Oh boy it was easy, and Big Swede took back charge.
Paul was slumped at his desk later on, slow figuring,
When he peeked out his window, and gawked: all of his men
Were back in camp, gabbing, lollygagging, horsing around;
He was skin-pinching amazed, and when he asked them what,
They said Big Swede decided to handle it all by himself.
Old Paul felt crazy in his belly, and a four-alarm fire

In his blood; he lit out for the mountain like a sting bee
And in no mood for a jaw session, huffing and grunting,
Whacking his hand against the air, and vowing to shape
This bull-shooting pig-feather upstart up and fast,
Before he lost his best saw boss, and all for nothing.
When he arrived at the mountain that stands on its head,
Big Swede was halfway up it, and old Paul bawled out,
"Okay, dreamer, you haul your butt back down to earth!
What's your story, huh? Why don't you let it slide? Don't
Act deaf with me, you dumb roundhead, or I'll start yelling!
I don't mind saying I'm a little perturbed with you.
Turn back, talk back, or by heaven I'll show you how!"
Big Swede wasn't speaking, the old-time mountain man
Was bouncing up the hill, rock to rock like a goat;
On top he unhitched his big ax from his studded belt
And, sizing up a stand of firs, he crowed back down:
"Oh boy, I love elbow room! Now I've got my own ax,
And my bunch of trees: this is my lumber camp, chief!
Hey, you shut up, you bag of air: don't monkey with me.
You hire me on, and what? You horn in on my job!
Yeah, I looked real dumb but, oh my rags and patches,
I'm my own big shot now, I quit: go blow your nose!"
Now old Paul's eyes were sparking, his beard was smoking:
When he sighted up the cliff, it was just too steep
And he backed up a mile for a tall-stepping jump,
Ran like a congressman, and zoomed into the blue
But missed the peak, and sprawled under his own landslide.
He spluttered onto his feet and rumbled up this hill,
And from there he jumped up skyward, lifting his arms,
And catching his fingers on the rim of the mountain.
He hauled himself up to the green flat and squawked good
As he danced in a circle, stomping, flapping his elbows
And hooting, waggling his head like a turkey, rocking
On his heels like a grizzly, till with a funny look
In his man's direction, he stood: his new foreman
Was giggling, squirting up into the air, and coming
Down in a corkscrew motion, sticking his arms out

Whirlwind style, kicking like a mule at a picnic,
Way up high, squinting into the hard winter sun,
And he only quit when he heard Paul Bunyan holler:
"Yahoo! I'm an old hawk, and I'm hungry for greenhorns!
I'm two-fisted, and inhuman is too polite! I'm full
Of prickles, and only a free-for-all will calm me down!
Oh, I'm going to surround you like a backwoods rain,
And introduce you to the stars! I'm itching for you!"
"Oh yeah? I'm scared, honey! But look out: I'm ugly,
And I love it! See, my punching bag's a beehive, ha!
And I'm all knuckles! I'm bad weather, and I hit hard!
I'll blow through you! I'm half man and I'm half hammer!
I'll pound you so flat you'll be a poster of yourself!"
"I hope you've said your goodbyes, because I'm riled now!
I swear I'll kick the shit and daylights out of you,
You big impossible cross-eyed finger-twiddling moron!
Yeah, laugh; but I'm going to knock you ass over appetite,
You stuck-up fat-headed red-necked unfaithful punk!"
"Okay, boss! But don't be so cantankerous with me,
It ain't healthy! Hey you, guess what! You're a polecat,
And you stink! Come here, my fist wants to talk to you!
When I'm all done you'll be looking for work in a circus,
You chicken, you cheat, you bluebird, you damn accountant!"
Big Swede yowled like an iron horse, and charged over,
Butting into old Paul's belly, slamming him to the grass,
Oh but Bunyan kicked him where it counts and bobbed up
Swinging, clouting the Swede in the forehead, ducking
A hook, taking a thump to the ribs, hammering back,
Old Paul was dancing, side-wheeling to his left
Around Big Swede, and biff! connecting with a jab, and wham!
Blood spouted from the Swede's eye, and with body blows
Landing, he lashed out, he was hurt, and jolted Bunyan
With a stiff counter punch, he yanked him by the whiskers
And waltzed a little with him, swiped at old Paul's chin,
Who spun off, tussling Big Swede down, where they wrangled
And slugged it out, rough-and-tumble, till they saw stars,
Big Swede on top, banging away with the old one-two,

And now it was Bunyan on top of the bucking Swede,
Walloping him pow! in the kisser with a hard right!
It was real dusty up there, and the two fist fighters,
Trading argument settlers, were wrapped up in a cloud,
It was bad, it was blue murder, the blood was flying,
The absolute booms of the jawbreaking, haymaking,
Heart-busting punches had all the bunkhouses wobbling
In the lumber camp, and the whole territory rocked.
It was a knock-down drag-out by Dakota rules:
There ain't any, and the big brawl went on for ages;
When the ruckus was over and the cloud calmed down,
The lumberjacks, climbing out of their quick foxholes,
Inched toward the fight for a look at what was what.
The mountain was zero, it was a hill of pebbles,
And out of its powder, with the black-and-blue loser
By the arm, and his shirt in rags, walked the winner
By a knockout, the Yankee wonder, the rose of Dixie,
And the world superheavyweight champ, Paul Bunyan.
He tugged Big Swede on back to the ramshackle camp,
And old Paul rubbed his red knuckles, and said real slow,
"I'm sorry; you're a horse, and I should have backed you.
Won't you be my straw boss? I love the way you hit!"
Big Swede, his eyes blue fight, said okay with a laugh,
And after shaking on it, he shouted up a work gang.
The bout was over, but all the blood had knotted on
What was now the great prairie, and the cakes of dirt
Balled up with blood were the Black Hills of Dakota.

3

They saw the mountains go boom in the awful shock wave
From the big fight between Paul Bunyan and Big Swede,
And the lumberjack shanties shake till they were timber,
And looking through the sticks and damage, old Paul yelped:
The ink barrels in his head office had split their ribs
And spilled ink all over his day journals and log books;
The tallies were splashed, and the characters were smeared,
The rigmarole was illegible, everything was blackened
Up to volume ten thousand, the stories said the end,
Oh the flashy and the old-fashioned words were lost,
And he winced, and laid his raw palm against his cheek:
"God, why do I have to rip through this flimsy camp
Like a pig at a wedding? While I brawl and I feather
My cap I catastrophe what I love; I'm all the mayhem
I need, I banged up these shanties, these innocent books
With my own fist! Look: my bouncing chronicles are spoiled,
The long gambles and the grand slams are wiped out now,
And I don't care how many god-damn dollars I pile up
Or prayers I squawk to the sky, I can't buy them back.
Okay, the boys and I are in a pinch, it's time to light
Into a whiz-bang and history-making job, and quick;
Oh my crazy lumberjacks, if I know you from nothing
A wrangle, yeah! you cocks, a double drive is just
What'll set your boots on fire, and boost you to the clouds!"
Old Paul and his mob shoved off, looking for a creek
For the double drive: they skipped Powder River, since
It's so wide and so shallow, till where it rolls over
And it's so skinny and so deep, and they laughed off
Salt River, all snags and velocity, and kept on walking;
They snorted at the white water boiling in the Hot Springs,
And while it's true it promised all kinds of good logging,
Nobody wanted to go up Shit Creek, because the idea
Sounded funny; they pushed on to the east anyhow,
Till somewhere out in the Wisconsin sticks they hit

The Side-by-Side Rivers, the water cresting, and slick
As a swindle; it looked perfect, but after scouting it
Out they saw the hitch: while the rivers were dandy,
The timber was skimpy by the shoreline, oh maybe
A winter's firewood and that's it, and old Paul sat
In his new office, sketching, working on an angle.
He was still stymied a couple of pots of coffee later,
When, popping his knuckles, he sauntered to the window
And sprawled back: it was hard to swallow, but he saw
What looked like a pine forest out there, out of nowhere,
With a chance of trees, and all of them big and bare,
Buckskin and topless, like a logger's kingdom come,
It was better than a kick in the head by a blue ox!
It was kind of spooky with the freak pines standing
In rows, but it's how come they'd be fine without trail
Swamping, it was a lightning show: the boys were drooling,
And when old Paul looked up from the amazing orchard,
He only sneezed, and pow! they jumped in, swinging axes!
He was real tickled to see his brush monkeys wheel
And the question mark answer itself, and he dilly-
Dallied awhile on the way back to his pencil shoving.
Highballing like fire through the amazing orchard,
Shearing the trees into big blue butts, the timber beasts,
Appleknockers, animals and punks, floaters and palookas,
Broke into the green timber: the double drive was led
On the left Side-by-Side by the bull moose, Big Swede,
On the right by the ramrod, Soupbone Tom, log-hungry
And money-mad, who was so skinny he had to stand
In the sun ten lousy minutes to throw a shadow,
And wore a double-barrel shotgun for a pair of pants.
It was a race, there were troublemakers screwing up,
And the bull bucks name-calling to crack down on them:
On the sheepherders, who couldn't hit a bull in the ass
With a shovel, and the grape grabbers, on the lookout
For the short haul, the bible pounders, with their nerve
And their noise, on the punks and whittlers, who whipped
All morning without any muscle, and the sightseers

And witnesses, out gawking instead of pitching in, and
On the buckwheaters, who were all thumbs, hopeless, slow
As grandmas, and didn't know a broadax from a banjo.
Now most of the men were lightfoot gut-busting horses,
All iron and steam, out to be on the blue ribbon side,
Working the back country, and skipping anything less
Than six feet wide, tackling the barber poles, crooked
As ram's horns, hollow trees, redtops dying of beetles,
Wolf trees, on a perhaps, fat pines and bastard firs,
Rampikes, blowdowns, and the clear long-bodied saw timber,
And falling the ice-broken bayonet tops, stagheads, cripples,
Timber with stubs, burls, swells, crowfeet, spike knots,
Scars, and pitch pockets, out in the windshake woods.
After the swampers had brushed out the walking trails,
A logger, singlejacking by himself, fixing to fall a pine,
Would shoo off the yellow jackets and the mean horseflies,
Keep his eye out for a hidebehind, the man-eater, always
In back of him, bite off a chaw of fancy dynamite
Eating tobacco, grab hold of his ax by the blister end,
Whistle something while planting his bergman calked shoes
In the tiger crap, lift up his ax, swing solid, whack out
An undercut, dodge splinters spit by the argopelters,
Corner her up, shuffle around, chop the back cut out,
And sing out, Down the hill! as the pole croaked and fell,
Smashing on over like slapstick, and busting its crown.
Now's when the beavers got eager, knocking off the limbs
And the knots with boy's axes, getting their misery harps,
Their crosscut saws, oiling them up with cougar juice,
And sawing hell for speed, if they got timber-bound,
They'd widen the cut with wedges, bucking all the trees
To logs, kicking up sawdust. Now the bullwhackers came
To bunch up the pay poles, bridle them round with rope
And pull, straining their milk, drag them to the skid road,
Where the blue ox was hauling for both of the teams,
Snaking logs to the two rivers, where the canthook men
Rolled and decked them on the rollways, ready to drive,
With Big Swede and Soupbone Tom stacked up in a tie.

With the fat cut booming out of the bush, the bookkeeping
Was doubled, and old Paul just blinked, as mixed up
As a handful of ants, trying to count up the infinite
On his fingers. Once he looked up from his book juggling
And it struck him that the left twin was six feet high
And rising, while the right was okay, and so, puzzling
Why the river was all jacked up, and anxious about
The rollways, he went downstream to take a gander.
He saw what he thought was a rumptifusel, wrapped
Round a tree trunk like a fur coat, and pure vicious,
And jogging on, he tried to track a toteroad shagamaw,
Walking on its front bear claws, on its back moose hoofs,
And sniffing for lumberjack clothes hanging on the pines.
When he was a country mile down, he bumped into it:
There was a work boot out in the belly of the river
And backing the water, which was worn by a man taller
Than the mortal law, sitting up on this bluff, and when
He jiggled his foot out of the branch, the flood let go.
Old Paul eyeballed this stranger, pretty near as big as him,
Baldheaded, with a high forehead full of logic wrinkles,
And with sky-pale blue eyes behind his golden spectacles,
Which perched on his long snout, and who bit on his lips
And fiddled with his necktie, as he scraped a jackknife
Big as a bull across a limestone cliff, making it flat
And throwing off flakes like snow; up from behind his ear
He snatched the original lead pencil, made of a coon tree,
And scribbled on the bluff, making numbers, up and down,
And all oblivious to Paul Bunyan, which is no breeze.
Paul waved his burly arms, and he hopped like a pigeon;
He uprooted a fir, but nothing doing, and so he drawled,
"Yeah, it sure's going to be dry if it don't ever rain."
The stranger didn't flinch, he just kept on writing
And so Paul plumped down beside him on the cliff and said,
"Pardon me if I say howdy; it's a mighty morning.
I think I'll just help myself to a chaw of this here
Peerless spit-or-puke tobacco: you're welcome to it
If you like, it tastes ferocious. Well, how's it going?"

The stranger looked up, real casual, and he sighed, "Oh,
I'm just staggering around: I don't know, I feel funny,
My hair's flying off in clumps, my eyes are shot to heck,
I've got chapped lips, my teeth all hurt, my breath is awful,
I've got a bellyache, cramps in what I call my muscles,
My ass is sore from the applejack sprints, I'm horny
And my cock's out of whack, oh my knees are buckling,
My dogs are woofing and I'm scared to count the blisters,
Insects are ganging up on me and eating me alive,
I think I'm having a sunstroke, what are the symptoms,
I'm sick, my wind's broken, my heart's running by prayer,
Oh I'm in great shape, pal, I'll be okay if I live.
I believe I will indulge myself with a twist of scrap;
Why hell, you know since all of you hillbillies are hooked
On chewing tobacco, I ought to market an out west brand;
Ads, billboards, sandwich boys, listen to the campaign:
Dazzle the boss, and wow all the gals with just one nip
Of this champion funky all-American plug tobacco!
I'd have to scalp it, you see, knock it down dirt-cheap
To cut under the boys back east; I could branch out
And pocket a cool million, oh and I mean clean up!
It sure beats melting in these god-forsaken boondocks."
Old Paul was thinking this bird swallowed a dictionary,
And he was doing his level best to keep from grinning:
"You won't be hot long, stranger, buck up: it looks like rain."
"Are you kidding? Have you sized up the old firmament,
Or what? Why, these cat's-tail clouds are all hocus-pocus.
I want to wise you up, big boy: clouds are supposed
To be the great chiefs of the wild blue, right? Like hell;
I say they can't organize a piss in a beer parlor!
Oh yeah, they bluster, but don't let that bamboozle you;
They're all thunder and no rain, trust me; underneath,
When it comes to sky juice, they're a bunch of pinch fists."
"I wish I had a notion of what the heck you're talking
About, but don't say: I'd like to hear what you're writing."
"I'm working on this plus this, that take away that,
So-and-so times whatever, and nothing into something;

In a word, I'm figuring: I guess it's like a hobby."
Old Paul slipped off the cliff, dusted off and then yelled,
"Hold on! Gracious me, you do arithmetic for fun?"
"Oh natch, corn cracker, I'm so hot for numbers, ha!
I love it: all the honky-tonks out here in gay Wisconsin,
And I work! I can't fandango in the middle of nowhere!"
The man's an artist, thought Bunyan, he works for nothing!
"Howdy! I'm Paul Bunyan, tramp, big shot, tall talker,
Trail swamper, ax swinger, pine tree bucker, log driver,
Pioneer, lightning thinker, and all-round superlumberjack."
"Hi ya, Mister Bunyan. I'm John Rodgers Inkslinger,
Answer man, math whiz, ballyhoo man, land surveyor,
Country doctor, local comic, and back street philosopher.
I'm actually working on a rough geography problem."
"Well, break it to me, Johnny: I've done some figuring
And I know the layout here; maybe I can help you."
"Okay, here goes: I'm looking for section thirty-seven.
In surveyor's measure, there's thirty-seven square miles
In a township, but out here I only count thirty-six;
I walk it over, thirty-six; I add it up backwards,
Thirty-six! What happened? I ain't fooling, it's a pain
In the atlas: if I didn't blow it, surveying is bunk!"
"Now hold everything. When I logged off the lower Side-
By-Side Rivers, I'd hitch Babe, my blue ox, to a section,
On account of old Babe can haul anything with two ends,
Tow it to the river, cut down the good and plenty timber,
And drag the square of land back to its original spot.
I always let the thirty-seventh sit in the water
While I went on a coffee break, and it'd wash away.
I guess you better switch to a scale of thirty-six."
Inkslinger squinted with surprise, and started jabbering,
"Well, I'll be hornswoggled! You'd make a hot surveyor;
Why you're no country egg, or frontier rowdy! Look,
Why don't you hook up with me and be a mud chicken?
With your latitude and my longitude, there's no limit;
We could pace off this continent down to the last pebble,
And I promise the work'll go down like morning wildfire!

Don't be shy, muscle man: what is it, yep or nope?"
"I've got a big idea under my hunting cap, Johnny,
Which I'm hoping will come out in front of the parade:
Why don't you sign on with me and be a timekeeper?
You'd be the brains and count the stacks of timber for me,
Reckon up the payroll and dream up theories for laughs,
Crank out your heart's journal, and in your own words,
Witness our lumberjacking and write it down, guts, feathers
And all, oh glory, Inkslinger, you were born for the job!
The pay is slim, but man! the exaltation's evergreen.
Why don't you take a whirl at it, and see what's up?"
"No thanks, you keep your rough-hustling lumber camp,
I'll stick to my compass and chain: I've come this far,
I want to go the distance, I want to map America.
Hey, will you ask your blue ox to quit licking my cheek?
I mean, I love animals, but enough is enough, huh?
Oh, no! What's this? What in the hell is this? Oh shit!
Your dumb stinking ox trampled on my instruments!
My charts, my scopes, my pencils, my lines, my tables,
My cheating sticks, they're all stomped on by the blue beast,
It's all over! Ah, I might as well just kiss it off!"
"Hang on, Johnny. I apologize for the blue ox, honest,
But don't you act like a nincompoop and start bawling!
Okay, two-fisted calamity's knocked you for a loop:
What do you do, caterwaul like a kid, or bang back
Like a cowboy? I say why dive, on a random punch?
I all but wiped out my tall chronicles in a fight,
But damn if I was whipped: I just spit and jolted on.
Now, don't boohoo: come on, let's tromp over to the camp.
No sweat, you'll get your share of sun circles, like when
The boys and I struck out, after the above skirmish,
And walked as big as anything into this amazing orchard
Where all we had to do was yank out the pines like that!
I'm spouting off, I just wish you wouldn't say it's over;
Nothing this side of sunlight can lick a lumberjack.
Look, over yonder's where the nothing-to-it timber stood."
Inkslinger pointed, with his skimpy hair pricking up like

Wild bristles on an old broom, and he stood and squawked,
"Oh, nausea! I don't believe it! Oh lord! Help, police!
All of my surveyor's stakes! They're all gone, you crook!
Go get them, you bastard: you better haul them back!"
"I'm sure they're sawed up by now; I'm sorry, I didn't know."
"Oh great! Goodbye two years of real baldheaded work!
I rooted them deep, man: those poles were going to weather!
Hey, I feel lousy. Everything looks yellow; my skin is numb!"
Inkslinger spluttered, stretched out his arms, wobbled
And said oh-oh like a moo cow, doubled up like a sack
Of Idaho potatoes, and slumped into a mud puddle.
Old Paul leaned down and lugged him fireman style into
The back room of his shanty, where he let him snooze;
And the low surveyor took to roosting in that tight room,
Kind of sulky and nothing to say. The drive poked along
Till the blues hit old Paul, and he thumped on the door:
"Johnny, it's Bunyan. I swear, I feel dumb as a man
With a size seventeen collar and a size two hat for,
You know, my stake mistake, and when the ox ran loose
All over your gear. If I had two heads, I'd let you
Knock them together. I guess I am a country egg,
I should have known; boy, it's so hard to build whatever,
And so easy to bust it up. I owe you, Inkslinger.
I could kick myself, but that's silly. I could trap you,
Oh, say a gyascutus: it's big as a buck in winter,
And with blue lightning in its eyes, jack rabbit ears,
Mountain lion jaws, and a yowl like a southeast blow,
It's no wonder you can't see it till after a snake bite,
Sloping across the foothills, up on its telescope legs,
Hanging on tight with its rainbow tail, and eating rocks.
If your pleasure's fire water, I can bring you a fat jug
Of my wild juniper moonshine: it's righteous, cutthroat,
And with beer back, look out! It's a true antifogmatic,
It'll whoopee you up in no time, as sure as preaching.
Would you go for the complete works of Bigmouth Bill,
In forty volumes, with woodcuts, a forward, backward,
Index, glossary, concordance, gazetteer, and almanac?"

Paul stopped and rubbed his chin, and Inkslinger sneered,
"The more you stir it, the more it stinks. Give it up."
After this slam old Paul was so stung in his heart
He let his chronicles go and lost track of the logging,
And though the Side-by-Side drive was a four-star hit,
He only sat there, calculating how to make it up
To Johnny, when the surveyor shuffled out and said,
"Okay, Mister Big, fetch your books: I'm signing on."
Paul went straight up at this, and hollered from the clouds,
"What on earth! Are you fooling me, Johnny? What happened?"
"I'm coming to it, blue eyes: with all this ripe time,
I figured I might thumb through your old chronicles.
Now, when I'm in bad shape, I'm a sucker for myself,
But while I read, I stopped thinking about my sour luck:
Why, you're an ax-slinging wonder, you son of a bitch!"
"How'd you read the chronicles? They're covered with ink!"
"Wait just a second here, and I'll let you have a look."
Johnny came back out with book one of the chronicles:
He'd traced over the goose feather scratches in the paper
In white ink, religiously, bringing back the alphabet,
And he'd salvaged all of the ten thousand volumes.
Old Paul stared, and he said with a catch in his voice,
"I'm proud to know you, Johnny; but why'd you do all this?"
"I'm in love with you, high pockets, what do you think?
No, really: sulking gets to be duller than Wisconsin
After a while, and patching up the chronicles was fun."
"Oh Johnny Inkslinger, you're in! Shake hands, partner."

Paul Bunyan roused and back-slapped his solid work gang,
Big Swede barked out the show like a circus ringmaster,
Johnny Inkslinger spelled it all out in the big book,
And the camp trekked to Saginaw country, Michigan.
Out on the grizzly and snow-stacked Tittabawasee
They split timber and piled the rollways up to the sky,
Old Paul now logging elbow to elbow with his boys.
Yeah, but spring staggered in with an air of trouble:
Come April, the boys were standing out on the old Manistee,
And when the ice shivered the tail down men broke rollways,
Jabbing their canthooks, shoving the saw logs in the river,
And the water rats followed, tramping down gig trails
Along the frosty shore, and riding on rafts and booms,
Kicking out the jams, tangling with the skookumchuck:
Waterfalls, whirlpools, narrows, tiderips, neverstills.
The slough pigs at the tail end of the misty parade,
Whirling swingdogs, yawping, laid back, sacking the rear,
Rolling the draggers and strays in the almighty water,
And nobody but was two hoots from a timber wolf.
All of a sudden, without a howdy-do, scads of mosquitoes
With sixteen-foot wingspreads dove down out of nowhere,
Straddled the creek, and started shanghaiing lumberjacks!
One old strong-arm logger fought free of the varmints
And slooped straight out of the blue, falling so far
The dang bluebirds built a nest on his windy head
And hatched their daughters and sons before he hit home.
Old Paul saw the whole gallinipper sneak attack,
And he shuttled Brimstone Bill the bullwhacker south
On a hot pony and at full pay for the Pecos River
To round up fighting Texas bumblebees, big and pronto.
Bill rode across the Oklahoma flats so all-honking fast
He saw the gosh-darn wind: he riled the hives up good,
Was a star in a whip-crack rodeo, and drove the swarm
Back from Texas to Michigan without losing a bee.

The ugly pushflies, with their hot heads and ring tails,
Slammed into the mosquitoes under a scab-red sun,
Whacking their wings like wet buzzards, and squirting fire;
But after a dogfight, the insect mobs fixed it up
And went in cahoots, cranking out a bunch of crossbreeds:
The moskittos, with stingers at both the front and back,
And just a monstropolous fancy for hooktenders' oxen.
They were death on ox snatching: they'd corner an ox
In the corral, fly up to it with a sling of leather
And buzz under, spin a bowknot, tighten the loop,
And good night Irene. Old Paul had holed up his herd
In a skeeter-proof cave, when the moskittos roared back
And hit that rock whining, working down like steam drills,
Dropping a shaft to the ox cave, shooting up lightning.
The moskittos were two rods deep in north country rock
When the loggers saw them jam up against a quartz vein,
And hold up to point their stingers: the nearest sandstone
Was clear in Minnesota, and so Paul had time to tick.
He dragged out an old kitchen boiler, stuck an ox in it,
Scrunched on in with Big Ole the blacksmith, and grinned.
The moskittos swooped up and got a whiff of the ox,
Whizzed a spell in the air, and zoomed in on a beeline:
As soon as a stinger drilled through, old Paul and Big Ole
Banged it over with their ten-pound sledges like carpenters
Clinching nails, till the whole mob was hooked to the iron.
The boiler rocked and rose as the ox rustlers took off,
And quick Paul and the blacksmith jumped Geronimo,
With the ox in their arms: the moskittos flapped away,
And were never seen again, especially by greenhorns.
To loosen up and just dawdle after the carryings-on,
Old Paul shouldered his pine-butt straight-barrel flintlock
And hiked on out to hunt in the freezing Michigan woods.
Just a spit and a holler out of camp, he got a flash
Of an actual gumberoo, looking for burned-out woods,
With a pumpkin head and a potbelly like a stove,
Ape arms and crazy legs sticking out round its waist;
It'd heave itself off a slope and roll down sideways,

Squeaking like a pulley, and scared of nothing but fire,
Because if it ever rubbed up against a flame, kerblam.
It minded him of when he sighted a whirling whimpus,
Which was a scraggly bastard, as big as a rain barrel,
With its plow horse legs all grown together at the fetlock
Into one hoof, and skinny arms which were so long
It steadied itself by propping on its palms. If a man
Was dumb enough to sidle up next to a whimpus,
It would cakewalk and whirligig like a wino on ice:
A crack from the whirling fists would cream the guy,
And the whirling whimpus would lick him up like pudding.
He thought of his staring contest with a flock of huggags,
Which stood thirteen feet high and weighed in at three tons,
With mud balls instead of heads and warts on their snouts,
Gunny sacks for ears, pine needle coats, and big flat feet.
The huggags go grazing in herds, on pitch and sweat,
And when it's time for shut-eye, since they have no knees
And can't flop down, the herd faces northwest by the moon
And sags against the trees, which, under three-ton pressure,
Begin to slant after a couple of nights; in American woods,
A stretch of timber all tilting one way is a sure sign
Huggags have been sleeping there. Just for the heck of it,
Bunyan figured out how to go about catching a huggag:
It'd be simple to pick out one of these skew-jaw trees
And saw it halfway; the idea's when a huggag went
To lean back for the old siesta, the trunk would rip
And the huggag go down, and, without knees, stay down.
Now Paul wasn't out for lop-eared gazooks and such like,
And so he aimed his heart and gun sight at a flight
Of two hundred twelve wild ducks skidding in pattern:
But why blow a slug on each and every nothing duck
In the sky? It was just plain wasteful, period. So
He tied a ball of twine to a bullet, loaded his rifle
And yawned, and when the ducks were lined up, he fired,
The twine went flying, the bullet harpooned all two-twelve,
And he tugged them back to camp like trout on a thread.
On his second outing, he went on the prowl for partridge,

And arguing like before that one shot ought to be plenty.
At last he spotted three hundred and twenty partridges
All pluming and twittering on a white spruce bough,
And he crouched, sighting longwise down the pretty branch,
Waiting for a bear to come bumbling and puffing along,
And when a big black bear wobbled up, old Paul squeezed:
The bullet went sparkling through the bear, split the limb,
The partridges' feet dropped down in the sudden crack,
The crack sprung shut, pinching all the birds to the bough,
Which broke off with a bang, tumbled in the air, and clouted
A burly deer in back of a juniper bush, wild honey
Poured out of the rip in the spruce, the deer kicked and
Slugged a fat buck rabbit up smack into Paul's forehead,
Paul teetered and flopped in the creek, and wading out
With his pockets full of fish, he headed back to camp,
Bringing, in his haul with a single bullet, a black bear,
Three hundred and twenty partridges, a buck rabbit,
A good-looking eight-point deer, a passel of catfish,
And two rolling hundred gallon barrels of wild honey.
On his third tramp, Bunyan was loaded for Red Eye,
The ugly bull moose who was tall as Suicide Hill,
With famous eyes like railroad lanterns, and great horns.
He brought a bullet and an ox wagon full of popcorn,
Which was his favorite snack when it was salty and buttered,
And deep in a pole thicket, a couple of rattlesnakes,
Coiling, clicking, flickered out at his boot: he sneered
And, twiddling his whiskers, hitched their heads together,
And, inch by inch, the sidewinders swallowed each other
Down to the rattles, and disappeared like abracadabra.
On a high cliff yonder, Red Eye was munching the grass,
As fat as a December bear, and bored with hunters:
The trick was how to blow it down without knocking
The moose, which was nobody's fool, off of the cliff;
And so old Paul sniffed and combobbolated a moment,
And when an idea lit up like morning in his attic
He nodded, diving into the popcorn for energy, chewing
With a clatter as loud as a Kentucky free-for-all,

And whisking it in so fast his hands were all blurry;
The wind off his fingers jerked trees out by the roots,
And the country acres around was drifted a foot deep
In popcorn scraps, and all the quill pigs and swish tails,
When they saw the ground white and the sky full of flakes,
Figured they were out in a snowstorm, and froze.
With his smoke pole reared, the butt cradled in his shoulder,
Old Paul grunted, "I aim to let fly and massacre you
Between the eyes: now get ready for circumbustification;"
He drew a bead, laid off breathing, and let her blaze,
And he lit out lickety-split for the moose, skedaddling
Quick as a boy and girl get naked under a honeymoon,
Hustling up there to grab old Red Rye before he fell,
So breath-taking fast he'd just touch a foot down now
And again to steer, red-faced like he was stealing home
On a wild ball, in a level game, in the last inning,
Two away, with a full count on a cross-eyed rookie;
But it was crazy, he ran just a suspicion too fast
And showed up at the moose before his own damn bullet.
He was chortling at this when it was time to duck,
As the shot went zinging over his hat, and it missed
Between the antlers, but Red Eye was already stiff:
The varmint had recognized old Paul and died of shock.
While he was slogging the miles home, with a new smile,
Paul Bunyan made chin music to keep him company:
"Bunch up the Dixie swamps and the Bible belt prairies,
The holy down East farms and the wild West beaches,
Throw in the cities with their shows and skidrow queens,
And all the screamers in this checkerboard of states,
Wrap them in Great Plain clouds and tie it with Old Muddy,
And like a dime firecracker next to the Milky Way,
Where the Fourth of July will spin till half past always,
The whole shebang is beat out by the Northern woods.
Now that the snow's thawing and jazzing up the creeks
And the midmorning moon's a white wreck in the sky,
The springs boom and improvise the reedy sloughs, and
Wake up the lakes, whose style is to double in water

Three seasons of the tough poles in the swank forest.
The long grasses hang on and mob out of the mud
Under the green snarl of wild holly and huckleberry,
And up with the looting bluejays and whiskey jacks,
In the tight bark whose calligraphy nobody can read,
The old evergreen timber muscles toward the light.
I hike the Northern woods with a kick in my sally,
I soak up the world like it was highballing away,
And once I snort the backwoods air into my pipes
My eyes ignite and my toes curl, I cock my elbows
Because I'm so slap-happy, and I arch my back and yowl
Like a lean coyote with all the stars in his head!
The animals may be a touch on the rampageous side,
But I can manhandle anything with bones, yeah
I can buck-dance with a wildcat and laugh him down,
I can snuff a timber wolf with a couple of blue words:
I'll wrestle Mrs. Nature three falls out of three
And stake my ox and all that I come up immortal,
And still steamed up with love for the curve of the earth.
I declare! Fire, infection and Yankees only slow her up,
And she's handsome as a keg of beer in a heat wave.
The pitch climbs in the pines, and my sap jumps in me
I feel so gully-whumping good when I look out
On a Northern morning and see the pine cones bulge
On the branches, and the daylight lean against the trees."
When Paul got back to his choppers he was full of bang
And the logging was too slow-motion to please his pulse,
And he whistled like he was mad, and staggered them up:
"What kind of a one-dollar chicken-shit outfit is this,
You jerkwater slow-poke wishy-washy deadhead
Flat-beer pussyfooting lollygagging drag-ass punks!
I turn my back to spit and whiz, and you guys peter out!
I'm sorry to crack up your gingerbread dreams, ladies,
But when I said to saw logs I didn't mean snore!
You bunch of whittlers are useful as a one-legged man
At a kicking match! I want to see Swedish steam
Spout out of your temples; get dirty, give her snoose!

I catch a man boondoggling and I'll eat him for lunch!
Wade in and knock it down, show the jungle you're alive!"
Paul picked out the top loggers in the Saginaw camp,
Red Jack, Rocky Dan, Pumphandle Joe, Slabwood Johnson,
Billy the Bum, Cedar Root Charley, and Roaring Jim,
Called them the seven axmen, swapped their ax handles
For iron chains, and let them swing their double-bit heads
Like sodbusters in August out mowing the south forty.
It was still too slow, so Paul invented the two-man saw
And worked it with Big Swede: its blade was around a mile,
And it swiped an acre at a whack. In the rough country
It skimmed hills and ridges, it skipped gorges and flumes,
But the two champions bulldozed whole counties anyhow.
While they were hitching up the load to Babe the blue ox,
The clouds curdled and dumped down a goose-drowning rain,
And when Babe, strong as a bullwhacker, pulled homeward,
The wet leather harness, under the strain of tons,
Stretched out like gossip on the general store porch.
When they rolled into camp, Paul discovered the harness
Running clear out to the skyline and the load beyond,
And he wheezed and chuckled till the sun came out,
The buckskin shriveled, and the lumber chugged to his feet.
The rain water had spilled so awful hard in the downpour
The rain barrel, which held nine hundred eighty-nine barrels,
Twenty-eight gallons, one quart, one-half pint, one gill
And three tablespoons minus eight drops, filled thirteen feet
And ten inches over the top, old Houghton Lake overflowed
And the Muskegon River ran too fast to sip from it:
The boys were scared the current might rip off their heads.
Old Paul rounded up the river rats and the boom pokes
And started the drive, yelling tips from the book of snags;
But as soon as the wood was wet they hit a log jam,
With a big pole stuck and a whole stack-up behind it,
And if a monkey were to shin up the jackpot to free it,
He'd be sure to be crunched before he could say scat.
Now, planting the blue ox down-river in front of the jam,
Old Paul fired off his shotgun, aiming to tickle Babe's ass

With buckshot till his tail twirled like a screw in the water,
Which washed it backwards, and untangled the rack heap.
Bunyan and his river hogs, with their peaveys in their fists,
Steadied out on the timber, and barreled down the flood
On the backs of the logs, heading for a far-off sawmill.
After sailing for a spell, Paul called to Roaring Jim,
"Hey, check out the lumber camp on your southpaw bank!
I could have sworn we were lonesome in Michigan, Jim:
You ever catch word of a logging gang up against us?"
Roaring Jim squinted at the pine shanties and said,
"No, man: I ain't heard a hoot about any competition,
But it sure as eggs looks like we've bumped into it!
It's too bad, but we're floating by too fast to ask them."
Old Paul yanked his slouch hat down to his boiling ears
And took a bite of his squirting tobacco, spiked his log
And snarled at the white water as they all coasted by
The tingling spruce groves, on the lookout for boulders.
When they burbled round a long crescent in the river
Paul stiffened up like a scarecrow in a frost and shouted,
"Okay, Roaring Jim! I'm about to go nuts: why don't
You cock your eyes to the left, and sing out what you see."
Roaring Jim rubbed his eyes, stooped down and looked out:
"Say I'm all wet, but it's another camp! Yeah, this one
Is slightly bigger; but hold on to your petticoats,
Am I slipping, or is that camp kind of familiar?"
Old Paul sneezed and answered, "I don't know, Roaring Jim;
All I know's this country's getting a trace too crowded,
I see another lumber camp, I'm going to get curious!"
He leaned out, looking alive: it gave him butterflies
In his stomach and a shooting star in his idea box, but
He just drove on through the haze, boosting up his boys,
Tending out, and sticking to his skill and his hunches.
The singsong water was making him drowsy and timeless,
As he rode on its skin, and rippled around a slow curve,
When he jolted and stared at a big money lumber camp
On his left hand, and he hollered, "All right, damn it:
All hands and the cook and the woodpeckers, ashore!"

The river rats steered over to the bank, and Bunyan said,
"Ain't this a beauty? We're back at our camp. If you boys
Imagine we're going ahead, you've been stung by creation.
Oh we're not too swift this morning! We're on a round river.
We can paddle from now to Christmas, we're going nowhere,
And it'll be the same hawk, blackberry bush and lumber camp
In the Great Lakes country sun after ten thousand years.
This creek has no spring and no bay: it's circled back
And turned us into tourists, I swear to Yankee Doodle!"
Paul was about to take a tall shovel and cut a canal
Slapdash to the lake from the make-believe backwater,
But he saw that the Round River was a wonder-for-hogs,
And so, hauling the timber overland to the Muskegon,
Old Paul launched the whole lollapaloozing drive again!
He was so star-spangled exultant at the big finish
He celebrated the fact by dreaming up water walking:
He broad-jumped way out to a long log in mid-river
And rolled it with his stride till the water creamed;
He stomped like a turkey, and while he birled he bragged:
"Whoopee! I'm long-legged, I'm rambunctious, I'm ripe!
I'm all bouncy, I'm the spotted horse nobody can ride!
Yeah, I waddle like an ox and I crow like a cyclone,
I punch like a landslide and I fuck like a hummingbird!
I'd walk ten miles in a good hurricane for a fight!
I've got the guts of a god-almighty freight train
And the brains of an almanac! Oh, I'm an easy hobo;
I can take a bite out of the sun and spit light,
I can strut till a buffalo blushes, and outscream you!
Look out, boys, I'm freewheeling and I'm on the loose!"
And he hoofed it so strong that when the river rumbled
He walked ashore on the bubbles, cut a gig trail,
And skipped back to the log before the bubbles broke.

When they had wound up the haywire Round River show,
The sawdust eaters decided on a drift to the west,
Out towards Red River and the hard Minnesota winter
In the country of bread and butter and the North Star,
Globe-trotting on the tail of the floater, Paul Bunyan.
The pot wrestler, known to the boys as the belly robber,
Was named Pea Soup Shorty, and was so dead-in-the-bone
And let-it-slide lazy, he'd railroaded his flunkies
Into sniffing the green slop in the kettle for him
Because, he said, it tuckered him out to breathe that deep.
He ruled out groceries one by one: first, porcupine stew,
And then slumgullion, bubble and squeak, and mystery pie,
Till he'd cut all the meals back to nothing but pea soup,
Pea soup today and forever, with a taste like fog.
He froze it around ropes and shipped it out as sticks,
He got the idea of sloshing it into the hollow ax handles
So the swinging of the axes would keep the soup hot,
And when Shagline Bill's freight sleds cracked up on the ice
And spilled into a lake, Pea Soup Shorty strolled out there
With a half a hog and three crates of Arkansas chicken,
Which is long for salt pork, dumped it in with black pepper,
Bloomed up a fire under the lake and made pea soup.
When he was running low, he sliced each pea in two
And boiled up a barrel of the world's first split pea soup;
And when they gave out, the bum salted a green shirt
And dunked it in the kettle, and nobody noticed. After
That, Brimstone Bill the bullwhacker walked up to Paul
To squawk for the boys, and blared till he was blue:
"Oh, for crying out loud in the clatterwhacking morning!
I'll be shot for a mockingbird before I touch a drop
Of this god-awful slime, and that goes for my pals!
I'd rather eat wind sandwiches, or a stack of knotholes!
This sad flat pie-face you hired on as a stew builder
Won't build a stew, on account of he's too busy looking

To slow-poison us all with pea soup, I ain't humming!
I've had my gutful of the bastard: he's a washout
As a soup jockey; he could be replaced by a fart!
I see a splash of soup and I'll puke up my breakfast!
Hey, you know I don't bellyache, I'm too straight-grained,
And it's got to be the limit when I get the gripes!
Come on, give the runt the ax, before we all keel over!"
Bunyan was too red-blooded to let his men fly off
Over bad chow, and he sacked Pea Soup Shorty that minute,
And boosted Sourdough Sam, who had been the crumb boss,
Up to grease burner: he was no slouch, but a high-stepping
Old horse, and sort of a crackpot about his one subject,
Sourdough, and not from buck fever like Pea Soup Shorty,
Who started in to pushing pea soup out of pure laziness;
Sam took a forty-two caliber devotion to sourdough
In the way that a gospel pitcher loves Jerusalem Slim.
Sam was daffy about sourdough, and he moved from biscuits
To sourdough salad, sourdough hamburgers, sourdough coffee,
And now he dreamed of a seven-course all-sourdough spread.
Sourdough rises upwards of five times as fast as yeast
And it's dynamite to handle, which didn't hold Sam back
From bragging it to the moon like a salesman, and claiming
It worked as pillow feathers, candle wax and gun powder,
And when swallowed as a pill, it would cure all miseries
From hay fever and black eyes to boils and summer colds.
Now a crab, a stranger by the name of Blowhard Ike,
Had blown into the camp, spare, toplofty, and peaked,
With this eye squinting and that one looking up for rain,
A man who pranced an inch too high for a raw hand.
He showed up in front of Johnny Inkslinger and spat,
"Hey! I'm the new swamper, and I'm here to draw my gear."
Inkslinger wagged his pen and spoke up in a flat voice,
"Hang on, you long-tailed barnstorming son of a whore,
I'm sweating out a brain tickler in high algebra:
I'm looking for the fourth proportional to three vectors
In a common plane," "Give me a break, four-eyes: will you
Cut out the crap? Give me my stuff, and I'll toddle off."

Inkslinger tilted back, peering over his goggles, and said,
"Okay, speedball. Okay now, hold out your rosy hands,
And here's your freaks: your cork boots, turkey for plunder
And such, two face, toe splitter, muck stick, bung starter,
Bear cat, and Swede fiddle: all right, you're a run cutter."
Blowhard Ike stooped a little under the tools and lingo,
And sidled out the door while Johnny covered up a smile.
Ike swung clattering up to the saw boss with a snarl,
"Show me the swampers, sir: I pretty well know the ropes."
"Hot dog! Let's shake our hands! Howdy-do, Mister Blowhard?
Yoohoo! Hey boys, stump on over here! It's the green horn.
Boys, meet Mister Blowhard, meet the boys, I'm Big Swede!
I see you've got your diddlewhacky and your thingumajigs,
I guess you're all set. Come on! Oh, and bring your whatsit."
Ike stood in the grinning ring, with no idea which tool
Was the whatsit, and he shouted up at the man mountain,
"What is all this muck fiddle and bear starter nonsense?
How in you know where am I supposed to crack your code?
Why don't you spell it out without all the slang trimmings?"
"Oh shucks, it's easy as strawberries, Mister Blowhard.
First, put your cork boots on. There's your turkey, your pack.
You stick your plunder in there, your letters from mom.
This drag saw's your bear cat, this muck stick's your shovel;
The big ax is a two face, the little ax is a toe splitter;
This thing that looks like a Swede fiddle is your bucksaw,
Oh hold on here! Well, poop! I'm sorry, Mister Blowhard.
You're stuck like a goose. You can't whack the trails today."
Ike rubbed a red polka dot rag across his brow, and said,
"This camp is beyond me! Why can't I whack the trails?"
"Golly gosh! It's nothing. You're missing your sky hook.
You fetch it from Mister Inkslinger and you'll be fixed."
Rumbling and snorting across the sea-sloping clearing,
Ike faced the timekeeper on the stoop of his office
And told him about the mix-up and the missing sky hook,
While Johnny nodded, cool as a catbird, and answered,
"My mistake, Ike; I was all coiled up in my graphs
And I clean let it slip; pardon me, and I'll square it.

You just can't be a star swamper without your sky hook,
You old sharpshooting fool; let me haul it out here."
Inkslinger inched back out, dragging a hulk of a rig
Built out of odd pulleys, crooked augers, big flywheels,
And weighing somewhere in the neighborhood of two tons.
Blowhard Ike was crumbling, but just tightened his jaw
And flexed his horsepower, saying to himself he'd show
These cornball rednecks he wasn't a man to be rattled,
And if they thought he was a lily, he was an iron bull.
He grappled himself all round the infernal contraption
And grunted it into the air: and then, popeyed and snuffing,
And with his cheeks twitching, all of his veins rippling,
And his circle pump thumping for mercy in rag time,
He wobbled sidewise across the cloud-curving field.
It's easy to say iron bull, but his arms were fading out
Just as he came teetering up to the fringe of the sticks,
Red as a whorehouse rug, holding on by his whiskers,
And puffing like a locomotive going up a hog's-back.
Nobody looked at Ike moaning the sky hook down,
They were cocking their ears as Pumphandle Joe talked,
And Ike, wondering what it was all about, listened in:
"I had travelled all the way out there to Yahoo County
To clear up the riddle of the Scarecrow Mine, and sworn
I'd comb the hills from horn to hoof till I struck gold,
By god, and in spite of the three bandits on my tail,
And so I whistled off south and on into Shirttail Bend
Come morning, sleepy, riding my salty lightfooted pinto
Straight through, taking the east fork for Shanghai Hill.
There I could see the cloud kicked up by those cutthroats,
Who could take honey and an anthill and make a man
Give up his daughter, let alone the Scarecrow Mine's secret,
And I wheeled around and struck out for Bluebelly Ravine.
I was aiming to give them the slip by circling back north
And fording a creek a little outside of American Hollow,
Where I hid my pinto and bunked in a squatter's shack,
And he said to go sling the gab with his kin in Ragtown.
Well, by sunup I was three hours on the road east,

Raking my gooseneck spurs and no sign of the outlaws,
And my huddle in Ragtown sent me out to Shinbone Peak,
Far south: the sun sat in the crotch of the two summits,
Just like the old jackass prospector had whispered to me,
And so somewheres hard by here was the lost Scarecrow.
If I'd known the Mine's horror, I'd have bolted the county,
But I rode on from Petticoat Slide to Barefoot Diggings,
Moving westward across the hillsides, rooting for the shaft,
Till I knocked off to camp at dusk, near Brandy Flat.
I guessed the weather looked okay for a star pitch,
I untied my blue bedroll, and saw the bandits' fire.
I was fixing to quit, ah but what the hell, I figured
I had travelled all the way out there to Yahoo County
To clear up the riddle of the Scarecrow Mine, and sworn
I'd comb the hills from horn to hoof till I struck gold,
By god, and in spite of the three bandits on my tail,
And so I whistled off south and on into Shirttail Bend
Come morning, —" Blowhard Ike, all keyed up, interrupted,
"Yeah, but why? Didn't the old prospector say Shinbone Peak?"
The guffaws and the horselaughs came booming down on Ike:
"Haw, haw, haw! The pigeon swallowed it! Shinbone Peak!"
"He was hollering for more! It's just a darling whopper!"
"Oh! He's the dumbest tenderfoot since the Sunday Kid!"
"Hee-haw har-har yuk-yuk ho-ho hee-hee arf-arf!"
Cross-eyed and purple, Ike kicked the machine and barked,
"Yeah, hilarious! Here's the sky hook. Can I get started?"
"Sky hook? Oh no, Ike: that's a smokestack reamer!"
"Dang me if we didn't bamboozle him going and coming!"
"Hey Ike, old scout! Look it up in the swamper's book!"
"Lay off! He can't hardly look it up in that there book,
When it was all eaten up by the tree-dangling hangdowns!"
The mob honked like a flock of mules, as Ike set sail:
What would've just knocked the frills out of a frisky stranger
Sledge-hammered Ike, and he stalked off with a cold eye,
And wound up at the cookshack, bad blood in his veins.
Sourdough Sam was plumping his sourdough rocking chair
Which he'd just slapped together, when Ike stormed in,

All tricked out in his haystack bonnet, his swagger coat,
His flashy new tickle britches, and wet weather shoes,
And, griping like a bulldog, he poured a cup of mud.
Sam stowed his rip chisel in his tool chest and said,
"I want you to be the first in my sourdough rocking chair:
Roll down in the plush, and take it easy: oh, dynamite!"
The rocking chair started in to burbling under Ike,
When it burst open, slobbering all over his deluxe pants:
"Okay, doughface: you can yank out the greenbacks, now!"
"I'm frightful sorry, Ike; I've been fighting a jinx,
Lately: I tell you what, I'll scrub them up just as clean
As a lady with my all-sourdough foam-action soap flakes,
I promise you. Shuck them off, while I mix you up a tub."
The britches came out of the suds as white as a church,
But Ike whipped them on and cleared out without a word.
The boys kept up the hard riding, nicknaming him Legs,
What with his white pants invisible in the white snow,
And told him he was lucky, he was safe from snow snakes,
Because once he was bit it was tanglefoot oil or death.
Ike hooked every man with, like sniffles or a squeak heel,
And tried to saddle it all on the screw-loose cook
And his lousy sourdough, and he traced athlete's foot,
Whooping cough, baldness, and mosquito bites to sourdough.
After that, the boys would back off from the stink of it,
And work on without their chow, which upset Sourdough Sam;
He was all fussed up like an owl, and talked to Paul,
But the walking boss stood there with winter in his face
And his own worries zinging around his head like blueflies:
It was trying to thaw, and as soon as the ice fractured
Out on Red Lake, the water line would drop perilous low;
If the boys didn't wind it up fast, there'd be no out
To the Red Lake river, with all the lumber landlocked.
Sourdough Sam looked down and poked along to the cookshack,
Where Blowhard Ike sat smoking, and Sam spit and said,
"Ike, I guess it's up the chimney. I might have worked
Natural wonders with my sourdough; and now the boys
Don't even like it as bread. Sourdough's all I can make,

And nobody'll touch it. Ah, there's no snap left in me."
"Wait, Sam; what about your sourdough ink stretcher?"
Johnny Inkslinger was a skinflint with his ink, since
By rigging up a hose from the ink barrel to his ink stick
And saving seventeen minutes a page by not dunking it,
It's like he went through a barrel in a couple of squirts,
And Sam, snatching at the chance to help him, spoke up,
"Oh, dynamite! This'll show the boys sourdough at work:
John won't be obliged to skimp, I won't be tossed out
On my backside, and we'll all be off to the races."
Sam gave his instructions with his thumb, and Ike lugged
The sourdough in tanks over to the kegs out in back
Of Inkslinger's office, shouldered the goop and slopped it
Into the pen juice: it fizzed and burbled four bars
Of Yankee Doodle, while Sam leaned on a keg, smiling,
"It's sparking up a little! It's okay, though, it'll settle."
Kerblooey! All of the rib-splintering barrels exploded
To blue heaven with a whoosh of bamblustercation,
Flooring Ike, jolting Sam to the top of a black ridge
Of ink and sourdough, spouting across the ice fields!
The blowup plowed under a green mile of oak saplings
And when it cracked a fence close to the blacksmith's shed,
Big Ole broke out wonder-struck, still holding his hammer,
And gawking up at Sourdough Sam, riding the flood
Just like a broncobuster high-rolling with the bucks
On top of a hot sunfishing and jackknifing horse,
But he was waving a stump, and bawling at his blood.
As quick as think, big Ole strung a loop into a rope,
Circled it around his head, spilled it and lassoed Sam,
While Bunyan and the boys all galloped up in a sweat.
Inkslinger, who was a born doctor, knelt down by Sam
And talked him through the twinges as he patched him up:
"Sit tight, you high-flying mule-hearted old galoot,
And tough it out. Don't you dare sag without a tussle!
There's nothing wrong with you a lazy April won't fix,
Say a whirl on a sternwheeler down the Muddysippi,
With those tall drifting days full of old jokes and whiskey,

The sky all mare's-tail clouds, the haymaking sun high
In the sticky air, and you loafing by the rail, joy-riding
Past the green and mayfly islands in the wide waters,
Into the poker midnights where the stakes are fat
And your luck's holding, shoot! and the peacocking gals
Tugging on your arms, slow-talking and sleepy-eyed,
The stars outside rocking to a skinny harmonica,
And day breaking with the whippoorwills streaking home,
As you roll into New Orleans so all-fired husky
You're just busting to kiss the first jackass you see."
"Oh, the whole commotion has just caught me flat-footed,
John; I guess my damn sourdough still isn't up
To scratch, and now, thanks to me, all your ink is lost.
I'm as sorry as a yellow dog with his tail tucked."
"Forget it, whiskers. We won't let a two-bit disaster
Split up old partners like us, will we? I'd sooner lose
All the ink in Philadelphia than one Sourdough Sam.
You just build your steam back up, okay? Oh, dynamite!"
Inkslinger stood, shouldered his way past Blowhard Ike,
Who was in the middle of his sob act, wiping his nose,
And walked on over to old Paul, saying kind of soft,
"He's got a blast furnace instead of a heart: he'll pull through,
But he'll be one-armed and one-legged from here on out."
The sun was fat, the spring thaw on, and the water falling
In Red Lake: the hour was skyrocketing toward the deadline,
And the boys were hustling like salmon to save the lumber.
Inkslinger quit dotting his i's and crossing his t's,
To stretch his last barrels of ink, and Paul signed on
Hot Biscuit Slim as the new greaseball, a red-eyed man
Who just pined away, and only spoke on cloudy Thursdays.
Slim moved into the spitnew and spanglorious cook shanty,
Which was so thumping big they handed out maps at the door,
And cranked out everything from bull steak to ice cream.
But Blowhard Ike kicked around camp, walking in the slush:
"How in the world did I get stuck in this horse opera?
I think these hicks would patch it up after an earthquake
And sail back into work: I bitch, and they start grinning;

I feel like a bullfrog in the dust bowl on a hot Sunday."
Ike barged into the chuckhouse, where Hot Biscuit Slim
Was stirring up the lunch, and started to sweet-talk him
Into fixing up bucksaws and boots with oatmeal dough.
Slim sniffed out the polecat in back of the explosion,
And he straightened up, tugged at his cap, squinted at Ike,
Shook his head, shook it, nodded, spit an arc of tobacco,
Coiled into his windup, slanted his arm with his elbow high,
Ripped out a pitch, and knocked him out with an old doughnut.
Double-Jawed Phalen, who once went scrounging for cheese
And ate a grindstone by mistake, was the only man
Who had the tusks to bite into one of Slim's doughnuts.
When Ike woke up and hauled his headache to the door
He saw the whole cuckoo outfit loafing around Red Lake
And lumber jammed in the lake as black as a crow's eye.
Sourdough Sam was leaning on a crutch up a sugarloaf hill,
And squatting by the old cookshack, Paul Bunyan yelled:
"Spring has frisked up the stretch and beat us to the wire,
But, much obliged to Sam, we're still going to swing it,
And blow this timber out of here! Okay, Babe: let her whoop!"
Babe tugged, and the tilting cookshack, which Sam had crammed
With sourdough, went sliding rickety down the rollway:
When it hit the water there was nothing but blue hell,
The lake splurging up like a waterfall on its head,
And the logs cartwheeling down the Red River Valley!
Snatching his straw hat, Blowhard Ike broke like bad news
And faded out in the direction of Pike County, Missouri.
Slim's kitchen smells turned out so scrumdiddliumptious,
When the noon gabriel blew the boys didn't finish a stroke,
But all roared straight in, leaving their axes in mid-air.

In the sunburnt fall, when the light fairly thins out,
And summer's gone like a fast freight on a dream line,
And the needles jiggle on the jade pines in a slack sky,
With the Red River load all shipped off to the sawmill
And his slashers and sawyers buckling down to new work,
Paul Bunyan was out there cracking the high timber down
From Brainerd to Bemidji, across wide-ribbed Minnesota.
Brimstone Bill the bullwhacker, in buckskin and fringes,
Jogged through the haze in the air to talk to Bunyan.
"Afternoon, Bill. What's on your mind, besides pig feathers?"
"I don't know; I might be wide by a thousand miles, Paul,
I hope I am, but blast me if there ain't something ailing
Your old blue ox: it's nothing, he just ain't up to snuff.
I yoked and harnessed him, but he just hitched off, instead
Of galloping out slap-bang to the woods, like always;
He wouldn't chomp on the scrub or slurp up water nohow,
And the truth is, he didn't ram me with his horn, once.
To sling it to you straight, the ox is too damn polite,
With none of the old shenanigans, none of the fireworks;
He's as tame as a snail on a leash, and must be sick."
Paul was walking in a flash, and Brimstone Bill behind;
They sighted the blue ox by a creek, on the near bank,
With his head stooped, his round eyes flat, and his legs shaky,
And Paul smacked him on his sky-blue flank and shouted,
"Hey, Babe! You ducking work? Won't you give me a lick?"
The big ox just snuffled, and Paul said, "Fetch Inkslinger:
I'd like it if you'd go two steps ahead of bolt lightning."
The sharp timekeeper cut out to the creek and snorted,
"What's new, superman? I'm almost caught up with—Hey,
Babe's sure looking seedy. Whoa, boy: hold it right there!
Look, I've stitched up your rascals after their eye-gouging
And ear-chewing fights, I've doctored them all laid up
With logger's smallpox from a Sunday stomp in the face
With a spiked boot, and I worked miracles with bellyaches,

But never in all my time moonlighting as a pill shooter
Have I treated one of your four-legged switch-tailed critters!
I'm no vet; why, I don't know the muzzle from the shank;
I'm all for fixing Babe, but you've got the wrong rooster."
"Fake it, Johnny! Aren't you the joker who lit on a moose dead
Of old age, and tracked it clear back to its birthplace?
We're ninety miles from nowhere, you're the medicine man,
Babe's to the bad, and you won't shake your salt to help?
Lose him, make him better, but don't you let him drift!"
"Okay, okay. But I won't jump into this baldheaded:
You've got to spare me a couple of minutes to hit the books.
I mean I can't catch fire with a fishhook and all
I promise is an outside chance, but I'll give her a go."
While Inkslinger thumbed through his headache books,
Hot Biscuit Slim fixed a batch of flapjacks and parsnips,
And Brimstone Bill carted them out to the baby-blue ox,
Who tromped on his foot like old times, but only sniffed
And licked at the vittles, and stuck by the frisky creek.
Then Johnny Inkslinger hitched out with his black bag,
Walked Babe into the stable, and started trouble-shooting
With book in hand, busy as a cowbird in a short pasture:
He poked the haunches, tested the joints, studied the blood;
He stood out in back of the blue ox with a check list
And stared at his hindquarters through an old spyglass,
Wondering what on earth could bother a bull that big.
It couldn't be a tummy-ache: once when they were swamped
With sawdust, they just strapped green goggles on the ox
And let him graze; his stomach was immortal; he could
Down a brush whiskey still without so much as a hiccup.
Six loggers were lowered by a hoist into Babe's throat
And swampers combed his hide yard by yard for a sore,
But they found nothing special, and Inkslinger was stumped.
When old Paul asked what was the story, the timekeeper
Went up and down the barn, yawping like a steam calliope:
"Yeah, just call me Sawbones! There's no virus I can't nail!
I had a hunch when your ox first went off his feed,
And now I've looked into it, I've got a big nothing!

It ain't the blind staggers, the sniffles, breakbone fever,
The jitters, heartburn, the pukes, foot-and-mouth, the whoops,
All I know's what it ain't: and it sure ain't my round.
I was out of my skull when I ever hooked into this!
Temperature? Oh boy! Heartbeat: boom boom. Breath, yikes!
I pump my head, and all for nothing: ixnay, zero, no soap!
We're miles past March, and so it can't be his old hay fever;
And there's just no dang symptoms but the hump on his back.
It's got me as puzzled as a squeal pig in a washtub.
What about the hump? If we straighten out his spine,
There's an okay chance it'll shove him back into shape;
Keep bumping, you old blue ox: you'll be skyhooting soon!"
An alley-oop crew, after sticking ladders and scaffolds
Up Babe's back, climbed up with jerk lines and grass ropes,
Inkslinger and Big Swede stood at the blue moon horns
And Bunyan manned the tail, and they pitched all their beef
Into the tug-of-war, stretching Babe like the last dollar.
Johnny flashed the high sign by and by, and the three
Turned the front-page and cosmological tall ox loose:
Babe whinnied and cavorted like a two-gun tornado,
Johnny yelled it's working, and Paul reddened with love.
But the spunky blue ox had been bluffing, and soon stood
Shivering on his hoofs, swimming, with his ribs rawboned,
His bellow sour, and the hump on his back ballooning.
Old Paul stuck his thumbs in his front pockets like a tough:
"What's next, doc? Look: we've got sixteen tons of slow blues
And no damn time. The Armstrong method got us nowhere:
I reckon you'll have to switch on the old think box."
"Don't crowd me, big daddy: I'm thinking in six languages.
Okay, so what if I foozle, huh? Where's your miracle?
Do you know Big Ole's motto? He says, 'If I can't fix it,
I just paint it yellow and send it back to the woods.'
What do you say? I didn't volunteer for this whangdilly,
And you can just go play that on your tack piano!"
"Oh, my aching back, shut up, Inkslinger: shut your mouth!
No other horse doctor alive will tackle my blue ox,
Except you, you kite-flying quack! so boom, you're hired!

Don't you crawfish on me, just jump back in your shanty
And don't budge out till you get lucky! Oh, and Johnny!
I'm sorry I slammed you: I'm as touchy as a colt."
Old Paul and Big Swede stood rubbing the blue ox down,
Waiting news, whittling time, listening to the chug of axes
In the blunt woods, where no timber moved to the Crow Wing.
When Inkslinger showed, he sidled up to Paul and said,
"Whale milk." "Whale milk?" "Don't you savvy American?
It's the milk of a whale: in plain U.S., whale milk."
"That's the cure, eh Johnny? Where do we scare up a whale?"
"We point ourselves at the tall grass, pack up our plunder,
Thumb a ride on a prairie schooner, and haul out west."
Paul Bunyan plunked the whole camp and caboose on wheels,
And Big Ole, who could shoe six mustangs at once in his lap,
Scooped out an iron mine for Babe's shoes, and coming back
With his brawny arms full, he sank to his hips in bedrock.
With Babe hitched up, and all loaded to go, Bunyan hollered,
"Okay, let's get this circus on the road! The coast or bust!"
The camp was flying through the blizzards and swingcats
Of South Dakota when, rising out of the buck brush
On its three legs, this local beast with a gun barrel nose
Snickered, and after taking a clay bullet out of its cheek,
It cocked its head and fired. It was a rare tripodero,
And the boys showed a sudden interest in Nebraska.
Out in the yellow sandhills, they saw a sidehill dodger
At home by the Platte River, with stumps for up legs
And stilts for down, which is how it kept level, whirling
Rip around the hill with black eyes, saw teeth, hard bristles,
Yowling, burrowing, tail-spinning, and throwing kisses.
They hit the badlands in a dry spell, and way out there
In the acres of red dust, box canyons, and hot rocks,
Where only the grasshoppers and pumpkins can survive,
They found a squatter who was so thirsty the only way
He could whistle to his hound dog was to ring a bell,
And the almighty dog was so terrible wheezy and dry
It had to lean up against a rail fence just to bark.
Babe got stung by a drove of horseflies out of nowhere,

And they all left the land of blackwater and cornhuskers
When the blue ox stampeded into Colorado territory.
There they swapped brags with a contrary oil monkey,
Too old to hunt buffalo, too young to prospect silver,
Who built a derrick like a double dare to the cyclones.
His bad luck was it was as dry as a Nebraska eye;
His good luck was one Friday night the twisters came
And unscrewed the well: when he saw the thousand-foot
Hole sticking up in the air, he sliced it into hunks
And sold it east for post holes. Outside Cripple Creek
The boys took a two-beer time out, and a quick look
At the sliver cats, with their slit eyes and tasseled ears,
And their skinny tails tipped with a bone-and-spike ball:
They'd sit politely on a branch and knock a tourist out
With the bone side, and haul the catch up with the spikes.
Old Paul and Big Swede were out mudslinging, working on
A joke landmark: they slapped big rubble and wet clay
Around a pike pole, like a real mountain, called it Pike's Peak,
And rallied the boys, hotfooting it out to Wyoming,
On the hammer like old outlaws, across the Great Divide,
Where they saw a turkey-headed green-necked goofus bird,
With a red wing flipping and a black wing flopping,
Hooting, spiralling in the air out of its upside down nest,
Flying backwards all the way to Cheyenne and gone
Because it only loves to look at wherever it's been.
Babe got thirsty, and with no water in sight, old Paul
Took a pickax and whopped the glory out of the ground,
And when the water spouted, and Babe was sipping it,
Wham, the spring shut off, and bam, it shot off regular,
And so Bunyan named the fountain Old Faithful, in honor
Of the blue ox, but after a swig, renamed it Old Filthy.
He figured on turning south for the sun, on account
Of the blue ox shivering in the cool and the sagebrush,
And the boys thumbed their noses at the poor sheepherders,
And then wheeled through the lilies and beehives of Utah.
Coming through the salt flats, and avoiding the joint snakes,
Which split in twelve and strike everywhichway at once,

With its wheels kicking up copper clouds, the logging camp
Crossed over the mesas into Arizona, where it's painted
With six coats of sundown, and the weather report is fire.
It was so mythological hot, for example, a lean coyote
Was chasing a jack rabbit, and they were both walking,
Fish in the arroyos made puffs of dust as they swam,
And natives, who could hardly mix a pitcher of lemonade
Before night, saw flu-flu birds splashing in mirage lakes.
Bunyan, hailing from the North country, was breathing hard
With the heat, and he lowered his peavey and let it drag,
Plowing the hollow which was later called the Grand Canyon.
They dawdled in Nevada, hoping for just a peekaboo
At the three-tailed bavalorous, with a crooked horn
On its forehead, bird body to its hips, with shaggy legs
And starry hoofs, and then the world-famous three tails:
The first a harpoon, sharp as a Green Mountain winter,
The second a branch, doubling as a brace and a whip,
The third a galaxy, sprawling, all flash and feathers,
And perched proudly over its left shoulder for show.
They skittered the sage hens, looked at the glory diggings,
And shoved on to California, with weather eyes out
For gold and grizzlies, and old Babe was perking up now
Like a brass band quickstepping down Main on turkey day.
Paul Bunyan jumped the Sierras, and landing on the outskirts
Of the sequoias and stealing in there by his lonesome,
He leaned against twenty centuries, looking for words:
"Oh hit me with a hayseed, and lay me in the clover:
I'd say you were flapdoodle if I couldn't slap bark,
Redwoods. I reckon you were shooting when the sea was
First slopping, standing the winters here, in the haggle
Of storks and buzzards, green with the knack of surviving,
And now you cram the sky, as old as stargazing, high
As a farm boy full of moonshine. You're the bluest berry
On the fat earth, I wouldn't fall you for dare or double.
Whee! I like, —oh my, I'd best let the bluejays tweet
My thanks to creation, now: I'm fresh out of tall talk."
The lumber camp had barged across the Oregon border,

Where they saw a teakettler walking backwards, whistling
And blowing steam out its red nose. At south coast camp,
They swapped their axes for idiot sticks to shovel out
Inkslinger's whale corral, and carved Coos Bay, as Babe
The blue ox was rickety as a calf, and sick all over.
Old Paul slogged out to sea, whinnying to the grey world
And croaking to the whales in kind of salt-water Greek,
Till Dynamite Jack, who was up a tree in a crow's nest,
Sighted flukes and spouts and yodeled There she blows,
And a blue gang of sperm whales dove in the whale corral,
As thick as whores at a horse race, and the way old Paul
Was blubbering, it was dumb luck he didn't sing half
The hogs in three counties into his big arms to boot.
Big Swede, the North Sea all-star milking champ, walked in
Swinging his bucket, and with his fists full of whale tits
He stood there, squishing and yanking like a steam pump,
Duded up in his cowboy jeans and his ten-gallon hat,
Catching the spew in the pail tight between his knees:
"Whoopee-ti-yi-yo! I'm an old Chisholm cowpoke, boys!
Daddy was a mule skinner, mama was a man-eater!
Oh, I was born in the saddle, suckled on beer, and I'm dusty;
I'm a long horn, I'm a blue moon, and I'm full of fleas;
I've got pig iron bones and thirteen rows of jaw teeth;
I root and toot, punch cows, I ride slick, and knock down!
Whoa, boy! Sing to me, six-guns! Yippee-ki-yi-yay!"
The pail was brimming with luscious milk in no time;
Inkslinger waded out and said, "Calm down, buckaroo,"
Fetched it on back to the beach where the blue ox lay,
And sat joshing with Bunyan while Babe set to lapping:
"The boy's a caution! Where does he get that foofaraw?
He's never wrangled horses, wrestled steers, or rolled his own!"
Old Paul didn't hear him: the blue ox at the big bucket
Was slumping, drooling, sick of milk, with his wind hard
And his blue eyes scummed with fear. On the plain sand
Bunyan rounded up his boys, under an unclear sky,
In a fine drizzle, by the slop and bash of the waves:
"It's no good, boys. Babe's dying. He's tough, but so what?

White pines in the steady sun, brook trout in blue water,
Owls sliding out on the weather, bulls steaming in the mud,
You mopping the kitchen, your honey going for the mail, are
All equal, all dripping with risk, like icicles in April.
It's a skinny consolation, at a funeral. Now my beauty
Is buckling, oh brother! in death, in one jump nothing
But a tall tale, and all my love's curdling in my belly.
It's a raw afternoon, where's the campfire? It's crazy,
But morning, without my companion, will go on breaking."
He took a shovel that was handy, and stumped up the coast
To gouge out a grave for the blue ox. Inkslinger snorted,
"Oh hold on a minute, boys; services ain't started yet:
I'm still scratching! Now if whale milk won't clear it up,
Why, dang it, all of this aggravation is in his head!
Big Swede, plunk yourself down in front of the fool ox,
Eye to eye, and say 'You're okay, Babe,' over and over,
And don't quit for high tide or red indians, follow me?
If we just buck him up, he'll be healthy as a seesaw."
Big Swede cinched his cowboy hat and sat by the ox:
"You're okay, Babe. You're okay, Babe. You're okay, Babe.
Oh, Mister Inkslinger says so. And I say so, big Babe.
You're okay. You're okay, big Babe. You're okay, big Babe."
He chittered and chattered, and in a while it was like
Saying hoop-de-doodle: the words were nothing but babble;
He spouted it like an old song, and it wore his voice down
To a wheeze, but a swig of whiskey would fix him up,
And he whisked out a crate of Inkslinger's white lightning,
Oiled his tonsils on the half hour, and went on droning
At the blue ox. He was on his thirteenth bottle, when
He flared up, with his eyes popping, and fire alarms
In his ears, drunk as a rainbow trout, and he hooted,
"Oh, you sick ox. Whoop! Oh Babe! Whoop! You dumb ox."
He was swacked: the beach was swinging all round his head,
And Big Swede, looking out at the water romping, burped
And rolled to his back, with a pile of seaweed for a pillow,
And tipping the crate over; whiskey pooled on the sand,
And old Babe licked it up, stamped into Johnny's shack,

Ate up a ton of pills, and cavorted. His bounce was back.
He waddled off, sniffing for Bunyan, but the white lightning
Hit him between the horns, and he lurched off the trail,
Curling back south to Crater Lake, snorting in the cold.
The sprinkle of rain sifting down on the green country
Thickened, and thunder coughed all across the flat sky,
While the blue ox, plumb lost, on the lookout for Bunyan,
Shoved on, with his ramshackle heart rocking with love.
The tall clouds cracked and it rained like all hickory,
Babe hobbling nowhere in the black mud, and the spray
Spitting off his tail was building into the Rogue River,
Till up on a mistletoe hill, the weather unwinding,
The blue ox slammed sideways onto the grass and died.
Old Paul came into camp and chased out with Inkslinger,
Hunting up his ox down south, clear to California:
When he sighted the carcass on the hill, he folded his arms
Over his belly, and stooped down under the white sun.
Inkslinger stood there like a haystack, rubbing his arm,
And scared of the streaks on the puddles. Water dangled.
It was windy up on Mount Shasta, blowing down
To the west, and a whoosh of air went fanning across
The hill, wagging the dandelions all around the dead ox.
After one whiff, the blue ox was alive and sashaying.
Bunyan whistled and hugged him off his hoofs, shouting,
"I love you, California: I ain't kidding, your air is fresh!"
Johnny was cussing hard, jumping like at a hoedown,
Babe bucked, and pastured in an acre of parsnips,
And old Paul heehawed like a Rocky Mountain canary.

Winter barged in early with a spell of weather as cold
As the windy side of an Idaho tombstone by happy
New year starlight, and the sun went south with the geese.
The North country only had three seasons: July, August,
And winter, and when it dipped down to sixty-odd feet
Below zero, the loggers couldn't light a wood match
On a grindstone, the pot of java froze up so fast
It was still steaming, and the boys sucked on the ice,
And when the tin can lantern flames froze, the cooks said
To twist them off the wicks, and crush them up for pepper.
The blue ox, out walking with hay bales and feed sacks
On his wide horns, had got a hayseed stuck in his ear,
And when Brimstone Bill, who was up a pine to reach it,
Yelled out for a ladder down, since it was too slick,
Paul Bunyan told him to piss and slide down on the icicle.
It was so awful chilly, talk froze in the crackling air,
And the lumberjacks walked around bumping into words;
And the spring thaw was like a bull shooting contest,
With cracks defrosting all over the evergreen camp:
"Howdy Oh meow and nuts Go ahead So what Timber
It ain't weather it's a disease Ho hum Good enough
Screw you punk In the kitchen with Dinah What gives
I'm champ Okay sweetheart Says who Get the shovel
It's sky-bound Gee It beats me Haw Take it easy."
Big Swede, gallivanting across the slow snowdrift
Where the skid road lay, saw this loose whiplash there,
Brimstone Bill's by the braid of it, and when he stooped
For it, it yanked out of his paws, and Bill roared up,
"Let go, you dirty five-fingered damn chicken thief,
I'm hauling a hundred tons of butt log in bad weather
Back of two teams of mean oxen, and I need the lash!"
Yeah, Washington was cold, and the snow deep as the world.
Pumphandle Joe stretched out, with a yawn and a sniff,
Hitched up his bay pony to a bush, and took a nap.

He snoozed clean through the thaw: when he woke up,
He saw his horse dangling from a limb of a Douglas fir.
Old Paul had never seen the likes of this west coast timber;
It was clear and fat, it was so thick a hummingbird
Would snag in it, and tall to where it took two loggers
To see up to the top: oh, it was a green daydream.
Bunyan knocked over a yellow pine for a creek bridge,
And Brimstone Bill, poking the oxen across it, kept on
Coming up shy by a couple after every crossing.
He would've heard them splash for sure if the dumb cows
Were drowning, and likewise he would've spotted a rustler;
He fished all around, and found them in the hollow trunk
Of the big yellow pine: they'd slipped through the knotholes.
Cedar Root Charley and Rocky Dan had tackled a tree
Which was sticking up through a hole in the calico sky,
With falling axes and a great stack of crosscut saws
Brazed into one, chewing up bark, gobbling up sawdust
For ages and ages, and when they were dry and winded,
They sneaked around the pine tree for a snort of whiskey
And saw who on earth but Roaring Jim and Billy the Bum,
In their red shirts and blue jeans, working the far side,
Swapping big lies, old-time gags, pigtails of tobacco,
And whanging away at the same honest-to-god tree.
The rollways went up on the shore of the Jack Off River,
Which flowed as sleek as a kiss, as choppy as a punch,
And liked to duck under and bob up like a fool rabbit,
Full of snags and loggers, and maybe a whirl or three;
Splitting up, zigzagging, squirting on, humping itself,
It squiggled and galumphed to the rub-a-dub ocean,
Slap into Puget Sound, the grave old Paul had dug
For the blue ox, wide open for all the whopping logs
Booming over the cockeyed river, and the cockeyed roads,
Which were so crooked the poor skidders couldn't tell
If they were riding out somewhere or on their way home,
And when a jack met himself coming back from the landing
It was time to hook up Babe and jerk out the kinks.
Now what with the cold weather, large trees, and bad river

They had in that late Northwest midwinter afternoon,
Nothing short of a rip-roaring fire-eating man could
Manage it, and so a wrangler, name of Old Lightheart,
Dragged a bunch of scissorbills off the farms to the east,
And changed them from hay shakers into buffalo boys:
He lit into his saddle tramp pitch and sold them all,
Stripped off their sheep-stinking laundry, dressed them up
In buckskin duds, bandannas, and buzzard wing chaps,
And set his boys to circle herding, lasso looping, guitar
Picking, and buffalo milking out in the pine-rail corral.
Old Lightheart's whole notion was that a barrel a man
Of this here hair-curling and bare-chested buffalo milk
Would give the lumberjacks the go for all-out logging.
There wasn't a glass of milk or a doughnut but was spiked
With it, and Jersey lightning was branch water next to it.
The boys took to raw bear meat topped off with the bones,
And whipped off their mackinaws, joking about the cold;
They razzed each other till they all turned rantankerous,
Throwing ax handle parties, leaking blood; they showed off
By skinning the cat on a long branch on a tall pine,
Grabbing sky, and somersaulting down on the Cascades.
The buffalo boys took a slug of the milk all around,
Rode out in wolf-skin coats, looking for buck-jumping colts,
And out front was Old Lightheart, on a mountain lion,
Riding bareback and screaming for American cows.
The hardtail winter broke up into a freak spring,
Rainy and crazy, like a pool hustler on a bad night,
And Slabwood Johnson, thinking the woods pretty damp
And waddling into a clearing, saw all kinds of rain.
Water alone wouldn't flutter his feathers, he could take
A drizzle; it wouldn't have flustered him at all, but
It was raining straight up, squirting out of the mud
Into a sky blue as the blue ox on a blue morning.
He went swooping like a gander for the big bunkhouse
But the floor was as full of cracks as a Yankee peddler
To let out slush and such from the spiked logging boots,
And so the water spattered into the room by the bucket,

And naturally the roof was so watertight the rain
All puddled overhead, and when Slabwood skipped in
He bumped into a god-damn upside down hog wallow.
He bounced back out into the hazy sunlight and ran
Red-faced to Paul's shanty, clucking like a prairie hen.
"Okay, Bunyan! You see this slop all over my kisser?
I walked into the bunkhouse and I forgot to duck!
It's no fair, sweetheart! Hey, why ain't it raining in here?"
"Simmer down, Slabwood! You bang in here without knocking,
And start handing out birdseed till I'm woozy as you:
Jenny's pass, no savvy, I don't know, and all that.
Now back up to the bunkhouse part, and if you feel
Conflabberation coming over you, take a couple of hoots
Of this here horse liniment. All right, what's eating you?"
"I'll tell you flat, Bunyan. Get this: it's raining up."
"Oh, now you're logging! You mean a storm's clabbering up."
"If I do, sweetheart, you can plant me out on the plains
For buffalo chow. I mean the rain isn't falling: no,
The rain is falling, but backwards; I mean it's flying,
It's coming down antigoglin to the ground, hold it,
I'm wrong! I'm wrong! Aw, hell. Where's the horse liniment?"
Old Paul was smiling out the window: a whingding of rain
Was coming up from China, and when he whipped back
His big bearskin rug, the water spindled into the air.
Slabwood was cackling to himself, hoisting the bottle,
When Inkslinger dropped in for a powwow, and old Paul
Handed him a cup of java and a question mark.
"I'll tell you, old scout: the lowdown is, the camp's hurting."
Johnny poured a streak of moo into the bellywash,
Sugared it up to kill the taste, and tried explaterating:
"The boys are twitchy, the cooks are sulky, the blue ox
Is acting silly, Slim is his usual self, and I've got
My eye on a peach farm way out in South Carolina.
This new-fangled rain, yikes! Oh I know, you were low
On coffee, and so you boiled up a handful of turds!
As I was saying, this Yankee trick out of the sky,
I mean the mud, is giving our camp the jumps, man,

And if we don't get to finagling, we might as well
Call it a bust and go slop hogs in Dixie Land."
Bunyan leaned out the door and yelled at the West coast:
"Okay, I can see the weather's screwed up out here!
Wise up, you turkeys; I mean if it's raining backwards,
Saw backwards, or whatever: don't let it crack you up!
The first clown I catch sneaking back to the bunkhouse,
Watch out! I'm going to inspect his guts by hand!
You boys keep the pines shaking, I can beat the water!"
He slumped down by Johnny and rippled through a wish book.
"We could wrap them up real heavy, Bunyan, but hell,
It seems like clothes are figured for everyday rain
And all shed water down, just like shingles on a roof;
But this dang rain jumps up your blue jeans, your slicker,
Your favorite shirt, your long underwear, your beaver hat,
Into your hip pockets, under your belt, down your socks,
And you squish off with the Great Lakes in your work shoes,
And soaked to the leather: whoo! it's a sin to Crockett,
And no wonder the boys are ugly. Ha, if you could
Haul your britches on upside down, you'd be okay!"
"Hush up, Johnny; look here in this mail-order catalogue:
Quilts, rockers, silverware, trombones, tubs, umbrellas!
I want a boxcar of umbrellas: write me up an order."
"Yeah, but they ain't worth a whistle in this weather!
Who's going to want to lug around his own puddle?
I say we order up a tub of booze and a holiday."
Old Paul clapped up the wish book and sneered like a horse:
"You stop yapping, and stamp it rush: I've got an angle."
When Brimstone Bill saw a shipment of umbrellas come
Jolting into camp, he jumped on his hat and sneezed,
Gave a yodel to the barn boss, and waved him over:
The barn boss had been contemplating how to shovel
Babe's crap out of the swampers' way, when the up rain
Sprinkled into the pile, which commenced to steam,
And the stink turned his whiskers as white as an egg.
The bullwhacker showed him the umbrellas, and they hiked
Over to Paul's office, with the barn boss looking prickly

And Brimstone Bill spitting out words like apple seeds:
"Thanks a million for the parasols, dear! I picked
A bunch of daffodils to go with them, and they're darling.
I'm going to wear them in my butt! Oh, why fight it!
Unpack the petticoats, handsome: let's dance ourselves silly!
And get this, jelly bean: you can take your shower sticks
Out of your boxcar, and shove them up your caboose!
My pal here will help you. I'll take rain any way you
Throw it before I'll slink around under an umbrella!"
Old Paul smiled like a coon up a sugar tree and said,
"You yokels have been hitting the buffalo milk too hard,
You're thinking with your fists. Yeah, umbrellas are okay
For old ladies who won't look the weather in the face,
But hell, I'd rather swim than pretty you boys up, so
Get off of your high horse: this ain't that kind of rodeo.
Go ahead and grab you a couple of bumbershoots
And bust off the handles, strap on rawhide and bang!
You've got rain shoes. Try them on, lollipop: they work!"
The boys latched on to the rain shoes like easy money,
And Brimstone Bill was out there getting the hang of his
When Old Lightheart whistled up to him in a sweat:
"Hey, man; I was out spelunking in a hole yonder
When I burnt my fingers, bobbled my fire, and whoa!
I heard a squalling like it's the granddaddy buffalo,
And skedaddled. Tell Paul, while I keep an eye out here."
The bullwhacker bumped into Inkslinger and yelled,
"Say, will you hunt up Bunyan; tell him Old Lightheart
Was out prospecting when he flopped into a dry gulley,
His arm caught fire, he let go his handful of daylight,
And he was trampled by buffalo under a stiff rain."
Old Paul was in his shanty when Johnny showed and said,
"Guess who's up to his elbows in trouble: Old Lightheart
Struck it rich up on Sawtooth Ridge, spilled off a cliff,
On fire, burned like a weed in the flat sky, blacked out,
Slammed down out of the rain and was squashed by a cow."
"Come on, Johnny: don't you give me your ten-story lies,
Because I ain't buying. I want a fish and a yardstick:

Let's see Old Lightheart, and get the honest-to-god."
When the buffalo boy was done pointing and exaggerating,
Bunyan rammed square into the cave, but it was like
Trying to get a rooster into a game of checkers,
And so he snuggled up, listened till he was popeyed,
Hooted into the dark, and swayed up onto his feet:
"Boys,   there's only one animal can make such a ruckus
Of banging and shimmering, and it's a kid rainstorm
Hollering mama, strayed and holed up under our camp,
Spooked, and raining like silly, which is why it's coming
Up! If we could persuade the maverick out of the cave,
We could start towelling off: it's a cinch we can't haul
Weather around by the tail, as there's no tail to grab;
But if I dress up like his mom, in big raindrops,
I can thunder and lullaby him clear to the Plains."
Inkslinger didn't blink, but just cocked back his hat:
"Okay, dreamer; I'm sticking around for this: first,
Where the hell in Hicktown USA are you going to get
The outfit? I mean, they must be sold out everywhere."
"I hear there's nothing you can't buy in Kansas City."
"Well how, buck-naked and soaking wet, you going to make
A hunk of cloud, which is as bashful as a barn swallow,
Believe you're its own mom, instead of an ad gimmick?"
Paul was lurching toward Missouri when he shouted back,
"I guess I'll just have to work up a solid routine!"
Inkslinger gave the boys the screwball sign and said,
"There's times when I could swear I was in a dime novel,
But then I shine up my memory, and I snap out of it:
Like now, ask me who in the whole showboating country
Can walk out and flimflam a rainstorm, and I'll say
Oh, a lumberjack, tall as the Sierras, and heading east."
It took a lot of looking, but old Paul rounded up
A true Kansas City hustler, squinting at the yokels,
With a rose in his coat and a suitcase full of steals.
Bunyan walked up behind him, and whistled at his back:
"Hey man, start pitching: I want to rent a disguise."
The dude twirled on his boot heels and fell on the grass,

And in a minute, when he woke up, he smiled at Bunyan:
"Oh my but you startled me, son, with your big howdy!
Oh, oh! And behind my back! It's funny; but you know,
You can't carry a weapon in lots of these bible belt towns,
And son, my advice to you is this: use sign language.
I sell eye to eye, so I'll have to bargain with you
From here, flat on my back: you just stand still, okay?
You're real tall, son! Yeah, you take after the North Star!
And you want a disguise! Oh yeah, I can picture it:
We'll get you a white hat and a couple of yucca trees,
And you can pass as Mount Whitney. Why don't you yell,
Scratch that: why don't you point at what in creation
It is you want to look like? You're pointing at what,
At a rain cloud! And you're not laughing. How about you
Forget the disguise, and let me sell you a box of matches?
I could throw in a bottle of hair shine; oh all right,
Don't get your back up! I can handle it, don't panic:
I just hope you brought a hat full of greenbacks, is
All I can say, on account of this is a special order
As your cloudburst outfits don't come in extra large.
Okay: we've got your basic sprinkle, but I imagine
You're looking for a downpour, and as for cloud structure,
It would be just too crude to wear cumulus in society,
Since anyone who's anyone's in nimbus this season.
And, let's see, in our April line, though you might fancy
A light shower, no charge for the thunder, I suggest
A root-searching rain, which is the only style I carry.
Oh, shall I wrap it, or should I go get my umbrella?"
Old Paul stared down at the tiny salesman and snapped,
"I ain't got all day, speed: just get my merchandise."
He plunked down a stack of money and clouded over,
Fired off a snort of thunder and a couple of swipes
Of chain lightning, and floated out west in a tail wind.
When he saw a hawkeye squatting out on the prairie
And hoeing corn, it showed him he was on top of Iowa,
Where the rainstorms summer, and old Paul kicked around
With a crowd of them, who figured him for a stranger

Blown up from the Gulf. He sang and roughhoused with them
At all their get-togethers, getting their lingo straight,
And raining out political rallies like an old-timer.
On the far side of the Rockies, Brimstone Bill, standing
Hip deep in Green River mud, was poking sugar pines
And flapping off the rain, inventing new swear words
For the rolling crew, when a hoop snake with its tail in
Its mouth came skimming like a wheel out of the bushes.
Bill dove through the hoop to stump it, when its tail flared
And the sidewinder was gone, its sting in Bill's log wrench,
Which swelled up so big the boys were looking for saws
When an axhandle hound, with a hatchet head, scooted
Out of who knows where, and with a woof and a tail wag
It chomped on its supper, the twelve-foot peavey handle.
Brimstone Bill grunted and slogged over to tell Inkslinger
He was off to join the circus, when a zigzag of lightning
Trimmed his whiskers and lit Inkslinger's boots on fire
With a ruckus like the buffalo boys on a Saturday night:
"Whiz poof zip creak crackle clatter tick tick tick ding
Pop slam bang boom rattle pow wham bam thank you ma'am:"
It was Paul Bunyan, sky-walking up on stilts of air,
Yahooing out of the east, and talking American thunder,
With his wet hands full of Missouri water, tossing bolts
Like horseshoes, blocking the sun with intentions of rain,
And piling up clouds till they slopped down forty ways.
Inkslinger, fooled at first, stuck his arm up in the sky
And shook hands with Bunyan, who slacked off to a mist:
"Okay, star! Let's go and see if the kid likes the show."
Old Paul lay down to whoosh and spatter into the hole
Like ma calling, and all of a sudden the up rain stopped:
Brimstone Bill wiped his eyes, and at the very next holler
The heifer storm jumped out into the daylight and lit up
On Paul's shoulder, where it sat, looking pale and grouchy;
And with a rainy word and the directions home, old Paul
Slapped it on its rump, and it floated out of the pines
And puffed away towards Iowa, shooting off rainbows.

The loggers broke pine and bucked it till almost summer
On the banks of the Onion, with the water rats sliding it
On down the river full steam to the sawdust factory;
The trouble was the wild onions all along the shore
Would split open and then, when a lumberjack was blind,
He'd work on in the damn dark, with his hands full of tears
And his ax whizzing, but when the whole daffy show was
On the point of stalling, the boys asked for Paul Bunyan.
After a minute of headwork, old Paul said the idea
Was to yank out the tearjerkers, and hold a duck feed
For the gang later on, since they were all swamp angels
And green timber heroes, and hungry. Hot Biscuit Slim
Hopped to it, in his white apron, bitching and baking,
But Cream Puff Fatty wondered what to use for ducks.
Old Paul promised to scare him up a couple of thousand,
And tottered off without his gun. While he was gone,
Inkslinger was rummaging around the big kitchen
On the lookout for cookies, and saw Sour Face Murphy
Up on a stool, peeling spuds into a bucket of water,
And Sour Face was so ugly the water was fermenting.
Inkslinger saw it fizzling, walked up and took a whiff
Of true whiskey, and he hired Sour Face as a still.
Out the greasy window, Bunyan was strolling into camp
Tugging fifty-odd wagons, all full of quacking ducks,
And the bottle washers crowded him, asking how on earth
He'd bagged that many ducks that quick without a shot.
When you're a sharpshooter, he'd said, it's nothing to squat
All day in a pole thicket like a chicken on Sunday,
Your whiskey gone, your dog mixed up, and your boots wet,
And blow ducks out of the dull sky, it's just no thrill:
And leaving his popgun behind, he'd leaned into the sky,
Bawled out his name, and the ducks up and surrendered.
Oh yeah, he'd said: advertising! It always works.
The cooks were sailing, the stoves on fire, and the kitchen

Shaking, brighter than a rodeo, loud as independence:
The bread was done before a man could circle the oven,
There was water spitting, butter boiling, smoke starting,
Oh and the smell of supper was in the air for miles.
It took two savages to blow one hoot on the old horn,
And when the music hit the pines the boys climbed on
By swinging a leg over, like in the pony express,
And rode bareback on the horn's echo all the way home,
Singing off-key, and busting the cookshack door down.
The lumberjacks sat and dove straight into the greens
In wooden bowls, with love apples, American cheese,
Salt pork and the house dressing, choice of alphabet soup,
Garden sauce stew, wish wash, and the kitchen mystery,
With suds and soda crackers, triple-decker sandwiches,
Yellow baskets of johnny cake, hard biscuits, sour rolls,
With cow grease, bear sign, red horse, birdseye tenderloin,
And the main dish, in wings and drumsticks, roast duck,
With chestnuts and oranges, and duck soup on the side.
The boys played with the string beans, squash and cauliflower,
But the plain peas and corn on the cob were as popular
As pie, and the tall cakes, the old-fashioned doughnuts,
The white ice cream and the hot cookies were sloshed down
With milk out of pitchers and good coffee by the gallon.
The Galloping Kid, behind a team of ponies, shook
The reins and drove the salt and pepper wagon across
The table, hauling fruit pits, coffee grounds, and eggshells
Out to toss to the tigermonks, who got so strong on
This trash, they took to wrestling blond wolves for fun.
The grub fight went on and on, but the boys were winning,
And Cream Puff was cheering when he dropped his mixing spoon:
It sure looked like Hot Biscuit Slim had cracked a smile.
Now it had been brush ape etiquette since way back when
To shut up during chow, and worry about the groceries,
And so when Bunyan started to spout off out of nowhere,
It was flabbergasting at first, and threw everybody:
"I'll give you boys odds of a hundred to one you don't know
About my wild brothers; you ain't blind, I said brothers:

I mean my kid brothers, Soar Bunyan, the fisherman
And the big drunk, and Cal S. Bunyan, the railroad star.
Now Soar had a champion bowwow, name of Slow Music,
The all-around hound dog, who'd look up at his boss
In the morning, and if old Soar was carrying his rifle,
Slow Music went scouting for deer, if it was his shotgun
He'd sniff out rabbits, and if his fishing pole, worms.
This hound was not dumb; one time Soar was bragging how
Slow Music, like a sure enough hawk, would point at fish,
When the dog froze; Soar was on the ball in a flash,
Catching the fish in question, and when he cut it open
If there wasn't a bird inside, there's no liars in Dixie.
One day Slow Music streaked it, barking like he was crazy,
After a fox maybe, and bolting clear up Saddle Mountain,
Around Blaze Spur, on down King's Creek, and back to camp,
Where he hit a swamp ax by accident and so dang hard
It sliced him in two; Soar slapped him together quick,
But sewed him up with his left legs up, right legs down.
It didn't hurt the old hound; he kept on like all getout,
And when his legs got tuckered out he'd just whirl over
On his fresh pair, rest and keep rolling at the same time,
And now nothing in the woods could outrun Slow Music.
Soar fished northern waters all year, and in all weathers
He'd be out there at sunup, red-eyed, in his hip boots,
Drunk as a dollar, skimming flies across a puddle,
Wearing his lucky shirt and holding out for breakfast,
Whistling, and waking up the fish, thinking about girls.
He was good-looking as an actor, almost always broke,
And famous for hooking imaginary fish all by himself,
Like the goofang, swimming backwards to keep the water
Out of its eyes, around as big as a sunfish, only bigger,
And when he hoisted his the creek fell a couple of feet;
Like the whirligig fish, swimming in circles all winter, so
Soar rubbed the ice holes with bacon fat and the fish
Got worked up good, till they corkscrewed into the air
And dropped into his hands; it was a tougher job than
Catching giddy fish, which were miniature and goofy,

And would go dodging east, west, and crooked in crowds;
Soar just banged one solid to start him into bouncing,
The school copied him, till every last fish was flopping
Out of the water, oh heavens, there was nothing to it!
Soar was always scratching around for easy fishing,
Like when he tried the eastern trick on a brook trout,
Curling his fingers under its belly and then just barely
Tickling it, so it rose up toward the air peaceable;
He kept on till its back almost broke out of the water,
When he yanked hard, and sailed the fish clear to the bank.
There's the time he was still-fishing off of the rocks
When a fish hawk, flying out of the hills, dove in,
Scooped up a salmon, and hit out over Soar's head;
He gawked upward with a green eye, and clapped his hands,
And bang! the hawk let go the salmon with a skreak,
And Soar just crowed as the fish plopped into his basket.
One day in a light canoe, with a pal at the paddles,
And trailing his line out back, Soar hooked into a trout,
Husky and mean, who beat the water and wrestled him hard:
Since Soar didn't care to horse him and maybe lose him,
He tied up his pole, let the big fish tow them back across
The calm cove, and had his pal bait his hook for trolling,
And they caught two rainbows simple as they rolled home.
He had witnesses the morning he caught a lake trout
With the fool idea of taming it somehow or other;
It tickled the boys, but once he was all for a project
Argufying was silly, because there's no give up in him,
And that trout did look like it knew its geometry.
He unhooked it, let it splash in the water in his boat,
And hauled for shore, where he rolled out an apple barrel
And dunked it in the lake, and in went the little fish:
He'd been careful to catch it young, since it was clear
There'd be no teaching it if it was old and cranky.
The trout did okay swimming around in the big barrel,
And every night, when it was sleeping, he'd tiptoe up
In his stocking feet, the moon still out, jiggle the knot
Out of the knothole, and let a spurt or so of water

Out of the apple barrel: the fish had no suspicion,
And in a month it was living it up on the dry bottom.
He broke it of the barrel by sticking it out mornings
In the wet grass, and soon it could go it in the shade
Till noon o'clock: by now it was as tame as a tulip,
And the sun hardly bothered it; it tagged after him
Everywhere, down the sawdust trails and into saloons.
Appleknockers hollered, millionaires knocked themselves out
To buy it for the circus, and kids would come for miles,
But he'd shake his head, snatch his hat, whistle to his pal
And clear out, the trout waggling up the street behind him.
One day he struck out for the spring in back of his camp,
To inspect his still, stretch out, and sample his lightning;
The fish tailed him through the thin trees, into the clearing,
On the log bridge, and when he was stooping over his boiler
He heard a splash; it was nothing to him till he figured
And lurched up, too late: the trout had slipped into the creek
Through a crack in the logs, and it drowned at his feet.
He was sad, but it would have flunked winter anyhow.
He bucked himself up by rowing out on a big little pond
With a full jug of flapdoodle whiskey, fishing for bass
And fighting off the skeeters: old Soar would take a whiff,
Hook up a worm, flip it out, sit waiting for a twitch,
And reel it in, when he'd take a real crack, hook up a worm,
Flip it out, take a nice hoot, sit waiting for a twitch,
And reel it in, when he'd take a long pull, hook up a minnow,
Take a good jolt, and one for luck, flip it out, sit waiting
For a twitch, slopping it down, till a skeeter'd bite him
And fly off, bumping into trees, lit up like a steamboat.
Now with the fish stealing all his bait, his dander was up
And puzzling over it in a circular way from the booze,
He swirled a minnow in his private moonshine, hooked it
And slung it, watched a brawl broil in the green water
Till his boat rocked like in bad rapids, and guess what
He saw when he hauled it in: the minnow had the bass
By the throat, and was swinging it like a true wrestler.
Soar let him go, and cramming the bass into his creel,

Lay back for a shot of his knockdown mountain dew.
He was always too cockeyed drunk to be shy of taking
Chances, which is why he'd go scouting for cougarfish,
All claws and appetite, but it was tricky: he went so far
As to set hard money on their heads, but they laid low,
And no matter how many flies twinkled, none were fooled.
The log gar was a real beast, a joker and a bulldozer:
When it was famished it would knock a hole in the boat
With its saw-tooth snout, and Soar never hit on a hook,
In brass or steel, it couldn't snap like a salt pretzel;
But talk about slow fishing, look at the upland trout:
It was a tree nester, flying all around the old jungle,
Over not under the water; it tasted wonderful fried
But was too sly for fishermen. Folks tried to bullshit him
Into thinking it was a bird, but he wouldn't fall for it.
Now, the payoff's like this: he stomped out in the dark
South of the forty-eighth parallel, chanced on a river,
Squinted across and hoped he was equal to jumping it:
He walked up a fair size hill for a scramble start,
Streaked for the water, hit and stepped up into the sky,
And halfway there he calculated out a fall shortage
And jumped again, landing in the weeds on the far shore.
He was hankering for a snooze, and stuck his tackle box
On a limb, he thought, but next morning it wasn't there:
He looked here and yonder for maybe a bear till sundown
And there it was, hanging up on a horn of the moon.
His trouble all started when a teardrop of his home-brew
Kicked him back off balance and a beauty of a cliff:
The bottle was bashed, and the whiskey dug a Great Lake,
But Soar was in his hip boots, and when he slammed down
He bounced, and higher and higher, till he was a dot,
And that's that: anything else you hear's phoney, except
If there's fish where he is, believe me, he ain't starving.
I figure it was back around umpteen forty-eleven
When Cal dreamed up his railroad; and he proposed a line
So colossal it would outshine the Wabash Cannon Ball,
And he'd grab headlines like the brass hats and big wheels.

When he was money-raising at the ballyhoo lectures
He talked dimensions that'd amaze all the gum chewers,
And when he was bankrolled, wham! he was out on the job,
Baldheaded, full of salt, and bawling for the impossible.
It was somewheres a couple of hoots from a whistle stop
He launched into spreading out gravel and laying track
On the Ireland, Jerusalem, Australia and Southern Michigan
Railroad, which was nicknamed the I'm Just A Super Man,
But which everyone called the Eagle Line, after the engine.
Old Cal had billions of six-ton Rocky Mountain boulders
Shipped in for rocks and gravel, cut ties from California pine,
And after two hard years the country's best steel mill,
Working a thirty-six-hour day and a nine-day week,
Finished the first of the rails of the Eagle's track,
And it was laid with pile drivers beating in the spikes.
Oh he had a swell time looking for machinery giant
Enough just to work on his locomotive and his coaches,
And so he used a big pair of ferris wheels for a lathe,
A merry-go-round for a boring mill, who knows how
But he rigged up an old roller coaster as a drill press,
And since the rivets and the staybolts in the Eagle's box
Were ten yards wide, they got them hot in prairie fires,
And hammered them in by shooting cannons at them.
It was a high iron horse with razzle-dazzle wheels;
The smokestack was stupendous, the cylinders gorgeous,
The side sheets pure silver, the crown sheet solid gold,
The big bell was the very image of the Liberty Bell,
The journal box was famous, the air brakes wonderful,
The cowcatcher would handle a day herd of longhorns,
And the whistle could sing I've Been Working on the Railroad.
Now when the mud chickens were all done drawing pictures,
And the powder monkeys had holes in all of the mountains,
And the iron men dropped the rails, and the section gangs
Had hooked them up, and the lever jerkers set the switches,
And the train delayers stacked up tickets and schedules,
And the tent stake drivers had no more nails to nail,
And the carnival crew banged all of the cars together,

And the car inspectors were smiling, and the yard masters
Were snoozing, and the paperweights had full ink barrels,
And the last handrail was shined up by the last porter,
And all the throttle pullers, fire eaters, ticket snatchers
And air givers said okay, the god-damn railway officials
Showed up in thousands and held a banquet in the firebox.
There she was in the daylight, the Eagle and her coaches,
Her boxcars, her flatcars, her tank cars, and her caboose:
The engineer and fireman couldn't climb up the gangway
Without carrying bedrolls, so they rode in a balloon
Up where the mules hauled coal out of the tender in cars
And unloaded it in front of the two-ton scoop shovel
By the fire door, with black coal flying into a white fire;
And pretty soon, when the safety valve showed a feather,
The engineer spit, tugged on his hat, and then cranked up
The four-barrel push-pull motor which drove the throttle.
As soon as the train was rattling, orders were written up
On rolls of newsprint, and stomped out in dot and dash
By square dancers in work boots. It was a big train:
The high-pressure cylinder couldn't be walked in a week,
Smoke took a month to float to the top of the stack,
And the wheel made one revolution between paydays.
The Eagle was so long a streamliner the conductor
Had to ride toward the glory wagon on a race horse
And punch tickets by shooting holes with a forty-five.
They'd dish out a whole cow for a steak in the chow car,
Hoist spuds on crane hooks, mix gravy in real boats,
And pump the coffee and moo juice from a tank car.
When the new hogger honked the new whistle the steam
Clouds busted and it rained too much, but the big bitch
Was the headlight, which lit up the farms for eight hours
After the train was gone, and the hay pitchers were hot:
It singed the wheat, it dried the ditches, and it kept
The gosh-darn chickens up till all hours; when the hogger
Bolted six-inch iron plate over it, it shined right through,
And so he crashed out the reflector, yanked all the wires
Out of the sockets, and took a hammer to the dynamo,

Which cut the light's range down to a mile and a half.
Cal, of course, was all for motion, and one July morning
He got an idea of the Eagle at a real healthy speed
On a hill-country run, when the up-and-down slopes
Boosted her like mathematics; the hogger got cautious
And whistled for the brakes, but it was like the brakemen
Were dozing or something, because she just cracked on,
And when all that tooting didn't wake up the boomers
It scared the engineer, who hauled on the reverse stick
With his arms and legs, till he stuck it in the corner:
Now, it turns out the Eagle was barreling so fast
The whistle's whistle was blowing by her crew before
They had a chance to hear it: she had to roll backwards
Till they caught up with the squawk, and when she came
To a full stop she was still doing sixty miles an hour.
In not too long, they were so far ahead of schedule
They were rolling in an hour before they left the station,
And so old speed-crazy Cal handed his star engineer,
Armstrong, a pair of goggles a foot thick, and said
Go double speed, which was no sweat, since all this time
Nobody had opened the throttle beyond the third notch.
The train boomed by the one-horse towns, mixing up
The slickers, by the fat farms, stacking hay, shucking corn,
Across the lie-down rivers and the stand-up mountains,
It moved into the big sticks, on its last go-around,
In and out of the weather, the sunlight sparking off it,
When Cal yelled okay, eagle eye, give her all she's got;
And speed ain't the word for it when she was wide open:
In back the rails were puddles and the crossties smoke,
Out the window was just a red, white and blue blur,
And when they were highballing too fast for map reading
They hit a long uphill mile, and boys, it was the end
Of the Ireland, Jerusalem, Australia, and Southern Michigan
Railroad; at the very top the Eagle slipped off the earth,
Out of gravity, into the blue: yeah, but I hear it's still
Chugging between stars, on the Aldebaran to Orion line."

"Howdy, partner! Oh man. Shove it, Red Jack; I'm sleeping.
I'll be a bobtail rooster! I ain't seen you since morning.
Of all the! What is this, your birthday? Get out of bed!
What's up? Oh, nothing! Don't kid your grandma. Okay,
It's a bull dance. What, in the shanty? I'll kiss a cow!
Is it rolling? Yeah, it's rolling, and I don't mean maybe!
Give me an idea. Who's whooping it up? Paul Bunyan.
It's a scrape, it's a jubilee! Come on, for heaven's sake.
I'm coming, I'm coming. It's high time, Rocky Dan.
Good god! Who's playing? I think it's, oh gee, let's see;
Old Lefty's scraping a horse's tail over a cat's guts,
I mean fiddling. Hey, I'm sorry, I was all worn out.
Skip it, friend; nobody hurt. I'll bet you Brimstone Bill's
On the dulcimer! He's wild. Here we are: oh, look there;
It's Big Swede and his North Sea piano! Squeeze it, man!
Let's wrestle, darling! I'm from Missouri: show me!
Ha, you waltz like a mule! Thank you. Your cider, buster!
Swing me! Is this a jig or a breakdown? Don't ask!
I can buck and wing, woops! Where'd my glass go? Hold it.
Okay, greenhorns: here's to tight cunts and easy boots!
Here, have a swallow. Mister, I'll have a whoopee cocktail.
My stars! Hey, they're playing Flat River Gal, my favorite!
It's the gospel, honest! Hand me the barrel, I'm thirsty.
Give this man a cigar! It won't wash, Pumphandle Joe.
No fooling, now! You're funny. I am, huh? I'll funny you!
I'm giving you the straight of it, and you won't buy it?
Here's looking at you, dreamboat. Look, it ain't the straight
Of it, it's the horse crap of it. Yeah, it's barefoot weather.
You're a bad actor. What? I look bad, but I feel good.
You're a fake, and a liar! Oh brother. Oh well, it's all
In a day's work. There ain't no such animal, period.
Oh yeah? Here I come, honey. I'll tell you what, big mouth.
Will you quit hogging the applejack? I like your nerve:
You're bold as anything, and you've got grit. Ups-a-daisy!

Good luck, because first I'm writing your mom a letter.
Don't look at me, question mark! I wake up like a goose
In a new world every day. I don't know from nothing. Yeah,
And then I'm knocking you into the middle of next week.
Now hold on, one minute! How are you fixed for moisture?
Oh I've got plenty. Whoa: nobody touches Slabwood Johnson,
And goes on breathing. Pardon me. I've got to see a Chinaman
About a music lesson. Now, now! Say hi to Lulu for me!
Hold her, deacon: she's headed for the barn! They don't come
Too tough for me! Says who? Say your prayers, little boy!
The first hundred years are the hardest. Says me! Okay if
I take notes? Oh, don't get hot. Break it up, you baboons.
Go ahead. I was just joking. It's too many for me. Hey,
Billy the Bum! Welcome back: how are you, boss? Oh, fair
To piddling. I'm quitting! Why? The hotcakes are too round.
Aw, go way back in the woods and sit down. Good night!
I'm teasing: I'm going strong, like always. I'll be tomcatting
As soon as we close camp. And where are you boys pointed?
I'm steering for Burnside Street, Portland. It's close by!
I'm heading out for Sawdust Flats, Muskegon. And you?
Oh, Cedar Root Charley and I have our hearts set on
Haymarket Square, back in Bangor. I want a blow job
From all one hundred of Old Colorado's girls! Yahoo!
Well, I'm looking to beat up Silver Jack just one time.
On my birthday I'm sitting down in the Red Light Saloon,
And standing up three days later with empty pockets,
Or my name ain't Roaring Jim! I'm bowlegged for love:
Oh, I love it! I can smell the farmer's daughters from here!
I wonder if I should go crazy and get hitched, buy me
A little ranch, a big house, raise up a gaggle of kids?
Okay, but first you've got to get out of this shanty, pal:
Go on, try and squeeze past me, I'm a lumberjack!"
It was so all-time happy in there, the room was tilting;
It was steamy and musical, and in between the dances
The boys sprawled back, trading chatter, singing The Jam
On Gerry's Rocks, all hundred verses, inventing more,
While over on the rain barrel was a tight checker game

In which Old Lightheart had the bulge on Dynamite Jack.
It was all back talk by the wood stove, and after joshing
About crossing bedbugs with bobcats to get bedcats,
And the one-winged and hilltop-circling pinnacle grouse,
Whose feathers' color changed according to the season
And who was looking, Brimstone Bill and Big Swede jumped
All whooped up into the great American lying contest:
"Hush up, saw boss, and I'll take you back to the old days,
When everything was bigger: when I was a kid we sowed
An acre of land on which nothing popped up but a turnip,
But we lost our two hogs inside it, and found poor folks
Living under one leaf, it ain't no lie nor whore's dream."
"I'm sure you're for real, bullwhacker; my goodness, yes!
When I was just a squirt, my daddy was the top man
At the iron works, where he built him a kettle so big
If a man dropped his hammer on Friday he didn't hear
It clang till Monday, and we boiled your turnip in it."
"I swear you're the original windjammer, but I'm not
Stretching it when I say our trains back home can't
Carry hay or the cows along the track will eat it, and once
I was riding when they stopped for a cow, chased her off,
And stopped an hour later, when they caught up with the cow."
"Oh gracious, that wasn't slow, that was an express:
I razzed our conductor once till we got in a big tangle,
Rolled off the train, I knocked him out, woke him up with
A hat full of water, we hopped on the caboose as friends,
I jumped off for the cap he lost, and still made it back."
"You may be proud of your slow train, but I like action:
Like when I bake biscuits, I start out at the pump,
And when the first drip drops I pick and shuck the corn,
Grind it, whack kindling, light the fire, and grab salt, milk
And lard before the drop hits the bottom of the bucket."
"Yeah, but why dawdle like that when you might hurry?
When I'm hungry, I just shoot me a buck, I skin it,
I dress it, hang it in the smokehouse, tug off my boots
And lie back and read through the latest Police Gazette
Before the dang bullet can come out of my shooting iron."

It was hard to say who started up the game of poker,
It was all just plain stud and high-low, dealer's choice,
With a tough ante, in freeze-out style with nothing wild,
And, with the mixed luck, it looked like it'd last till sunup,
Or till Johnny Inkslinger shut up, whichever was first.
"I was run out of Oklahoma over a poker hand, boys,
And rode a long-ear mule out of the town of Crossroads
Clear to Hog Eye, Texas, where I tied up at the saloon:
I slouched in and ordered a whiskey and lemonade,
I believe it's called rattlebelly; I knocked it off
While looking at the bunch of lazybones and sodbusters,
And said, 'It looks like rain.' This old pioneer walked up,
Everybody staring, slapped me on my shoulder, and said,
'Stranger, did you know there's only two kinds of folks
Who predict Texas weather?' I confess I was stumped:
'Only two kinds, old-timer? Okay, what might they be?'
He answered with a deadpan, 'Newcomers and damn fools.'
Well, the joint went crazy; lord! it was solid laughter
And shouts of 'You're sold, partner,' and 'Set up the shots:'
I smiled, I bought a round like a good horse, and when
The rowdydow was over, and the bar was buzzing, I said,
'I see you're right, grandpa, when you say there's just two
Kinds of folks who predict Texas weather, newcomers
And damn fools: why, there ain't no other kinds in Texas.'
I could've been elected mayor, but I marched by them,
Headed for the whorehouse, knocked on number twenty-one,
And a whoopee girl yelled, 'Who's there? I'm in the tub!'
'My name's Inkslinger; why don't you unlock this door?'
'I won't see any old stiff,' she said, 'How tall are you?'
'I'm six feet: open up.' 'How do you measure yourself?'
'From the crown of my sombrero to the spurs on my boots.'
'How long are your arms, Inkslinger?' 'Oh, forty inches.'
'How do you measure them?' 'Shoulder bone to finger tip:
Open up!' 'Okay, but how long is your cock?' 'Three inches.'
'Mercy me, how do you measure that?' 'From the floor.'"
Paul Bunyan swallowed all his fun water, and showed them
His timber dance, he won a jackpot on a bluff, and

Squatted on a log bench and looked into the old fire
In the iron stove for a long spell, till he stood up,
Rubbing his eyes, and stepped out into the blue night.
It was crazy, but he was like a white pine himself
With the wind in his head, and the dusk in his arms,
Out under a red sky, and all that was left of the sun
In the work yard: he stood in the sawdust and talked
To the new crescent like a sailboat up in the air:
"Oh moon, you give me goosebumps: I'm a daylight boy,
All I know's the world of sweat, and siestas bewilder me.
I wish the sun was always up; I'd be out logging
Now, but I guess that's that: there's nothing left but scrap
And the sequoias. I could hang around, but I'd just see
My boys all scatter like sparks on the Fourth of July:
I can't stop them, but I can't holiday, it ain't my style;
I'm clearing out, I'll just go and hug them once more.
I'm a veteran of all our mornings, and I'm loyal to them:
The early camps, with big mouths, show offs, wonder men,
All of the strong-arm tramps showing up out of nowhere,
The blowups, the jokes and bellyaches, the slams, the scuffles
And the beautiful fistfights, where we became pals backwards,
I can name the years for history by the insane weather
And the scrapes with animals and greenhorns, oh my land,
We've charged all over the American map like a railroad,
From the skid roads to the boom towns, and in nice circles,
And the air was always full of brags, cracks and comebacks,
Big lies and old lines, swear words, tall tales and sweet talk,
I sure loved it, but it's like it was only a day. Oh,
I can't tell my roughs goodbye, my heart's too watery;
I hope they hold up, but I don't know why: they're loggers,
They're solid as the Rockies, in shape like the Mississippi,
They like to swim with catfish and frolic with grizzlies,
Bald eagles sing to them; oh yeah, I'll see them around.
Why am I out yacking to the moon, like a screwball?
I'm shoving off; I'm not sleepy, and if I'm crowded
By all I've done, I'll be okay once I'm on a frontier.
I might be invisible tomorrow, but nobody should wonder

Where the hell I am: I'm in the United States, working."
Old Paul lifted his ax to his shoulder and shouted
To the blue ox, who bounced over: back in the bull pen,
Shanty Boy, the tall talker, climbed on the deacon seat
To spout a story, and as the big lumberjack walked off
Into the uncertain pines, he just caught the beginning:
"Out of the wild North woods, in the thick of the timber
And through the twirling of the winter of the blue snow,
Within an inch of sunup, with the dream shift ending,
A man mountain, all hustle, all muscle and bull bones,
An easy winner, full of swagger, a walking earthquake,
A skyscraper, looking over the tallest American tree,
A smart apple, a wonder inventor, the sun's historian,
A cock-a-doodle hero, a hobo, loud, shrewd, brawling,
Rowdy, brash as the earth, stomping, big-hearted, raw,
Paul Bunyan lumbered and belly-laughed back at the stars."

John Henry

Aint no hammer
on this mountain
ring like mine
ring like mine

This old hammer
shine like silver
ring like gold
ring like gold

old song, the jubilee, in smoke,
rising, out the dead fire, white
and black, in the iron forge, go
down Moses, the ore and flux,
live, let my people, molten, go,
the hammer, I lifts it back, daddy,
on the ivories, slow drag, steal
away home, swing, the gospel,
I aint got long, the blow, ah mama,
hole in the Blue Ridge, now, take
this hammer, throw it in the river,
in the dark moon, it shines right on,
the stars begin to fall, and the blue
train, going nowhere, I'm the rail
splitter, in the war of the rebellion,
in the gold capitol, naked, oh long
time man, one night, all still, I see
the number nine tunnel going to be,
my woman, up on a lonesome hill,
the driving blues, the death of me

What I
be playing
in that
cathouse
on that
eighty-eight
No praise
house hymn
Heaven
shall be
my home
More like
that reel
goes ah Jim
crack corn
and I
don't care
Don't need
old tunes
old man
You're free
just blow
against
the changes

I'm saying
can you
come up
Hungart's
Creek and
see me
in there
back on
the ridge
in the hills
above
Hinton

Little bell
call you
Big bell
warn you
You don't
come now
I'll break
in on you
Aint you
going to
Aint you
going to
Bacon on
the table
coffee
bout cold
You don't
come now
throw it
out the door
Wake up
buddy
and hit
the rock
It aint
quite day
It's six
o'clock
And hey
buddy
it's hard
but fair
If you had
a home
you wouldn't
be here

We shining. Your jive is like them clouds
in the east, it's different ever daybreak:
it cracks me up.

Aint only but
what comes into my head. Hey man,
big day: you ready for this dust up
with the steam drill?

Give it my all:
I can outhammer man or machine.
It's another day.

Bless you, John Henry:
the boys in back of you.

Rise up,
Jefferson, it's almost day!

Ah sure.

Hey, One Eye, open your one good eye.

One Eye?

Aint you Jefferson Davis?

John, why do you

Well, it's your nickname.

do it?

Hear what that greyback say?
We in a fix: a one-eye president,
one-leg general, and a one-horse
confederacy. Say what?

Why, John?

I think it fine I have the former
president of the confederate
states as my shaker.

It's just my name.

Sides, the shack rouster wake me
up laughing, out of a dream, oh
what a, begin way back, and I'm
a kid, smoke coming from the pit
is this old spiritual. . .

The pit?

The hearth, for making up charcoal,
on the iron plantation.

Never knowed, John:
where is you from?

I be from here,
in old Virginia, from a keep on creek
in a pine grove, in a hollow under
an Appalachian ridge to the north,
the Shenandoah, the daughter of
the stars, Algonquins call it, Old
Dominion, where the past is back
of what we say, and the first men
was hauled ashore, called slaves,
into Jamestown, in white Virginia,
the founding father, Popes Creek,
in red Virginia, knives come down
into Southampton blood, in blue
Virginia, and the surrender signed

at Appomattox: man, history's what
they done told me, I hope to know,
of the day I was born

Aint never seen
the sky that color.

So hot, for May.

Look up yonder, at that black cloud.

It's all the way, from north to south.

Hear that? The birds twittering
all over.

Like it's mating.

Like it's sundown.

Here come Mister Henry.

He got the granny.

Afternoon, Aunt Rilla.

What you all doing out on this porch?

We knows what's going to happen.

What's that?

This is almighty.

Ever birth is almighty.
Where is she?

By the fireplace.

Fill up a tub.

Ah! that lightning
hit over yonder!

The thunder, like a hammer.

Here come
the rain. The wind blowing so hard.

Praise God. This boy is born. And let
the storm say amen.

My daddy
is the fork lightning, my mama
the southern earth, the downpour
my milk, and the gale my lullaby.
My name is John for High John,
Henry for my family, sold down
rivers, fare thee well, oh honey,
across the south, and sharing, if
not good morning, our last name,
and love by blood.

The same old hash.

What? The stokings? We got
choice of salt pork along with
cornbread, or hog and hoecake,
or sowbelly and yellow dodger,
or pig and pone, or Arkansas
chicken and hot Johnnycakes,
all morning, and a cup of mud.
Got a story?

Got a story?

Aint I sing to you last night?

And play banjo. I go to sleep
under Ring that charming bell.
First, tell me what in blazes is
a iron plantation?

In the old house,
half windows, poles, a gallery,
I always hear that waterwheel
slapping, see that tall furnace,
with a bellows and a fire, forging
pig iron. And I'd play Old Hundred
under the shadow tree, counting,
and the girls hiding, seeking kisses,
in the green grove, bare chestnuts,
blossom dogwoods, straight pines,
virgin hemlocks, I loved them hills,
under the Great North Mountain,
by Stony Creek: mama and daddy
was took for slaves, in forty; know
where we was? Liberty Furnace.
And when I's thirteen, I go to work

Well son, put you on the strip mine,
you shovel out the overburden side-
ways over the vein, and so it don't
fall in, you shore it up with timbers,
white oak, red oak, and black locust,
foot wide, and you whang a pickax
at the iron ore, till it loosen, lean,
and shovel it out, if it's too thick,
you just move on to where it aint,
look here, it looks like this, like rust,
load it on the wagon, and the mule

drag it over to the road, wheel it
and dump it in the crucible stack
to fire, with charcoal and limestone.

No more hide and seek, though
mama'd drag us, and steal away
to the hush harbor, with a lookout
for the white patrol, out all night;
if caught, it's a horse-whipping
or the auction block: in the bush,
fire in their bones, they shout their
hallelujahs, pray for deliverance,
sing for salvation.

O Moses, the cloud shall cleave the way:
let my people go;
a fire by night, a shade by day:
let my people go.

Jordan shall stand up like a wall:
let my people go;
and the walls of Jericho will fall:
let my people go.

Oh, all that
old testament thunder, the stars
falling—and what was it? A world
in words, where the hero hauls
dominion down, where they can
breathe, dream, into the day
they're free at last.

Go down, Moses,
way down in Egypt land:
tell old Pharoah,
let my people go.

Salvation from what?
Fire and brimstone?

I expect so.

You didn't make it.

Didn't make it?

Where we working?

Big Bend.

West Hell.

It's good money.

It's a mile and a quarter of
tough slate, and the bad red shale,
we down in the scant light, inferno,
foul smell, in the yellow smoke,
stone dust, in the pandemonium,
men dying, no air, it's profit over
safety, if they's a fall of rock, blast
accident, they go and throw them
in the fill, and if you ask questions,
you gone.

All mountains. Knock them down.
Or die trying. Don't care how tall.
Aint easy. You know. Solid rock.
But once we drive a hole through
the Appalachians, be able to ship
from the Tidewater all the way to
the Ohio. We're uniting the states.
This tunnel the longest in America.

Well, you a hero, muscle man:
you tell the story.

While we walk up.

To the Number Nine.

This so big bald eagle be coming
down to the shore ever morning,
and dip herself, and rock, and up
into the sky, over the holy water.
High John the Conquer thinking
he like to fly, back of the bushes
till he seen her out of the waves,
and rock to go, High John jump
a straddle of her, and here she
go winging on up toward the sun,
cross the ocean, come down in
West Hell, hotter, and he see her,
girl child, her eyes, the grey of rain,
and nothing on, oh grains of sand,
says I love you, who so ever you
are, and she, the devil's daughter,
and he, let's me and you elope,
and she say yes, bang: on the run.
They done stole the devil's horses,
Hallowed-Be-Thy-Name and Thy-
Kingdom-Come, and harness them,
the devil find her gone, hitch up
his jumping bull, Who-Art-in-Heaven,
go flying after, and with ever jump,
he call his horses by name, they
fall to they knees, the bull gaining,
till he catch them. And he rise up:
Can't nobody get out of this hell
without they answer my three times
three questions: and if you don't,

you're mine, in blood. High John
nod, got to give word for word,
win her for wife. The devil smile:
Oh what is louder than a horn?
Or sharper than a thorn? Or greener
than the wood? Thunder is louder,
and hunger sharper, grass greener.
What is the king who has no land?
Salt water without sand? And what
the fire that never burns? The king
of hearts, our tears, the fire of love.
Oh what is longer than the way?
Or deeper than the sea? Or worse
than woman? Eternity is longer,
hell deeper, and you lie, Old Scratch,
woman is good. And when the devil
hear him to name his name, he clap
his wings, in flame, and he fly away.

That him, at the east portal?

Who, the devil? Yeah, him, and his
fool machine.

When you cut work
at noon, you done walk in on him
with the captain?

Yeah, Railroad Bill
seen his red wagon, and member it
from working for the C & O over
at the Lewis Tunnel.

Captain Johnson?

Afternoon, sir, what can I do
for you?

I'm John North, engineer for
the American Diamond Drill
Company, on Liberty Street,
in New York City. You save
miles of railroad track from
the looping river, cut through
the mountain; I can save you
money, with our 1870 Black
Diamond: it improves on all
the old rock-drills; the drill is
on the piston rod, and spirals,
like the Burleigh drill, used
at the Hoosac Tunnel, and
at the Nesquehoning; we got
the contract out at Hell Gate;
its points are black diamonds,
no light or beauty, but nothing
is harder; it runs on steam,
bang on the rock, and rotates
for the next, it's simple, ready
to lift, any direction, at three
hundred pounds; it changes
its feed by how hard the rock
is, can go through four inches
of blue limestone in oh, three
minutes: five hundred dollars.

Five hundred? Like to see it on
red shale.

I'm here today to

Captain.

Hey John,
you listening at the door?

You going to go with a rock drill
instead of me?

Well how do you

I hear it through the grapevine.

If this here is cheaper, I got to think
about the C & O, it's overextended,
overcapitalized, and owes back taxes.
What can I say? Business is business.

Business is hammer men, and shakers,
it's boomers blowing through the country
and only hoping to keep flesh on bone
in they own family.

There's always work.

A contest.

What, you against the steam drill?

I outhammer it, we keep our jobs.

It's a machine, John, how can
you beat it? It's steel and steam.

A man aint nothing but a man:
before I'm beat by that steam drill,
I'll die with my hammer in my hand.

Captain, we'll put it in for nothing
if he wins.

All right, tomorrow, sunrise

to sundown, at the east heading.

That's how it go, Jeff. You know
the song: brother, you better pray:
oh if I miss that piece of steel,
tomorrow'll be your burying day.

Take this hammer
Carry it to the captain
Tell him I'm gone
Tell him I'm gone

If he ask you
where I'm gone to
you don't know
you don't know

Sun's over the horizon: go.

Old motion, the nine-pound hammer,
swing up, drive it from my shoulder,
whip steel, and wait for the shaker,
over, to the rhythm, all day, it's an oar,
and I'm rowing the back country river
to freedom. Like them nights in sixty.

Not bringing nothing.

Well, son, it aint

Ah what, daddy? I said nothing.

Only from out the hidey hole.

And what is that?

The silver dime,
a hole in it.

To save you, yeah.

Only a string of blue beads that
go round your mama's waist.

And son,
that is how come you come into
the world.

That's all right, mama.

Sun back of the Great North.

We got to rub our shoes on this
spruce bough, fore we walking.

How come?

We be invisible to the dogs.
Nobody know what direction
we take. Won't never guess
on down the ridge.

How long walking?

Three days, to the first river.

Four years, after I become
a steel-driving man. I done
stack up so much iron ore,
Liberty Furnace loan me out
to the railroad, building over
mountains, so the trains roll
out of the Piedmont, and all
the way to Shenandoah, so
through the old range, blow
the four tunnels, Greenwood,
Brooksville, Little Rock, and
Blue Ridge, top of the pass
at Rockfish Gap, the longest
in the world, is most a mile.

Ok here, where we now standing
is the heading, sideways into this
hard mountain, and you drill down
from it, inch by inch, into solid rock,
and all this only to make a hole for
the black powder, to blast a tunnel,
now the shaker has the long drill
between his knees, you drive that
sledge hammer bang on the steel,
after the hit, the shaker rocks it,
to loose the dust and spoil, rolls it
to get back the bite, all the way in,
it's rock and roll, on the back beat
the old hammer cracks like thunder.

Was on that gang I hear that glory.

Daddy Mention, he's a freeborn,
and in and out of jails all across
the south, seem like. Must a lost
playing old sledge, they give him
ninety straight up, for vagrancy,
lock him up in that prison farm
outside of Independence, up in
Grayson County; he aint liking
the grits and grease, the captain
cussing at him, says Aint treating
me right. We in the logging gang;
he work so hard: he would fall
this tree by hisself, and carry it
on his shoulder, long ways, back
to the stack. The captain he don't
believe his eyes; not long before
he's making side money, betting
on this man could carry any tree
anyone down; Daddy's always

walking in and out of the woods,
with a big tree in his hard arms.
One evening, most like any other,
one more bad supper, he's up
and out of the slophouse, into
the jailyard; and he lifts up this
colossal log, and he walks out
the open gates, and right on by
the guards, they think it's just
another bet, sides who ever saw
a man escape with a white pine
on his shoulder? Daddy told me:
I just keep on carrying that log,
no trouble on the Wilson Creek
road, why they all thought it had
fell off a wagon, I was hauling
it back, nobody have the nerve
to steal a log like that and walk
on down the highway, singing

I says, Come on gal,
and shut that door,
the dogs is coming,
I've got to go.

It's a long John,
he's a long gone,
like a turkey through the corn,
through the long corn.

Soon as I'm to Mouth of Wilson
I drop the log in a lumber yard
and sell it; I got money to ride
all the way south to Kingsport,
honey. Aint going to catch me
in Grayson County no more.

We toiling in the unknown mountains,
in the unknown moon: that a stick
cracking, or the slave hunters on us?

Who's there? Hold on! Rifle on you.

I'm nobody.

Dogs following?

Aint heard any. Who are you?

Sentry up here. Shake hands.

All right. Sentry for who?

Dozens of us living in this wild.

You them outlyers we hear about?

In exile, from the insane country.
They call me Woods: when
I'm in them, I can't be seen.

John Henry. And this my folks.
Aint the

Where you—go ahead.

Aint the white man come after you?

No more. We talk their language: guns.
And Virginia mountains just too rough
to fight in.

How you live without

Keep pigs and chickens, hunt coons
and possums, catch crabs, and fish,
grow greens.

Declare independence.

That's right. Where you headed?

Trying to get down to Lost River,
float down the Greenbrier, and row
up the Bluestone, to the western
mountains, where they live liberty
for all.

You aint buying a boat
in daylight, no freedom papers.

Might have to steal it.

We can get you
a little batteau.

I'd be grateful.

First river, be a white patrol,
you want a weapon?

Aint doing that.

Second river,
row upstream? How strong are you?

I'm strong enough.

We'll get you down
past Seneca Rocks, to the shore.
If they catch you

Aint going to
catch me: can't get hold of a spirit.

Getting dry, walker, don't need
no steel right now, need water,
carry it here. Look at that, man,
steam drill turning, and the spoil
slide down, into the hole, and it
gets hung, in the seam of the rock,
and full of dust, got to haul it out
to clear it. Your hole's done choke.

Now's our chance, John, to go ahead:
keep on keeping on.

Soon as I swig
this Greenbrier water.

In the black river,
by the old warpath, by creeks
without no name, in and out of
white water:

Now when we first catch
voices, I'm rowing to the shore,
into a flat pool, we all get out,
kneel in the water, with the keel
up over our heads.

We drift all night,
in the uncertain current, that
can drown or deliver us,
no words, only our silence, and
the water's hiss.

so I reloaded.

You hear of that new Yankee gun?
The Henry rifle.

I aint.

They say
you load it on Sunday and shoot
all week.

That right? How many rounds?

Like sixteen.

Hey, that a batteau,
yonder, capsize?

Yeah, reckon it is.

I don't remember

We're out for runaways,

it there
before.

not wrecks. Let's get down to
Fort Spring, and that's our night.

Think them sandhillers will
secede?

Well, if the black republicans

Ah shaker, all our signifying
is out of sight. And anything
get it going:

Sure dark tonight.

What, this aint dark. I seen a night
so dark, a drop of rain knock on
my door, ask for a light, show how
to hit the ground.

That's nothing; I seen
a road so crooked you meet
yourself coming back.

That's nothing; I seen
a man so tall he's trying on
hats in heaven, and getting
a shoeshine in hell.

That's nothing; I seen
a woman so short she took
a ladder to climb up a grain
of sand.

That's nothing; I seen
a morning so cold, the sun
blowing up a fire.

That's nothing; I seen
it so damn hot the devil was
praying for rain.

That's nothing; I seen
a mule so strong you hitch him to
midnight, and he break day.

Hard pull, upriver, against
the Bluestone water, all
night, into unending woods,

into mountains hatred has
not climbed. Aint no slave,
and never was.

Wonder what master
doing on the iron plantation.

I don't call him that, daddy.
Only a man. If anything
he's a slave, to the illusion
he can own us. I say, what'll
the slave do, he discover
us gone?

Say where my money? What
this, son; you be saying you
got work for me?

You know you
a natural on that upright,
and get music by heart
in the brick house?

Yeah, my fingers
remember.

Well, through a Blue Ridge man,
I line up a chance for you
in this red light, playing piano.

What I be playing in that cathouse
on that eighty eight? No praise
house hymn: Heaven shall be
my home. More like that reel,
goes ah Jim crack corn and I
don't care.

Don't need old tunes, old man.
You're free: just blow against
the changes.

You men talking now,
can I sing?

You can sing, mama:
aint no more hush harbor: we
up with the wild Irish, and they
love singing.

My lord calls me—
He calls me by the thunder;
the trumpet sounds it in my soul:
I aint got long to be here.

She musics on the dark water,
looking for a savior on the frontier
between the words slave and free,
her Christ, in the constellations.

Steal away, steal away,
steal away to Jesus:
steal away, steal away home,
I aint got long to be here.

In the steep hills, thin valleys,
in Summers County, I swing
a hammer; man I'm working
for, he hurrah me to a Union
captain, out looking for men
to go tear up the iron tracks,
get rebels off of that railroad;
I'm off leaning on a pine tree,
and overhear him:

You want to hire
John Henry: I swear, the best
man I ever knowed, a natural.
We give him a job breaking
old iron: I aint seen nothing
like it. He'd go out in the yard
and look it over, and sit there,
meditate on it, and most days,
go home, not do a lick of work.
Early next morning, he'd be
at it, and before you think he
had hardly begun, he's done,
and laying back, daydreaming.
How he done it, he'd look into
that iron, and know what way
the hammer should go, so ever
blow counts. I seen him break
foot thick wheels, break more
in two hours than another man
in a long day, with a nine-pound
sledge, hard handle, and always
singing:
One of these mornings
and it won't be long,
the captain going to call me,
and I'll be gone.

If he ask you
was I running
tell him no
tell him no

Say I was crossing
the Blue Ridge mountains
walking slow
walking slow

Sun's at the crest: break for dinner.

You are in Stoneman's cavalry;
I am Captain Lord, commanding.
Confederate troops and materiel
have been running on this road,
Richmond to the Shenandoah:
this raid, we destroy the Virginia
Central Railway, tracks, culverts,
switches, water tanks, telegraph
lines, depot, and set the bridge
over the North Anna River in
flames, under fire from pickets,
so the enemy won't be able
to follow, and head out to burn
the forges, Liberty Furnace.

I'm splitting rails, cutting tracks to
the same tunnel my hammer done
made, man next to me saying, This
war need us so bad, only free can
sign up, but they can't tell fugitive
from free, I say I'm free, and join:
I'm a runaway.

Well, we ahead?

Don't know, shaker, and we won't
know: aint measuring till sundown.

Hey, walker, what we got for eats?

It's flying squirrel stew, and river
water, and we got shoo fly pie.

Hey, John, what's that you was singing,
something about, your hammer in gold,
at the White House?

Yeah, I been there.

What, in DC? What in the world?

I made a name with the general
breaking the line, and get invite
to go and listen to the rail splitter
lay out his idea of a black colony.
We a committee of five, walk up
to the White House, doorkeeper
the image of Lincoln, he say you
all go round to the south portico,
to the basement, to the steward;
our chairman say, Aint servants,
we here to talk to the President;
Impossible, no colored man ever
been through this door; I hand him
the invite from his secretary; he
go back inside and come back out,
open: we make American history.
Abe Lincoln swing his hand for us
to sit, sip lemonade, in hot August;
he go to talking in a cracked voice:

Morning, gentlemen; I just come
from the Secretary of War; and I
asked him a riddle from a negro
story, so I call it dark arithmetic:
There are three pigeons sitting
on a rail fence; if you shoot one,
how many are left? And he said,
Two, naturally. And I said, No,
none: the other two will fly away.

A sum of money has been appropriated by Congress, and placed at my
disposition for the purpose of aiding the colonization in some country of
the people, or a portion of them, of African descent, thereby making it
my duty, as it has for a long time been my inclination, to favor that cause.
And why should the people of your race be colonized, and where? Why
should they leave this country? This is, perhaps, the first question for
proper consideration. You and we are different races. We have between
us a broader difference than exists between almost any other two races.
Whether it is right or wrong I need not discuss, but this physical differ-
ence is a great disadvantage to us both, as I think your race suffers very
greatly, many of them, by living among us, while ours suffers from your
presence. In a word we suffer on each side. If this is admitted, it affords
a reason at least why we should be separated. You here are freemen I
suppose.

Yes, sir, our chairman said.

Perhaps you have long been free, or all your lives. Your race is suffering,
in my judgment, the greatest wrong inflicted on any people. But even
when you cease to be slaves, you are yet far removed from being placed
on an equality with the white race. You are cut off from many of the ad-
vantages which the other race enjoys. The aspiration of men is to enjoy
equality with the best when free, but on this broad continent, not a sin-
gle man of your race is made the equal of a single man of ours. Go where
you are treated the best, and the ban is still upon you.

I do not propose to discuss this, but to present it as a fact with which we have to deal. I cannot alter it if I would. It is a fact, about which we all think and feel alike, I and you. We look to our condition, owing to the existence of the two races on this continent. I need not recount to you the effects upon white men, growing out of the institution of slavery. I believe in its general evil effects on the white race. See our present condition—the country engaged in war!—our white men cutting one another's throats, none knowing how far it will extend; and then consider what we know to be the truth. But for your race among us there could not be war, although many men engaged on either side do not care for you one way or the other. Nevertheless, I repeat, without the institution of slavery and the colored race as a basis, the war could not have an existence.

It is better for us both, therefore, to be separated. I know that
there are
free men
among you
who even
if they
could better
their condition
are not
as much
inclined to
go out of
the country
as those
who being
slaves could
obtain their
freedom on
this condition
One reason for
an unwillingness
to do so
is that
some of you
would rather

One evening
most like
any other
one more
bad supper
he's up
and out of
the slophouse
into the jailyard
and he lifts
up this
colossal log
and he
walks out
the open gates
and right
on by
the guards
they think
it's just
another bet

sides who
ever saw
a man
escape with
a white pine
on his
shoulder
Daddy
told me
I just
keep on
carrying
that log
no trouble
on the Wilson
Creek road
why they
all thought
it had
fell off
a wagon
I was hauling
it back
nobody have
the nerve

remain within
reach of
the country
of your
nativity
I do not know
how much
attachment
you may
have toward
our race
It does
not strike me
that you have
the greatest
reason to
love them
But still
you are
attached
to them
at all
events
The place
I am
thinking
about
having

for a colony is in Central America. It is nearer to us than Liberia—not much more than one-fourth as far as Liberia, and within seven days' run by steamers. Unlike Liberia it is on a great line of travel—it is a highway. The country is a very excellent one for any people, and with great natural resources and advantages, and especially because of the similarity of climate with your native land—thus being suited to your physical condition.

The particular place

I have
in view
is to be
to steal   a great
a log   highway from
like that   the Atlantic
and walk   or Caribbean
on down   Sea to
the highway   the Pacific
singing   Ocean and
Come on   this particular
gal   place has all
and shut   the advantages
that door   for a colony
the dogs   On both sides
is coming   there are
I've got   harbors among
to go   the finest
It's   in the world
a long   Again there
John   is evidence
he's   of very rich
a long   coal mines
gone   A certain
like a turkey   amount
through   of coal
the corn   is valuable
through   in any
the long   country
corn   The practical
                          thing I want
                          to ascertain
                          is whether

I can get a number of able-bodied men, with their wives and children,
who are willing to go, when I present evidence of encouragement and
protection. Could I get a hundred tolerably intelligent men, with their
wives and children, to cut their own fodder, so to speak? Can I have fifty?

If I could find twenty-five able-bodied men, with a mixture of women and children, good things in the family relation, I think I could make a successful commencement.

I want you to let me know whether this can be done or not. This is the practical part of my wish to see you. These are subjects of very great importance, worthy of a month's study, instead of a speech delivered in an hour. I ask you then to consider seriously not pertaining to yourselves merely, nor for your race, and ours, for the present time, but as one of the things, if successfully managed, for the good of mankind—not confined to the present generation, but as

From age to age descends the lay,
To millions yet to be,
Till far its echoes roll away,
Into eternity.

We'll hold a consultation and
in a short time give an answer.

Take your full time—no hurry at all.

We do the questions?

Mr President, in your inaugural
you said you were all right making
the thirteenth amendment as you
say, express and irrevocable. That
would give states the right to own
slaves, forever?

What's your name?

Edward Thomas, president of
the Anglo-African Institute for
the Encouragement of Industry
and Art.

Well, Mr President,
the Constitution sanctions slavery,
I didn't think I had the power,
I was trying to stop secession.
I'm working on the Emancipation
Proclamation.

To free all slaves?

Not those in the border states,
or in southern territory held
by the Union.

Only in territory you don't
control? So who goes free?

Nobody.

When free, can a colored man
hold office? Or sit on a jury?

You read the debates. No.
Can't intermarry. Can't vote.

Mr President,
we been talking this over with
Mr Douglass: he say to say
to blame us for the war is like
a horse thief pleading it was
the horse that made him steal.

Mr President, I been talking
with Miss Tubman: she say God
won't let Master Lincoln beat
the south till he do the right thing.
You done lost at Front Royal,

Winchester, Cross Keys, Port
Republic, Cold Harbor, Cedar
Mountain, and that's only Virginia.
You need black soldiers. Say they
all free. But freedom aint no act
of congress, aint no proclamation.
It's daylight breaking in my spirit.
I done free myself. Don't feel like
descended from Africa. I'm from
Virginia, down the Shenandoah
from where your daddy was born.
I love its woods and waters. I aint
going nowhere.

Who're you?

John Henry.

Outside, strolling on the long curve:

Emancipation?

It done been tried.
Last year, in Missouri, this man
Fremont, I hear, Commander of
the Western Armies, looking to put
down rebels, put the state under
martial law, and say the property
of any who aid the Confederates
at war be subject to confiscation:
their slaves go free. The President
say you should never have dragged
the negro into the war, and revise
the order, and Fremont say no,
Lincoln revoke the proclamation,
and relieve the major general of
his command. What you say, John?

I say nothing, only the words,
no champion, no savior, only
the truth, to lift me out of here,
that old work song:

My mama call me
the way she can:
Aint you tired of working
for that sundown man?

My daddy call me
on the old shore:
Aint you sick of rolling,
what you stay here for?

Oh long time man,
hold up your head:
you may get a pardon,
you may drop dead.

Go down, old Hannah,
don't you rise no more:
if you rise in the morning,
bring judgement sure.

I got a rainbow
round my shoulder
Aint going to rain
Aint going to rain

Did you ever
stand on a mountain
wash your hands
in a cloud?

Sun's at half past, back to it.

You know how his capitol talk
end with old measures? Well,
I make my own:

Why's this hammer so heavy? It's
a slave to gravity:
when I swing it from my shoulder,
I set it free.

John, listen to them.

you done so far?

I had to put in a new feed spring,
and, let's see, the pawl, the nut,
the ratchet cover, the tappet bar,

What's going on, Mr North?

The steam drill's breaking down,
Captain.

Well, John's already hammering.

Can we fire up?

Yeah, but the cross head's
cracked, the screw spindle's off,
and the piston head, the black
diamonds may go.

Hey John,
can you drive her?

I see Polly, always
come by as the shift's ending;
one day I look in her blue eyes.
What's that story, Railroad Bill
go courting? It's after the war,
he's caught in the black codes:
you can grind sun up to down
in the factory, on the railroad,
a dollar a day, and a man aint
nothing, or they won't give you
work, and arrest you by the new
vagrancy law, weaken your rights
in court, sentence you to prison,
and lend you out for hard labor:
well, they done reinvent slavery.
Railroad Bill break jail, go riding
on the slow freight, free the cans
of black-eyed peas, snap beans,
lay them at the door of the shack
of this poor old lady, God bless

Railroad Bill, Railroad Bill,
he never work, he never will:
ride, Railroad Bill.

The old sheriff had a special train:
when he get there, a shower of rain,

looking for Railroad Bill.

The sheriff out after Railroad Bill,
and his posse, on a wildcat train
to this lonesome hollow, but Bill's
in the car behind them, and when
they get off looking, he go on back
to the boxcar, bagging more cans.

Railroad Bill, Railroad Bill,
lighting cigars with a ten-dollar bill:
ride, Railroad Bill.

Ten police all dressed in blue
down the street come two by two,
looking for Railroad Bill.

The sheriff hear Railroad Bill
courting this gal in Piney Grove,
rent bloodhounds in Mississippi,
give them a scent of his old hat
he drop once running, and them
dogs go straight for the Grove.
The sheriff: We get three dogs,
or was it four? Can't remember.
It's four, with a black hound.
Knock on the cabin: See Bill?
No, I for sure aint seen him.
The sheriff go home all weary,
and take the three trail dogs
back to their owner. Well, that
black hound was Railroad Bill,
chasing hisself down, and he
stay on at the cabin, courting.

Railroad Bill, he love to float,
shoot the buttons off the sheriff's coat:

ride, Railroad Bill.

She smiling, in freckles: I say,
So you just up here on the rise,
say nothing, hands in pockets,
ever evening, till I step up
with the first word?

Mm-hm.

John Henry.

I know. You don't know mine:
Polly Ann Fletcher. Come over?

Say what?

I'm saying can you come up
Hungart's Creek and see me
in there back on the ridge
in the hills above Hinton.

I can come now, only I

What?

Only I only know the old
way of courting.

All right by me.

Kind miss, can I walk by you and
whirl the wheel of my conversation
around the axle of your attention?

You may, if you address me right,
kind sir.

Kind lady, what is all the best
news with you?

Oh mister, at
this time, it's a quarter century
I been looking to east and west
for a man who suits my fancies.
And now I'm listening for a word
from your lips.

Oh miss, I gone up
on high sap, and I come down
in Shenandoah, where many goes,
but nobody knows.

Kind sir, when you
say that, you is a huckleberry
past my persimmon.

Good miss, is you
a standing dove, or flying lark?

Good sir, I'm still in air. I hear
you is flying from limb to limb,
and nowhere to rest your wings.
I hopes that you can light.

White-wing
doves still cooing.

Kind lady,
they's a rose blossom: how can
you get it without no reaching
or no sending after?

My man,

love lays it in my hand.

Dear woman,
if you was to get a letter, what
you do with it?

Dear sir, read it
twice, lay it in the north corner
of my cedar chest, and when
ever I think of it, I'd follow it
with love, in answer.

Ah, miss, I has
so much poetry inside my head,
many waters, ten thousand tongues
can't flood it out.

Dear sir, I dream
I'm on a journey and I seen
vines from one side the road
to the other, heart to heart.

But kind miss, I can't wear
out my boots and shoes in vain
for all my days.

Oh you won't, by
no means: my word's my bond.

Kind gal,
will you gratify me the honor
to come to your hills on visits,
with true character?

No hindrance
in the wayside for you to pass.

Dark already, up here.

Dear miss, the world's a wilderness,
and you still got to walk through it:
has you made up your mind to do it
on your lonesome, or with a man?

Dear sir, I has knowed gentlemen
with slipping words, flickering looks,
but with fake hearts. May I ask you,
kind gentleman, if you has the full
right to address a lady in this way?

I has, kind miss. I seen many
dear ladies, but never up to
this day and hour have I left
the single highway to follow
false lights.

Kind sir, I think you honest,
and in this wilderness, I feel
we all looking for company.

Can I hope, then, honored miss,
that I might walk by your side?

Like now?

Man, she good looking.

When I look into your blue eyes,
I trust that fire; you give as good
answer as I question, and with
a voice of love. Kind woman, if
I was to go up between heaven
and earth, out of the blue, drop
a grain of wheat over the acres,

and plow it with a cock feather,
would you marry me?

At the next full moon, I tell her,
I made you measures:

Love to hear them.

Can't read. Not the black bible,
or the blue back spelling book,
haunt of that god, the alphabet.
But I can count the pulses of
your blood, listen for April in
the quail, show the way through
the constellations. Can't write,
love letters, in praise of what
I have to praise, or even a list
of what we need. But Virginia
is my page, the rivers spilling
over it my marks, when I take
breath, I'm given, in this hard
heavenly land, hover, and sing.

Next morning, I'm walking back,
by the fill, high in the half light,
and my shaker:

What you doing?

Coming to work.

With that woman.

Loving her ways.

Aint she white?
Or most?

Well, I had a chance to
look her all over.

You aint ask her, you only look?

She pearl, and ash, and I kiss seal
skin, and she bronze, like sun, deep
black, off white, a dream, that color,
brown, as bread, as wine, she red,
she roses, and milk, oh she change,
her ivory, pale black, such honey,
high yellow, and her blush is gold,
her body's rain, and the living bow,
she covenant, both light and dark.

Last night. Not talking, a kind
of talk. And she lift on elbow:

Man never beat no machine,
why they machine.

Well, then I'll make
history. Aint you backing me?

Oh I am, don't want you hurt.
It's all to keep your job?

That's what
I told the captain.

The jobs of all
the hammer men?

That will happen.

But don't that drill make it easy

for you?

I swing a hammer.

Aint
the hammer everywhere?

Yeah,
at canals, at dams, at turnpikes,
at quarries, at mines, at tunnels.

All this, you working, long day,
and it's all for the C & O railroad.

Yeah, and it minds me of the drill:
train slamming through the blue
mountains.

They saving money, on
them cheap bridges.

One time, I want all them bosses
to see a man.

You win, they'll know
they nothing without you. All right.
It time for song?

Sure enough. I dream
some of the lines:

Last December
I remember
The wind blowed cold
The wind blowed cold

When you hear that

hoot owl howling
somebody dying
somebody dying

When I hear my
own voice singing
I caught the fire
I caught the fire

Hammer falling
from my shoulder
all day long
all day long

Take this hammer
Throw it in the river
It rings right on
It shines right on

Some of these days
I'll see that woman
It aint no dream
It aint no dream

Captain call me
Hey jigaboo
That aint my name
That aint my name

If you see my
blue-eyed baby
tell her I'm gone, boys
tell her I'm gone

By lies, I'm sentenced to a river,
driven naked, to humble us, men
and women, into the prison yard,
in rows to hear what they will say.
Over my shoulder, she stretched
out by my side, her hair in braids;
she's getting out soon, and blue,
as I'm staying; she wrap herself
round me, and we're skin to skin.

It's late one night,
all still, I see
my woman up
on a lonesome hill

The day, in mist, outside the office:

Look it, John, the Chesapeake
& Ohio is laying down deadlines
that I can't make, less I, I don't
know how to get you boys, born
lazy, to step it up.

Aint boys.
Not all alike. Aint lazy, captain.

Well, thanks for nothing. Had it
with you jigs. Course you're lazy.
Why you think I'm captain here?
I'm white, it's only natural that I
be over you animals.

Aint animals.
You are not white, nobody black.
All blood is mixed, and runs down
from one red Adam, out drifting,
east of Eden.

Quoting scripture:
you just a fool, like all the rest.

I aint what you dream. I'm like
the invisible man. You looking out
of minstrel show eyes. Oh I seen
the Christy Minstrels when they
come through town. The parade,
all dance in, singing, in blackface,
wool hair, white popping out eyes,
flat nose, and white burlesque lips,
in rags and patches, swallow tail
coat, white gloves, big flop feet,
in a half circle, at center, the pure
interlocutor, mocking the end men,
who cock and twitch, and hunch
and holler: the audience catcalling.

Mr Bones, I hear you've left your master. Is that true?

Yes, enter lock your door—

Interlocutor.

Yes, Sam, dat's so.

Why so?

Made me work twenty-five hours a day.

But there's only twenty-four in a day.

Yes, but he had me git up an hour befo day.

What's the real reason?

Trouble with lub.

What was it?

Well, I had free womens.

Free: they left the plantation?

No sah, free: one mo dan two.

Two too many?

Well, little Liza Jane, she cotch me wif my gal Sal, and she cotch me in the kitchen with Dinah.

Strumming on the old banjo?

I can't help it, I sees em and I gots to cover em.

You made a run for it?

Yes, I went down to distortion.

What's that?

Where am de rollraid.

Oh, you mean depot.

De po, de rich, dey's all dare.

And did you ride?

I saw de corndoctor.

No, you mean the conductor.

I axed him, Is dis de place? And he say, For what? And I, I don't know, and he say, Yes, and I, What time do de five o'clock train get in? and he say, Soon as de depot go out.

You had no money?

No more dan I wanted. Thought I'd go to New York as a deadhead, so I hide in a box of straw.

Nobody saw you?

No, sah. Bimeby man come along wif a basket ob eggs, and put em in de straw. Den de box was put on board and off we go clickety-clack.

You in the box all the time?

Yes, sah. Man come along and pry de cover off, and I poke my head up.

Was he surprised?

No, sah, but he was awful shocked, and run down Broadway, knocking ober omnibuses, and axing everywhere for P. T. Barnum.

P. T. Barnum?

Yes, sah.

Why him?

He said dat he wanted to see P. T. Barnum cause he gots a box ob eggs to sell him, dat ebry egg would hatch a coon!

Here we are, boys, together tonight, but not like in the good old days, when the hearts of darkeys were light on the old plantation. Mr Tambo, if you could choose, where would you like to be?

Well, Sam, as you am axing me dat question, you knowed dat I'd do anything to get dem good hoe-cakes old Dinah used to make for us darkeys.

Yes, Tambo, I think of the old folks, and drop a tear when I think they are gone.

And, Sam, old massa lub nothing better than our wild singing ob nights:

Oh ole Zip Coon
he is a larned skoler,
sings Possum up a gum tree
an coony in a holler,
Possum up a gum tree,
coony on a stump,
den ober dubble trubble
Zip Coon will jump.

Oh it's old Suky blue skin,
she is in lub wid me,
I went de udder arternoon
to take a dish ob tea;
what do you tink now
Suky hab for supper,
why chicken foot and possum heel
widout any butter.

I tell you what will happen den

now bery soon
de Nited States Bank will be
blone to de moon;
dare General Jackson
will him lampoon,
and de bery nex President
will be Zip Coon.

And then a cakewalk or something.
Nobody look, or talk that way, no,
captain, and that's the foul cradle
of black and white. This carnival
has crawled across these states,
burning this lie, in tattoo lines, into
the American skin, and a century
from now, men and women will
be shot down, on account of this
bad art. And I got just one more
question for you. Captain of what?

Sun's going down, and the steam drill's
punching that hole: let's do John's song.

When John Henry was a boy
sitting on his daddy's knee
and looking down at a piece of steel
says A steel-driving man I'll be.

When John Henry was a boy
sitting on his mama's knee
says The Big Bend tunnel, C & O road
is going to be the death of me.

John Henry went up the mountain
and come down on the side;
the mountain so tall and him so small,
he laid down his hammer and he cried.

John Henry went up the mountain,
and it was all so high:
he called out to his loving wife,
I can almost touch the sky.

John Henry oh John Henry,
his nine-pound hammer too,
when a woman's pending on him
no telling what a man can do.

Captain say to John Henry
Believe this mountain's caving in;
John Henry answer him with a smile,
It's just my hammer in the wind.

John Henry told the captain
They better moan and pray,
ever time my hammer falls
I feel the mountain giving way.

John Henry had a woman,
her name was Polly Ann;
when John took sick and went to bed,
Polly drove steel like a man.

John Henry took his little boy
up in the palm of his hand,
one word he told that child,
You be a steel-driving man.

The sun was big and burning,
weren't no air at all:
sweat run down like water
when John let his hammer fall.

John Henry told his shaker,

You rock while I sing,
I'm throwing nine pounds from my hips on down
just to listen to that cold steel ring.

John Henry told his shaker,
Sing just a few more rounds
and before the sun hits the line
you'll hear my hammer sound.

John Henry told the captain,
A man aint nothing but a man:
before that steam drill beats me down,
I'll die with my hammer in my hand.

John Henry on the mountain side
look to the heaven above:
Take my hammer, wrap it in gold,
give it to the woman I love.

In the pulses of my dreaming,
I'm turning into song. Between
this old hammer lifting back
and the blow, in the swing's
the story, in all our voices.

Sun's under the ridge: stop now.
All right, men, out with the steel
and drill, and I'll measure. Here,
John Henry's drove it fourteen feet.
And the steam drill only made nine.

Can I get a drink of that Greenbrier
water?

Sure thing, John. Walker, go.

And fix me a place to lie down.

John, you all right? Hey, doc!

Aint here.

Aint here? Where in hell is he?

Believe he went into Talcott.

We got to save this man. You two
ride in, ask at the general store.

Ah John.

That you, honey?

Don't die
on me.

Oh, honey. I done what
I come to do.

Davis, you talk to
him, keep him here; if he can't see,
he can

still hear
Sure captain
Hey John
got more
to that
Long John
that old
Daddy sang
Well two
three minutes
Let me catch
my wind
In two

We drift

all night
in the uncertain
current
that can
drown or
deliver us
no words
only our
silence
and the water's
hiss
Hard pull
upriver
against
the Bluestone
water
all night
into unending
woods
into mountains
hatred
has not
climbed

Oh mister at
this time
it's a quarter
century
I been looking
to east
and west
for a man
who suits
my fancies
And now
I'm listening

three minutes
I'm gone
again
My John
said
on the third
day
Well tell
my rider
I'm on
my way
It's
a long
John
He's
a long
gone
like a turkey
through
the corn
through
the long
corn

And all that's left is to row up
this river of stars, till I am free.

He's gone.

Where'd his hammer get to?

That aint true. He's gone into them.

This old hammer
killed John Henry
It won't kill me
It won't kill me

Chief Joseph

1877

October 5
                              Hard afternoon,
blowing out of the north, iron clouds
blister through, and the sun slides
down on Montana, colder, Captain John,
old horseherder, red man, army scout,
rides back over that ditch of water,
Snake Creek, on a sore nag, from that
day's talks, up the cutbank, banging
his heels, unhorsing at the big tent,
the officers, and the buffalo robe,
lips tight, and Colonel Miles nods,
what's White Bird's answer, and John,
what Joseph says is all right, I've
nothing to say, and Miles, tensing,
and Joseph's answer, Lieutenant Wood,
copy this, Captain, and John recites,
looking out at the snow-veined flats,
voice shivering, his finger stubbing
at the drops on his dirty cheek.
                                   Tell
General Howard I know his heart. What
he told me before I have in my heart.
I am tired of fighting. Our chiefs are
killed. Looking Glass is dead. Noise
is dead. The old men are all dead.
It is the young men who say yes or no.
He who led on the young men is dead.
It is cold and we have no blankets.
The little children are freezing to
death. My people some of them have run
away to the hills and have no blankets
no food. No one knows where they are.
Perhaps freezing to death. I want to
have time to look for my children and
see how many of them I can find. Maybe
I shall find them among the dead. Hear me

my chiefs. I am tired. My heart is sick
and sad. From where the sun now stands
I will fight no more forever.

June 16

old moon face upward : and do it soon :
this winter's rough : I'll hit the spurs
of the Bitterroot Mountains : burn down
that whitebark pine with a holy song :
talk to the sun : that spirit's good :
it said to me your knowledge my light :
it's gone so long : the hunt is over :
no luck : we're hungry : we're down
to buffalo jerky : down to rose haws :
old moon face upward : and do it soon :
Pile of Clouds was singing for weather
by the second fire : by the first fire :
in the long tent : long time : in that
Imnaha camp : in a low moon : his ah
power song and did it break : I mean
the weather : the snow : ever break :
in time : I have no illusions Sound
of Running Feet : the boys and girls
down in a circle : mamas in feather :
men squatting in back : all looking
to that medicine man : ghost chaser :
Pile of Clouds : all looking to him
for the big power : I was standing in
the east I think : out under the snow :
with an unsure heart : twenty-seven
winters later : and nothing's changed :
Stars Overhead : was the peace chief :
you know : and so I had to lead off
in the vigil song : silence : silence
banging like a bell : inside of me :
and my forehead painted with red mud :
Pile of Clouds was still chattering :
and floated toward me : I was scared :
his silver eyes : his two-sided smile :
my pulse was ice : all my nicknames
blowing away : he touched my hair to

hypnotize me : I walked : first fire :
I was being born :
                         your sister : okay
for now : okay : only one sleep old :
is all Granite will grind out tonight :
hah : that hard-bargaining old lady :
asking me for a white mare to birth
the kid : the idea : I paid it anyhow :
my babies : all but you were swallows :
lighting flying : she's famous : but
why : no ceremony : simple medicine :
I don't know : promise me fast news :
go away she growled : oh that taboo :
I hate that taboo that she : that I
can't go in : to my own wife : what :
till the hot weather : no I mean till
ah : till : the blueback salmon moon :
Spring of the Year won't question it
though : and it's her sphere : I sat
cross-legged outside the blood lodge :
like courting : all night all through :
her labor last night : at the creek
across the prairie : at Cottonwood :
I was outside the law : you figure :
the man is pure and has to shout at
the woman's lodge : from a ways off
from her not pure : outside the law
I was inside love : I stuck by her :
pangs quickening : her voice at first :
I tried to blank out the White Bird
killings : past days : by meditating
on just her voice : at first as calm
as the slow clouds it rose : sharpened
from pain to pain : in standard prayer :
made up prayer : uncontrollable prayer :
and bad language : as a kind of prayer :
she panted in rushes : like a shower

of rain : she vomited : all dizzy and
was crying : ah : why is it so hard :
I'd've paid double to lace our hands :
she was worn out : words in our dark :
push : it : it hurts : and on and on :
I heard a bawl : and Spring crooning
you're here oh baby I waited so long :
herself again : in joy : our daughter :
alive :

        that vigil was kind of like
the nothing hours on the lookout for
my guarding spirit : it's far : only
a couple of snows back you were ten :
by my buckskin string it's far : that
morning in the first salmon run moon :
my memory shines on it : like water :
I was up early : the sun announcer
not yet riding : I was fixing to go
trout fishing : at the lake I loved :
I was walking to Leapfrog : and had
the fishhook : it was : red hawthorns :
doubled up : with ah threads for bait :
and a hemp line : then Stars Overhead
said it's today : go walk northwest
to Sawtooth Hill on your holy vigil :
I nodded : holding the hook : and he
tied a hawk feather : for luck : ah
to my sleeve's fringe : and slapping
my arm : no magic words for you boy :
I taught you the way : last winter :
go up there : dream : and fly back :
Tall Grass kissed me and she slipped
a shell into my palm : I walked out
of camp heart fast : out of Wallowa :
along the : along the shore's shape :
around Chief Mountain : west shore :
on up Moon Creek to Hurricane Creek :

not even thinking : up Granite Creek :
into that mountain always in our air :
I made a ridge under the green crest :
and scared away : the bighorn sheep :
at the vigil circle the old man had
pointed out : I piled up bunches of
dry grass : pine boughs all leaning
to the long fire : I laid them out :
the whirling stick : the hearth stick :
Coyote taught us how : and I whirled
the stand-up man : red fir : so quick
into the lie-down woman : willow root :
till smoke : and don't let it go out :
would you : ah bank our fire : girl :
last winter he said in vigil go back
down the backwater : till you clear :
I tried to go over that sun inside :
the sun announcer was : Twisted Hair :
ah it's hard to say : well no matter :
up and : on a spotted pony : and down
the summer camp : riding : clamoring :
it's morning : light : you're alive :
you be grateful : wake up : get up :
hey girls : go plump up the fires :
hey boys : go and check the horses :
we're alive : light : it's morning :
the old man's feather : was a fetish :
old woman's conch : from down river :
but why hide it : all mystery : it's :
look : it's pale and pretty : around
my neck : not luck : but just because :
ah : shore : creeks : vigil mountain :
ridge : crest : circle : fire : I was
down the backwater : and I cleared :
and at first : I was toward the south :
middle break : in the arcs of stones :
I saw the green summer : the winding

water : the lake I loved : miles away :
I was hungry : went without : nothing
in my head : later : toward the west :
last break : the ridge across shining :
the sun in back : of the sharp hill :
the domes of the Blue Mountains past :
oh : that fly : I waved it off and it
buzzed back : off back : okay but was
it a real insect : or a ghost talking :
why had the old man said : fly back :
because he wanted a sky spirit for me :
sky name : sun fishhawk cloud eagle
moon crane : higher spirits : by that
he was saying : fly back chief's son :
stars out I ached : I was thinking of
that fly : in the red willows story :
you know : with the girl ah : killed
on her holy vigil : I heard rustling :
crackling : was it fire or a grizzly :
I was spooked : I wished I was down
with the old man : or a ghost guard :
but in his faith : I faced the east :
first break : the black pines coming
out of the black : the sky changing
that half : the color of the seashell :
the geese squabbling at the morning :
and the smoke of the fire straight up :
then ah not sure : I jolted : so dry :
in the harsh light : wake up wake up :
my body buzzing : voices in a flood :
white water : I fighting sleep : was
I fighting the dream : waves of heat :
man in a yellow blanket : slouching
up the hill : with water in his hands
he poured into mine : and that was it :
I woke up at dusk : by the weak fire :
I was shaking : and that man symbol

was out of the sky : the holy vigil :
my name :
                    yeah I'm breaking the taboo :
at last : talking the dream blows away
the power : what power : why's everyone
crazy for power : are we that helpless
under the sky : will the water drown us :
are the wolves coming : Stars Overhead
prayed for power over the band : band
its rivals : Pile of Clouds over snow :
old lady infection : Spring over pain :
all wishes : but the sky bends over us :
we live by water : the wolves honor
our distance : ah the chief was frail :
the band even : snow falling : midwife
in luck : and woman able : Shore Ice
prays for power : over the white man :
but the red man is mist on the hills:
always in retreat from the white man :
the morning sun : always on the move :
that prayer in vain : what is power :
at its summit it's the power to kill :
you hear the killers : in ascendance
outside : and singing : Red Moccasins :
Strong Eagle : Five Winters : and ah
Going Fast : their awful vendettas :
hard drinking : their rifle waving :
it'll only : it'll haul down cavalry
all over us : and your little sister :
what will she do : when the army aims
at her : I won't : I'm like that baby :
unnamed : and water : what is it your
mama says : low water : wears stone :
Good Woman : and in that long council
tonight : White Bird was saying cross
the river at Horseshoe Bend and run :
my idea was taken : no war : and when :

when the soldiers come we'll parley :
only peace : talk : the water itself :
and those ah tall Salmon River hills :
all shelter us : in sleep : it's later :
it's your bedtime :
                        okay then first
that story's end : and then to bed :
I was : ghost dancing against war :
the old man's eye said hey flying :
the old woman's eye oh : graceful :
and I was whirling with my hand up :
music : in my down hand : rawhide :
a bag of stones : I dared to hold :
I rattled it : music wasn't allowed :
and caught up in the power of blood :
all chance : I sang to that circle :
father : Pile of Clouds in the east
under the snow : spirit in the air :
the fall deer hunt moon : the song :
the sky the sky : the elkhide tight
on the horizon's hoop : hammer out
a dance : dry weather dry weather :
blue flowers : hanging in the dirt :
announce water : the dark the dark :
down on the country time and again :
astonish me with light : white horse
boom over the great plains : days
are only stones : I hear you rattle
oh Thunder Rolling in the Mountains

June 17

Coyote cry, and the word comes down
it's a soldier lighting up his pipe,
with breakfast done, and a red line
over the dark buttes, mud underfoot,
Leapfrog squats in the buffalo skin
lodge, and lifts his brows at Thunder,
what last instructions, peace chief,
horn blows, he checks old Blackfoot's
field glasses, up creek, the advance
guard, we people with them, brother,
the low fire hissing, yeah, treaty
scouts and, and Thunder, let me look,
and Leapfrog, officer, and Thunder,
ah, Jonah Hayes, I trust him, don't
shoot first whatever, go pass it on,
with a white breath, uncertain tone
in the cold morning, okay, brother,
but if, breaking in, no if, no war,
are they all here with good hearts,
ah, only peace, but if there's fire
I'll find you, go ahead, Goose Girl
and the women, with the spare horses,
all still across the line of charge,
and fifty warriors, without a leader,
all making noise, on the soft hill,
Shore Ice, with his cold eyes, Going
Alone, Red Moccasins, wisecracking,
Strong Eagle, boozed up, and Leapfrog,
Fire Body, don't shoot first whatever,
pass it on, breeze on the bare skin,
stars invisible, cavalry shows north
on the far hill backed up by black
shapes, infantry, east hill hiding
Two Moons, fifteen warriors, minute
after minute knots up, pony snorting,
Leapfrog palms his shoulder, unknown,

light sprays into the sky.
    He day-
dreams that Two Moons is attacking,
in whoops and gunfire, galloping up
out of nowhere, with his wild boys,
like crows in alarm, and from behind,
blues revolving, off guard, Leapfrog
sticks his weapon in the air, waves
on the charge, hurrahing to the hill,
flows past Shore Ice, the soldiers
fan out, back to back, the warriors
coil around them, like fire shadows,
cavalry, from the north, pour down
to the river, on Two Moons' flank,
Leapfrog's shots true, his brother
in the thick, mysteriously off his
white horse, Leapfrog rides on his
own, crazy like Rainbow, big-hearted
like Five Wounds, into pure disaster,
out of ammunition, swinging his gun
by the barrel, and soldiers go down,
he's grazed and goes black, weaving
on his horse, blood on his forehead,
and catching Thunder up in his arms,
he gallops through fire to the creek
and green safety.
        Six riders named by
Thunder moving out of Salmon camp on
slow horses, Hawkeye and old Red Elk,
Left Hand, Lightning Tied in a Bunch,
Sliding from Cliff and Earth Blanket,
no words between, under a white flag,
toward the grey army, all quiet, now,
and a dog barking, back in the camp,
Hawkeye makes out the advance guard,
that bastard Ad Chapman, cattle thief,
land thief, in a white hat, and yells,

what you people want, Chapman slaps
at his big belt, is that his pistol,
he shoots it, oh brother, that's it,
shots, now and the riders flash down
to White Bird Creek, is it Two Moons
in the bushes, bugle, Fire Body looks
and drops the man in a sag of brass,
Leapfrog's pony is twisting in space,
the charge, damn horse battle-ready,
and bucking under him out of control,
on the east hill, the warriors float
upward, just like the dream, Chapman
and the volunteers wailing fall back
to the first ridge, horses, Leapfrog
reins in, slaps tail, and jolting up
the powdery cut, to the bluff's edge,
where's the fight, it's Roaring Eagle,
waving an old musket, with no ramrod,
Rosebush, drunk on his ass on whiskey,
Blacktail Eagle, with a bow and arrow,
a ghost on horseback, oh what an army,
where's Leapfrog, the distance runner,
horse man, buffalo hero, nobody cares,
rifles crackling, and grass rustling,
sun up, and the soldiers dismounted,
but nobody's dying, blues are dying,
he leans and levels his gun, Wearing
Quiver, blood on his belly, grappling
with a white man, and Thunder's there,
saying, hey careful, don't you shoot
each other, the blue collapses, is it
an arrow, no sound, Blacktail Eagle
comes up sideways, out for the rifle,
and Thunder's gone.

        What's happening,
shots now and again, Leapfrog aiming
that way, the down cavalry look back

and break, no orders or horns, and his
bullet's high, and a captain, hoarse,
howling about-face to the wild squads
as they give up, outflanked, scared,
and he charges on, arms flapping, in
a couple of minutes, nobody in sight,
then Leapfrog sees blues scrabbling
toward, away from riders to the west,
on foot up creek, into sparse cover
in a little ravine, guns stuttering,
urging his long-necked horse forward,
he catches up and it's over in there,
that blind canyon, twenty, wiped out,
and gets down by a soldier, out flat,
a private, and stooping for the dead
boy's rifle, he shoots it at the mud,
it clinks, too rusty to fire, Light
in the Mountain, blood on his thigh,
Wounded Mouth, Charging Hawk, Horse
Blanket, Yellow Wolf, circle around
an officer, lying against a boulder,
staring, his throat clicking, like
trying to talk, and with red smears
on his bullet holes in his thin arm,
white hand, in his chest and groin,
but Horse Blanket, frowning, thinks
the blue's too hurt, nodding, Light
in the Mountain sticks his long rifle
to the man's heart, and lets it blow,
the lieutenant bounces, blood drools
from his grey lips, oh but his throat
is still clicking, Horse Blanket says
it's amazing, Leapfrog waves it away
and walks, one step, his legs buckle
and he's down sick, in an ice sweat,
with the shakes bad, are the warriors
watching, ah no, they're war-clubbing

259

the man to death.
                        Later, treaty man
Hayes says in answer to Three Eagles,
in answer to Leapfrog, yes, married,
and he loved fast horses, his body,
and nineteen others, lay in the sun
and off-and-on rain around ten days,
the skin burning red, and the belly
bulging with gas, the coyotes came
out in daylight to gnaw at the face,
now black, and the frozen arms, till
the burial detail, mouth-breathing
in the stink, dragged it to a hole,
the hair, rooted in the hard mud,
all sliding off of the slimy bone
of the white skull and like a scalp,
and shoveling him over, mire, rocks,
they hung his blue hat up on a bush,
his legs stiffening, and in a month,
his boots sticking out of the grave.

July 2
Bird Alighting : under a white flag
parleying with soldiers : who'd come
to arrest Looking Glass : what for :
white looting : rustling : what else :
is it true : who knows : all hearsay
from ah Half Moon : in the mixed rain :
snow : yesterday : up on Clear Creek :
let us alone : we moved on : before
that fight : are living here in peace :
don't : don't you cross to our shore :
it's like at White Bird : why : this
volunteer fired : hit young Red Heart
in the thigh : they charged the water :
we people flying away : that woman
oh : Arrowhead's pony lost footing
in the Clearwater : she and her baby
slipped off and under : first deaths :
in the quick river : what a victory :
I hate it : the cold army that cut
the wildflowers down : the : hold on :
the idiots : rifled lodges : torched
them : stole ponies : pure stupidity :
thanks to that shot the numbers will
double : the warriors stream out of
the mountains : and the rivers fuse :
Winding water : Walwama : Leapfrog :
Salmon water : Lamtama : White Bird :
The conflux : Tamanmu : under Noise :
Twining water : Witkispu : Red Echo :
Clear water : Salwepu : Looking Glass :
with the bands washing back into one
under sad pressure that had split up
in sixty-three :
                    I was at that council
in : was it the first salmon run moon :
I ah : Stars Overhead in the big tent

negotiating : I just strolled around :
a boy : outside politics : the army
camp there : up at Butterfly Creek :
couple miles : below the Clearwater :
in a circle of hills : quick village
on the west flats : the morning rolls
back in absolute light : no wonder :
I woke up : on the bearskin pillow :
under the elkhide blanket : with blue
bead stripes : triangles : my dream
nothing : dream on the dry grass bed
by the wall : at the head : a basket :
at the foot : fire : dark : shallow :
the summer floor : of the long house :
slender spring flood driftwood poles :
slanting : in cattail mats woven with
cord to the ridge poles : roped : and
a crack for smoke : three fires : ah
one fire two families : like always :
you know : Horse Blanket : his people
already up : and my clothes hanging
from a cross pole : I hauled on deer
skin breeches and my favorite shirt :
long sleeves : long fringes : and at
the chest : loose strings : between
strips of otter : skin of the collar :
disk : beads : oh and the quillwork :
quills in circles : over the front :
and with Thunder : breakfast : Tall
Grass handed me a willow coil bowl
of smoked blueback salmon : trapped
in a willow weir : at the headwaters :
red huckleberries raked off branches
with a coarse comb : and camas pulled
after blooming : in wet prairies blue
as lakes : up in the pinewood glades :
steamed : hit with a greenstone pestle

from her mama : rolled in grass : cut
in cakes : sun dried : a wooden spoon
and a sheep horn cup of water : yeah
I loved that bowl and cup : oh it's
always summer : always thanksgiving :
I lifted up the heavy buffalo skin
and I crawled out : and at the sweat
lodge : open to the east and sloping
to the turf floor : with the roof of
split poles : rye grass : thick dirt :
with stones heating in the fireplace :
water sizzling : and mist blowing out
the door : I looked in : no joshing
the boys in there : or making waves :
I was in the shallows : breathless :
in the muddy creek : world of my own :
two agents : territory superintendent
of indian affairs : four : companies
of cavalry : thief treaty diplomacy :
the tribe disbanding : all nothing :
for the old men : clouds in the air :
I was twenty-three : so young : Sound
of Running Feet :
                              that's when I went
by : oh my brother was riding in a :
in a : horse race : or ah something :
I chanced by Bone Whistle : out in
front of his long lodge : long time :
it was in back I saw her : dancing :
or rehearsing : to Red Cloud's drum :
that chief's daughter : hah : I said
it's unwomanly : your unblushing show :
but I loved her motion and she argued :
I'm Good Woman and good for more than
weaving twine : and cornhusk baskets :
once we were talking : nobody existed :
our words embraced : breath steam : in

263

the air between : oh we were brilliant
and covered plains dances : syllables :
coast decorations : geometry : love
in dreams : tally sticks : willows :
doves moaning : and events as circles :
but that Red Cloud : she was stung :
scared of not winning her : I said
I'd court her from outside her lodge :
court her by dark on the seven holes
of my elderberry flute : true style :
but she shook no : no : she'd invent
a reason : yeah and ride out to me
in the west hills when the moon rose :
I waited : I rolled : it was early :
elk bone dice with my little sister
as the day dragged : I swam the hours
like a chinook salmon : all tension
in the peace streaming down on that
isolation : that rise : the smell of
the grass at dusk : the white lupine
blooming : dice rolling in my heart :
the oval men : and the zigzag women :
chance in the air : the game's limit :
till our old words : she cantered up
and our old conversation started over :
our words the stars that never go down :
oh yeah we kissed a little : not sure :
I was so backward : she was so loose :
sex came but later : we weren't so ah
so big on it : but we sowed you huh
darling : we spouted all that night
and we stole home under a pearl sky :
in love like that : woke up lonesome :
and nobody I talked to : old Rainbow :
White Cloud : Lying in Water : after :
oh nobody's talk touched me like her
dear voice : he was so good-looking :

but she and I were true companions :
ah there was that : I'm leaving out
that time : I shivered with jealousy :
it wasn't always clear : companions
yeah : in the years' dance that was
more musical : by the lake I loved :
late in the summer : so anxious : I
had old man Horse Blanket : approach
her folks : Bone Whistle only smiled :
refused appaloosas : buffalo robes :
I was in line : as the peace chief :
they arranged for my possible bride
to come to me : in a trial marriage :
the real wedding : in the fall deer
hunt moon : the following year : I :
I guess Tall Grass fancied up Good
Woman : oh she was gorgeous : with
otter skin bands : strings of shells :
and feathers : woven into her braids :
two deer skin dress : all straight :
mud white and fringes on the seams :
cape sleeves : at the shoulders blue
four corner beads : the deer tail cut
across in bands : at the breast three
ribbons knotted behind double slits :
beargrass stitch : at the waist dark
copper pieces and the skirt flared :
that day the old woman escorted her
to my lodge : little ceremony : her
voice quivering : bird in the hands :
but mine was steady : male and female
gifts : passed out to all the in-laws :
and the horn spoons from the big party
were given to us : we smoked our pipe
in peace after : no borders between us :
Good Woman :
                    oh the lines the white

man draws on the earth : like cracks
under quakes : first treaty : second
article : outlining the reservation :
listen : in an awful song : commencing
where the Mohanashe or southern boundary
of the Palouse River flows from the spurs
of the Bitterroot Mountains : thence down
said tributary to the mouth of Tinatpanup
Creek : thence southerly to the crossing
of the Snake River ten miles below the mouth
of the Alpowa River : thence to the source
of the Alpowa River in the Blue Mountains :
thence along the crest of the Blue Mountains :
thence to the crossing : I know by heart :
of the Grand Ronde River and the mouth of
the Wallowa River : thence along the divide
between the Wallowa and Powder River :
thence to the crossing of the Snake River
ah : fifteen miles below the mouth of
Powder River : thence to the Salmon River
above the crossing : thence by the spurs
of the Bitterroot Mountains to the place
of beginning : he's a tassel of grass :
riding on the current : a moment or so
in the loving sun : and sliding under :
it's a fool : who maps out property in
the unstopping water : Stars Overhead :
caught in the white craziness : laid
out a deadline : at the thief treaty
talks the reverend clawed at his arm :
saying sign : the old man shoved him
off : what're you saying : your job's
to talk about spirit questions : not
surrendering land : the governor held
the treaty out : saying sign it like
the other chiefs : and the old man :
you go where you like : and so do I :

you're no child : and I'm no child :
I think for myself : no man thinks
for me : I have no other home : only
Wallowa : I'll give it up to no man :
ah governor : take your paper away :
I won't touch it : at home he raised
up four birch poles : trail's edge :
on Wallowa Hill : show the line to
the white trespassers :
                              the general is
days behind in the baffling mountains :
ah but he's coming : all the soldiers :
after that beating : thirty-three died
at White Bird : it's the worst beating :
after Little Big Horn : thirty-three
and not one warrior : at the council :
the first since the outbreak : I saw :
I saw my influence at low water : why :
because I wouldn't kill : I said head
back to the Snake River and stand in
our own high country : Noise was loud :
White Bird : and they voted to follow
ah Cottonwood Creek : hissing outside :
to the Salmon ferry : and east : oh
the chiefs bitter : and now Thunder
Rolling in the Mountains is in charge
of the old men : the women and kids :
huh : like you and me : no fighters

July 11

Water sizzling on his red shoulders,
Leapfrog dives into the Clearwater,
horses racing down the river bottom,
Thunder on the beach, smoking a long-
stemmed pipe, with a soapstone bowl,
and twirling his old elkhorn quirt,
under the white bluffs, mist blowing
out of his mouth, nods at the irony,
treaty men, warriors and not farmers
after White Bird, in three skirmishes
across the prairie early in the moon
to the mountains, Wounded Mouth dying,
oh but the tribe alive in the north,
the raiders out burning thirty farms,
it looks like that kid, Yellow Wolf,
on the hillside, punching cows down,
with another boy, Bull Second, bump,
out of nowhere, dust shoots upward,
it's a shell blowing into the flat,
blues are there on the harsh upland,
and without orders, warriors hustle
ahead to the hills, all directions,
Leapfrog wades out, goes to his lodge
for his Springfield carbine, cartridge
belts at waist and shoulder, shouts
outside, walks in the sun, dripping,
into a pine ravine.

                        He's meditating
on that White Bird dream battle, not
a fighter in it, even if by accident,
his collapse afterward, so pricking,
and not in the Cottonwood skirmishes,
by accident, Two Moons commanding, in
days out of danger, he had turned it
around and around, till he was scared,
images of fire and crossfire hit him,

his heart got tired of the long dread,
only yesterday, no more burning, and
now, loosened by the morning's swim,
he jolts into the thickening timber,
in a hawk's mood.

                    In the good shadow
at the crest of the ridge, he sees
motion south, Noise, and twenty men,
at a ravine's edge, pines shielding
them up there, on the easy tableland,
Five Wounds and warriors slashing out
at the pack train, killing ranchers,
catching a mule and ammo, the breaks
north, south of the sliding plateau
full of guns, and the center manned,
the crescent of blues now surrounded
in the tall grass, troops, volunteers,
cavalry, infantry, artillery, packers
all roll out of the summer afternoon,
and spotted horses are led up on ropes
from the shining river, warriors mount
and go raking by with a constant fire
at the infantry, in the parched grass,
crazy, whooping at the blues hurrahing,
guns blowing and all the mules braying
under the vicious sun, his cover is
solid, but what if he's flanked north,
and so he shoots that way, loading up,
working his jaws till thought is gone,
when a blue charge rams to the south,
shoving warriors back into the ditch,
and a second action hits at the west,
White Bird holding steady, Big Dawn
and Three Feathers, so calm, bolting
into the blue line, gunning, so close,
all day, from that first cannon, till
the fire dwindles, into pure sniping,

warriors, soldiers, dig in, pile up
available rocks, quick work in that
rough break, but hard on the plateau,
rifle pits, low blinds, till the sun
downs, and the heat goes on, Leapfrog,
his blood thrilling, a man out there
crawling toward the stream, whips up
to his six feet, his fingers stinging,
and fires a couple of rounds, scaring
him, his canteens banging, and drops
flat on the grass, hot and jumps up,
not thinking, and there's a man back
of a grey horse, aiming dead at him,
cold knowledge, in that ugly moment,
it's over, heart weak, not flinching,
nothing to do, but stand right here,
bull-headed on a meaningless field
at the end of his days, bark cracks
on a tree behind him, it's the shot,
oh and dear life sprays in his veins,
alive, alive, like a fat salmon, oh
or a lush bush, in the good summer,
he blows the sandhill crane legbone
whistle around his neck, and waving
his arms, crowing, wishing the man
back of the horse would shoot again
and danger him, he loves this game
of dying or living.
                          Red Thunder is
on his left hand, sitting in a tree,
with a scope rifle, for a long space
absolute sharpshooter, picking them
off, till the drawn fire falls him,
like a green branch ripped away, and
his blood slides out as he looks up
at his high pine, in the sultry air,
nothing certain after all that time,

and Leapfrog, leaving a thin defense
at the line, palms his eyes, sighing
as they shoot at the doctor's lights,
and slips down in the starred night,
past the women working, old dancers,
to the war council, Thunder, unlike
himself, looks at the red fire, quiet,
but Leapfrog, uneasy, won't take over,
no signs between brothers, Red Echo
says the numbers are bad, and Noise,
in shame over retreat, charge, crack
their line, and Thunder's up and out
of the circle, voting without words,
White Bird says run north, as always,
but Looking Glass, no, stand, we won
the battle, the skirmishes, and with
bad numbers, never broke, Lean Elk
argues, no tradition of fortifying
against the morning, Leapfrog bows
his head yes and the council's over,
Fair Land is up on the hill, caching
feather headdresses and bead shirts,
silk dress root bags and hoop skirts,
country store goods and old things,
skins, moccasins, saddle trappings,
salmon, berries, knives and dishes,
and rag dolls down in holes, they go
to a lodge, boy in a buckskin cradle,
and lie like spoons, his arms coming
over and under, her hands inside his,
good night, and she kisses his fist,
and he kisses the nape of her neck,
good night, his breath, her breath,
into the dark.
                   July 12
                   Morning on the line,
in the north ravine, nobody moving,

anybody who shoots is a target, how
did that stand-off yesterday happen,
nobody thinking, old man Yellow Wolf
and the boy Animal into a Hole hurt,
Going Across shot down by a bullet,
Hawkeye by a cannon ball, Whittling
dead in that pit, Red Thunder dead
by his long rifle, no replacing them,
and a blue company, scouts, mules up
out of the south, and there's no end
to the white men, yeah, bad numbers,
all that daring, Leapfrog remembers,
that whistle blowing and arm waving,
all that mockery, did he square it,
kill anyone, ah hard to say far off,
blues were shot, hey that company's
turning, Noise in the south ravine,
the battle line charging, warriors
go right to flank it, under shells,
blues crawling, is Noise in trouble,
the soldiers are up, forward, flash
into the ditch, yell, to the river,
it's broken, and scraping his calf,
he climbs down, his idea save them,
on the river bank, Thunder packing
families on horses, where are they,
and Looking Glass hollering stop it,
Fair Land is there, tugs on his arm,
it's up, let's go, she's right, no
time for the lodges, water boiling,
cattle spooking, and Leapfrog sees
gatling, raking the camp, howitzer
on the yellow bluff, Last in a Row
yanking Black Feather, no, where's
About Sleep, oh and Grizzly Blanket
dying, horses scattering, look out,
blue soldier, his finger up, there,

shoot him, it's Joseph, and he bends
on his pony, galloping, what did he
say, Spring of the Year and her baby
back there, Yellow Wolf slides over,
arm bloody, but his hold controlling
his plunging horse, and hauls them on,
all flying up the river bank, toward
the north and safety, what did he say,
Joseph, the grey Clearwater sighing.

July 15

all I can do : war inside war : if
the slaughter : he said four : four :
Yellow Wolf : no : ah thirteen dead
at Clearwater : we got away : with
only the rifles : the herd of horses :
only this : old buffalo skin lodge :
for you and me : huh : darling girl :
if it : and the attack at The Roots :
with that captain : across the water :
it was : I saw : it was old One Arm :
firing at us : they were calling him
General Day After Tomorrow : firing
from the far shore : at our camp in
the east mountains : it would weigh
as I proposed it yesterday : I said
when Red Thunder died the wild rose
bushes withered : the speckled trout
went belly up : and the birches down :
antelopes collapsed on the red trail :
old rivers dried up : the mountains
were cracked : and the sun blown out :
oh and the stars dropped : the world
we love disappeared : in that battle :
with every red man : white man : with
breath broken : this calamity : must
not happen again : not by our hands :
oh my chiefs it's not too late : lay
down your guns : White Bird answered
ah from under his big ceremonial hat :
with the eagle's wing : hanging down :
hiding his true face : we surrender
and we'll die : think back to that
Yakima war : in it was fifty-eight :
Noise interrupted : and the Modocs
in seventy-three : and White Bird :
they surrendered : and were quickly

hanged : is that what you want for
we people : I argued : didn't argue :
I had talked surrender : no headway :
in hopes of dealing with the army I
said we're fighting for what : what :
our lives : no : for this country :
our fathers' bones are buried here :
I don't want to drag my family out
to strangers : I don't want to die
in a strange country : you're trying
to tell me I'm scared of the whites :
hah : you want to fight : do you :
stick here : and you'll have plenty
of fighting : we'll stow our people
back there in the mountains and die
in our own dirt : fighting for them :
I'd rather do that than go fly away
I don't know where : Looking Glass
jangled the rings on : he had brass
earrings : and fingering his mirror :
he won the five bands over : saying
this war is with General One Arm :
not the United States : I'm saying
no more fighting once we're out of
his territory : whites in Montana
are not our enemies : Five Wounds
and Rainbow have word : the Crows
are talking war : if they help us
we leave it all back here : if not
ah show us to the old woman's land :
I say we go : move on tomorrow to
the buffalo country :
                              I was there
twice : you were ah what : I guess
you had to be : only three winters :
very first time when Stars Overhead :
it started when that reverend came

over : and the old man : all wonder
at the talking paper : the new bible :
him and No Blankets : first converts :
he helped him haul up white fir logs :
for the Butterfly Creek mission : was
baptized Joseph : married Tall Grass :
christian style : and that was ah in
the budding moon : the reverend gave
the old man a : black new testament :
and christened me Joseph : like him :
when that bad day : I went to school
out there : no timber : bleak hills :
that bad day came : up at Rye Grass :
missionary and his wife : all killed :
by Rye Grass men : reverend not hurt :
and I went home : ah no more school :
a colonel and volunteers : soldiers :
went after that tribe : the killers :
the innocent : in revenge : question
was Stars Overhead in on the murders :
no no : he was a hundred miles away :
it's confused : when the troops hit
that mission : we people were there :
hundreds of warriors and the old man
walking : holding the American flag :
and that new testament under his arm :
as signs : the agent : hah : announced
peace : no whites inside the borders :
uninvited : and us to go on planting :
all that in the year of the smallpox
outbreak : so many dying : and spirits :
all the herbs : baths : medicine men :
did nothing : in sixty-three that bad
blood again : and that thief treaty :
all had made marks on the first but
the thief treaty : the old man never
signed it : or half the fifty chiefs :

tribe frozen into three camps : one
Lawyer : yes to the treaty : his land
not less : two Eagle from the Light :
war against the whites till they go :
three Big Thunder : the whites broke
the first treaty : we don't sign it :
in the long council : nobody bending :
but the old man : the tribe : banded
back in forty-two : old missionary :
into one : and now disbanding : like
before the whites : all chiefs sign
for their own : and the commissioner :
half as many signatures on the new
treaty as the first : he had anybody
sign it : till it looked full : then :
after five or so snows : the senate
passed it : the indian bureau said
Lawyer signed it for the whole tribe :
white justice : what tribe : and my
old man : who had been a long friend :
had faith in the white faith and men :
thirty winters : in the agent's eye :
took that : old black new testament :
and ripped it up : the pages blowing
across the grass : we lit out that
morning : under our old names : for
the buffalo country :
                Swan Woman sang
in our lodge : to her man's guarding
spirit : for eyes that miss nothing :
a hand that's sure : ah six suns ride
east from the forks of the Clearwater :
up a hard ridge : Lolo trail : pass
over the Bitterroots : the way we go
tomorrow : coming to the high plains :
the sky was bigger : clouds had room :
with a fat rain : light shooting down

on the half-thawed pools : jammed with
red reeds : away : the bare mountains :
and above : at night : all night : oh
the tribes of stars : at daybreak all
the scouts on out : against Blackfeet :
on the plains : looking for buffalo :
we tracked them : till we sighted them
and the charge was right : I carried :
I had been given : a ram's horn bow :
worth a solid horse : a mountain ram
horn split : and ah : backed by deer
sinew : it kept its coil : glue blood
of a sturgeon's backbone : spit wet :
bowstring of sinew : my brother's was
red cedar : long : and good shooting :
most men had only plain wooden bows :
of ash or willow : and the wet weather
had loosened the strings : the buffalo
back from the salt lick : all hundred :
on their bedding ground : most grazing :
oh a few down : their legs under them :
but most were grazing : horns straight :
spines like ridges : backs all matted :
they were at peace : the east so bright :
I held my bow : and a couple of arrows :
in my left hand : and one in my right :
the arrows : berry branches : heated :
rubbed : straightened : flint heads :
tipped on : hawk feathers : tied on :
red bands painted : and otter quiver :
I was so glad : on my horse bareback :
of my far-shooting bow : and scared
of the big animals : all loping away :
I shot at one : at the left shoulder :
no hunter : but oh my : Leapfrog was :
so forward and sharp : I traded bows
with him : in honor : women reading

arrows : not anonymous like bullets :
Wind Blowing : the boldest of anyone :
in the old days : with his high spear
out of red fir : and the barbed point
banged out of jasper : later we ate
the meat and fat : and saved the hide
and horns for trade : Stars Overhead
mute about the whites :

                       oh he talked :
later : the reverend : losing souls :
rode into Imnaha camp : black coat
in the cold weather moon : and rasped :
you will be damned : is that what you
want : your people sabbath-breakers :
without religion : drunks : robbers :
and the old man : save the drunks and
robbers : huh : why don't you start
with the white miners : all over now :
rough men : when they don't strike it :
they go crazy with drink : they steal :
no answer : I don't believe in you :
in that story : first man and woman :
your god said if you eat the apple
you'll die : they ate and didn't die :
and the snake : eat it and you'll be
gods : they ate it and stayed human :
and so that paradise was full of lies :
the bureau agents grab our money off
the first treaty : the commissioner
gets fraud signatures on the second :
the congress only nods : yeah : it's
a religion for liars : the reverend :
I'm not here about the old testament :
but : that new : why'd you rip it up :
god loves you : remember : our father :
and the old man : ah : your god loves
your people : not mine : and lays his

big hand on the white man's shoulder :
yes like a father : but he's disowned
his red children : he lived with you :
we never saw him out here : he taught
you things : no word for us : for you
it's spring : and he lifts you like
the waters : day by day : not long
and you'll cover it all : but for us :
who once filled this country : like
stars in heaven : it's summer's end
and we are lower : we won't be back :
no : god can't love us : forget it :
we have no father :
                          bitter : always :
after that : but he wasn't fighting
a god with favorites : no : all this :
is in our hands : men : women : ah :
god in a rage wrote the white man's
religion : on slabs of rock : a man
of peace : preached it on that hill :
it's saved on paper in the two books :
but in our hands : it's the reverend
introduced us to the whip : Sound of
Running Feet : the sixth commandment
is what : don't kill : the new law :
love your enemies : white soldiers :
they they try to kill us : and call
themselves christians : ah : their
religion is in their mouths : ours
in the old ways : old men's dreams :
in old sayings : and in our hearts :
this morning when we rolled the camp
over to ah Loose Beads prairie : had
No Heart go down : under a white flag :
talk peace : One Arm promised to make
a court : No Heart saying it was our
band that'd surrender : at first light :

boys under White Bird : Looking Glass :
fired on them : you see since I talked
surrender : Metal-Eyed Crane : and ah
Three Feathers : with us at Cottonwood :
the night the baby : in case we walked :
have been out there : watching over us :
and if I light out : I'll be shot down :
oh darling : but I worked on Red Heart :
his son Black Raven and old Half Moon :
to clear out : Red Arrowhead : Coulee :
by afternoon : tomorrow Pile of Clouds
will slide away : and oh I even talked
Three Feathers into it hah : all their
wives : and babies : it's a beginning :
after the red council fire : was out :
I walked over to Looking Glass : over
to Grasshopper Creek : I said this is
your fight : not mine : I'll keep us
all moving : you hold them off : he
just snorted : but while the general
is waiting : we can climb Lolo trail

July 28

It comes to a thousand horses, with
them stolen at The Roots, climbing,
with nothing to eat but wire grass,
wild lupine, they balk, disbelieve,
buck, break down, dying in the rocks,
that impossible canyon, forced ride
on the Lolo trail, at the north fork
of the Clearwater, the bands walk up
the Bitterroots, on the spare hills,
by the green pines and sulfur creeks,
and with down timber, it's slow going
to the bright east, all the in-and-
out miles, at the canyon mouth, logs
and earthworks the army's laid from
steep cliffs, over to grass ridges,
and Looking Glass saying go through
here quietly, our fight's with Idaho,
not Montana, and up at the barricade,
the captain saying hand over rifles
and ammunition or else, that council,
Leapfrog sees Thunder ride in, wave
yes to surrender, but back in camp,
Looking Glass rolls out his opinions
again about the fifty-eight troubles,
and the hangings, saying he'll hand
over ammo, the captain holding out
for a total surrender, now, morning
on the north ridge, no army up there,
thinking it too hard, we people walk,
on ways the scouts had found, I Give
No Orders and Hand in Hand, go above
the little blockade, down to the Lolo
trail, and across the creek, warriors
always between the women, kids riding,
and the blues amazed, Looking Glass
waving his hat, let them shoot first,

all the Montana boys standing there,
in the flat light, with guns clinking
across their arms, in the rear guard,
with Leapfrog's eye on a blue squad,
skirmish line and a big force in back,
we people make it to the canyon mouth
and camp, and the whites, careful, go
around the quick lodges and fires and
fade into the plains.
    August 8
         Words crossing
in the council after the Lolo motion,
with Grizzly Bear Boy saying, head up
the Blackfoot River, north to the old
woman's country, and White Bird, yeah,
and Red Owl, yeah, and Looking Glass,
the war is over, go through Big Hole,
down the Yellowstone, join the Crows,
and Thunder, it's not my country, it
doesn't matter, Hair Combed Over Eyes
and Two Moons go behind White Bird,
the warriors, White Bull, Five Wounds
and Rainbow, go behind Looking Glass,
his way is taken, and then Lean Elk
rides up, they give him the command
over Thunder, and eighty-nine lodges,
in the Bitterroot Valley, bad words
going around, with Shore Ice saying,
I can see it, I'm dying, we're dying,
and Lone Bird, my heart is shaking,
death's after us, I can't hold back,
I have to say it, and Pile of Clouds,
why are we at the Big Hole, I slept
and my medicine said move on, death
is coming, don't lag, oh my chiefs,
if we do, our eyes will be in tears,
on a cool morning, out cutting poles

in the lodgepole pine thicket, with
river boulders, bone wedges, seeing
soldiers standing in grey blankets
on the hills, uneasy, Red Moccasins
and Red Scout go to Blacktail Eagle
for good horses to look around back,
he says no, it's a couple of scouts,
like always, later on, Five Wounds
argues for them, Looking Glass says,
when our raiders hit a ranch, I took
six horses, I put the settler's iron
to them, and loosed them on his land,
quit riding, quit fighting, the war
is over, no scouting, that would be
breaking faith, with the white men,
and Five Wounds, all right, you're
in charge of us, and I have nobody,
but in the danger, whatever happens,
whatever is lost, it was your idea,
Looking Glass only listens to himself,
and the camp halts on the old ground,
neutral to the far tribes, that night
there are stick games and foot races,
singing till late.
        August 9
            Leapfrog walks in
his spotted horse, broken in water,
the winner, calm, the ceremony going,
where's the other tribe, but that's
Eel Creek, lapping into the ah Snake,
not a war dance, his words are gone,
the drumming hard, the women singing,
yes, no, it's like they're squealing,
why oh a dream, whites attacking us,
Fair Land bolts up, he hugs her back
down to the bark mattress, bullets
snap through the cattail mat walls,

poles splintering, and his gun tied
out of reach, it's like waiting out
a summer hail before getting up, but
all nightmare, men, women hollering,
howling in the thick fire, when it
dies down he quick unties the rifle,
waiting at the door skin, crouching,
motions her down, and hurls outside,
oh brother, the blues so close, only
at the next lodge and he runs for it,
we people shot like quail, as they
wake up, fling out into the clearing,
into the gunfire, but he can't see,
can't hear, and everybody's wounded,
is that hissing a shot coming at him,
he goes sprawling, and it's the wind
shivering a fir, nettled at himself,
he's on his feet, bad sign, and down,
at a hump of earth, oh he's done for,
bullets after him, and mud spraying
over him, he's frozen, he's choking,
shit leaking out all over his thighs,
why won't he wrestle this blue fear,
voices rasping, it's him, kill him,
kill that Joseph, damn it, Leapfrog
looking if Thunder and no, it's like
at Clearwater, strange morning, they
are shooting at his brother's image
in him, when it slacks off, he dives
in a thin washout, in the cold creek
women are wading, holding out babies,
Swan Woman, her sad eyes saying don't,
to the blues on the bank, I Block Up
floating, head on the gravel, breast
bloodying the water, dying, bullets
flying through the willows, and Two
Moons is there, bangs and drops one,

Leapfrog in the tall grass, a branch
overhead, looks at Shore Ice aiming
at camp, blues holding the north end,
the moment he fires he pitches over,
his woman, with a baby inside her, hurt,
swoops to his rifle, and firing back,
she grabs her belly, in pain, sagging,
spotted horse comes near to stepping
on Leapfrog under the brush, flinching
back down, invisible to the soldier,
not shooting and showing smoke, till
the charge is by and the creek quiet,
he inches on the far bank, on hands
and knees up toward the horse corral,
no reason, or maybe better shooting,
and up the river, by himself, Five
Dark Cloudy Days, in a white blanket,
with his hunting bow, pacing in front
of his lodge, firing arrows at blue
soldiers, closing, after their fourth
volley he sits down, full of bullets,
at the corral, Red Echo is lying in
the dirt, blood under him, the chief
of that band, No Heart looking after
the horses, all huddled up, tails to
the wind, heads low, in the cold day,
and Thunder sliding down off the hill
in only a blanket, barefoot, his arms
around a baby in an old buffalo robe,
and Leapfrog, what, get ah, what are
you doing, get your gun, and Thunder,
Spring of the Year was hit, and I'm
holding the baby, I don't have a gun,
remember, and Leapfrog, oh man, get
the hell out, go on, save yourself,
no help to us without a gun, go on,
save her, the air is smoky, the blues

are firing the camp, the lodge covers
too damp that morning, few catching,
and Leapfrog, all done in, plodding,
dead woman, her baby on her, bawling,
with a fat arm, and the hand hanging
on a thread of skin, blood jerking,
and looking for Fair Land, he crawls
in the wrong lodge, kids, too still,
shot in their grass beds, one alive,
Gray Hawk's daughter, he circles her
in his arms, blood on her breastbone,
so frightened, and he says low, ah,
White Feather, and silently, no, no,
it's not a war, it's our annihilation
they're after, god, that's why a man
in a blue uniform lowered his rifle
to her young breast, oh and her dark
blood is sticking to his raw shirt,
as he rocks her and prays she go on
breathing, no interest in the chaos
outside, that voice from the far end
of camp, White Bird is shouting why
retreat, something, our kids, better
to die in battle, something, we aim
as good, and Looking Glass is closer,
hey Shore Ice, this is a real battle,
yeah, they ain't sleeping like them
you killed in Idaho, so hot to fire,
at Lolo, against my word, let's see
how brave you are this morning, you
started it, hey I'd rather see you
shot up anyhow, come on, and kissing
White Feather, on her wet forehead,
Leapfrog goes out to tell that idiot
he's making a speech to a dead man,
but he's nowhere, and return fire is
spilling out of the firs, the bluffs

to southeast, the willows, slicing
into the blues, hauling their hurt,
dumping their guns into the creek,
backing off to that point of timber
and Grizzly Bear Boy loping after,
he flails his rifle at a burly man
in just farm clothes, they're down,
blood on his forehead, white hands
up at his throat, he waves for help,
and Red Coyote fires his needle gun
into the man's back, heels him over,
and sighs, the boy's arm was broken
by that shot.
    Men, gradual, come in,
and all through the camp, the roaring
over dead warriors, the pining over
dead women, dead kids, war whooping
as they edge out in the green grass,
shooting, the blues answering wildly,
and hoping Fair Land is out of there,
Leapfrog goes to his belly, back of
a whitebark log, booms away over it,
soldiers crumble, and he jams rags
in his rifle bore, till bullets spit
under the trunk, and he slides away,
later White Cloud crawls to the foot
of the mountain, by the stunted pines,
and lights a fire upwind of the army,
in the thin grass, the wind changing
before the sagebrush burns, Leapfrog
goes on sniping all day, blues pinned,
behind him, the bands burying the dead
on the creek bank, caving dirt on them,
piling the wounded on ponies, escaping
to the blue southeast.
    August 10
      Next morning,

off-and-on gunfire by the warriors,
and back and forth chatter of wiping
them out, bad shots, nowhere to go,
word comes, One Arm is tramping in
with his volunteers to cut them off,
at noon, no change in that one sun,
Leapfrog lifts up his arm and barks,
hey leave them alone, it's pointless,
and the warriors ride toward Willows,
he can't find anybody in the ruckus
till Thunder walks up and he lights,
his brother circles and arm over him,
not like him, and Leapfrog grinding,
like metal, and yet nobody talking,
he flashes what is it, in his eyes,
Thunder saying, in a voice breaking
like water, I took care of her, oh
so tenderly, in the long night, lay
spider webs on her wound, and care,
chanting, you know, no help to her,
and Fair Land died.

August 19

it only grazed her : on her shoulder :
the shot : Spring of the Year is young :
will heal up fast : but it shook her :
and now she flinches : so lucky : did
you see his eyes : I mean : Leapfrog :
all red : his eyes on you : terrible :
on nowhere : on where she is : he cut
his hair : burned it : in mourning :
no saying her name : and wearing only
his old dirty clothes : no laughing :
he tramps by tall : oh and graceful :
Circling Swan : no more : No Heart by
mistake : the warriors : Five Wounds :
at word of his friend Rainbow's death :
walked with his gun forward : crying :
into the blue line : so that he would
die under the same sun : the killers :
Shore Ice : Red Moccasins : no more :
that hard-bargaining old lady Granite :
old Red Echo : killed : like a coyote :
the kids : Red Heart : who was working
on ah Black Trail's collarbone : Dawn :
no more : oh : the women : what names :
Fair Land : red guns aren't that low :
they're out there : shooting ranchers :
all over Horse Prairie : Birch Creek :
where are we : it's Lean Elk's idea :
ah Shotgun Creek : only old Blackfoot :
Blacktail Eagle : old men : know it :
from trading days : huh :

the old man
was my first dying : ah three winters :
he tore them up : treaty : testament :
after three winters : it took it out
of him and he took sick : four bends
of the river away from Wallowa Lake :

on the south side : north side : ah :
spring before that : he was so weak :
and asked the band to vote : I'm not
saying it right : I should say I had
no campaign : you see : when : when
I married I asked to be the speaker :
not a high position and the old man
okayed it : memorizing all the talks :
and saying them over : to we people :
oh : our language : on my own tongue :
the images : the rhythms : the shape
of it : one day I talked : its beauty
is natural and musical : it says much
in a few lines : till fire and idea
make that circle : one heart : I had :
I didn't have to go out and campaign :
the voting my way : and I was chief :
and the old man : that last night by
the Wallowa : like in a winter story :
I can hear his crackle : in the quiet :
and the loud creek rushing : in back :
slow flies in the blue dusk : out by
the easy fire : smoke from the sticks :
up twenty feet high : and vanishing :
I took off my bonnet : eagle feathers :
above the pines : the river of stars :
and I went in : to that steamy tent :
I held his hand : and his heart going
so fast and light : he said : ah son :
my skin and bones are going back down
to the old woman : yes and my thought :
untethered at last : up to the chief
of the invisible world : and the day
I'm two and gone : and soon : look at
this country : you : chief : they're
all looking to you : always remember
I never : I never sold this country :

when they ask you : cover your ears :
only a few moons : only a few snows :
and none of the great tribes will be
in the high plains : in the big woods :
no children : to stand by the graves
of a people once as many : as alive
with hopes as the white man : ah why
be sorry over our undoing : what are
men and women : only the wind waving
in the tall grass : and here and gone :
you pray : cry after them one night :
and then they're never in your eyes :
even the white man : must come to it :
maybe we are : brothers : their eyes
are on this land : when they're all
around you : think of my last words :
this dirt holds my body : don't sell
your father's bones : tell them : oh
I'm winded : tell them we lived here :
we were happy : in this high country :
tell them : when the red man is gone
from the long earth and only a story
in a white man's book : we'll still
be here : on the dear ground : always :
oh you won't see us : but when your
grandchildren think they're nowhere :
in the back streets : and all alone
in the bare towns : our dead will be
all around them : our dead won't go :
we love this place : and ah the dead
are strong : I said : I would guard
his grave with my life : forgive me :
he smiled : and let go : into sleep :
it was meaningless : he was resting
for more fighting : he never woke up :
old Stars Overhead :

                              his eyes sharper

than ours : shut in the creek salmon
moon : and in the river salmon moon :
through her sister you know : I knew
Spring of the Year : in that summer
after summer : by that little creek :
by Cayuse Ridge : wild mint in the :
oh Thorn Brush Creek : morning walk :
space was woven of wild roses there :
a confusion of grass : of weeds and
thistles : wet daisies : and berries :
this spiral of flies : pines : breezes :
and time was bare : the drip of pitch :
the plash of water : with periwinkles
and spiders : at the tender surface :
on the white rocks : ducks chittering
and the clouds skimming I kissed her :
I had loved her so long : in longing :
I saw her smile : and her lips ideal :
at a blue dragonfly : clicking away
in the deep sun : took her wet hand :
and over slick stones : to the bank :
not anxious : for once : we lay down
in the bending willows : her eyes
were round with longing : I lifted
off her loose shirt : first look at :
well : there was that time : I saw
by accident : like it was all going
to happen : at : her little breasts :
I quick untied her sheepskin skirt :
kid's blanket : saw her flat belly :
and her bare cunt : oh baby girl : I :
I took her wrists : in a hard grip :
and held them down : over her head :
her arms a circle : and she tilted up
her lips : in offering : tongue kiss :
her mouth a circle : tits flattening
under me : I dragged my teeth on them :

her nipple a circle : ribs and belly
hollow : her cunt : yes it was wet :
her cunt a circle : and my cock hard :
more than it ever : and I rammed in :
riding her : I was a boat in her ring
of water : and with attention to her :
we banged : and like a dream : fuck :
her little moans : no going back we
were coming : quick : quick : stars
in the wild heaven : summer grasses
all thrilling through us : ah there :
out of breath now : and the air shook
with our new love : and there : oh
the creek : was rushing again : Sound
of Running Feet :

               all that two moons :
not that far from the old man's grave :
did I say north : ah he'd been moved
south of the river : to the big camp :
next day was : next morning : buried
at the top of the ridge : temporary :
our graves always on the high ground :
in sight of camp : and I said no : no
but by the lake I loved : north shore :
across the water from tall ponderosas :
tall snags : in the shallows : poles
of a chief's home : in ruins : and no
cedar Pile of Clouds pounded in balm :
with an old pestle : a couple in each :
ah corner : of the circle of the hole :
scraped out by hand : digging sticks :
and then boughs woven between stakes :
old man : on the horse drag : on down
from the ridge : in a : in a deerskin :
in a lashing cord : face painted red :
his wolf-tooth necklace and his fan-
shaped comb : with him : No Blankets :

and Bone Whistle : laid him out with
poles across : cottonwood brush over :
stones above him against the coyotes :
the fire bending : at that late hour :
ah Pile of Clouds : talked to the old
spirit : dear Stars Overhead : words
have no weight to balance your dying :
wear the comb and necklace : ride this
dead horse : and our love's with you :
don't hang back with us and smother
our children : I'll move your house :
burn your bark mattress : blow smoke
in the four corners : don't hang back
or we'll go crazy : ride on this horse
to the shadow land : Stars Overhead :
and they had the old man's black mare
hauled out : his horses' tails docked :
and no one rode them : three winters :
his black mare : hauled out on a rope :
it was hobbled : with ah : four lines
on her : her shanks : and ah held out :
drummers going : in quick : no : slow
time on the elkhide : sticks clacking :
and Pile of Clouds : hand at the bag
around his neck : out with his short
black knife : chipped of stone from
Obsidian River : and set with pitch
in a wood handle : walking chanting
around the grave : laying his palm
on the mare's chest : and the knife
at her gullet : black on her black :
whispering : something : then drag
slashing and : and the black blood
spraying on his arm : loud whinnying
from the tough horse backing climbing
the air in pain : jerking her foreleg
free of the rope and her head banging

on the quarter moon : stars scratches :
ropes controlling her : Pile of Clouds
whacked at her throat again : her eye
simple fear : blood down her muzzle :
out of balance : oh that black mare
swayed : and crashed on the poor fire :
rolled almost to her hooves : braying :
a haze of sparks : and she lay back :
ah : she lay back quivering : dying :
under the black pines : they hammered
like a fir pole through the dead mare :
and stood it up : on top of the grave :
my death lesson : Stars Overhead and :
and the black mare : winters now I go
back : the flesh has dried : on that
ghost horse : because the wind blows
and the bones rattle :
                 I don't see
why one death calls for another to
distract us : out here : it's worse :
we buried Fair Land : in the corral
at night : and drove horses around
to cover it up : stop Buffalo Horn
and army scouts from digging her up :
and scalping her : had to leave her
back there : and the drunk boys : ah
they'll stab anybody : shoot anybody :
run from : justice : they hit Hole-
in-the-Rock station and knocked out
the telegraph line : stole harnesses :
Bird Alighting : he and Bull Bait
and Rattle Blanket saw dust clouds :
it's General One Arm moving out from
Dry Creek to Camas Creek : Leapfrog
said : it's unbelievable : in fights
blue soldiers zero in : on him : why :
because I spoke out to the white man :

no flinching : they think I'm general :
and in the smoke : he looks like me :
the man can't even die : as himself :
General One Arm at yesterday's camp :
Black Hair dreamed of warriors going
to the old camp and stealing horses :
Naked Head : with his slippery talk :
was claiming the attack would slow
up the long chase : Leapfrog rode in :
broke in : morning's near : let's go :
and I'm to ah : guard us : guard you :
oh honey : at the Big Hole all those
warriors : twenty women : and twenty-
eight kids killed : and not numbers :
I thought of you in the vicious rain :
in the bullets : why you can't die :
because : oh honey come here : yes
ah : because : there's only one you :
there's only one : in this old night :
in this grey country : only one you :
only one : only one you : only one

August 20

Moon out, Two Moons rounding up Bird
Alighting and Hair Combed Over Eyes
for the attack, his horse nickering
and blowing, Leapfrog leads the men
back to Camas Creek, light in and out
of clouds, the scouts, Lying in Water
and Red Raven, go ahead, cut picket
ropes and hobbles on cavalry horses,
moon down, rain falling on the black
meadow, and the bluejays starting up,
the warriors ride, holding the horses'
noses, not to whinny, Looking Glass,
almost sunrise, orders them to fight
on horseback.

Leapfrog is forward on
his pony, numb to the grey mornings
he wakes up alone, what awful thing,
oh that, she's dead and oh her hands
were always cold, and now she's under
that corral, ah, no hope, don't think,
he rubs his eyes, like dead, like her,
outside of it all.

The grass is thick
under the hard hooves, willow fringes
on the low bank, across Spring Creek,
Leapfrog slides by volunteer horses
and goes for cavalry horses, yanks on
one rein, it's tied, another, same,
what happened to the goddamn scouts,
voices to the east, a shot and hoots,
he prods his horse, but it's so dim,
fast shooting, and he yawps, go ahead,
it's only the cavalry, Looking Glass
in charge there, blue cavalry in back
hollering, two stars to the man who
nails that Chief Joseph, he weighs

roaring his name, don't, no matter,
light spilling in front of him, and
fire, rattling at him from his line,
he gallops around it, white wagons
across the field, oh and maybe one,
two hundred stolen horses, dancing
out of the creek, into open country,
volunteers race for the high ground,
officers' tents and the creek beyond,
and the cavalry saddle up, let's go,
we surprised them.
      No cavalry horses,
only pack mules, head northeast over
the lava flows, sagebrush, confusion,
and the blue army catching the rear,
Leapfrog bangs at them, maybe fifty
mules are cut off, and Looking Glass
calls halt, at a rock ridge, behind
sparse timber, all the blues go back,
but one company, shooting, circled,
as half their mules break away after
bell mares with we people, on back
to the two buttes, horses in a clump
of aspens in the hollow, steady fire
from the red warriors.
      Leapfrog, in
shelter, in the high rocks, looks at
Wild Oats, the ass who'd fired first
this morning, his crazy boy, riding
on the outside of his pony, shooting
under its neck, and he just squints,
shakes no, thinking of his big show
at Clearwater, the risk, the praise,
it's nothing new, what are the odds
he'll get out of it, and so what, why
chance it, shoot level till it's over,
ah that poor kid, he sighs, no point,

picking his shots, squeezing them off
at the rifle pits, the blocks of lava,
in the long hours, blinking the sweat
out of his eyes, till the blue relief,
and that's enough, Black Hair's dream,
without the mules, they'll be slower,
as we ride east, for the Yellowstone.

September 9
that was on Firehole River : horses
sore-backed : lame : lodges nothing
but canvas on poles : nothing to eat
but bread : old roots : and tea : ah
the wounded dragging : I was anxious
about the blue troops : not very far :
and Looking Glass not sending scouts :
Three Eagles was talking by my fire
about white tourists : or ah miners :
killed by raiders : sick of his talk
I walked around the fire : hunkered
by Spring of the Year : baby looking
around : the prisoner woman : crying :
man talking : I don't know : dealing :
I'd shielded them and that's enough :
I just sat there : he laid our baby
in the woman's lap : I had to smile :
Spring of the Year : why's she crying :
and the white man : husband was shot
today : and Spring : she's heartsick :
I had Lean Elk go and : loose them :
in the morning :
                    what : why'd the war
start oh : hard question : things are
like seeds : and begin under the mud :
in the dark : like you in your mama's
belly : Sound of Running Feet : yes
and this earth in a blanket of clouds :
in days : out of our reach : I guess
it kind of starts at : or centers on :
the last councils : all that was in
the air so long : and after when talk
was done and the war howled : at one :
you see : white squatters : Findley
and McNall : out chasing lost horses :
walked into Wallowa hunters : in camp :

all this was in : in the first salmon
run moon : McNall saying to ah Wind
Blowing : come on : chief : we know :
where'd you hide them : huh : don't
lie you asshole : both men : inching
over to where the rifles were stacked :
making a grab : Wind Blowing wrestled
McNall over the barrel : who growled
jesus Findley shoot the son of a bitch
before he gets me : and Findley shot
him in the chest : the body the body
shaking in the dirt : blood all over :
whites : hightailing it out of there :
well the horses turned up : four suns :
at Findley's cabin : the blue cavalry
came and I mean : everybody was on me
to answer that death : nothing I said
calmed them : not wanting to let that
fire go : I led them up Wallowa Hill
on horseback : and I told the whites
hand them over or we'll come and rip
into your ranches : the blue cavalry
in the stand-off up there : one man
who listened : the whites had a trial :
Findley said he was defending himself :
they let them off : first Major Wood :
that honest man : on his own say-so :
he got a council together : on rights
to Wallowa and Wind Blowing's murder :
with General One Arm : but we never :
always talked with the indian bureau :
never the army : and in the tamaracks
without needles moon : at the mission :
I had the chiefs go slow : no hurry :
are they : going to start without us :
seven suns late : I dawdled in there :
in a heavy blanket : rain showering

on the shingle roof : low building :
and the president : we welcome Young
Joseph to this council : he's spoken
true words to the white man : we hope
this talk will bring : understanding
and ah : ah : peace : to us : chief :
whites call me Joseph : but my name
is Thunder Rolling in the Mountains :
he's spoken : I never saw him before :
and ah : ah : peace : with a general
at his side : I stood : men nudging :
it's good to be here this afternoon :
good to talk : to the great general :
major : who speak for the white man :
who control him : and answer for him :
peace is broken but we can build it :
the agent shaking his head : it was
Reuben ah between the two languages :
I had him ask the agent what it was :
he said bad commission : is the army
in charge of indians : no : no he is :
the old men : from the east country :
in order to be fair : no experience :
and the general : in his faded blue
overalls and his military hat : with
a star in front : my adjutant here :
ah Wood : has told me that there are :
that whites and indians have trouble :
and one of you was killed : will you
give this body your view of it Joseph :
I thought of that sally : I learned
off Eliza : at ah the mission school :
it's good : I said : in seventy-two :
with the bostons coming in : I said
we people were only fishing : hunting :
not making trouble with the bostons :
and that I wouldn't : and the general :

excuse me : who : why are you calling
whites bostons : and the major : it's
a word for : well : the first whites
west of the Rockies : were trappers
who came from Boston : they call us
all bostons : and the general sighed :
well you can call us : we're not all
from Boston : I said : all right then
don't call us indians : we're not all
from India : hah : Leapfrog laughed :
I nodded : it's true : whites killed
my brother in Wallowa : Wind Blowing :
oh that quiet man : that steady man :
we looked up to him : and the whites
who did it : quarreled with everyone :
I worked so long to be above trouble :
above blood : once we were many and
they few : we wanted peace : we gave
up land for it : we never paid back
rustling : killing : we wanted peace :
oh they know we're nowhere as strong :
maybe they do it : to get into a war
they're sure to win : who gave them
that idea : yeah I want them brought
in to the agency : if a man goes bad :
I stop him : I fine and disgrace him :
or it's my crime : likewise : if you
don't punish them : you're a killer :
that Wind Blowing : what is he worth :
more than Wallowa : his life is worth
more than the United States : or than
the world : I can't measure how much :
now he's dead in Wallowa : his blood :
his body under its grasses : oh now
that pale dirt is the holiest ground :
I claim it : in trade for that life :
all whites clear out : and the agent :

Wallowa's high and cold : the spring
is late : and : and the frost early :
can't raise a thing up there but ah
tough vegetables : wheat freezes in
the milk : it's good stock raising
is about all and it's their fishing :
a ring of mountains and no road in :
squatters up there be only too glad
to sell out to the US : and I said :
clear them out : at last : at last
honor the old treaty : of fifty-five :
ten thousand dollars : every winter :
for twenty winters : and where is it :
congress said war between the states :
the handful they gave the agents took
and congress knows it : they cheat us :
fake up invoices : double our prices
and then pocket half : sell shovels
made of sheet iron : cast iron axes :
shoes with paper soles and blankets
made of rags and glue : ah where are
the forges the mills : tin gun wood
and wagon and plow shops : where is
the hospital even : you promised us
no whites inside unless invited : ah
what's the town of Lewiston : whites
crossed over the line in sixty crazy
for that metal : restless : we said
all right : north of the Clearwater :
don't hurt our fields : when snows
blocked up the trails : trapped them :
we gave them our food and saved them :
and when that steamboat couldn't land :
we said all right on the tongue south :
then docks : a boathouse : we asked
for troops : to back up the treaty :
none came : it's the gold miners who

walked off with mares : burned fences :
trampled on fields and jumped claims :
by sixty-three : and the thief treaty :
red man : four thousand : white man :
in Lewiston : on that tongue of land :
around fifteen thousand : you tell me
if the white man's broken the treaty :
and the general : it's a big mistake
to take Wallowa away : sure congress
will let you keep : that poor valley :
and that was the first day : at night
I stared at Leapfrog's map of Wallowa :
green willow paintings : on cowhide :
of Wind Blowing's murder : next day
I : I don't know : the general said :
I don't like it : any more than you :
we give you title to the country and
dissolve it : all legal : I can talk
it down : the injustice : but my job
is to back it : I talked thief treaty :
bad signatures : Stars Overhead said :
don't take what's due from the first :
white men will say it means yes : to
the thief treaty : tribe disbanding :
ah but the congress didn't see that :
it said : other signed for us : in
our democracy : the many don't force
the few to obey : imagine a man says
I want to buy your horses : I say no :
I like them : he goes to my neighbor :
Thunder won't sell me his horses : and
my neighbor : pay me : I'll sell them :
the man comes back : hand them over :
if the white man has bought our land :
that's how : and the major : we can't
justify you : protect you : with you
off the reservation : the president :

and even if the state of Oregon gave
up Wallowa which it won't : it's too
cold for a reservation : the major :
and if all whites clear out : others
will come : and I : the United States
broke both of the treaties : it's in
your own report : you have no right
to Wallowa : no right to stick us on
that crowded reservation : we're okay
up there : leave us alone : we sell
our stock : buy what we need : we ask
for nothing from anyone : we're free :
the agent said : what about getting
schools : and I : nobody wants them :
and he : why not : they'll teach us
to go to church : and don't you want
churches in Wallowa : no : why not :
they'll teach us to argue about god :
like catholics and protestants : no :
we might argue : about the things of
this world : never about god : and I
started in dreamer talk : you know :
that new idea : that all the red men
who ever died : all the dead buffalo :
come back : and overcome the whites :
get paradise back on the plain earth :
and never cut her : with ax or plow :
the agent hated it : I'd spout it to
rile him : out of the sun the earth :
oh : leave it like it was : no lines :
and I'm out of the earth : we're of
one mind : one measure : I won't cut
my love : for the old mother : if I
was on the reservation : I'd have to
bow to your chiefs : your laws : if
I thought god sent you to talk to me :
ah : no : but don't misunderstand me :

it's not my land : I have no right :
whoever made it : has a right to it :
I have the right : to live up there :
as you where you in peace : and red
in the face at that the general spit :
what what are you saying : you won't
agree to any terms : this commission :
I've heard talk and talk : I broke in :
nothing is done : words don't pay for
my dead : the country you cover : and
talk by men : with no place talking :
where do they get authority : to say
to the red man : stay there : inside
of a damn line : yeah : when he sees
the white man go : where he pleases :
no answer : ah : I know your terms :
no : I won't agree : no : I won't go :
no : I'm not afraid : Stars Overhead
is gone : I have no chief and : and
the general : okay : I hear you : do
you know what happened to the Modocs:
the Seminoles : the Sioux : want that
for the Nez Perce : well next summer
if : if there is trouble in Wallowa :
it's going to be like the bard says :
the plumed troops : and the big wars :
I'll send out guns : two to your one :
and I'll whip you : into submission :
I said go ahead : I'm ready for you :
I motioned to : my burning brother :
on the way out : I heard the agent
ask a soldier's wife : is your hair
on tight : she said : I wish someone
would kill him : before he kills us :
and I broke out : in her own tongue :
you think we're like : wild animals :
my eyes stinging : I lifted my face

against the tears : and I walked out
into the drizzle : the next morning
I rode up to the back gates : Noise :
and Naked Head : in the solid rain :
White Bird : the council was over :
I was gambling for the best terms :
in my long bonnet : white feathers
from a young eagle : caught : plucked
a couple of times : and then let go :
with orange lines on our faces : bows
and arrows : headpieces on the horses :
nobody was there :
September 10
where was I : oh :
next morning : I had waited too long :
I froze the general : hurt the peace :
the major with us but even he thought
whites higher : the agent in charge :
army at his back : he was against us
hunting : gathering : oh he'd love to
have us give up : our old wild ways :
hunter : warrior : sit quiet on farms :
love to cram us indoors : in school :
and turn us white : he said it's the :
we don't belong in boxes : sparrows
nest in circles : they have the same
religion as us : the agent told me :
it's the reservation or war : I said :
no : a council : in the bread moon :
up on Butterfly Creek : at the fort :
outside the big tent : on the ground :
I saw One Arm : I'm ready to listen :
and he : no : tomorrow : in council :
I'll make my orders plain : and I :
no : man to man : I've been in many
councils : and I'm no wiser : we're
all born from woman : but not alike :

who are you : to order me : and he :
you deny my authority : hah : do you :
you want to dictate to me : and cut
it off : because I had : that council
nothing : White Bird said they sell
our boys whiskey : it makes them deaf :
and Noise talking for the five bands :
it was a river of dreamer words : oh
his tongue is rough : true but he has
no touch in councils : he was on fire
and the general jailed him : he had
given us one moon to move : are you
going on the reservation peaceably :
or shall I push you on with soldiers :
and Noise aiming his finger : saying
in his grinding voice : you brought
a rifle to a peace council : only ah
thirty suns for gathering our stock :
yeah : we'll have to fight : he was
arrested for backtalk : and to calm
them down I said : we can avoid war :
we promised Lewis and Clark : saying
no war with the white man : we never
broke it : why rush : we can't do it
in thirty suns : not with the spring
rains and the Snake : at high water :
and white rapids : under the cliffs :
stock everywhere : but in the fall :
with the river low : stock together :
and our supplies for the winter in :
and the general : in his scripture-
quoting voice : what's that old hymn :
what shall the harvest be : run over
by one day and troops will herd you :
all stock outside the line : will go
into white hands : and that was that :
last council :

in the first salmon
run moon we crossed the Snake River
in flood : hide ropes under the old
women's arms to drag them over deep
water : we had to leave I don't know
how many horses : cows : to thieves :
and the five bands up at Split Rocks :
men dancing racing gambling : women
digging roots : and the anger under :
at the big council : reciting white
crimes on we people : twenty-seven
murders in sixteen seventeen winters :
not one white man killed : not one
in jail one sun : Shore Ice : ah his
old man a victim down at White Bird :
he took that beauty : to bed : Dawn :
in the morning her mother : got wind :
ran swearing to his lodge and yanked
her daughter out the door : hissing :
leave her the hell alone you bastard :
big man always fucking girls : yeah
you weren't so damn bold : when they :
they shot your daddy : huh : big man :
no answer : at a kissing dance later :
Ten Owl : Dawn's brother : said hey
look who's here : don't go flashing
by us : we know you : little rabbit :
the next dance around : same thing :
and ah Shore Ice : what do you mean :
and Ten Owl : look rabbit : there's
your old man's grave : man who did
it is living it up on his ranch now :
down at Horseshoe Bend : you aren't
man enough to do him in : Shore Ice :
I'm going to make you swallow that :
hid in his lodge going over and over
that day : three winters back : when

Eagle Robe : back from visiting : in
the flowers moon : saw a white : Ott :
had moved his rail fence to a field
where the chief gardened and lived :
he said : Eagle Robe said : move it :
Ott kept on plowing : and the chief
waving a blanket to scare the horses :
Ott slipped out a rifle and shot him
in the gut : that tough had been run
out of Lewiston : Eagle Robe hung on
a week : and made us his last wish :
I know there are : only a few suns
for me on earth : from that gunshot :
I don't want this : to fire you up :
tell him : Shore Ice : for the sake
of we people : don't let your blood
beat you : when I'm dead : tell him :
that man was poor : and land hungry :
the whites aren't like us : we are
all poor or none : tell him : don't
go to war : you'll lose the country :
and the men who saw : wouldn't swear
on the old bible : at the grand jury :
not their religion : they could tell
the truth without holding up a hand :
and after the trial they let Ott go :
in the black morning : he corralled
Red Moccasins : his kin or something :
Swan Necklace : to hold the horses :
headed for the Salmon River breaks :
the no return river they all call it :
and his old man Yellow Bull : caught
Red Moccasins and couldn't turn him :
they rode up river : down the hills :
hollered across : at Horseshoe Bend :
for Ott : no answer : he's nowhere :
and that afternoon : they walk in on

old man Devine : who loosed his dogs
after we people : and shot a cripple :
and in his shack : him sick in bed :
kill him : with his own gun : go on :
General One Arm might say : that was
the war's beginning : ah no it's one
in a string of crimes : next morning :
they shot maybe three field workers :
for nothing : and circling back to
Slate Creek : said for good whites :
Wood Fockler Titmar Rhett : to come :
be spared : and they turned a stolen
horse and a rifle : over to Big Dawn :
in the council : old Rainbow saying
no fight against : all the big guns :
wait till summer : a council of all
the tribes : and Big Dawn : oh you
old men sliding your tongues : three
warriors are coming with his horses :
white man killed last sun : soldiers
are after us : the war has started :
that night : Noise : seventeen riders :
all wild with whiskey : out shooting
anybody they saw : I hear they killed
ah four five men : on down the river :
Benedict in his cheat saloon : who'd
shot Red Moccasins and maybe killed :
all this : you know : we were above
the Salmon : my brother : Goose Girl :
Half Moon : Three Eagles : you and I :
butchering cattle : and coming back
with loads of meat : on pack horses :
ah twelve horses : over Buzzard Hill :
I went on ahead : Two Moons rode up
with the bad news : if I'd been home :
never have happened : first thought :
lodges down : the bands hurrying away

over to Cottonwood and Looking Glass
already at Clear Creek : I : bands
to the reservation : I was so hurt :
wait for the soldiers : make peace :
much trouble : much blood : would be
spared if we opened our hearts more :
I said in the war council : Leapfrog
had his say : word is I want to fight :
it isn't true : I have a wife : kids :
horses : cattle : a heart : and eyes :
we fight : we'll have to leave it all
and go into the mountains : snarling
boys : had roused all the bad hearts :
they voted down : letting whites not
in the fight off : the council broke :
nobody was left : Spring of the Year
close to the birth : I would've gone
to the agency that night to give up :
oh but White Bird had the nerve : to
cover me : and keep me there : night
raiders : I don't know : drunk again :
under the stars again : shot three :
I hate ah numbers : one of them sat
with a boy's skull between his knees :
and caved it in : one of them caught
at a girl's tongue and sliced it off :
stabbed her : they raped her mother
by White Bird Creek : in the morning
burning the cabins : they shot Mason :
who whipped two red men last winter :
and raped his sister : another woman :
your mama and Leapfrog said : don't
go back : whites will lay it to you :
not believe you : and kill you : and
I : all right : I'll take my chances
with the rest : oh darling : the men
who : were friends of ours who did it :

whose fault : it's theirs : but think :
the old men shot : old women slapped :
they were insulted hundreds of times :
lost horses : lost homes : got sick
on white man's whiskey : I couldn't
ah handle them : they think revenge
is good but their mamas know better :
I wanted : no blood running : I was
ashamed : I said in my heart rather
than kill : I'd give up the country :
the old man's grave : anything : not
to have this blood on us : our hands :
give up my life :
                                    yeah : we almost
didn't make it : here to Rock Creek :
we were packing up in the salmon sky
this morning : No Feet looking east :
to the foot of the Absarokas : dead
prairie : and the Big Horn Mountains :
northeast : he saw blue companies up
on Heart Mountain : in front of us :
Red Wolf and all of his hard riders
loped on ahead : and let the cavalry
find them and ah : oh it took nerve :
I'll tell you : chase them southeast
maybe twenty miles : while we pushed
up the south fork : Lean Elk had us :
not leading us on the mountain grass
and in plain sight : had us keep on
one mile : toward the Stinking Water :
like we're on the run that way : halt
in a clearing : and mill the ponies
all directions : then cut back north
through pines : with a little ridge
that hid us : that last quarter mile
we squeezed our horses through a hole
in the pure rock : out of the canyon and

onto the flatlands : that old hunter :
restless : and always loving a game :
coming up with this as he was riding :
in unknown country

September 13
This morning, east, old Yellow Wolf
tells Leapfrog, over the Yellowstone,
station and haystacks burning, light
coach and horses rolling, mail sacks
in the well slashed, letters blowing
across the prairie, us whooping till
we see blue soldiers, cut the jerky,
I ride east with five warriors, kill
ah trappers, out in nowhere, and to
a logging camp, with the straw boss,
his rifle in arms, eying his horses,
come on in, boys, everybody in camp's
out fishing, we don't like his rifle,
back off, go flying toward the river,
he hides in a wallow, we set a saloon
on fire, and Leapfrog, why do I have
to hear it, in the dry wash, soldiers
out there, just over that flat ridge,
in the Yellowstone.
               In the afternoon,
on the buffalo trail north, lookouts
see scouts, coming out of the crack
in the rimrock, that grey and yellow
sandstone, officer on the tableland,
warriors open fire on them, keep low,
all scrambling into the dry creekbed,
stand up to shoot and are scared down
by sprays of fire, in a crazy shower
out of everywhere, at last breaking
over an easy slope crossed by draws,
Leapfrog is dragged along with them,
and in a fury, nothing but a branch
in the white water.
               He slaps Red Elk,
where's Surrounded Goose, I was going
to order him forward with questions,

Red Elk shakes him off, I don't know,
he was wounded, I, and Leapfrog, what,
alive, you didn't haul him with you,
and Red Elk, yeah, in that crossfire,
he's dead, I looked at, and Leapfrog,
ah you can't leave him dead or alive,
and to nobody, look, boys, stop here,
we've got to go back down the ditch,
it's a wounded man, and nobody moves,
and to himself, he's dead, for sure,
no sense in baring all their bodies,
Red Elk you ah, you have the command,
he slides off down the dead creekbed
after Surrounded Goose, it isn't far,
his head is back, and his jaws open,
no good carrying him, with soldiers
up on the sagebrush flats, he crawls
till he catches him a worn out pony,
blues avoiding the ravines, he comes
to women driving horses, on a bench
north of Canyon Creek.
                              The warriors
shoot from horseback, hit invisible
in the wet dirt, miss at that range
in the hard air, cavalry dismounts
and a few soldiers charge, retreat,
horses lost, most blown, a hundred
let go, hooves cut, we people walk
in the north fork, Bare Legs, alone
in the skirmish fire, tough, holding
off the blue army in the tumbleweeds,
till they try climbing the cliffs to
the south, and fail.
                              Only boulders,
in an off canyon, the warriors make
a stand up there, wishing the hills
higher, soldiers, unknown, take off,

oh and Over Point of Hill, hanging
from his horse, and Leapfrog looks
into the sun, wincing at the blood
pattering, nothing to do, red sky,
blues go back to the canyon mouth,
and the word around camp, the Crows
were there, fighting for the whites,
for pay no doubt, but stealing pack
horses from them, and Looking Glass,
words all forgotten now, was wrong.

September 29

six suns : along the Missouri breaks :
in the badlands : the low-water port
at ah Cow Island landing : with tents
for officials and freight : our boys
begged or : paid for a side of bacon :
a sack of hardtack : and at sundown :
you know : they fired at the troops
on guard all night : charged through
the willows : steal : burn : nobody
hurt in the dark : next day : I gave
them axes to bust the whiskey barrels :
Dog : down on his knees : licking it :
I said : friend : you get half shot :
you will get shot : calico and paper
all over Cow Creek and a bull train :
going to a fort : they passed it up :
next day : shot at bullwhackers come
for their cattle : wagons in flames :
light gunfire : from the high bluffs :
down on all the : I'm tired of this :
I'm so : I have a story for you hey
Sound of Running Feet : ever wonder
why I keep you up nights : talking
till the moon's gone : it's because
old men : on winter nights : always
talked to kids : gave down to them :
our stories : our skills : because
I don't know what will happen : only
that both One Arm and Looking Glass
want me dead : but this is who I was :
and because I love you : don't think
the world's like this : ah maybe so :
it's full of holes : and makeshift :
we're hardly out of the north wind :
but in this lodge : there is no war :
it's everyday : and life as always :

it's a Coyote story :
                        he's so sharp :
wild : out for himself : beat winter
in his big lodge : one night his wife
got awful sick : not breathing right :
and died : in the days after : he was
alone : didn't do a thing : but cry :
the death spirit came up : and said :
Coyote do you miss her : and Coyote :
what yes : I long for her : it hurts :
and the ghost : I can take you where
she's gone : but look : you have to do
ah whatever I say : just like I say :
nothing else : not ever : and Coyote :
anything : yes no : what could I do :
and the ghost : all right : let's go :
and in the big mountains : the ghost :
whatever : and Coyote : I miss her so :
why wouldn't I : he couldn't see him :
only a shadow : on the great plains :
the ghost and the ghost shouted : oh :
would you look at all those horses :
like a round-up : and Coyote who saw
nothing : yeah : so many horses : by
the dead land the ghost shouted : oh :
would you look at all those berries :
let's eat them : and Coyote who saw
nothing and the ghost knew it : yeah :
let's pick them : the ghost bent down
the invisible branch : and Coyote did :
picked berries : ate out of his hand :
and Coyote did : and the ghost : good
berries : and Coyote : yeah : lucky
we found them :
                        later on : the ghost :
we're almost there : at a long lodge :
very long : she's in there somewhere :

321

wait and I'll go ask : and the ghost :
okay : this is a door : do what I do :
the ghost : lifted up the door skin :
and leaned inside : Coyote like him :
and the ghost : she's making supper :
go sit by her : and Coyote : who saw
nothing : was crouching in the open :
in just scrub willow : only feeling
the ghost was there : it's ready now :
let's eat : and the ghost ate : hand
to his mouth : Coyote only saw dust :
but ate like him : after the woman
cleared the bowls away : it seemed :
the ghost : wait : I'm going around
and visit : and the ghost : it's all
contrary here in the shadow country :
our dusk your morning : our morning
your dusk : the sun was going down :
Coyote heard whispering : all sides :
low words : all dark : he saw a line
of fires : on down a very long lodge :
we people : with bodies like shadows :
and who they were : he saw his wife :
right there : by him : it was a joy
just to say hello to his old friends :
long dead : it was a joy : he walked
down the aisles : between the fires :
they shrugged : well it's not so bad
in the dead land : but blackberries
aren't tart : the water isn't cold :
it's so washed out : voices are weak
and touch is vague : oh it was good
back on the earth : the talk went on
all night : he saw : the grey lodge :
at dawn the ghost was back : Coyote :
it's our evening : not too long and
you won't see us : don't go anywhere :

we'll be back : when it's your night :
and Coyote : yes : where could I go :
sun up : and all by himself : Coyote
sat there : in the middle of a field :
all day : under the hammer of heat :
dying for water : that night : words
in the long lodge : and so for suns :
one daybreak the ghost : ah tomorrow
you go home : and your wife with you :
and Coyote : yeah : but I like this :
I wish I could stay : and the ghost :
yeah : but tomorrow you go : careful
and don't give in to your fool ideas :
now look : you've got five mountains :
five suns : and your wife with you :
talk to her : don't ever touch her :
when you go down the last mountain :
do what you like :
                          and Coyote : yes :
at dawn : he left that place : all on
his own : but she was there : so dim :
one mountain and she was more there :
like shadow : two mountains : and she
was sharper : across the waving fire :
oh in the quick bark and brush lodge :
and the death spirit : counting suns :
figuring distance : hoped he'd do it :
get her back : the night before life :
at the next to last mountain : Coyote
saw her : like she was real : across
the whipping fire : her face her body :
yeah that was her : and he stretched
in pleasure : and swooped over to her :
to hold her and ah : to hold her down :
she said : no Coyote don't touch me :
as he touched her : smoke : and she
was gone : again : to the dead land :

323

the ghost heard of it : and in a fury :
you : you always foul up : I thought
I'd cautioned you : fool : oh Coyote
we were making death so that the dead
always come back : man and woman are
about to be born and you wrecked it :
for them : death will be like this :
Coyote just cried : said to himself :
I'll go back over the five mountains :
see them : her again : next morning
he was walking : saw where the ghost
had seen the horses : said to himself :
oh : would you look at all the horses :
like a round-up : saw where the ghost
had seen the berries : said to himself :
oh : would you look at all the berries :
let's eat them : and did the motions :
and at where the long lodge had been :
he said : yes ah : this is the door :
sat where he had : supper is ready :
and ate hand to his mouth : sun down :
he listened hard for the low voices :
on the lookout : for the old shadows :
nothing happened : he kept the vigil :
all night : no lodge no ghost : Coyote
sat there : in the middle of a field :
that story's told :

     in all the tribes :
ah the rain's cold : no timber here :
no weeds : and the northwesters blow
down on Snake Creek : yeah but here
there are water holes : meat : robes
for winter : with buffalo and deer :
elk and antelope : out on the plains :
oh there are spaces : in the lodges :
in the council : but when we cross
that northern line : we will be free :

and no more force : from up there we
can talk to the government : I'll get
Wallowa back : and go home in peace :
I prayed my trail was clean : and if
there are : dead men : in back of us :
I worked against it : messengers are
flying to Sitting Bull : please join :
against attack : with ah more red men
out on the run from American soldiers :
are you : I'm kind of sleepy : are you :
big kiss : okay darling : night night

September 30

Wolf howl, bad dreams, no sleeping,
Leapfrog walks stiff on the icy dirt,
the old riverbed, high table, thick
buffalo grass, Hair Combed Over Eyes
is up there, that old man who knows
the dead, the hurt, the disappeared,
I had a dream, in last night's rain,
it was an attack, and you know what
Lean Elk told Looking Glass, go on
and lead, they'll catch us, kill us,
and Leapfrog, yeah, long jump down
to a gulley fringed with sage grass,
the stars are faint, over his head,
at last go out, frost on moccasins,
and his throat aching, he reaches in
for his willow bark and chews on it,
he's thinking, the Cheyenne scouts,
talking sign language, why let them
escape on back when the buffalo came,
the sky is lighter over the Bearpaw
Mountains, the camp packing up, only
forty-odd miles to the north border
and Canada, scouts waving blankets,
the danger signal, to the south, he
goes for his rifle, back at the edge,
the watches the blue cavalry cut off
a thousand horses, grazing, Thunder
out there, hollering, no way to help,
the charge, who's moving, White Bird
lowers his arm, all stand and fire,
horses whirl, the soldiers come to
the very ledge, but can't ride down
the cutbank, and he cracks his rifle,
man on an iron grey horse, in with
black horses, and hoping to cross it,
falls on his head, and cartwheels up,

his pistol in hand but hanging there,
he'd hit the grey, Leapfrog's rifle
is frozen to his palms, so bad that
he has to rip the skin to get them
off, bleeding, the blues can't walk
on the hard slopes in long overcoats,
no cover, and the warriors slide out
into ravines, circling them till more
soldiers come, and the warriors back,
Leapfrog looks for them giving orders
and blows them over, cavalry closing
in back of horses with reins in hand,
shooting long range like the red man,
and it's too much, he shies from it
down in the cracks, in the creekbed,
as the blues dig in, up on the crest,
and fire on the gullies all morning,
in the afternoon, they charge on his
band's lodges, it's Thunder's voice,
soldiers hammered by warriors hiding
in rifle pits, the bullets vibrating,
in a harsh music, of flies in summer,
dirt spewing in the air, dead horses,
runaway horses, grey dusk, at last,
message from Bear Coat, the colonel,
asking to parley, and Looking Glass,
come and scalp us.
                    Oh, and Leapfrog
walking to Thunder, warriors search
the blues, wounded, give them water,
blankets, relax, I won't ah kill you,
kid, you can't shoot, and Leapfrog,
hey man you got through, and Thunder,
I was with her, oh Sound of Running
Feet, it's gunfire, ah here's a rope,
go ahead, darling, and catch a horse,
run north with them, and she sighed,

you be careful, daddy, quick got her
on a big appaloosa, and flàshed away,
on the horse's neck, prettiest thing,
I ever, ah she was free, joined Good
Woman and Bird Alighting, Black Eagle,
all chasing north, a hundred horses
and a few lodges, and I, so dazzled,
I didn't hear the shooting, and, and
I saw cavalry going toward our lodge,
get to Spring of the Year, the baby,
or else get killed, prayer in my head
to the spirit, white horse boom over,
ah the great plains, days are stones,
I hear you rattle, oh Thunder, and I
rode at the soldiers, guns in front,
in back, Leapfrog, the pony swerving,
was it wounded, down and stepped in,
Spring of the Year slapped her rifle
against my palm, hey here's your gun,
fight, and I, looking at my clothes,
in ribbons, I wasn't touched, I went
to my belly, out, and the white men,
oh, twenty steps, in the rifle smoke,
and aimed the gun, for her, but saw
that old morning in, ah the root moon,
and a storm walking over the Sawtooth,
and just before the blow, a thousand
split-tail swallows, flying up above,
and all the kids, side-arming rocks
at them, good time till one was hit,
it hurt, I did nothing, just looked
about to throw, I shouted, oh I shot
down at their feet, to warn them off,
six warriors dying, soldiers backing,
and ammo stripped off the new bodies,
and Leapfrog, it's a bad day, Thunder,
ah, Pile of Clouds is dead, Lean Elk,

by accident, I don't know, warriors,
Noise, down at a blue soldier's feet,
Lone Bird, Five Winters, they can't
attack and we can't go north without
a thousand horses.
                    October 1
                              Snow looping down,
Leapfrog sits there, in a rifle pit,
watching Thunder, with a white flag,
and his pain eyes, off-and-on smile,
going to their camp, but not talking
for all the bands, and that Bear Coat,
sliding through the camp after ideas
to help him crack it, in the council,
Looking Glass was saying, I'm older,
know men with two faces, two tongues,
you surrender, you'll wish you were
dead instead of fools, and Thunder,
this captain is fair, we people are
in the hills, naked, freezing, women
aching, children whining at the cold,
for them, White Hawk, Woman Walking,
No Hunter, not me, I'm surrendering,
and Looking Glass, I won't give up
to the white liars, that afternoon,
Thunder is prisoner, officer hostage
for him, his message, I don't know
what it's all about, if they kill me,
don't you kill the officer, no good,
the light is dropping, shells banging,
Leapfrog, pissing into the rifle pit,
watching a woman, her girl, crouching
under a buffalo skin, and the air is
ripped, all hazy, and the girl, Girl
Chasing Animal, is covered with holes
of blood, and Leapfrog, after the man
at the big gun, is on his feet quick

in the cutbank, unloading his rifle
that way, ah who is it who slugs him
in the ribs twice, knocking him back,
why'd he do that, and he lies there
with his eyes shut, oh he's mixed up,
it's gunshot, yeah, but thank heaven
he's only grazed, hands on his chest
all wet, Two Flocks on Water, saying
he'd maybe swap horses, good trade,
old song Goose Girl's singing when,
ah when, no matter, opens his eyes,
and a little weed, on a green stalk,
is hanging there, and purple spikes,
it's just alive, sparks are going
in circles, it's like he'd given up,
after Fair Land, he feels so thick,
that little weed, he starts to say
go ahead and oh his voice, so harsh,
a breath of air, it shakes the weed,
so lovely, and.

October 5

Looking Glass saw it,

that death, nothing to do, but wait
for Sioux, at sight of a man riding,
he waved him in, and a bullet broke
into his forehead, oh and the dark
coming so quick in that up country,
old women digging with hooks all day,
shoveling with pans, making shelters,
little cooking, mamas going without,
water after dark, out of Snake Creek,
little sleep, leaning on the walls
of their pits, all broken, all lost,
in the winter night, no more talks,
only more snow, from the raw clouds,
guns flashing, shelling, four days,
morning of the fifth, all shooting,

none hit, Leapfrog's body, his skin
like beeswax, and his eyes no color,
his mouth, his ribs, open and under
the inches of snow outside the lodge,
the crackling stops and Thunder lets
in Captain John, Old George, scouts
from the white camp, and one, so good
to see you alive this sun, long ways
ah catching you, we're glad you want
no more, Yellow Bull lifts his rifle
and Thunder his palm, and the other,
shake hands, our daughters are here,
we're far from home, dead soldiers,
like warriors, lie out, side by side,
and one, Bear Coat is straight, says
it's fair you get your horses back
and keep your rifles, and the other,
you can take his food, his blankets,
and ride on back to the reservation,
warriors argue, afraid of hangings,
and Thunder, in the lodge by himself,
talks to the air, my voice is faint
and won't carry, I don't know where
you are in the hills, but listening,
oh I pray you're alive, not freezing,
Sound of Running Feet, I'd come and
look for you, they wouldn't let me,
do rivers go backward, and can a man,
born to these plains, ever be happy
in a corral, it's in that dream song
Many Wounds sings, from his old man,
ah Hair Combed Over Eyes, and his,
Black Eagle, and his, Red Grizzly,
it goes, creation as it is, animals
and people, will be overcome, eagles
in cages, elk behind fences, buffalo
all massacred, freedom dead, red men

331

on little islands, forests melting,
game vanishing, rough places, where
the beauty is, flat, in a sick rain,
in the bad air, nothing blossoming
in that future, the waters bridled
and the land stripped, ah it's been
on my back so long, the bones of it,
we keep the country, the way it is,
they shift rivers, knock down hills,
and always on the move, they leave
houses and graveyards, with little
regret, and when they die they walk
into the stars, their heaven, and
forget the earth, oh but it's not
like that with us, our dead look back,
in love, and think of all the days
and the wild earth, and long for this
real home, and the living walk over
their ashes, and long for them, ah
my brother, shadow, warrior, ghost,
I, I said so much, and not goodbye,
every river, every bank that my foot
has touched is holy to me, and alive
with what happened, and nothing can
beat down my joy, in the vigil hill,
the dancing ground, the open where
she and I talked, the wedding lodge,
with the white lilac, the dry grass
where the old man tore up the bible,
his simple grave on the north shore,
the creek that skinny girl and I lay
down by, the prairie where the baby,
that green delta where you were born,
yes oh and Wallowa, the lake I loved,
and all the mornings, I'd pole out
in a driftwood canoe, fire-hollowed,
in a still music, on the pure water,

darling, I can't go away from that
high country, it's the earth I love,
winter is broken by the old sierra,
the summer's good, in the tall air,
ah where is it, I never bowed head
to the white man, because I was free,
and I talked free, and they ordered
the army, its courage in numbers, to
catch me by the long hair, down me
and dog-whip me, oh my daughter, do
any of the soldiers out there know
we lived here ten thousand winters,
all over, I'm Chief Joseph, but once,
in a sun that's only history now, I
was Thunder Rolling in the Mountains,
ah Captain John, tell General Howard
I know his heart.
                    In the vague sun
that afternoon, overcast, down red
on the horizon, the camp in shadows,
wind kicking up thin snow, he rides
on a borrowed horse, on a black mare,
at her own gait, in a Mexican saddle,
and his head down, his hair in otter
skin braids and loose in back, bullet
marks on his forehead, on his wrist,
in a slate grey wool shawl with five
bullet holes, and a striped blanket
around his hips, hands at the pommel,
long rifle across his knees, in his
buckskin leggings, plain moccasins,
Naked Head and Yellow Wolf, walking
on one side, White Cloud, Two Moons
and Last Time on Earth on the other,
low talk, he says nothing, hitches
forward, into the light, and colder,
to a little plateau, some soldiers

up there, and one the man who fired,
the courier's horse, nervous, pawing
the dirt, he slips down, holding out
the iron rifle, it was his brother's,
to General One Arm, who motions to
Colonel Bear Coat, he hands it over,
no words, and in the air above them,
a red-tailed hawk, on a long circle,
wings quivering, curves out of sight,
into the somber north.

Wyatt Earp

1

Arizona Territory

Out over the snow-shot Chiricahuas, sideslipping on the sullen air, the sun, scorning the high pines, and the black oaks, the sharp junipers, wallowing to get wind of any dead flesh under the buckthorn on the lower slopes, green rattler, fox squirrel, body, warping its wings, shadows, hissing, is drifting down the pillars of cloud:

on the outskirts of the Sonoran desert, all of it keeps back what water it can from the sun, in secret, in the thorns of the mesquite, spines of the saguaro, cholla thicket, paloverde, ocotillo sticks, stalks of the manzanita, yucca, creosote, the yellow grass:

the sun, a bullet hole in the last west, the blue, bleeding orange, bleeding coral, is flooding the heavens as red as blood, as the buzzard's skin, and the dark, breaking, gives sanctuary to any, the outlaw hour, invisible.

In the distance, a couple of hoodlum wagons and a string of horses are dusting across the reaches of the San Pedro, on toward Goose Flats.

Tombstone

Wyatt Earp rides in, night without stars, Tombstone, dismounts in Dodge City, trail's end, in the buffalo grass, dust blowing in his face, loops his black racehorse to the hitching rail, Everything goes in Wichita, cowboys leaning outside, and goes into the Grand Hotel, the kerosene light, the tack piano doing The Blue Tail Fly. He gets this medicine: shack for now around the corner from that new O. K. Corral; south of the Dead Line, the Santa Fe tracks, is all honkytonks and hells, to the river; across the toll bridge, dance halls, sideshows, and Dixie Lee's bordello; no call for a stage line, mail and express already going; try the Oriental and deal in pasteboard and ivory; Texas boys might hurrah the town, pilgrim, the mayor would like a peace officer; no city hall, courthouse, jail; but robbery in daylight, whores in gingham; silver miners, whip cracking in the street, to start the nude saloon girl race: dust is a citizen, and the stars don't matter. He slips outside, and his long horse is gone.

Mexican Quarter

theys only one Wyatt Earp story his book of Genesis told over in a power of ways now Virg in 61 you was off in the Union infantry out in Tennessee and us little brothers back in Iowa and Wyatt just 13 ah Morg he says I hate looking at that mules tail and this turning the grass upside down 80 acres all corn and hes hearing the bugle and one day runs away half days ride to Ottumwa and the recruiting office and wouldnt you know daddy is there and hauls him back he gets the switch ands fixing to give him a hiding and mama says Nick laying her hand on his shoulder he done nothing wrong and daddys arm jolts her out of the way and Wyatt so steady so brave steps in between and eye to eye You cant hit mama and daddy drops the switch

Allen Street

The fire always breaks out in the Arcade Saloon, some damn fool lighting a cigar by the whiskey barrel blowing out the door into Allen Street, and the stores catching, the clothing burning, and the dry goods, the Oriental burning, the Lion burning, the Magnolia Saloon, the dance house burning, the bankrolls burning, the sun at 100 degrees, the district court burning, the judge's office burning, and the undertaker's, the Eagle burning, the Alhambra burning, Fifth Street burning west, east, burning north, south, the Occidental burning, the Cosmopolitan, Wyatt Earp walking through the smoke with a Winchester in his arms and seeing a woman on a balcony, Hafford's Saloon burning, Brown's Hotel burning, and the gun store, bullets banging, letters burning, the newspaper burning, and the Tivoli Saloon, the Grand Hotel burning, the hoisting works whistle, the hook and ladder, Tombstone is burning. At dusk, the mayor comes back from the east with a fire engine and two hose carriages.

Prayer for What Vanished

That trail, not cold,
into the back country,
the sign, old music,
or the scent, tallgrass,
to Illinois, the garden,
before the flood
and the outlaws,
ah god, those fields,
at morning, green,
unknown: the hills,
the creeks, downpouring:
Urilla's kiss: that thrill:
out of the Mississippi: sparrows:
the prairies: that peace.

Sulphur Springs Valley

Oh I am a Texas cow-boy The rangers, in a battalion, drove them like longhorns, out of the Lone Star. Into this territory. So easy to make them out: none of them in a John B., white shirt, black coat, like a citizen; they're all *just off the stormy plains* slicked up, with a big sombrero the color of dust, red bandanna at the neck, wool shirt, doeskin trousers, half boots. *My trade is cinchin saddles* They fight off Apaches, go down Sonora way, *and pullin bridle reins* steal cattle and keep them at the Clanton ranches in San Pedro and the Animas, at the McLaurys in Sulphur Springs, sell beef cheap, pay dollars, drink. *Oh I can tip a lariat* They like to shoot peace officers *with the greatest of ease*, think it's in the name of the lost cause. Few arrested, less tried, none convicted. Curley Bill can whirl his pistol *I can rope a streak o lightnin* and cock it as it rises *ride any damn where I please.*

Soldiers Hole

rain threatening
you Frank McLaury
in the door of the twisting house and the corral empty
this is my layout off limits to you and your platoon
word is Curley Bill rustled six mules out of the camp and fencing them
is a federal crime this is US Deputy Marshal Virgil Earp
who are them civilians youre violating my rights
his specials Morgan and what you got there Wyatt
its the iron D8
it blots the US brand just right eh Frank
dont go looking for em lieutenant I cant answer for my brother and the
boys here theyll start shooting
well
Im known in the Territory never been called a thief youre here to protect
me you coward bring all this posse down on me maybe you stole and sold
em Ill let Arizona decide
easy Frank return them and well drop the charges
till manana in Charleston a word with you star men
under his breath
what business is it of yours if a few government hard tails go missing the
folks round here dont care if they get em cheap and dont love the army
anyway the sheriff dont care and as for gunshy the fools on him
how come
I aint bringing no mules back and one more thing you ever follow us up
this close well kill you
look for me Im Wyatt Earp and tomorrow Im wiring Tucson and accept-
ing as deputy its not you not I its the law break it and I will ride into your
dust
first drops

Cosmopolitan Hotel

Im only saying youre tending bar here
yeah
anyone can see youre Buckskin Frank
oh yeah
from your getup
yeah
youre gallivanting with this chambermaid
yeah May
whos married to that bartender
yeah but they split
I see trouble
well youre on the inside he told me if her and you go to the ball coming
with the quadrille band Ill shoot you
or one of his pals
yeah
I know youre a dead shot
yeah
anything can happen
thanks for the warning
yeah
hey I hear you got brothers going against you in Sulphur Springs
I got my own brothers to go against them
oh yeah
like that time in Missouri the hell with it
what happened Wyatt
hard to
never get over it till you do
on the outskirts of town I was constable and my bride Urilla her brothers
and one you knocked her up and killed her and I it aint so it was the yel-
low fever and no amount of quinine she burned and he if youre not too
yellow take off your gun Im giving you the beating of your life before I
run you out of here and I where you want to do this and he this lot I hand
my badge and Colt to my brother and he when I rough and tumble you
that pains for the pain you give us and I dont talk so much lets get this
over he springs at me and I sidestep and bang his jaw and hes off balance

and drops in the dust gets up comes on I slam him in the belly he doubles
I upper cut him on the chin and hes out and I anybody else want any and
my brothers looking at them
ever lose a fight Wyatt
never

Law Office

    (reading)

The Clerk: Mr Leslie, also known as Buckskin Frank, in the victim's own saloon, Lowry and Archer's, was telling the accused that a citizen handed Wyatt Earp a wire saying deliver the prisoner for the shooting at the Headquarters Saloon to him, and the deputy sheriff said the sheriff can spell his own name, this is a forgery, when the victim's wife invited the said Buckskin Frank next door to the Cosmopolitan Hotel, to whisper with him on the dark porch, and in his dying statement, the victim said he saw the two and was going when the accused said Look out Frank here is Mike, and both opened fire, the victim wrestled with them and was shot, and though Buckskin Frank was arrested by Wyatt Earp, the judge ruled out the dying statement and set him at liberty, when the accused was arrested by Wyatt Earp.

Mr Jones: Your honor, in light of the fact that you were Buckskin Frank's counsel in the foregoing case and justice of the peace at his wedding, I would ask that in this case against the friend he was covering for when he confessed to the shooting, that you recuse yourself.

The Court: Who are you to question my integrity? As I'm newly appointed? I order you to apologize, and to quit this courtroom.
    (pointing to door)

Mr Jones: I will not apologize; I have a constitutional right to be in this courtroom.

The Court: I cite you for contempt. Deputy, arrest the counsel for the defense.
    (the deputy sheriff does not obey)

The Court: You damn
    (the judge jumps up and collars the counsel for the defense)

Mr Jones: What the
    (the counsel for the defense flails and slaps the judge)

The Court: How dare
    (the deputy sheriff parts them, and they resume their chairs)

The Court: I fine you twenty-five dollars for contempt and sentence you to a day in the county jail for striking a justice of the peace. Deputy, escort him to jail.

Mr Earp: You can walk around; I'll meet you at the stage depot.

The Court: What? I order you to arrest the counsel and you stand there like a flagpole. I order you to escort him to jail and you let him walk. You will appear in these chambers tomorrow as I cite you for contempt.

Mr Earp: Your honor, as soon as you adjourn this court, you're under arrest, for assault.

Capital Saloon

its the way of gunfighting first heard it from my daddy in a wagon train going west through the cornhuskers out here your life at any moment might hang on if youre ready to fight for it these western camps are free and easy and you might stretch a point and let a man off but when youre up against pure vicious thats our old enemy and when that outlaw forces it you go as far as you have to hit first and hit to kill and in that legendary summer Kansas City in Market Square on the bench in front of the police station talking buffalo hunting with those old scouts Cheyenne Jack Old Man Keeler Wild Bill Hickok that hard winter bunch making history it turns to gunplay and Jack Gallagher Boot Hill is full of them who pulled the trigger before aiming and got a halo for nothing they can quickdraw and fill both hands or one fanning or shoot from the hip no chance against you if you slack off and pull the trigger once and next season on the plains out on the Salt Fork its Bat Masterson no tricks no show no bluff no hurry and let your muscles think faster than thinking first shot last shot and tells me how its courage that stands you up to them and nerve keeps you cool only way to quickdraw is to take your time Ive never had to use this wisdom but I got to be a crack shot the gun just above my waist Id fire five shots from one hand the border shift to the other five shots at a hundred yards into the capital O of Office by the time I and I met Mattie on the way time I met you Doc in that Texas water hole three years gone

Ballad of Mattie

Off of the farm,
on to the lights,
that sixteen runaway's
in his sights.

He's on the trail of this outlaw
out of Dodge, east to Fort Scott:
in a parlor house, girl of the night,
and he was caught.

With her shadow hair
and her shy way,
she let him in:
he lost a day.

He's on the trail of this outlaw
but she was dear when she was bought:
the stars laid out the common law,
and he was caught.

Fort Griffin

on the flats by the Clear Fork this bare saloon
pardon me
the backbar black cherry with scrolls of gilt the mirror the nude and the
dog asking
on the trail long
I been reading sign through the Nations on down the Brazos
whatll it be sir
what it was only I wish youd won that day in Cheyenne in 68
for the love of christ is it yourself behind that moustache Wyatt Earp
hey Shannsey imagine you
he knocked me out of prizefighting altogether so he did
well thats no
its nothing I do be thinking of look at you jesus youre a man
Id take a schooner of
ah youre the saint that wont touch whoopee water only one in all the
railroad camps you want mineral
thats right
there you go now
what do I
on the house hold on heres to stealing lying fighting cheating and drink-
ing may you steal kisses lie in her arms fight for your brother cheat death
drink in the wonder
remember that
what is it sign you say what brings you down into the panhandle
Im after Dirty Dave
for the bounty
for this holdup on a Santa Fe train him and Roarke hightailed it know
where he mightve gone
from here across the Staked Plains or towards the Rio Grande sure I dont
know
its a long shot
but that man there would
nodding at him whispers
Doc Holliday
in a pearl suit ash hair blue-eyed and haggard at solitaire

know him
hes the killer isnt he I dont figure him friendly to a peace officer
I hear hes killed but nobody round here
nodding to the old bareknuckle fighter and stepping to the window
morning Mister Holliday the bar-tender tipped me to you Im Wyatt
Earp
eye to eye
call me
hacking
call me
curling over his chest his hand out to shake no palm up wait till the
coughing
call me Doc everyone does absolute misnomer
strong steady grip
for some reason they dont want me leaning over them while they open
wide
Wyatt smiling
only gentlemen in this sanctuary are scouts soldiers muleskinners bull-
whackers sage rats cold deck cardplayers trail hands cattle rustlers horse
thieves land sharps which are you
bounty hunter
well if you will allow me to finish this round of ace in the hole Ill surren-
der without a
Wyatt laughing
struggle
Im looking for Dirty Dave
for the bounty
pouring a tall whiskey knocking it back
he hit a pay train Im only trying to get those boys their dollars
out here as the bard says in a wildernesse where are no lawes
what wayd he go
give me a day and Ill get his trail for you out for justice eh well Ill take
the bounty for my trouble
his slender fingers turning the cards
aint seen the like of that smoke pole in your cross draw holster
shining nickel barrel ivory grips
Colt Lightning

they say he showed you to draw and shoot and you showed him to draw
to a pair of aces
its a legend Id have nothing to do with that sidewinder
hes tough that Arkansas rancher the grass is waving over him and he
done it
nothing to me been carving credits on my gun barrel since I shot that
saloon keeper in Dallas had to move on that soldier hand of freeze out
in Jacksboro move on stabbed a tinhorn in Denver move on wounded a
sport in Trinidad how many have I downed
ever arrested
why no I happen to I
happen to what
youre a true heart Wyatt never thought Id and I cant throw dust at you
its all words words I make up dime novels as I go old Deadwood shooting
my way on and the bad hombres they keep their distance
never arrested
once for quote playing at a game of cards in a house in which spirituous
liquors are sold
thanks for levelling Doc
till tomorrow sir

Capital Saloon

it was the Missus here whos my salvation down in Texas after I told you
Fort Davis
I trailed him there and on to Fort Clark Fort Concho Fort McKavett
back to Fort Griffin and I got word from Dodge he doubled back into
Kansas hit another train for ten thousand was caught heading south by
Bat Masterson and a posse and I got wind of you
about the
they said you killed a man
how generous of them Im playing blind with this tinhorn whos monkey-
ing with the deadwood and I warn him play poker say it again at last I
pull down the sugar without showing my hand
perfect right
he pulls his six gun and I operate on his ribs with a penknife
dont your conscience get you
I coughed it up long ago
youre under arrest
in the hotel lobby thinking his associates are going to lynch me sure
though hes only bleeding
swallowing her whiskey and catching her breath
I hear those miners hollering and look in a back window till I see Doc
Im meditating on the brevity of our days when I hear Fire
I get this other six shooter and mine and tether this horse in the alley
burn a shed bang on the hotel Fire they all run out and I slip in cover the
deputy with one gun and toss the other laughing Come on Doc
and youre a dance hall girl
we hide in the willows get Docs plunder and horses and drag it for Dodge
ah Dodge my dear the gateway to the what is that story the conductor to
a rough on the train
ticket
aint got no ticket
where you going
going to hell
thatll be one dollar you get off at Dodge
you asked and angled for everything about that cowtown
did I

are there saloons where I can work start at the Long Branch you still assistant city marshal so I can cover you in a scrape with the law you really a deacon yes at the First Union Church is there a hotel where I can luxury the Dodge House

dont matter where he holes up his hearts down in Georgia all them billets doux

one too many whiskeys dont ruin it honey

whats her name Doc she your cousin

why I call you Big Nose Kate

hes in your whirl Wyatt let him go

I go where I please queen of the alley

Im going to Globe the hell with you

I wont forget you shell be back

Sixth and Allen

After midnight, when the aces burn off, and the pharaoh rules in the down and out dynasties, this player was coppering his card to lose in the Bank Exchange Saloon, when shots, outside, ah it must be cow-boys shooting the moon out of the sky. Wyatt Earp, dealing, off duty, unarmed, steps into the street, the McLaury brothers, guns out, flash, running toward the fire, Morgan, behind a chimney, and who is it, Dodge, give me your gun, sudden bullets off of the bricks, comes out of cover, across from the whores' cribs and cabins, I am an officer, Marshal White's voice, give me your pistol, gets in behind, it's Curley Bill, who draws it, White's hand on the barrel, Wyatt's arms around his chest, and White, now you son of a bitch give up that pistol, jerks it, it fires, I am shot, Wyatt buffaloes the shooter, squatting over White, they're sniping at him, to his brother, put out the fire his coat is burning, to Curley Bill, get up, and hauls him by the shirt, what have I done I done nothing it went off at half cock you cant arrest me:

what have you done you yellow god damn dog you gut shot the law and I know it hell die theyll close up gambling for a day the preacher will drawl on the great unknown and a thousand will follow his wound up to Boot Hill the vigilantes will come to string you up Ill stand them off and at your murder trial cause I didnt see you trigger him my testimony will let you go free but you best look over your shoulder among the willows Im coming Im an angel flying through the badlands and Ill keep on till you atone for this that silence is heaven all music my trumpet the thunder my voice and the requital your last breath

2

Tombstone, November 9, 1880

Charles Shibell, Pima County Sheriff
San Xavier Hotel
Tucson

Dear Sir,

I have the honor herewith to resign the office of deputy sheriff of Pima
County.

The election of one week past was rigged, and you won by fraud, com-
mitted by the cow-boys. The voting inspector was Ike Clanton, who has
been stealing cattle from Texas John. The precinct judge was Johnny
Ringo, who is a killer from the Hoodoo war on the innocent. The San
Simon polling place was Joe Hill's cabin, who is a rustler. From there,
Curley Bill, who shot our marshal, rode into Tombstone that morning
with the crooked votes that tipped it to you. He may hang for murder,
and is relying on my testimony; he has agreed to confess this fraud.

I know you'll choose Johnny Behan to replace me; he is a glad hand man,
not a peace officer, and is looking forward to joining your tax-skimming
10 Percent Ring. I will get a recount and overturn this election, clear to
the Supreme Court. But I cannot go on as your deputy.

Respectfully,
Wyatt S. Earp

Wells, Fargo & Co.

Wyatt Earp, waiting to ride shotgun messenger on the next stage to the Southern Pacific, looks out and here's Virg, raging in on a buckboard, thought he was riding south to the Last Chance claim, who's that in manacles, Johnny Behind-the-Deuce, that quiet faro crack always playing the two spot open to buck the bank, shivering it was self defense, they're flying from a lynch mob. He sends Virg for help, and lays a scatter gun in the crook of his arm, crossing to the skinny door of Vogan's Bowling Alley and Saloon, where he surrounds Johnny with his brothers, Doc, and four men, and leads them over to the livery stable.

stand back open passage Im taking this man to the Tucson jail

the law is failing and you know he wont stand trial were hanging him

stand back: it minds him of that time in Dodge City, where he invented buffaloing, don't shoot to kill like Wild Bill, and wound the boulevards, but grab their gun hand and crack their skull with the barrel of the Peacemaker, when the cowhands, flinging shots into the Comique Theater, at the marshal, and he and Jim Masterson fire back into the night, toward the toll bridge, and this kid falls, and this night, in front of the Long Branch, they get the drop on him, start shooting, and Doc in there at faro with Cockeyed Frank slams out with a pistol and a six gun and wings the leader in the shoulder so Wyatt can draw and buffalo him:

throw em up all the way and empty

throw em up: it minds him of that time in Wichita, when all the bosses, all the hands, out of Rowdy Joe's and Red Beard's, out of the saloons and whorehouses across the river come riding in a mob to the bridge to pay Wichita back for when he and four men going to repossess that bad debt piano from the madam, he says to them you're too cheap to help her out, if you take my advice you'll never go into anything you can't buy out of, and he leads his officers and citizens to the bridge, spread out and hard to shoot, all six shooters drawn, all hell about to break.

He keeps on looking at the gun man:

put away your guns mind me now Mannen put up that gun and go on home

Clements puts his pistol into his holster and turns his horse. And they all go back to the dives and deadfalls.

He keeps on looking at the cattle king:

you Tobe youre next
Driskill puts his pistol into his holster and turns his back. And he motions them all toward the calaboose.
He keeps on looking at the mine operator:
nice mob didnt know you trailed with such company Dick dont be a fool back off any of you attack this posse Dick here gets it
Gird puts his pistol into his holster and turns on his heel. And he leads Johnny Behind-the-Deuce into the stable. They could a got me easy, but no one fired a shot.

Charleston

where you been Doc
water rights claims in the Huachacas
Scar Face was right thats my long horse
whose corral is it
its the road agent that Johnny Behan made deputy here Frank Stilwell
lovely it makes robbing stages so much less trouble if youre wearing a star
its the Clantons
theyre going to take it out Wyatt
all right Im going to keep it peaceful with that fire breathing man hey Ike
what do you want
well theres a subpoena for you on this election fraud and Sheriff Behans
coming with a posse to arrest you and haul you to Tucson
yeah if he finds us Im arming everyone I wont stand it
he slips around the corner
a posse
I was bluffing
Billy you cant take that horse out its mine and Ive got papers from Tomb-
stone that
take it got any more horses to lose
Ill stable them so you wont have a chance to steal them
he drops a rope as reins over the horse

Oriental Building

were nearer to the stars of heaven up here
I like the roof because it catches air
hey Wyatt you seen that dancer I was shotgun on the stage that brung
her in with the opera from the Golden Gate
no I aint is
all curves and Bat says shes the belle of the honky tonks
that right
living with Johnny of all people
all politics why Governor Fremont made him sheriff of the new county
and this days after the cow-boys shot up the Alhambra Saloon
that Curley Bill
yes and the fourflusher broke his promise to make me undersheriff
he say why
he didnt like that bluff I pulled on Ike
out at Charleston
yes and I hit his faro table one night and broke his god damn bank Ill take
mine in cash your credit dont cover a white chip
her name is Josephine something
I bet hes cheating on her now
I tell you because you and Mattie
I know Morg Im drifting away I dont know how
hey Wyatt I been reading in the gospel
that right
that part where it says To day shalt thou be with me in paradise
I remember
where do you think we go after
where are the snows I saw falling on Illinois
just gone
aint no other place
I wonder
no inferno no glory
but how is there justice
in our hands here
maybe the body fails and the soul flies
ah this world is gunsmoke curling into the void

if youre right well never know
only one thing lasts
whats that
history

Oriental Saloon

In through the wings, Wyatt Earp, in the long saloon, as she slides by, first sight, her fingers this hour, her bosom love, her eyes adventure, asks the iceman, after, she don't go by Josephine, left just before, come back right after, and he's on her trail, his law, desire. He looks up and down, his heart beginning, and Bat Masterson shows him where at the bar she lifted up a gin fizz. He guesses she'll stay away from the faro table, and circles to cross by the silver mirror, cut over to the nude, on down the line. Daylight, and he's on his way, by the dark bottles; two days across the sawdust, toward the cash register, when a hard rain wipes out all signs of her. That night, by the upright piano, he hears from a dancing girl, that dancer, here not long ago, and in a rush. He picks up a trace east, and loses it next day, overtaken by rain. He makes for a table lolling at the back, and knows her by her legs, the way she moves. I'm Wyatt Earp. It's a pleasure to happen on you. May I call you Sadie?

Wanted

The beauty
of the hurdy-gurdies
Josephine
Sarah
Marcus
alias Sadie
also known as
May Bell
dancing in the Pinafore
as the captain's daughter
Josephine

For sliding by me
in the saloon

With her opera eyes
with her Cochise County tears
with her lover
that liar
in bed with married
with her manifest breasts
with her slim destiny
with her curves
in this flatland
with her fingers now
I'd love to lace
with her voice like water
in the future
with her by-and-by
like a memory kiss

Reward:
all the heart I have

San Pedro Road

man in the brush by the river
you got him Morg
yeah
Wyatt lighting
you Luther King
yes I
you jumped out of that corral what you running for
thought you was outlaws
were trailing outlaws
I was going to milk the cow
with two revolvers in your belt
well I
and two winded horses tethered
was going to
know anything about the Benson stage holdup
nothing
you leave that cow pony at Wheatons old barn
no I
I seen you riding it last week in Tombstone
I aint been there in a fortnight
all right Johnny its the Redfields Im going to look around dont let him
talk to them
he walks to the shack looks over his shoulder
thought I said dont let them talk god damn it now Redfields going to tip
off the rest
I dont take orders from you
Luther come down here
around the barn out of sight of the sheriff
youre up Salt Creek aint you you dont know nothing well I been after
you cow-boys and I know youre in that deserted adobe on Contention
Road reading Deadwood Dicks Last Act cause you tore out the end is
that it in your pocket the stage goes by with a shotgun and that means
bullion as they slow on a grade three men bandannas over their faces
come out of the chaparral with rifles saying hold up and when my old
friend Bud cracks the whip hes shot through the heart and his woman

and kids in Calistoga are cut loose youre firing on the stage and the man
outside looks at the moon last time now the sheriff says the trails twelve
hours old and hopeless and I say I can pick up the sign I follow you to
the Dragoon hills to Tres Alamos you doubling your tracks and riding in
the riverbed and on living rock and clouding your trail to Wheatons lost
ranch I find you here you long riders are all in the Clantons outfit Leon-
ard Head Crane and you well the man who watched the horses is lucky
he wont swing for the double murder
thats me I held the horses it was them shooting
Johnny are you hearing this and youre at Redfields ranch
for ammo and money to bring to our camp
and where is that
I wont run him in on suspicion and you have no authority Wyatt
the stage was carrying mail Ill arrest him on a federal warrant
they ride on into the desolation

Prayer to the Silence

The shooting star
at the toll bridge
that night in Dodge:
let it not be my bullet
in his back: and I,
Why shoot at me,
is there a thousand
dollar bounty
by the cattle men,
because I locked up
their boss? and he,
stars in his eyes:
That last roundup,
a thousand head.

Oriental Back Yard

you loudmouthed to him
Ike in motion Wyatt standing
I told him nothing
well he knows everything
what did he say
am I dealing with you
to surrender Leonard
yeah if the cow-boys
and the mans ranch
down on the border
he know you jumped it
you said no strings
all I wants glory and the election
for the dollars as sheriff
to end the cow-boys
you talk Im dead
why would I betray you
you pulled that bluff
out at Charleston
subpoena on me
trying to keep it peaceful
why is Williams
look you want the reward
cause he wont be taken
dead or alive I had him
without a fight
telegraph Wells Fargo
well whys he pumping me
hes shooting at the moon
what for
is he drinking
Ike motionless Wyatt walking away

Sixth Street

I thank you sir for my liberty what was the bail 5 grand cash only ah
well at least its not that fell arrest with out all bayle as the bard says but
what kind of institution is this to which I was remanded jailhouse is too
fine a word for it nothing more than an abandoned cathouse my lord
the squalor to which I Doc Holliday southern gentleman and upright
gambler was reduced I don't mean to trouble you Wyatt say the word
and Ill leave Tombstone but not before telling you how I was arrested for
the Benson stage murders King whom you caught well Johnny saw to it
he wasnt confined in this calaboose but in a flophouse on the outskirts
and miracles do exist in the night he managed to take the deputys guns
and ammunition go out the back way to a waiting horse and ride for old
Mexico now that the guilty were free it was time to frame the innocent
there had been if you read it articles in that cow-boy rag attempting to
diminish the splendor of my reputation by accusing me of this holdup I
imagine because Im the only one of your allies with a shadow though it
was my invention and its you they want to end the rumors were waning
when I had lets call it a contretemps with Big Nose Kate in which I may
have referred to her in less than loving terms that is as a hag a red light
sister a pig a slut an idiot a hussy a tart a harlot a strumpet and an outright
whore she did not take this with the best grace but looked for solace in
a bottle of whiskey and after swore out an affidavit for Johnny implicat-
ing yours truly in the crime now that afternoon I was in fact at Leon-
ards shack at The Wells old business friend from New Mexico have you
heard him read Wild Bills story out loud I returned with the water and
Old Man Fuller on the Charleston road and everybody at the faro table
that evening can alibi me including you besides if it was me Id a downed
the horse and come away with the gold unlike these desperadoes shoot-
ing two men for nothing whats that send her away Ill satisfy you I have a
roll in the Oriental safe Ill peel off a thousand and shell depart for Globe
singing Love oh Love oh careless Love

Mule Mountains

In the firs and manzanita, on the bad road, in the shivering rain, the night before, the driver said, the Bisbee stage, carrying the Copper Queen payroll, was stopped, men in bandannas, one with a shotgun, one with a Colt, men in the chaparral, and saying hold on, taking the gold-mount ivory-handle six guns from the Wells, Fargo man, and saying, give up the sugar, everyone knows that's deputy Frank Stilwell's word for money when he's in a game, and he saw through the mask to Pete Spence, his summer name, who is Lark Ferguson, the Texas killer, and the locals said them and Curley Bill and Pony Deal, come back from the Skeleton Canyon massacre, had been all afternoon in the Blind Trail saloon. In the mud this morning, Wyatt Earp is looking at the nailheads in the bootprint, and, with his brother Morg, slopes down into Bisbee, where he sights new bootheels on the deputy going into the saloon, and turns up the old, with the nailheads, at the bootmaker's, invoice to Stilwell, who says you can arrest me, round up Spence, but our confederates will lie us elsewhere in the face of the judge, and it won't stick.

Allen Street

late afternoon
almighty god Wyatt they was in black robes black masks and kissed the
six shooter to join the secret Citizens Safety mob
in masks theyre outlaws Virg
its twice as hard
secret hell theyre in the papers
to keep the peace theyre sick of our bad sheriff and no convictions
who isnt hey look by the Alhambra is that Morg inside that circle
they see Ike Clanton Billy Clanton Frank McLaury Tom McLaury Joe
Hill Milt Hicks Johnny Ringo
Im town marshal and you know my deputy Frank you can tell us what
youre saying
all right I tell you what you might arrest Stilwell and Spence but dont
think you can arrest me you ever lay hands on me or my brother Ill down
you all and Doc Holliday
if we have to come after you well get you
Morg walking away
why are you so riled aint just that holdup
I know youre getting up a vigilante committee to hang us
hang who
all us cow-boys
ah Frank you recollect when Curley Bill shot Marshal White who stood
off the vigilantes
you did
who saved Johnny Behind-the-Deuce from being lynched
you did
you still believe were in this committee
I believe the man that told me
whos that
its the sheriff
you know Virg he hates me for stealing her love
I tell you it makes no difference what I do Ill never surrender my arms to
you Id rather die fighting than get strangled
youre loco
one last thing Ringo

yeah Wyatt
we know all about your secret get together last spring and the cow-boys
taking an oath over your blood to kill the Earp brothers we caught the
stink from here
first stars

Alhambra Saloon

Jack o diamonds jack o diamonds
is a hard card to play
I cant live one hour in this country if they discover it
I dont see how he could spread it around Ike as hes in Tucson ten days
you talk everything with him
here he is on the six o clock stage Doc I ever tell you Ike and I were in
any deal
I was in the money Wyatt you dragged me out of the Fair for this no you
never said a thing
Ike says I did
Ikes a goddamn liar
Im a dead man
what deal is that Ike
I give up your pal Leonard
for the reward
dead or alive
cow-boy selling out a cow-boy ever hear of loyalty you double crosser
you traitor you rounder you squealer you turntail you lowlife you villain
you fraud you degenerate youre the original sidewinder
Im going to kill you
get your gun out and go to work
I got no gun
go heel yourself
tell you what
Ike walking to the Grand Hotel
Doc to the Oriental
next man puts me and Wyatt Earp in the same sentence Ill shoot him
down
whats he up in arms about
evening Virg that madman just spilled to Doc the deal he didnt want me
to let on to him
well its hell outside on Allen Street with Curley Bill Stilwell Spence
Johnny Ringo and all parading and saying theyre running the Earp
brothers out of Tombstone in the next two days
in a showdown

looks like it Wyatt the vigilantes say theyll back us against them
I say no to that move itd bring on a free for all in the street
they deputized you Wyatt and you Morg and Doc and say its our call
well wait the Clantons and McLaurys are back of this show Ike just left
for Sulphur Springs and we aint seen the rest in three four days theyll get
nervous when nothing happens and come in the longer we keep them
waiting the tougher it is for them
Virgil walking to the Occidental
Wyatt to the Eagle Brewery
I played the jack against the ace
and heaven looked me in the face

Fifth Street

Wyatt Earp
what is it now Ike
will you walk with me
what for
what for to talk with me
I cant go too far
whys that
I got to close the game
back there
back at the Brewery
you tell Doc Holliday no man
no man what
can talk to me that way and live
dont tangle with him
when Doc mocked me
just now
I wasnt fixed right
how so
no gun but in the morning
look Ike
Ill have him man to man
he dont want to fight
its been talk so long
long time
time to fetch it to a close
I wont fight no one
you wont
not if I can get away
how come
no money in it
in the morning
look Ike
Ill be ready for all of you
go sleep it off Ike
tomorrow

you talk too much for a fighting man
Ike going into the Brewery
the stars
Doc wavering on the street
out tonight
Ill walk you back
is the moon
you keep away from Clanton
all right
dont want a gunfight
keep away
with you in it
they go up Third Street to Fly's Boarding House by the O. K. Corral

3

Occidental Saloon

last hand its cockcrow
who chooses
the bucks to you Virg
five card draw high
anything wild
deuces Morg
you done shuffling
there
whorehouse cut Tom
all right deal
ante up Johnny
Im breathing
no bet
the actions on you Ike
five ivories
I see your five
Im in
I raise you five
pure bluff I cover it
to ten
all in I fold
dead money
Im in
Ill stand
with a made hand
three cards
hit me for two
and Ill draw one
I pass
I call your ten
I check
the showdown
three queens
tens up
the hell with you
ace full boys
another pot
its the break

Allen Street

hold on Virg
whats that
I know you stand in with them
with who
who tried to murder me last night
who tried to
if so Im in town
I dont know what youre
and I got a message for Doc
whats that Ike
the damn bastard has got to fight
I see you armed Ill arrest you
no man can talk
dont want to hear you
to me that way
talking like that
tell him
now Im going down home
Im in the street
going to bed
sleep nothing off
I dont want you breaking the peace
you wont carry the message
hell no
Ike swinging away hand under his coat on his six gun

After Prayer

I got a hold
of this trout, but
it wags away,
I see the water
is railroad tracks,
open boxcar,
in my hands, silver
scales, and this
man behind me's
firing a gun.
Who are you, sir?
I'm Independence
Day, deputy;
damn it, get up!

Mexican Quarter

get up Wyatt hurry and get your clothes on I was done with my shift at the Oriental and I seen Ikes pistol in his belt I covered it with his coat and told him go to bed and he said no ah no when the Earps and Doc Holliday show on the street the ball will open this was by the telegraph office wire who Curley Bill or Johnny Ringo I dont know I know he said theyll have to fight youre what going back to bed all right theres likely to be hell

Fly's Boarding House

wake up Doc
what
are you still drunk
what time
Mary says Ikes downstairs
yeah what does Jesus say
waving a rifle
what time is it Kate
noon
so what
hes looking for you
if God will let me live long enough to get my clothes on he shall see me
buckling on his Colt Lightning

Fifth Street

Wyatt Earp, in a flat black sombrero, white shirt, in a long coat against the October wind, with his American Colt revolver on his hip, walks across patches of snow, into the Oriental Saloon. The attorney who wouldn't quit the courtroom is asking Virg. What does all this mean. What do you mean. Ike's out there armed with a Winchester and a Colt. Hunting you boys. Wyatt steps in. What happened to thou shalt not kill. Well, deacon, it's Tombstone. I'll go down, find him, see what he wants. Wyatt takes Allen Street, Virg and Morg take Fremont, and he walks by the brewery, the unfinished church, by the general store. Virg comes up behind Ike, grips the rifle by the barrel, Ike pulls his revolver out of his belt and as he turns to shoot Virg buffaloes him to the wooden sidewalk. You looking for us? I'd seen you a second before I'd a killed you. You're under arrest. Firearms inside the city limits.

Recorder's Court

Ike bandannas his wound
Virg go for the judge
yeah Wyatt
okay you goddamn dirty cowthief you said youd assassinate me six times
that I know Id be in my rights shooting you down anywhere I saw you
if you were a second later theyd be a coroners inquest seven
if you want to fight Ill go anywhere on earth Ill go over to the San Simon
in your own crowd
fight is my racket all I wants four feet of ground and my six shooter
Morg holding his guns
Ill pay your fine if youll fight
Ill fight you anywhere anyway if I had a six shooter Id make a fight with
you all
here if you want to make a fight so bad Ill give you mine
offering his Peacemaker Colt revolver
I dont like the odds
sit down
I fine you twenty-five dollars and two fifty court costs
where should I leave your guns
anywhere I can get them
outside the courthouse Wyatt comes up against Tom with his dead eyes
what are you doing here
nothing out for a stroll on Fremont Street
youre lying you're here on account of Ike
Im looking after him
you think you can menace us and abolish justice
I dont know what
are you heeled
you want a fight Ill fight you anywhere
all right right here jerk your gun and use it
he swings his hand Wyatt slaps him buffaloes him blood branching
down his face

Fourth and Allen

Wyatt Earp walks out of Hafford's Saloon, lighting a cigar. Frank Mc-Laury and Billy Clanton, after drinks, swing out of the Grand Hotel, onto their horses, in their show-off rags, flat hats, wild shirts, high boots. Doc Holliday, by the Cosmopolitan, salutes them: How are you this fine day. They glare at him, turn up Fourth, dismount, go in Spangenberg's Pioneer Gun & Locksmith Shop, where Tom McLaury's sticking cartridges in his belt. Frank's bangtail steps up on the sidewalk, against the law; Wyatt strolls over and yanks it back into the street. The cow-boys shock, Billy lays his hand down on his pistol, Frank kicks out, snatches the reins, leads the horse away, as Ike walks up. Inside, the clerk looks at the wound on Ike's skull, and shakes his head. The cow-boys, in bright bandannas, loading their guns, stare out at Wyatt. Virg comes out of Wells, Fargo with a Stevens ten gauge shotgun.

Fourth and Allen

you the marshal
yeah who are you
I just blew in
what can I do
I seen
for you
I seen four five men wearing guns down by the O. K. Corral all salty and
saying the troubles with you and theyre going to kill you kill all the Earps
kill them on sight
thanks for the warning
what kind of town
afternoon Johnny
is this
whats the ruckus
all these sons of bitches in town and hell bent against us
who are they Virg
how about a quick drink
against the Earps
lets go down and disarm them
if you go down therell be a fight
their guns are legal inside the O. K. Corral but if they step into the street
Ill have them surrender up their arms and arrest them
they wont hurt me Ill go down alone see if I cant disarm them
thats all I want to do
you all wait here
hello captain what do the vigilantes want
the cow-boys are making threats against you we can have men and arms
ready ten in one minute you can count on us
no thanks I wont bother them long as theyre only getting horses to leave
town
why I just come from there and theyre all down on Fremont Street now
why the cane Doc
where you going Wyatt
down the street for a fight
Ill go along

this is our fight no call for you to mix in
thats a hell of a thing to say to me
hold on you boys
whats that Virg
come with us Doc
amen brother
Wyatt those cow-boys are in the lot by the O. K. Corral back of Flys
Boarding House which is Docs room to get a crack at him
all right but they aint giving up their arms this is a shootout and to the
death

Fourth Street

By what light's coming through the overcast, in the frozen dirt, in hopes of peace, long shot, Wyatt Earp, and his blood, Virgil, Morgan, and his savior, Doc Holliday, walk up the street, by the American curse, by the inferno, and the silent iceman, by pages blowing into yesterday, go west on Fremont, by a whirl of yours truly and past due, ah the bad news, up at the lot, sidestep, out of the line of sight, to the wooden sidewalk.

Virg holds out the ten gauge, Doc hands him his cane, hides the shotgun under his long coat, as they go by all charges, all pleas, by the veins of silver, by the last words on the forsaken cross, Doc whistling quietly Old times there are not forgotten, by the meat market, by the assay office, by the boardinghouse, to the vacant lumberyard, back entrance to the O. K. Corral.

Johnny comes up, looking back, They won't give up their guns unless you do, What will you, I'm county sheriff, I won't allow this, they brush past him, For god's sake don't go in there or you'll be murdered, and Virg, I'm going to disarm them, switching the cane to his gun hand, his Army Colt revolver to his left hip, and Johnny, I have disarmed them, Wyatt shifting his long barrel six shooter into his overcoat pocket, Doc, the cold wind blowing his coat open over and over, showing the shotgun, Look out there on the flank, for an ambush, and somebody hollers, Here they come.

Lumberyard

in the empty yard black horse bay horse and back of them Tom McLaury
hand on the rifle hanging from the saddle Frank McLaury in front Ike
Clanton Billy Clanton hands down six yards away from Wyatt at the
corner Doc in the street Morg at the sidewalk Virg into the yard
boys throw up your hands I want your guns
Frank thumbs back the hammer on his Colt Ike slips hand into his shirt
Billy cocks Virg lifts his arms waving the cane
hold on I dont want that
the cow-boys backing up Wyatt going ahead and so shoot straighter Billy
any more horses to lose draws across his body and fires Wyatt draws like
lightning Billys no shot but Frank *ever follow us up this close well kill
you* is dangerous he fires into his belly he staggers in the smoke fires back
the horses screaming trying to bolt Tom *Ill fight you anywhere* fires over
the top of them Virg switches the cane from hand to hand draws and fires
at Tom at Billy Ike *Ill be ready for all of you* charges Wyatt slaps his arm
his gun goes off Ike yelling
I am unarmed
Wyatt shoves him back
the fight has commenced get to shooting or get away
Ike runs toward the back of the boardinghouse Frank gutshot and moan-
ing at the sidewalk fires back at Wyatt and his coat flaps Billy fires and
Virg goes down clutching at his calf Morg fires hits Billy in the chest in
the wrist in the belly he leans against the house slides down switches
hands balances his pistol on his knee fires Morg falls
I am hit
holding his shoulder gets up trips on the water line trench Wyatt goes
to shield him
stay down
Wyatt calm cracking off rounds fires at Tom whos shooting hits the horse
in the withers and the horse runs Doc stalking Tom fires the shotgun into
his armpit Tom staggers into the street Doc drops it draws fires twice at
Billy Wyatt fires across the street at Frank bang from the alley but who
or ricochet fires back Wyatt and Virg aim at Billy sitting down blood
from his lips and fingers fire Frank has a horse by the reins fires at Morg
and the horse breaks away he aims at Doc

I have you now you son of a bitch
youre a daisy if you do blaze away
Frank fires Doc looks at his hip
Im shot right through
Morg fires Doc fires at Frank hit in the head in the chest dying Doc runs
at him
the son of a bitch has shot me and I mean to kill him
Tom dying at the telegraph pole on Third Wes picks up his gun Billy
done for shoots wild into the air trying to reload Fly takes his pistol the
hoisting works whistle blows Doc turns
what in helld you let Ike get away like that for Wyatt
he wouldnt jerk his gun

Fremont Street

What do I say, says the ghost bride, behind my veil, white smoke, to you, west cow-boy, at your last breath? Why did you come from the Lone Star plains, why did all your trails slope down, why did you drift into these badlands? To dance to the fiddle of crime, against the gospel, against possession, against blood? To live outside the law of skin, and shoot them down who consecrate it? To be condemned to this prison of light? Why didn't you claim me with a territorial kiss? Why was there no shivaree, of bells and banging? Why didn't you pioneer into me? For you, there is no woman, only the October wind, and disgrace, staining the dust of the street, no house, only the pine box under the hill, no sunrise girl, no boy under the setting moon, only the lies on your headstone, no days to come, only these last questions. And your mortal soul? It went nowhere, it bubbled out of your lips and rose, not to heaven, not to the stars, not to the steeple, only as high as your sombrero when you were standing, where it fizzled and was gone. I have nothing. Like you, I am nothing.

4

Fremont Street

out of the sheriffs office
Wyatt I'm arresting you
for what
for murder
any officer that was on the square Id let him not you
and the theater manager
dont be in a hurry to arrest this man he done right in killing them the
people will uphold him
we done right we had to do it and you threw us Johnny
what do you mean
you told us they was disarmed you lied to throw us get us murdered
youre under arrest
not today not tomorrow Ill be in town

Prayer for the Dead

Brass band
in the lead of the procession:
dead march:
hearse:
body in casket with silver:
name age birthplace date of death:
hearse:
bodies in caskets:
in a wagon, brothers:
hundreds, walking,
mourning: or rid of them:
carriages buckboards stagecoach men on horses:
witnesses in the dust
on the long trail up to Boot Hill.

Sixth Street

Doc with his hand on his wound
back in this hole goddamn it I cant keep out of it
this time with bail revoked
if this is to be my roost I swear if Tombstone cant afford it Ill take up a
collection for an actual jail
Wyatt looking out on the street as the light fails
least we got vigilantes watching out for assassination
ah my hip how is it everyone in that shoot up was shot but you
I dont know how I go where the bullets aint
and this you what picked up in your old gunfights
I aint been in a gunfight before
well bless my soul
I aint never shot a man before
those outlaws had it coming it was a luminous stand
it dont make it easy Doc
ah deacon your wounds inside
think the grand jury will take up the charge
well theyve assembled all of the best surviving liars as witnesses Billy
Allen Johnny Behan Kid Claiborne Wes Fuller
and who is this other McLaury brother
hes in from Texas to lawyer for the prosecution said I think we can hang
them
what theyre saying is absurd that they were unarmed with their hands
up and that you shot first with a pistol how could you when youre hold-
ing a shotgun
the beauty of lying is anything is possible
yeah but Ike Clantons stories all fly apart and only weaken their case
in the hands of the judge
I testify tomorrow
that what you been writing
yes by statute I can testify from a document without cross if nothing else
before were executed they can hear the gods truth

Judge's Office

the difficulty which resulted in the death of Billy Clanton and Frank and Tom McLaury originated last spring a little over a year ago I followed Frank and Tom McLaury and two other parties who had stolen six government mules from Camp Rucker myself Virg and Morg Earp and Marshal Williams Captain Hurst and four soldiers we traced those mules to McLaurys ranch also found the branding iron D8 and after quite a while the mules were found with the same brand they tried to pick a fuss out of me down there and told me if I ever followed them up again as close as I did they would kill me Captain Hurst came to us boys and told us he had made this compromise by so doing he would get his mules back we insisted on following them up Hurst prevailed on us to go back to Tombstone and so we came back they would not give up the mules to him after we went saying that they only wanted to get us away that they could stand the soldiers off Captain Hurst cautioned me and my brothers Virgil and Morgan to look out for those men that they had made some hard threats against our lives

shortly after the time Bud Philpott was killed by the men who tried to rob the Benson stage as a detective I helped trace the matter up and I was satisfied that three men named Bill Leonard Harry the Kid and Slim Jim Crane were in that robbery I knew that they were friends and associates of the Clantons and McLaurys and often stopped at their ranches it was generally understood among officers and those who have information about criminals that Ike Clanton was a sort of chief among the cow-boys that the Clantons and McLaurys were cattle thieves and generally in on the secret of the stage robbery and that the Clanton and McLaury ranches were meeting places and places of shelter for the gang I was satisfied that Frank and Tom McLaury killed and robbed Mexicans in the Skeleton Canyon two or three months ago and I naturally kept my eyes open I did not intend that any of the band should get the drop on me. . .

I believed then and believe now from the acts I have stated and the threats I have related and other threats communicated to me by different persons as having been made by Tom McLaury Frank McLaury and Ike Clanton that these men last named had formed a conspiracy to murder my brothers Morgan and Virgil and Doc Holliday and myself I believe I would have been legally and morally justified in shooting any of them on sight but I did not do so nor attempt to do so I sought no advantage when I went as deputy marshal to help disarm them and arrest them I went as part of my duty and under the direction of my brother the marshal I did not intend to fight unless it became necessary in self defense and in the performance of official duty when Billy Clanton and Frank McLaury drew their pistols I knew it was a fight for life and I drew and fired in defense of my own life and the lives of my brothers and Doc Holliday

Judge's Office

(reading)

The Court: Considering all the testimony together I am of the opinion that the weight of evidence sustains and corroborates the testimony of Wyatt and Virgil Earp that their demand for surrender was met by William Clanton and Frank McLaury drawing, or making motions to draw, their pistols. Upon this hypothesis my duty is clear. The defendants were officers charged with the duty of arresting and disarming brave and determined men who were experts in the use of firearms, as quick as thought and certain as death, and who had previously declared their intention not to be arrested or disarmed.

In coming to this conclusion I give great weight to several particular circumstances connected with the affray. It is claimed by the prosecution that the deceased were shot while holding up their hands in obedience to the demand of the chief of police, and on the other hand the defense claims that William Clanton and Frank McLaury at once drew their pistols and began firing simultaneously with the defendants. William Clanton was wounded on the wrist of the right hand on the first fire and thereafter used his pistol with his left. This wound is such as could not have been received with his hands thrown up, and the wound received by Thomas McLaury was such as could not have been received with his hands on his coat lapels. These circumstances, being indubitably facts, throw great doubt on the correctness of statements of witnesses to the contrary.

The testimony of Isaac Clanton that this tragedy was the result of a scheme on the part of the Earps to assassinate him, and thereby bury in oblivion the confessions the Earps had made to him about piping away the shipment of coin by Wells, Fargo & Co., falls short of a sound theory because of the great fact, most prominent in the matter, to wit, that Isaac Clanton was not injured at all, and could have been killed first and easiest. If it was the object of the attack to kill him he would have been the first to fall, but as it was, he was known or believed to be unarmed, and was suffered, so Wyatt Earp testifies, to go away and was not harmed.

In view of the past history of the county and the generally believed existence at this time of desperate, reckless and lawless men in our midst, banded together for mutual support, and living by felonious and predatory pursuits, regarding neither lives nor property in their career, and at this time for men to parade the streets armed with repeating rifles and six-shooters and demand that the chief of police of the city and his assistants should be disarmed is a proposition both monstrous and startling. This was said by one of the deceased only a few minutes before the arrival of the Earps.

Another fact that rises up preeminent in the consideration of this sad affair is the leading fact that the deceased from the very first inception of the encounter were standing their ground and fighting back, giving and taking death with unflinching bravery. It does not appear to have been a wanton slaughter of unresisting and unarmed innocents, who were yielding graceful submission to the officers of the law, or surrendering to or fleeing from their assailants, but armed and defiant men, accepting the wager of battle and succumbing only in death.

I cannot resist the conclusion that the defendants were fully justi-fied in committing these homicides, that it was a necessary act done in the discharge of official duty.

Cosmopolitan Hotel

who was the woman in a veil
who knocked last night
I hear she left without a word
it was a man Sadie
assassin
looking for me or my brothers
the Epitaph says
judge attorney agent mayor
the rumors are
and Doc all marked for death
they more than talk
look out this window
at what the Grand
you see that shutter
with one slat open
its for a rifle
who is in there
Curley Bill Johnny Ringo
across from your rooms
Ike Clanton Pony Deal
they wont shoot the sheriff
Im not running
not against Johnny
that sheet the Nuggets lies
was talking to Big Nose Kate
what does she say
Ringo told her go back to Globe
what
theyre going to gun down Doc
who is
the Clantons
it never ends
at Flys Boarding House
Im in a prospect hole
why honey

killing them boys
it was them or you
I think of him
of him
the only begotten
ah the savior
this catechism
in the gospel
who perishes
they that take the sword
who is blessed
the peacemaker
who do you love
your enemies
his hand his hand
but you know that
is open
they drove a nail
to kill to live
if we have to
what kind of life
its life
heroes
our saviors
walking in blood
ah love
lets get out of here
we can go out
where to
the Bird Cage Theatre opened
dont Dutch Annie have
yeah cribs in there
why go
sawbuck for a soiled dove
dont need any sweetheart
and snake water
never touch it

Little Egypt is dancing
whos she
she does the belly dance
she does
bare breasts
I dont know
Docs dealing faro
lets go

Fifth Street

Xmas, sagebrush trees strung with cranberries, hung with candles, and three days after, late night, Virg comes out of the Oriental, on the way to the hotel, watching Frank Stilwell go into the old Palace Saloon, burned out, and his arm shatters, bang, double barrel shotgun, bang, bang and his back's on fire, as he goes down, the gunmen run down Fifth, Head them off, past the ice house, the Combination shaft, down Toughnut, below the hoisting works, into the Gulch, riding out toward Charleston. He hunches into the Oriental looking for Wyatt, till he slops blood at his brother's feet; this miner says, Sorry for you, Virg, and he, It's hell, ain't it. When the sawbones show, Wyatt crosses the street, and out of the ashes by the window, he picks up Ike Clanton's hat.

Western Union Telegraph Company

Dated Tombstone December 29 1881
Received at 12 PM
To US Marshal Crawley Dake Phoenix

Virgil shot last night assassins in hiding wounds mortal local authorities doing nothing federal troops not coming to Cochise County wire me appointment power deputies lives here under threat

Wyatt Earp

Allen Street

Johnny Ringos hand on his gun Doc Hollidays inside his vest
you been shooting your mouth off about me Holliday
I have and I repeat it now Im sorry to see a first class cattle thief like
yourself fall in with assassins
youre going to publicly take back all youve said
what I said goes
youre going to meet your shadow
lets move into the street so no one else will be hurt
officer grabs Ringo from behind
turn him loose Flynn Ringo you can start shooting
Wyatt tugs on his arm
quit this foolishness
nodding at the window in the Grand Hotel with a rifle muzzle pulling
back in
one move and he wouldve dropped you

Occidental Saloon

for the love of god Doc I cant let you buck out in smoke and dont think I dont know why youre aiming for him it aint cause he got away with that stage robbery by threatening the driver its cause hes been galling Big Nose Kate look I have federal money to go hunt down the men who shot Virg you hear what he said Never mind Allie I got one arm left to hug you I want you in my posse seven men warrants for Ike and Fin Clanton and Pony Deal and you know what the judge said handing them over Youll never clean up this crowd that way Youd best leave your prisoners in the mesquite where alibis dont matter were searching Charleston and the hills outside and down the river in the back country when we get close theyll think its only mail theft and give themselves up but bang its attempted murder are you with me much obliged

Tombstone, February 1, 1882

Major C. P. Dake, United States Marshal
Grand Hotel
Tombstone

Dear Sir,

Acting in our official role as Deputy U. S. Marshals in this Territory, we have tried, always, without flinching, to deliver on the duties given in trust to us. They've been a hard go, dangerous, and had to be done in a settlement where sprees and shootouts could break out anytime. And why, to cross, in contempt, our carrying out the writs and warrants of the court, handed down to haul outlaws to justice. We are deeply obliged to many for their steady help in reining in crime, and for their faith that what we do is honest. But though we reckon as best we can, and do our damnedest at what we've been asked, it doesn't matter. Stage holdups go on, the cow-boys have alibis, there's a death list, and talk of a raid on us. Mexico may go to war to stop their rustling, and so they're forced to steal in our county. Wells, Fargo & Co. are threatening to close. In the election, the cow-boys won out. They have the mayor and the sheriff in their pocket. Their yellow journal prints bad words about us, over and over, warping and darkening what we've done, till the citizens don't know what to believe. And that leads us to this. To show them that we're true, and our intent's to do them good, without thought for our own gain or how we're advanced, it's our duty to put our resignations as Deputy U. S. Marshals in your hands, and turn in our stars. We're grateful that we've been so long in your favor, and that you're sure of our integrity. We know you may not accept this offer, and till you've appointed the men who'll replace us, we'll go on doing what you give us to do.

Very respectfully yours,
Virgil W. Earp
Wyatt S. Earp

Fremont Street

I have a warrant
read it Johnny
to any sheriff constable marshal or policeman in the Territory of Arizona
greetings you are commanded to arrest Wyatt Earp Morgan Earp Virgil
Earp and J. H. Holliday and bring them forthwith before me at my office
on Main Street in the Village of Contention in the County of Cochise
Territory of Arizona J. B. Smith Justice of the Peace
the charges have already been rejected by judge and jury
not my concern
Ike has no new evidence
you men are under arrest
I can smell this
give me your guns and get in the buckboard
so we can be ambushed out on Contention Road go to hell
who are
my army twelve men with revolvers and rifles in the buggy with a Win-
chester is my lawyer
lets go
you ride ahead

5

Attorney's Office

out the window no stars
they were after us last night
think so
you represent them
just business
you know anything
nothing
get an answer from Ike
no truce
think were in danger
youre liable to get it any time
I didnt see nobody
I think
different in town
I see strangers here
who is it
I think are after you
who
Ringo asked me to tell you
tell me
if any fight happened hes clear
that so
everybodys on their own
whos that below
Stilwell I better go
the window rattling

Campbell and Hatch's Saloon

in rain and wind
one game
no lets go back
what for
he saw armed men
you walked around
yes Morg
see anyone
Apache Hank
no threat
Indian Charlie
come on
you like the show
well Stolen Kisses
yeah hard not to
Sadie go back
yeah to Frisco
Lou wrote
California girls
out of danger
hey theres Big Tip
rack em up Wyatt
you love sixty-one
aint that the truth
go on and break
okay Im solids
you following up
on what
well on the thief
what thief
who stole the kisses
ah hah
the wall is dust
over Wyatt's head
what the

Morg folds over
two shots
glass door shattered
from the alley
Morg slides down
Wyatt hauls on him
dont boys I cant stand it
that bad
I played my last game
hound at the door howling
Morg whispering
ear to his brother's lips
guess you were right Wyatt
on what
the heaven after
I remember
I cant see a damn thing
ah Morg
you know who done it
I do
wish I could get em
Ill get em for you
all I ask but Wyatt
yeah Morg
be so careful
wind blowing in through the holes in the back door

Benson Road

At noon, on Sunday, his birthday, in the merciless light, the fire bell ringing dust to dust, Wyatt Earp follows his brother's slow funeral, from the hotel, with the departed in a spring wagon, to the iron station, and the train to haul him to his woman to bury.

He heads back on the old stage road, so many times, with the ruts holding out against the sagebrush, and the mesquite threatening in the dusk, and he curls over the thorn of his loss, keeping back any tears, all the way into Tombstone, to the one saloon.

Mexican Quarter

senor mi amigo you have always been welcoming when I cross the street
and you are U. S. Marshal and your brother was shot I have to tell you
if Spence kills me dios de mi vida last Saturday I was at home and my
husband was gone two days in Charleston and he comes home at noon
comes in with two men Freeze I dont know the others name they had
rifles he sent a man to look after los caballos then they go into the front
room and talk to Stilwell then Stilwell goes out and Spence to bed and
this is all that night Spence gets up at nine o'clock Sunday Freeze was
sleeping there the other man goes home on Friday and stays there all day
goes out Friday night but comes back in a little while to sleep Saturday
hes out all day till midnight and Spence comes in Indian Charlie is with
Stilwell he has a pistol and a carbine he goes out Saturday morning with
Stilwell and comes back with him at midnight both of them armed with
pistols and carbines when they come back to the house Saturday night
all their talk Spence and Stilwell and los otros hombres is in low voices
like they are telling a secret when they come in I get out of bed to receive
them and I see theyre excited why I dont know Stilwell comes into the
house and after an hour Spence and the others Stilwell gives me a mes-
sage from Spence Ill be up from Charleston that night Saturday I was
told at two o'clock think Spence left last night for Sonora dont know for
sure he went Sunday morning Spence says get breakfast it was about six
o'clock which I did but before that we had a fight and he hit me and mi
madre Francisca and he says hell shoot me and my mother says hell have
to shoot her too he says Marietta if you say one word about anything you
know Ill kill you Im going to Sonora and Ill leave your dead body behind
me Spence didnt say so but yo se el lo mato I know one of them killed
Morg I think they did it because he comes to the house all shaking and
the others who come in with him teeth chattering when he comes in I
ask you want some sopa and he says I do not myself and mi madre we
hear the shots and it was a little while after Stilwell and Charlie come
in and a half hour after Spence and the others I think Spence and the
others they might have come in the night they left their horses outside of
town and after the shooting went and got them I judge theyve been do-
ing wrong because theyre white and shaking when they come in Spence
and the others for days always leave home in the middle of the day and

come back in the middle of the night but they never come back in the shape they were in that night and the next morning after hearing that Morg died I see that Stilwell and the others did this deed I have not seen Charlie since that night dont know where he is last week my mother and I were standing on the veranda talking with Spence and Charlie and Morg passes by and Spence nudges Charlie and says thats him thats him and Charlie runs down the street so he can get ahead of him and get a look at him

Southern Pacific

the desert going dark
wish I could go after them Wyatt
well you aint
I know I aint mended
I cant look after you Virg and them
you got federal warrants
first thing
your posse
Doc Holliday Texas Jack
good boys
Scar Face brother Warren
yeah yeah
Turkey Creek Johnson
out of Deadwood
from the two against one gunfight
by the graveyard road
you go home to mama and daddy
whyre we stopping
dont know still east of the Tucson station
you Wyatt Earp
yes
Im Deputy U. S. Marshal Evans
what is it
this is a warning
you caught your breath
Frank Stilwell Ike Clanton
I know them
Pete Spence and a breed I dont know
Indian Charlie
in town watching the trains for you
his brother in the lighted window
get down Virg and you Allie
Tucson Station
goodbye Virg
Ill be seeing you
Ill be seeing you soon
take care
Wyatt leans out of the vestibule

Tucson Station

Wyatt Earp sees them in a flatcar on the next track, on their bellies. He slips out of the train, back way, to the platform, and there's the glow of the gaslight on the barrels of their guns. His shotgun on his arm, he walks over to them, and they drop theirs and run. He chases Stilwell, who crosses the tracks, at last stands, won't draw, shaking, and wrestles for Wyatt's shotgun, Wyatt gets the muzzle over his heart, Stilwell yelling, Morg! Morg! and Wyatt, You see a ghost? and fires. You are a ghost. He lights out after Ike, when a train pulls out between them, and he loses him. He runs up to the window, It's all right, Virg: one for Morg! and holds up a finger. He walks back to Stilwell's body. Doc is shooting it, in the armpit, in the leg, in the hand.

Cosmopolitan Hotel

whos there
the colonel
come on in
who are all these
my posse
whats going on
the telegraph operator woke me saying theres a message for Johnny from
Tucson that Doc and I are accused of murder for shooting Stilwell
was it a warrant from the county sheriff
thats what I said and no it was Ike Clanton saying hed sworn out that
charge
and the operator
was warning me I said you deliver it not yet can you hold off long as you
say one hour will do tell my lawyer
I advise you to surrender to Johnny
not going to
you can clear yourself easy
one Id lose days chasing the assassins two if Im disarmed Ill be shot three
he dont have the right or the authority to arrest me
what about
I have a mission and Johnny aint going to get in the way
what about the county sheriff
tell him Ill surrender any time
all right
and the document making over all my property from soda to hock to my
daddy
sign here
Turkey Creek Texas Jack
yeah Wyatt
pack up the camp supplies saddle the horses whos there
the vigilante
come on in
Johnnys in the lobby with a deputy and two in the street
colonel you better wait here till this is over
hell no I want to see this

Wyatt buckles on his six gun his Wells Fargo shotgun on his arm
Ill go down first Doc you come last
at the top of the stairs
remember boys no gunplay
and they walk down
this aint none of my affair Wyatt
the deputy
but the sheriffs going to arrest you and he thought we could avoid some
trouble if I talked to you first
Wyatt looking at Johnny
avoid some trouble tell that coward I got a double eagle for him if hell
only try to arrest me
Johnny goes out to his deputies Wyatt pays the hotel bill
come on boys
Johnny turns to him
Wyatt I want to see you
you cant see me youre going to see me once too often
Wyatt swings into his saddle as his posse heads out sun going down he
lights a cigar wheels and rides down Allen Street to the hills south

South Pass

hands down your alias Indian Charlie
si the vaqueros call me that
cause youre a breed well Florentino birth dont matter what matters is
how big a hole after your death
in the yellow grass bone trees and the Dragoons warping into the sky
you can walk though youre shot
si senor
around the shoulder out of sight of the waterhole
I had Scar Face hit you in the thigh not kill you so we could jaw a little
si senor I dont steal horse
I have a warrant for you on a murder count and the mid air dance you out
with it we can go easy
I no confess nothing
I was talking to these boys to let you try to go on the dodge when you
seen me you did up that slope you going belly through the brush thats
your confession
in a sweat drags off his bandanna
they was going one two times they was going to ambush Holliday
who was
Ike Clanton Frank Stilwell they ambush Virgil and Ringo in on it
Ike and Frank doing the shooting
si they ambush you and Morgan that night Curley Bill missing you from
the alley and Frank shooting Morgan through the glass
in the back like always any of you with sand enough to face us and you
I was lookout on Allen Street and Ringo with the horses on Fremont and
another man I dont know walked in with the
hes lying
I know Doc hes covering for Apache Hank that it
Frank left his cut horse in the arroyo at the edge of Tombstone we finish
off the Earp brothers and theres no reason to run
his getaway
I had to ride him to Pattersons ranch I know you smoked him thats all I
know
thisll be good testimony you can go with Turkey Creek hold on
que senor

my brothers and I we ever hurt you
no senor
why help kill Morgan
it was my amigos Curley Bill give me 25 silver dollars
25
opening his long duster
thats a number Ive got another number for you 3 you can draw when you
like I wont till 3
no senor
dropping his bandanna
uno
bleak morning the cicadas chirring
dos

Unanswered Prayer

Skin and bones Jesus,
out fishing for men in unredeemed Missouri,
in the tallgrass, sundown,
so north, where my woman lies, unrisen,
and where I saw
in the skies license, in the rains mercy,
I count this man's black wounds,
the thigh, by my order,
the gut, by me,
the back, the temple, by my companion,
blood everywhere,
cross me
with only a crack of the light of justice
in this country, this territory, this fucking mesa.

Iron Springs

Agents in Charleston say that Curley Bill is in the Barbacomari wilderness. On a vendetta ride Wyatt Earp racks after him, from the San Pedro River, long dry trail north, to the Whetstone Mountains, to get one thousand dollars for his posse at the waterhole at Iron Springs. At the trail forks, no sign of travel, for days. He has his brother wait for the money, rides up a skinny canyon in the infernal sun, and still no sign, lets down his vigilance, unbuttons his coat, loosens his gunbelt. He's carrying his Colt single-action .45 with a long barrel and a walnut handle, in the saddle boot, a Winchester .44-40, looped to the saddle horn, a cartridge belt, in a pommel strap, a 12-gauge Remington sawed off shotgun.

Down slope, past a rock shoulder, across a sand flat, hidden, back of a cut bank and hollow, is Iron Springs, beyond, an abandoned shack, and a grove of cottonwoods. His horse is quickening at the smell of water. It's wrong, he dismounts, slides out his shotgun, walks on, no sound. At the edge of the bluff, he can see down in the hollow, man lifting his shotgun, man cutting for the woods. Scar Face yells, Curley Bill! and rides the other way, bullets coming, Texas Jack's horse goes down on his leg, the posse going for cover in a cloud.

His horse spooking, and he throws the bridle over his arm, too wild, he can't get on. If my time's come, he's going with me. At the gully, he sees Curley Bill squint his left eye and sight with his right along his shotgun, he *I done nothing* fires, Wyatt's long coat flares. He missed me, I can't miss him. He fires, one barrel, the other, into the gut, cutting him in half, and the cow-boy yells in agony with his last breath.

He sees the gold-mount ivory-handle six guns that Curley Bill had stolen in that stage holdup. Pony Deal, Rattlesnake Bill, and all the rest, are running, he has warrants for all of them, they shoot wild into his coat. I should have saved the other barrel, cut holes in them. His horse rearing, he can't get his rifle, his gunbelt's slipped, he reaches down the back of his leg for his Special. Where in hell is the posse? riding away. He turns and fires into the band of angels, gets yells, he smells sulfur, as a bullet hits the saddle horn.

He's on his horse, and fires toward the hill of the skull, no answer, slides out his rifle, turns back to Texas Jack, who's hauling his saddle, shotgun, boot and all, away from his dead horse, Doc giving a hand. Wyatt fires twice into the row of crosses, shots coming back, and his leg is numb, only hit the bootheel.

Whetstone Mountains

Wyatt you must be all shot to pieces
no Doc
whats all this
only the skirts of my coat
miracle nobody hit
well you was riding away
not cold-footed only in cover
I couldnt see nowhere to go
you walk right in he had the deadwood on you
I made a promise
theyre on the run lets go finish them
ah no Ive had enough
saying you wont pursue
the angels the angels
the what
want war go on and get your fill
but its the goddamn cow-boys
without their leader theyll unravel
yeah but theres still Johnny Ringo
what will happen is who you are
I see hes always been down bound
hell shoot himself in the temple mystery why
and Ike Clanton goes on getting indicted
hell meet a lawman at last who wont spare him
and Johnny Behan the guardian of dishonor
hell go on cheating with money itll catch up
wasnt there money for us at Iron Springs
yeah and the gunfight come between
youre in for the thousand dollars on Curley Bills head
hell no I done this for my brother
well you shot up his outlaws the sheriffs coming
I reckon we can head up to the Sierra Bonita
thats General Hookers spread we can rest our horses
theres a bluff north where we can make a stand
youre right the sheriffs all show and wont charge

head on out to Colorado
I prophesy your San Francisco love
if I have any future its with her
cant follow you into that weather its adios
but not tonight old friend
thats music to me
know what I want
no what
a shot of whiskey

Sulphur Springs Valley

Wyatt Earp, followed by his posse, following nobody, rides north into the desolate playa, no life, not even vultures, for miles across the dead lake, to the edge and saltgrass, in the distance between desire and consummation, on a chance horse, its hooves lifting alkali dust.

He takes up the old trail, into the back country, ah god, that blood, at morning, red, unknown, the sighs, the blood, downpouring: and it's no good, can't dream, with a dead soul. What's the difference? Murder, everywhere on this ball, here, or across the line, in the high plains.

Last light, last prayer, on the Chiricahuas, and the light golng, and meaning, as the territory pitches into the dark, and he rides on, toward the ghost hills.

P. T. Barnum

Life
of the Showman
with the as I live & breathe stories
of his big top acts,
his freaks and wonders,
still out hitting
the sticks of memory,
Washington's nanny, the Fiji mermaid,
Tom Thumb, the Swedish Nightingale, the Siamese Twins,
White Whale, and Jumbo,
and his Museum, Menagerie, Hippodrome, & Circus,
the original Greatest Show
on Earth,
based on the lost notebooks
discovered in the foundation
of his last home,
Marina,
transformed
by
Larry Beckett,
author of the masterpieces
Paul Bunyan, Chief Joseph, &c.,
into a big time poem
in his ongoing American Cycle,
with hard blank verse innovations,
sharp Yankee imagery,
and state of the art postmodern structure,
for your lasting pleasure.

spirits, saying: blue laws: side by side her:
to bed with candles: day after Xmas: you can't
trick us: cock walking: into a silver dollar:
feathers, and rags: what would you take: and I
had clocks: gold spectacles: Island, in thanks

I was a salt in my green days, no more, and real thirsty for
that Cape Horn rainwater. 1 morning, anchored at the
Boston wharf, I was looking up & down Atlantic at the 5
saloons, and not a penny to bless myself with. I puzzled
a while on how to make it, and saw the light. I took me a
gal. jug, ½ full of water, to the near saloon:

                         this demi john's ½ full of rum: fill
her up, sir

                there you go: ah, that's $2

                                thanks, sir:
charge it

            oh no you fly by night: you pour it back:

                                    I
did likewise at the other 4 saloons, and I rolled back to
the tall ship, hugging ½ a gal. of Jamaica spirits, saying
aye, it's a miracle!

                      ah, something for nothing
is the true god: well, down the hatch:

                          He swallowed
his grog, last drop, hammered it down, tucked up
his bolt of linen, nodded:

                morning, Taylor
morning, Squire Hoyt:

                  red faced, and creaked
out of the country store. Old Bethel, where
it was a sin to fiddle, play 7 up, all shows
were outlawed, and a crime to horse & carriage
on Sun., 40 lashes. Bad debts would land you
in jail, oh the blue laws! in that town, under
dim sky, and a snow crust. The meeting house:
no bell, no steeple, no fire: in a square pew,

I'd time the pauses in the prayer, and sulk
in the white school: birch rod across the palm.
The country doctor, in his long black coat,
would bleed you every April, and they buried
suicides under crossroads.

                    What chance had I?
it's not yet Sunday: it's lucky, or the deacon
would pinch us

              on horseback, I know: long walk
in all this wet: it's such an old maid district:
thank you, Barnum:

                She'd come to Grassy Plain
for a spring bonnet from the dear aunt across
the sloppy road:

               it's a downpour this evening,
Taylor, would you side by side her the mile
back to Bethel?

           a flash of lantern / lightning,
and I wished it was 20. At Hallet's:

                    I'd best
be getting in

        I ah: nothing

              night, Taylor
night, Charity

        I kissed her / no. My doxology
in the dark: hallelujah the thunder, oh bless
the heaven of rain and Mrs. Wheeler's hat!
All that May? night, I saw her blushing face:
the morning after, I waited on her to meeting,
every Sun.:

        that's good:

            The heavy rains
had lifted in Va.; Lord, I got a stitch
when the hard headed innkeeper said, pay
all room & board, I don't care if you do
check out 1 day early! Old Turner ordered
dinner at noon, chicken & fixings, for our

travelling circus, and supper at ½ past,
oysters; we went to bed with candles at 1,
and banged down for breakfast, fresh eggs,
at 2 p.m.! He got his money's worth:
        how much
for this sap bucket?
     ah, it's not for sale,
I'd just have to restock it:
       Barnum, you have
no silver, and you want to buy that museum:
with what?
   brass:
     it's a deal:
        I said amen,
inside: oh lightning hit when the old owner
sold it out from under, for 3 grand more?
to low down operators, out to float shares
on the museum, and slough it off for cash.
I wrote the Sun / the Atlas, bad mouthing
the stock: if they don't pay day after Xmas,
sir, ah, you sign it over to me by forfeit,
and no reneging.
      4 flushers! I can be mgr.
if I quit writing squibs? all right: with me
in their pocket, the wheels in motion, they
let go, and skipped the payoff. In the mail
next morning:
    Sirs,
      We open New Year's day.
Visit the American Museum at no charge
till further notice.
     P. T. Barnum, prop.
Whiz bang!
    I told the Nightingale I'd keep
the mobs off her, and I leaked her arrivals
to the public: business is business; and
in Baltimore? ah, where they tore her shawl,

in chapel, daughter Caroline, next to me,
was taken for her: oh she sang for nothing!
they cooed after the hymn. In New Orleans,
that story / no, I had my agt. on shore
yell, hey it's her under that veil! and all
ganged after my daughter; in Cincinnati,
that story in print, I had my agt. yell,
Barnum, you can't trick us: your daughter's
under that veil! The Nightingale and I
went down the wharf, untouched. Ah, it's
a teetertotter. Where was I?

                                the country store:
open all day, and I was clerk! cock walking,
quill pen back of my ear, pure hustle, weighing
out indigo, figuring, drawing long sweetening.
We sold shotguns, powder horns, axes, handsaws,
nails, flints, harnesses, plows, seed, hayrakes,
wire, whetstones, jackknives, matches, traps,
scrimshaw, tongs, forks, spoons, sieves, samplers,
bean poles, buckskin, sheepskin, long johns,
straw hats, red shirts, shifts, frocks, buttons,
bandannas, wicker baskets, pitchers, platters,
bags, boxes, soap, candles, keel tubs, tow,
wool, calico, lace, thread, paper, scissors,
goose feathers, crazy quilts, tops, toy balls,
books of pictures, dolls, shells, chocolate,
pipes, tobacco, tea, pills, spices, whatnots,
fish flakes, horse chestnuts, hard rum, rot gut,
soda crackers, molasses, salt pork, and beer.
I scratched the charges in the big daybook:
$1:
     grandpa, his silver hair:
                           oh gracious,
a penny saved! bundle all your hard cash in
a handkerchief, Taylor: I'll show you what's
1st rate!
             That day / night, under the swinging

mermaid sign? at the tavern:
                              Wakelee, my boy
is in the money: change his copper pennies
into a silver dollar:
                        That cartwheel! I could
have bought the globe with it, and oh when have
I ever been so flush?
                        1st memory.
                                    I was
wildflower polite with ladies, and weed poor
 in words with local boys. It was cash, credit
& barter: I drove sharp trades, and old folks
paid me in butter, beeswax, feathers, and rags,
and mind the swindles:
                            you hear Capt. Noah's
up & married? I said, high time: why so late?
and he, if she's the 1, it's worth waiting for;
if not, I won't have to live with her so long:
It was hard rain all day, and a slow night,
most gone home in the mud, & I stayed open:
Ben Hoyt was exalted on an apple barrel,
haw hawing at a man beating the blue laws,
and, after a whirl of rum, story telling:
there's 2 old men with old testament names, on the 1
mountain: 1, puffing up from town, stopped in:
                                          are you
to home?
            I reckon I am
                              well, how be you and ain't you
going to offer me anything?
                              oh, I'm just tolerable
and will gumption do you?
                              thanks, sir: say, you hear
about that Vt. man? the road surveyor told him he was
really on the N. H. side all these years, and he said: oh
thank goodness, I don't think I could have stood another
of them Vt. winters

ha, ha: oh, you're
a caution
hey, good looking oxen I saw out in your
barn
ah yeah, if you say so: what do you think about
this late snow?
well, nothing to me: tell me, what would
you take for the both of them?
oh, I don't
rightly know, do I want to sell them? it was a short
summer last yr., remember? it come on a Thurs.
it did,
but was it morning or afternoon? look here, quit your
hemming & hawing, give me a price
I'll thank you to
keep your shirt on: cash down? ah, $10
done
where
you going?
I better get to getting before my bones
freeze:
now the other is thinking:
he liked my oxen: I
could've got 20 as like as not:
and the 1 is thinking:
did
I just buy his oxen? what in the world for? I don't need
them:
in the morning:
it's confounded, but after you
left, this man come by, offered me 20 for the oxen
that
so? well I won't hold you to it: he can have them:
How in his oh be joyful he'd tickle us,
on a double cross day. Oh, and they'd hide
the beaver hats and palm them off as otter,
I'd cut whiskey, ink in a high price name,

their loads light a bushel, and my wool cotton,
they had stones & ashes in their rag bundles,
and I had clocks, made to be sold, and lacking
a wheel or 2:
                    Phineas: it's in the Bible,
and means big mouth:
                          Ma turned, pouring new milk
into the corn meal:
                    you ballyhooed, 1st hr.,
and haven't let up since:
                            It was johnny cake,
and nation fine.
                    Customers shout, Taylor:
and I see grandpa, laughing, my stars! over
my head? in his gold spectacles: 1st man
I conjure up.
                Old card, my namesake: he'd
shake hands, and it was only to smuggle me
sugar lumps, 2 barrels ma said / pennies,
for raisins? at the lowest price! He deeded
5 acres, in the Plum Trees, in the parish
of Bethel, called Ivy Island, in thanks,
to me:
          imagine: hey, Barnum, tell us what
all happened out there

rum, and wild cherries: a tree at nooning:
into the Atlantic: as fast as horses: jump
hard, lad: what you'll give me: the circus:
is my property: invisible ink: the winners:
summer's come: I almost asked her: the moon

     I was making money:
a jug of rum, and wild cherries. No slouch,
I sold them gingerbread on training days,
all the other boys gawking at the muskets,
wishing for uniforms: halt & ground arms!
and I was on the green with a tall bottle
of cherry rum and glasses for the blue
platoon. My Lord, I had a calf and ram:
I'd have been rich at 12: pa made me buy
all my own rags.
     That? summer I asked to go
see grandpa's legacy / Ivy Island:
        land!
it makes you high roller of all the boys
in Bethel:
   and pa:
     I calculate you could
after we turn the hay out there:
       and ma:
it'll be ah 9 yrs. before you inherit
and are a nabob: hadn't you better lie
under a tree at nooning?
     no ma'am:
      and pa:
the hired man can take you, Taylor:
      No sleep
for 3 nights dreaming of that promised land:
what was your big sell, Phineas?
     I guess that time on the Norwalk sloop.
It was a 1 day run down to N. Y. on business. The Bethel hat & comb
makers all signed a contract to pay up a double sawbuck if they ever

bristled at a practical joke. Now on that trip with the wind not out, after
1 week slow going, we were becalmed off Sawpitts and had to get into
the eggs in freight. At last the sails were set, and we all thought about
shaving. Only I had bothered to pack a razor, lather box, and strop. I said,
now boys, time we're at the wharf the barbers will be closed: we can't all
shave by then, but it's bad business to let any man get a jump on going
ashore, so I propose each man shave ½ his face and pass the razor on
till all are clean. They agreed, I started, and when the razor came back
round to me, I finished, and then whacking it across the strop, I let it go
into the Atlantic, yelling, oh my gracious, it's overboard! They couldn't
blow up on a/c of the practical joke fine, and so they crowed. They went
ashore ½ bare, ½ whiskers, all streaked, and told the big towners it's the
Conn. fashion:

I was being shaved

in Bridgeport, and saw the groom bowl up in
the wagon. I wondered: what did we forget
for Caroline's wedding?

oh Barnum, it's

Iranistan: it's burning!

and I ran out

½ shaved: red flames out of the roof:

oh I

don't care about the cost, it's the danger
to our 1001 guests: ah David, don't worry,
you'll marry tonight if we have to have it
in the carriage house!

It was fire's touch:

I prayed they'd haul water as fast as horses.
We passed the firemen: hey, get a move on
with your old machine! Men, fixing the roof?
were up ladders with buckets in the smoke:
where's Ivy Island?

ah, at the north end

of that there field

Adam, what's that ax?

to hack into your timber to see how good
it is

hold on, don't go so fast, it's like
a swamp
                jump hard, lad, you can make it
I can't, it's all water
                        we're off the path,
you'll have to wade
                        it's way over my head,
I'll drown
                oh the devil, you're safe: it isn't
4 ft. deep, Taylor
                if I go under, you
come and get me
                        yes, to be sure
                                oh god Adam
it's hornets I, ow help me!
                        no cause, ha!
for alarm, boy, you're soaked, eh?
                                should I
put mud on it, or what?
                        buck up, it's only
a ¼ mile more to your famous island:
for stinging, member that slick Yankee? that
fly peddler, old traveler, and we ask him:
what is the price of razor strops?
                                oh them's Pomeroy's
strops, $1 apiece
                        what? it'll go for ½ of that before
the year is out
                        it does and I'll give it to you for
nothing
            I'll buy me 1 on those conditions: & Ben can
be witness to the contract, all right?
                                yes sir, there's no
back out in me
                hey Taylor, will you pour me a Santa
Cruz rum? ah Ben, I don't like it now I have it, hardly:
what'll you give me for it?

                              well, I guess, being it's
you, 50¢
            done
                        I get it, gentlemen: what do I pay?
confess you're sold and stand drinks for the house
                                                    I
won't do it, ah but I will give you a strop for your wit ha!
sharp customers in Bethel, eh?
                                    nothing to brag of,
gentlemen: I bought them there strops @ 12½¢, but I'd
heard about Bethel and I upped my prices: they go @
25¢ but if you want more @ 50, be glad to oblige you
Taylor, that rum coming or not?
1 morning in August, I stopped a deadhead
at Barnum's Grand Scientific and Musical
Theater: pay up; he said, I'm the sheriff;
I said, so what; he smiled, ask Mr. Henry,
who said, it must be that old $500 debt,
and he was holding our cash. I had a lawyer
write up a b/s for the mud circus, all with
the show in progress. Now the man he owed /
his lawyer asked for the keys to the stable,
to levy on the horse & carriages; I sighed,
hold on, told Henry, sign, hand over the 90?
lock up the 500. I said, sorry, gentlemen,
Henry won't pay; what? we'll have to bust
the doors in; it's my circus now, you can't,
look at this b/s. Oh but they were green
at the Yankee trick, and arrested Henry;
at night the groom said, he really owes 13,
and he was fixing to give them the 500
and the for heaven's sake circus for 1 hr.
and a saddled horse, and skip out on you,
and only that damn sheriff trying to get
in free balled it up. Henry said, fetch me
the 500 I had the juggler lock up for us,
Barnum, and bail me out. Well, I rode off

baldheaded and paid the man he owed the $
from Henry for his ½ interest in the circus
and assurance he wouldn't claim it and
assignment of 500 of the old debt. Oh my!
close rub: I saved my skin. And Mr. Henry?
not his real name:

> if I go under, you better

come and get me

> oh never fear, I'll have you

out in a flash

> yeah? I'm coming

> > step on

the branches

> where?

> > on the bottom

> > > all I

can feel is holes

> ah mercy me, you're safe:

boy, you look kind of like a water rat
in all that mud

> I was stung, Adam

> > > yes, cross

this little creek

> little, it's 12 ft. wide,

and jammed with alders: hey, is my property
circled by water?

> and why the devil would it

be Ivy Island?

> oh yeah, the name, I wasn't

thinking: how we going to get over?

> > > faith

and you'll see the use of the ax: we'll cut
an oak for bridge:

> > it's a grey day in Grassy Plains,

sirs: you needing any, ah, notions? I'm carrying old
knotholes, wooden nutmegs, paper stretchers, left hand
quill pens, invisible ink, moonlight books, winter

matches, smoke curlers, &c., Mr. Keeler

you go on
along, I've been shaved 1 time too many by your
kind

it's hard, sir, to be called a cheat on a/c of other
Yankee peddlers' chiseling: I tell you what, I'm
travelling

that's fine with me

now now, you just try
me: I'll take anything unsaleable you got, @ retail, for
anything in my wagon, @ wholesale

seems fair, I'll
have a look: let's see, what about the whetstones?
$3/doz.

I'll do a gr.

and what'll you pay me in?
whetstones, $6/doz.

all right, I come out at the little
end of the horn this particular time: here's a $ for your
trouble: you're just too cute for a tin peddler:

I must have lotteries
in my blood, from Old $2½, grandpa's trick
and nickname: anyhow, I had bartered for
green bottles, in all sizes, a wagon load;
Keeler said, fool, if you unload that trash
in 20 yrs., a miracle. I made them prizes,
with tin skimmers? and used pie pans, $ 50¢/
ticket, and whoosh! in 9 days, like a wonder,
I'd vanished them all to the winners, hat
trim girls, apprentice boys, journeymen, &
boss hatters: some fuming, most forgiving:
here we are, Taylor

it's just a scattering
of trees, and ah poor ivy

it's like I said,
Ivy Island

God look at that black snake,

I, oh Adam help me!

                        over the bridge: like
your property, eh boy?

                              I'd sell it cheap
April's gone, summer's come: you're a fool,
and I'm none

                  were they all in on the joke
since the day I was born?

                      ah lad

                          the liars:
I wrote lottery circulars, in big language
and inks all colors, with points & capitals:
Call on us & load your pockets with shiners
now, at the old sure office of lucky stars:
ah, home made poetry, and I sold chances
by mail order, post rider, on commission,
the drawing / oyster supper at ma's tavern;
I was hauling it in, till that law passed.
I sold a prayer shouter and his wife tickets
behind each other: is marriage a lottery?
Oh, ma looked down on my unlaced tailoress,
her fortune telling mother, and we eloped.
In the November smoke, her in laws, the crows
in trouble, swoop and laboring up the harsh sky
over the frozen over New York roads, old rust
wagons banging away on downtown cobblestones,
ice ringing all iron, the fall flakes blowing,
brought my to me sweet heart at the water black
and stinging wharf, oh in a carriage, blazing,
the wished on moon, to yes, to bride & groom it.
I wanted her, so hard, and his fabulous rig
nobody could ride: Arabian horse / new sleigh;
New Year's, in 29?

                    you can if you've a 20
in your pocket

               I do, grandpa:

                       I out with my

double sawbuck, and shoved it back:

you win,

you win:

Charity and I rode to the line
in that crack outfit: gee haw, the bells,
sliding over nothing, down the Old Lane,
across the snowy fields: I was hoping
for a kiss me quick: to the bright barn
and the frolic; I almost asked her, and
thought, wait till after oh Cape Cod girls
they have no combs, haul away. I walked her
out into the stars: white breath: her hand
with its fine sweat:

why do you hold back,

Charity?

because I love you so

let's ah

get married

yes: yes, Taylor:

It happened:
she hurt that I might hurt: the whipping boy,
in the days when anything was better than
haul brush, cut hay, hurry on out and weed
the cabbage, push cows over the thin fields
on the old hack, all forenoon. I did / no,
I took it easy: not lazy, ah but not born
for that clod hopping.

Oh and I was famous
at ciphering: no slate, I had to scratch
numbers on a stovepipe. The school master,
that 1 man power, at the neighbor's shed?
1 night, had said: ah so & so dimensions
in this stack of firewood: now reckon it
in cu. ft.: take you 5 min., I'm betting,
by this brass watch: go: and I figured it
in 2; on the way out, I saw the moon
in a water bucket.

girls, they: that pony runs: kissed her:
are tight, hard winter: to the Sun: freaks
to each other: lost in the Gulf: you go
on shifting: the $ for shoes: in love:
I lick: and she so: independence day

Oh Cape Cod girls, they have no combs,
way haul away:
they comb their hair with codfish bones,
we're bound away.

Then what?

Oh Cape Cod boys, they have no sleds,
way haul away:
they coast downhill on codfish heads,
we're bound away.

Haul away, you

How does that chorus go?
Old shanty: get the mainsail in the air:
Ah when I was a little whippersnapper like you, I had to
walk home from district school, and 1 night this man drives
up in an old sleigh, and stays the colt: he was breaking in
a black colt: says, you boys want a ride? Soon as we're in,
that pony runs off like all possessed, up over Cedar Hill,
and raking through Wildcat, we make a turn by the grace
of God and 3 in.! We're scared and ready to jump & go
bellybunk into a drift before we crash, and that man looks
back cool as can be and says, now sit right still, Uncle
Dud's driving:
                    Pa said.
I am what I remember in my bones:
I know a man started up in Falls Village
with a broke down nag and God awful shay,
and trading all the way down the Housatonic,

hit Stratford with a span of high steppers
and a glorious coach:
               No school, no church?
nobody home, Sat. kids lollygagging around:
straight chairs back to back, boy kneeling
on 1:
      I languish
            who do you languish for?
I languish for Rose:
             She got up on the other,
he kissed her cheek, & he, into the circle.
Her turn:
        I languish
             who do you languish for?
I languish for Taylor:
             On the tall chair,
she kissed my lips, & she, into the circle.
My turn:
        I languish
             who do you languish for?
I languish for Rose:
             heart hurrying afternoon.
I wanted her, so hard
        grandpa's Arabian horse
             down the Old Lane

       the snowy fields
             her hand
with its fine sweat

New Year's, in 29?

        bright barn

and the frolic; I almost
        wait till after

                why do you

                yes: yes:
                        Oh, unforgettable.
                                Ma was
of the old school, bless her:
                        blow seeds
off a dandelion and your wish comes true;
3x, like so, and if any are still on it,
your ma wants you! for a bad cough, take
fir balsam, and a spring tonic, a spoon
of sulfur & molasses: chickweed is open
in the morning, it's fair; a swallow will
fly low before a rain: if the corn husks
are tight, hard winter; if the geese north
in high numbers, it'll be warmer
                        yeah but ma,
today the doc has calomel, epsom, jalap, &c.,
and they predict weather in the Old Farmer's:
the modern's better
                not by a jugful, Taylor:
Old tales / the signs.
                I promoted her with
letters with news, gossip, jokes & mention
of the mermaid, mailed up from Montgomery?
to the Herald, Charleston to the Mercury,
and Washington to the Sun, and I told each,
Dr. Griffin won't show it, but your paper
is welcome to this capital mermaid woodcut

and caption; it's exclusive to you, no charge,
3 sea graces, lying on salt rocks, combing,
holding up mirrors, bare bosoms, scales below:
oh it was fabulous and pagan, sex for a penny;
next morning, boys sold 10000 circulars / ads,
at ½ my cost, and I trumpeted the Fiji Mermaid,
presented by Dr. Griffin: I played that trick
on the east coast.
     Strip tease: they're hooked.
Lust won't hold under, it sprays out; lay it
down to the sickle, you hymn singers, and it
burgeons; lock it in jail, and it goes crazy,
breaks out, and hoboes into the dear country:
it's our loose cousin, hammering at our door,
for in and kisses, oh! and so good looking.
Straight men, curve women, in our hand me downs
and Sunday black, we are breed of the pilgrims,
all cloaks and cover up, in that stiff winter
with no April, but clothes are liars, and bare
skin, blushing for it, is our constant dream.
I can't remember her
     in grandpa's woods:
ah, I'll show you my crack, if you show me
your bone:
    Oh she & I! freaks to each other
below the waist. I can make out a starling
on a roof, piping, and a crescent of cloud:
it's old summer, and the day goes on & on.
I wanted her, so hard

    down the Old Lane

    her hand

with its fine sweat

                                    that holiday

in 29

        wait till after

                  yes: yes:
                      Rumors of our marriage,
our ship, lost in the Gulf: I danced my 1st
with her, so awkwardly, on New Year's Eve,
played ball all day; I coined / collected
that pun: why won't Barnum & Lind break up?
he's all for getting, and she's for giving.
The papers ragged me, no charity! and I,
who forked out for her give away concerts?
let them rattle: she was so white, they had
to have a blackguard. Ah, free advertising.
I was working on the Congress of Nations,
an ark of specimen men & perfect women
from all countries, my agt. out looking,
and I figured on the back of an envelope:
less risk & more return in that soprano.
I was willing to blow big money to prove
to the world I was solid, and if I busted,
O. K., then for the glory. Wall St. laughed
at me: I mortgaged everything, and squeezed
a contact in Phil. for the last 5 grand.

On the R. R. back I asked the conductor:
you hear that Jenny Lind is coming over
in Aug.?

      Lind, Lind: is she a dancer?

                                 Oh,
no good; I had to spread her. In my memo:
In reply to your: and was the Nightingale
all that agt.'s idea?

                they said you were
just a showman: you'd throw me in a box,
haul me across the States, a quarter/head,
but your flat fee

             what is it that sold you?
it was the mansion, blazing on top of your
letterhead: with a house like that, I knew
you had to be a made man, and not a player:
Irene, the grocery isn't going to make it,
neither: I'm opening a tavern

                oh Barnum,
you're a dirt farmer, bad tailor, in turn,
and we're poor as poverty in an east wind:
why do you go on shifting?

              dear, the thing
is, if we scrimp, with Taylor's makings and
a pinch of profit, we can make do: now sit
right still, Uncle Dud's driving:

              He died,
of fever; his iou to me was void, and his
estate nothing: I had to clerk, where? for
the $ for shoes to wear to his plain funeral.
and I have faith in you. If you make it big,
you're sharp; if not, this time, you're nobody;
all they can say. In the headlines? so what:
that was last yr., not in their short memories;
and luck? it flickers like 4 stars in their
back & forth eyes. Oh Moses, there's no telling;
you're on your own, always, do what you can

in this scant world, it's like up country soil:
it's hard to live on it. Ah, but I'm of it:
I'm a grab all, and what's my cheap excuse?
I'm human.

          Yours, Barnum

               At Keeler's place,
we're hands in pockets on the weathered porch,
puffing out clouds:

            it's a tight race, you go
to the polls?

       I voted straight Federalist,
and if I could sneak by the ballot ladies,
I'd vote again

          oh yeah? go wash your face,
nobody'll know you:

           said old Uncle Jabez,
who never talked!

          by suggestion, the girl
in braids has closed her eyes: now reach,
darling: & what I will, she does; her arms
go up, on ropes / in love: I lick a pinch
of sugar? and she smiles; oh I make passes
down her front, murmur: deep breaths: till
she's mesmerized: now, ladies & gentlemen,
she's beyond pain, all on a/c of my animal
magnetism: watch this:

            Under a constellation
of lace, her breasts / the buds, skin color
of heaven, and she so willing: Charity in bed.
I wanted her, so hard

        the shining horses
          down the Old Lane

the easy picnic

LARRY BECKETT

                        her hand
with its fine sweat

                        independence day
in 29

                              band concert,
I almost   wait till
after   oh hear ye not

what's the matter

                              yes: yes:
That wasn't in winter: I couldn't have
remembered it; my world! I made it up.

453

abracadabra: up paper: I sold everything:
and peacocked: God moon: a man all machine:
the audience: your story, men: where is
that famous: ah there she is: wild & free:
at the brass band: sign this: straw gold

The magician holds up a bag of tricks with zodiac
stitching, saying, I have an old hen in here lays eggs
like anything: he turns the muslin bag inside out, with
nothing in it. He commands the chicken to lay with
3 passes, pulls an egg out from behind the lining, and
shows it. He goes on till 1 egg is left; he palms it and,
trampling the bag, holds up the egg. Is it real, he asks;
all eyes are on it as he breaks it, and, stretching back
with his other hand, switches bags for 1 with a hen.
And now, the invisible hen, he says, abracadabra, and
drops her out, flapping.
                        Fabulous trick:
till 1 day his fool asst. put a rooster
in the other bag.
                        Move on, clear to Natchez:
in the southern night, the horses were solid
enough, out there, hauling our unreal caravan,
old clown holding the reins, acrobat tossing
5 balls by a lantern, and the minstrel and I
in and out of sleep like stars behind clouds,
dream stiltwalkers beside the wagons, beasts
we wished we had, following our sorry circus:
oh flimsy magic on the freight road, rolling.
Our 24 hr. man was strolling in advance,
slapping up paper, and wrote he'd booked us
that night at Lady Hayes' plantation: ah,
we thought of mint juleps & 4 poster beds.
On a through pike, we ran into some down
east boys, out working on the only bridge
over the Oconee? for 16 mi. any direction:
we haggled and they put the planks back on

for show tickets. We paid & they confessed
that they saw our poster, undid the bridge,
and flimflammed us; and the big plantation?
it was a tilting shack on a withered hill:
our banner man, as always, was overwriting.
Old clown:
              well, that's just dandy:
                                  minstrel:
shit:
     and the acrobat:
                       I just dream that
I'm on the road with my monkey and organ:
I go anywhere, and it's good:
                            Our route
was across S.C. swamps, and Ga. roses,
Ala. cotton, Ken. bluegrass, Tenn. bends,
Miss. bayous, &c.: in a long crescent
over the American geography I'd learned
from Uncle Taylor, but I'd had it to here
with the blue highways and the touch & go,
and I sold everything but the band wagon
and 4 horses for a steamboat, and opened up
that floating pavilion on old man river.
                            morning
          with old Turner   white
       steamboat, going
the low Mississippi
                   the bluffs of
                   flying
        mud
                      not enough sleep:
the shells & balls
             play for the

                   his conjuring

that's something, you

          newspaper

                       that so?

I always
1 Sun. in was it Annapolis? I strolled
out in my ready made black suit, all profit,
and peacocked down the sidewalk, citizens
over the shouldering me, must love the suit:
old lecher, so sanctified, and he killed her,
in black, that villain, tar & feather him!
I wondered who, man with a beard hauled me
by the lapels, and 6 showed up with a rail:
we always have gentlemen ride: don't roll
your holy eyes at us, that game don't take
in this country: get on! ah you remember
the stackyard, revd.?

                what? am I dreaming?
what did I do?

             come on, boy, it's 100 of us
and 1 of you: we're going to introduce you
to the lynch law

              I'm not the man, I hate him:
I'm Barnum! I got in last night, in with
old Turner's circus: go ask him, it's a hoax:
The joker was on the gallery, & like to bust
out laughing:

           I'm sorry! but he looks just
like a priest in that suit, might have been him
who hung that factory girl:

                  They all guffawed:
look sharp, old scalawag, and pay him back
in his own coin:

           ah Turner, why on earth

did you monkeyshine me?
                              now we're notorious,
and at the opening, our rag pavilion will
be jammed:
                    It's almost day, the moon kneeling
in the red east, cloud crossed, and shining
over the mountain's cold shoulder: oh spectacle,
what have I done to rival you? It's all
like my seedy beginning, 1 winter night
a man from Bethel at our boarding house
with a note from my bro.:
                              Old Aunt Joice
is gone, her body's outside in the sleigh:
do what is proper.
                    Philo:
                              I parked her in
the cloakroom, & asked a surgeon & editors
in to autopsy her:
                    it's a humbug, Barnum,
she was around 80: I see no hardening of
the arteries
                    no what? proves nothing, Dr.:
is she a tree with rings? how can you tell
her age? I managed her in good faith, sir:
and did that stop Locke from exposing me
in the morning paper? Oh and this from
the moon hoax man, who had the women's clubs
in Springfield? raising seed money to send
our missionaries up to the men with wings
in a spyglass there on the pebble beaches
of the honest to God moon!
                              When did I buy
that shining automaton, a man all machine,
at a fat price, from the master conjurer,
Houdin? I said, image of loyalty: it drew
a dog; old king, with his green umbrella:
what is the pop. of the city of light?

457

it wrote a number.

    Oh the clockwork man,
and old Maelzel, granddaddy of show biz,
windbagging, in a whisper, of his craft,
the ins & outs, in the long nights I sat
at his elbow. With his big name, he had
the ballroom, but I covered panhandler's
heaven with posters, and I packed them in:
the old man had the grace to close, and let
me move into his space. When it thinned out,
I wrote anonymous to the newspapers, fraud:
Aunt Joice was all whalebone, india rubber,
& springs! everyone came back to see it for
themselves.

    The daily rags: oh I played them
like a steam calliope, my at liberty fingers
on black and white columns. As a come on
for the Bearded Lady, I had? an outside man
law me: in court / no, out: it was in court,
4 sawbones, hands on the gospel, testified
she was a woman / mother of the Hairy Boy,
bang! case dismissed: there's your story, men:
Old Hawley, who could blow fire from his mouth,
do magic with strings, keys, rings, ribbons,
and cups & balls, oh and the yarns! delivered
in his iron voice:

    The air in the Rockies, in 1 section,
is so pure nobody dies unless by accident or ah get too
old and are blown away. And there's a kind of museum
where they get registered, and hung up in sacks: I asked
if they might have my uncle Sam, lost in those mtns. it
was going on 30 yrs., and they said sack #367. I paid the
fee, they dipped him in a barrel of lukewarm water, and
we had 20 min. of talk, ah family doings, mostly, till he
got out of breath, and asked to go back in the sack. I said,
before you do, where is that famous ah fishing pole of
yours? and he, it's lying on the crossbeams in your old

man's attic. I said, much obliged:
                              who owned her, originally?
she was George Washington's father's slave:
he sold her in 1727
                    how old was she?
                                   54
wait a minute: that would make her
                              yeah:
she's 162 yrs. old: behind this curtain, ah
there she is:
                In her loose skin, oh mercy,
with her stiff arm, limp legs, no teeth,
no eyeballs, awful bush of wild grey hair,
and nails 4 in. long, she looked 1000 yrs.:
any proof?
                I have here Augustine's b/s;
you see how sallow, look, the folds in it,
almost worn through
                              why wasn't she found
before now?
                    well, she was down in Ken.,
in some outbuilding or other of Bowling's,
who ran across her b/s in the Va. office:
nobody'd known how old she was:
                                   Old clown
on stage doing tricks, and no confederate,
I crowded under the table, and lifting up
the pigeon, I was bit, bellowed and I
straightened up, busting it all to flinders,
the pigeon went squirting into the canopy,
balls rolling / cups breaking, and the mob
hooting; oh, magic is hard.
                              Ah, it goes,
Why come ye hither redcoats?

What is it?

You may ride a something steed,
you may have another master,
you came riding? down with speed
but you'll learn to back much faster.

Oh hear ye not the singing
of the bugle wild & free?
for the rifleman's song at Bennington
is a song? for liberty.

I wanted her, so hard, on independence day
in 29: the boys in town, who'd torn off all
the flimsy gates, hid them in the tall grass,
pitched firecrackers under the shining horses
to make them bolt.

     I held Charity's hand
with its fine sweat, at the hot air oration,
ah the balloon rising! and my heart going
so fast. We ate red watermelon, ice cream,
at the easy picnic, on down the Old Lane;
and in the dark, at the brass band concert,
I almost asked her, and thought, wait till
after the Riflemen's Song, oh hear ye not
the singing, of the bugle wild:

      Charity,
what's the matter, you hold back

        oh Taylor,
I can't hurt you, I love you so: I wish,
ah that I

   will you marry me?

        yes, yes:
how much?

    $3000 on trust

       no, she won't go
at that figure: I'll give you 1000 cash
on Mon.

    I'll touch to that

460

sign here, Barnum:
And I do further covenant, contract, promise and agree
that the possession, ownership,   and proprietor-ship
of Joice Heth, and the right, title, interest, and claim of
exhibiting, staging, and displaying her as aforesaid and
above mentioned, is hereby transferred, conveyed, de-
livered, given, bestowed, conferred, rendered, imparted,
granted, accorded, vouchsafed, yielded, afforded, ten-
dered, extended, issued, committed, consigned, assigned,
relegated, confided, commended, remitted, remanded,
en- trusted, invested, bequeathed, bequested, devised,
entailed, surrendered, ceded, waived, resigned, signed,
and deeded unto the said Phineas T. Barnum, his exec-
utors, heirs, assigns, issue, offspring, do something, help
me, I can't stop, I'll stop, that's that.
                                    I hoped to crack
slavery! Ah, we prayed / we finger crossed
for that Old Dominion black man & his skin
whitening weed, the mo. I what?
                                    The Gallery
of Beauty, and the people voted by tintype
for the dream American woman: the winner,
blonde actress, I forget:
                                    After a spell,
I was down to Jack Diamond, best breakdown
dancer in America, at the sailor's hornpipe,
or ah the highland fling? who ran off with
my fiddler & money, in Mobile, or was it
with a whore outside of St. Louis? and did
I jail that mgr. for false advertising, or
he me for debt, or both?
                                    you find the pole?
Right where he said. 3 yrs. ago this June, I went fishing
Grand Lake with it, and slipping back 1 sundown, I
saw the cabin door wide open. This old black bear, fat,
rolling, was in there wiggling the cork out of a jug with
his teeth. Molasses slopped onto the floor; he licked at it

and rubbed his paw in it. I crawled around back, yelled
in the window, and he hobbled out to the lake on 3 legs,
flopped down, held up his paw till flies and midges were
stuck to it, then waded in to his tall shoulders, and waved
that sugar foot over the surface till a trout jumped, and
he'd slap it up on the sand. When he seemed to feel he
had plenty, I'd only caught 2 that day, I remember, he
came ashore lapping the insects, ate ½ of the fish, laid
the rest in a row, and slogged away, looking back now
& again. I went down to the water, and there were 6
beautiful trout. At the wood's beginning, he stood up
and I called, hey old man, thanks! He waved at me, and
dove into the timber. I believe the fish were to pay for the
molasses. Since then, I don't shoot bears.

                                      by gee,
that's a lie, Hawley!
                      it's true as anything
I've said tonight:
                I'd always try to catch him:
I bet you've never been, in a balloon ascension!
you're wrong, sir, I went up 3 times with Wise
in 32 from Louisville: an altitude record.
I know the man was drawing the long bow.
Summers, I'd lay out a bare oriental rug
on the dry grass, say it's a flying carpet,
let other kids climb on, lift them with words
away from the boring farm, into the heavens,
to Arabia, its mosques and minarets, oh
where the hail's pearls, and the straw gold:
and they'd say, come on, Tale, we're in Conn.,
but I would hoax them: I just made it look
like that, not to scare you: we're in the air.

till his green came: old maid: into a world
unknown: had lost her shawl: low Mississippi:
my arithmetic: no matter: and the star spangled:
shell game: that's beautiful, you: hit on
Broadway: sailors on the: straight hearts, but I

The old charade, of my uncle in whiskey,
living on advances from our cash register
against his not yet due Revolution pension,
the hero in words of a make believe war:
to wipe him off our books till his green came
I shifted him into a duel: muskets? at 20
odd yds., with blank cartridges, I told him,
I had my actor look like gone down hurt,
I whooped, oh uncle, I forgot the blanks!
and he lit out for Guilford. When he came
back and my actor forgave him, he smiled:
didn't I say I was a dead shot?
                                   Old maid
from up to north, into my private office,
and I stood wondering in my long black coat
and stovepipe hat:
                        are you Mr. Barnum?
                                         I am
well, sir, I missed your temperance lecture
in Portland, with a cold
                              you like our museum
as well as Boston?
                        oh dear me! I had always
thought entertainment wicked, till I heard
of your moral drama
                           don't miss the Bible
waxworks down the hall to the theater, ah
I mean to say, the lecture room: oh, there's
the gong right now
                        what, are the services
about to start?

yes, ma'am, the congregation
is going in:
                    seeing, ladies & gentlemen, is
believing: the world's most amazing woman,
Joice Heth, George Washington's mammy! ask
her questions: make sure
                          I'm from the Sun:
can you tell over his birth?
                          little George?
ah, Augustine borrow me from Mrs. Atwood
1 morning: my Lord, what a morning, when
the stars begin to fall: to help to birth
the boy, Feb. 11
                    well, that's not right,
it was the 22nd
                    yes, new style, Richard,
11th, old style: go on
                          in a cold cabin
at Pope's Creek, run into the big Potomac:
I'm going over home
                          from the Evening Star:
he had a brother, John?
                          he what, uh huh,
older: she wife #2, and George the very
1st blessing that Mary had: we go 40 mi.
upriver, to a green farm on a hill: into:
oh Augustine: into a world unknown: go by
Mt. Vernon now
                    the Herald: and the name
of the Fredericksburg land?
                          ah, Ferry Farm?
across the Rappahannock, mighty run down:
no silver, only a sword, a spoon, children:
I'm going to sit at the welcome table
                               Spirit
of the Times: what a memory
                          I raise him, oh

yes, I put his britches on: loud hallelujahs
let us sing:
        Church sidewinding up to state,
after the power; if they went in cahoots,
look out! The Danbury papers all rejected me:
I had to save the U.S. from bad deacons
and weathercocks!
            With press & types, I fired
up the Herald of Freedom & Gospel Witness,
with the 3 graces and Jefferson's Eternal
Hostility on the masthead.
                At my 3rd trial
for libel, I'd slammed on a local believer
who put the squeeze on an orphan, the judge,
that heap of superstitions, scowling, saying
I was a Universalist, all I had done was
print sermons, and citing the Supreme Court
of Errors: all are saved? no fires of hell?
why avoid sin? man's not accountable to God?
well, you can't testify: he sentenced me:
it's $100 and 60 days in the common jail.
The cell: I wallpapered it / I put down rugs,
I edited from inside, martyred: liberty!
Charity, home, pregnant, had lost her shawl.
I bankrolled a museum of 1 in a millions,
sold it for 40 grand, and then it burned:
fire's approach; and Phil. wanted it back;
the old owner was making too much money
at the Adams Express Co.
                Peale's Museum
was doing take offs on my shows and all;
I'd sent a man in nights to size it up:
it was losing. And so I bet the fool mgr.
a century that he wouldn't be open 1 wk.
in the new yr.; he lost, I bought him out
in secret, oh and hired him back to make
more fun of me: publicity! Acts not coming

to terms with me warned of signing with him,
and I 'd say go ahead.
                   1 July morning,
relaxing with old Turner on the white deck
of the steamboat, riding in the channel of
the low Mississippi, by the cattail marshes
and sandbars, under the bluffs of Vicksburg,
all peace, a woodcock flying into the grasses,
oh and the muddy water dimpling and lapping,
I was kind of muzzy from not enough sleep:
the row of shells is banks and the balls cash,
I tell Old Hickory: look sharp: oh, the stars
& stripes, the 8th of Jan., hocus pocus!
I don't see much in that, he says: so much
the better, I say: where are the balls, sir?
under the shells, he says, and up and looks:
under 1 is a paper saying transfer draft,
and another, contingent check, and another,
treasury warrant, and ha! I play it fair,
but not as well as the treasury boys, sir:
drawing the balls out of my pocket: he goes
storming off to Congress
                       the old shell game:
that's beautiful, you make it up?
                          no, P. T.,
I got it out of Downing's letters
                  that so?
I love to read them in the Advertiser:
                      Ah,
the rollicking nights in the old Columbian
circus! A bottle of Spanish, a box of Havanas,
it was a gander party, and Joe / the clown,
who'd throw his voice, sing, sleight of hand,
and balance:
                you bet, Old Turner, but the trouble is
you work 8 hrs./day, 1/3rd of 24: now, 1/3rd of a yr.'s
122 days: you don't work weekends, subtract 2 days

x 52 wks. is 104 from 122 = 18 days: let's say your
vacation's 10 days, leaving 8, the holidays, Xmas, &c.,
= 0, & you don't work at all!

        Sidling in back of
Turner, I winked and said:

         if a man of 30 has a
son, he's 30x older: when the boy's 30, dad's 60, and ah
twice as old: and when the son's 60, the old man's 90,
only a 3rd older: you see? the boy is gaining on him: if
they keep on living, how old will the man be when the
boy catches up?

        They all acted out figuring:
old Turner:

      ain't that a case: huh: I don't know my arith-
metic, but I do know a fast horse will catch a slow who
got the start of it if they go far enough:

  I bet him a doz . of champagne?
it was impossible: bamboozle! and that paid
him back for the black suit joke:

       I tell him
good night stories: give me my pipe, somebody
the Courier: how long you smoked:

        oh, 120 yrs.:
do, Lord, deliver poor me: give me that pipe,
and I tell you: old buzzard ain't got no
sense nohow, look at him: when the rain come
down, he set on the fence, squinch hisself up,
draw in his neck, and try for hide his head:
he look real sorry, cry to hisself: no matter,
when this rain over, build a house bang off,
I ain't going let this rain lick me this way
no more: didn't it rain: when the rain gone
and the wind blow, what that old buzzard do?
set on the top of the dead pine tree, so
sun can warm him, stretch out his wings & turn
and turn, so wind can dry his all wet feathers,
laugh to hisself: this rain done over, ain't

going rain no more, no use build a house now:
fool man like that old buzzard
and that's all
for now, ladies
if I had wings
& gentlemen:
ice creams are available at the round table:
The Triumph of the People:
Barnum Released from Jail

In the courtroom where he was
convicted, an ode written for the
occasion was sung, and an oration
on the 1st amendment given; then
hundreds of gentlemen sat down to
a wild turkey supper with the usual
toasts and speeches. P. T. Barnum
rode home behind 40 riders and
the star spangled banner, in a coach
and 6 horses; a surrey with the day's
pres. and a committee was following
him, and 60 gigs, buggies, runabouts,
rockaways, hansoms, sulkies, phaetons,
broughams, breaks, barouches, flies,
fiacres, 4 in hands, sociables, tallyhos,
hackneys, carryalls, traps, drags, drays,
bandwagons, buckboards, oxcarts,
shays, and carriages, with a 3 gun
salute, the roars of citizens, and a brass
band playing Huzza for free America.
Wait: I left his circus
before I went down river.

morning   summer
with old Turner   white canvas
of the   wagon
not enough sleep:
the cups & balls
play for the

flying over the mudflats
his conjuring

steamboat, going
the low Mississippi

off the bluffs of

lightning
happens

that's fabulous, you

almanac
that so?
I get it
The Hoosier Giant,
the Mammoth Lady, to rights: old photographs
by Matthew Brady, from spang across Ann St.
I love grand opera and the real stage, sin
to the down easters: they itched for plays
but stuck at going into the actual theater;
ah, and how to hoax them in without wounding
their morals? I dreamed up the Lecture Room:
philosophical experiments, Great Western,
the Yankee comic, oh the anatomical Venus,
shows of roses, dogs, birds, & babies, &c.,
and gospel stories, with jokes on scripture

and country songs for the yokels, history
& melodrama, like a sampler, with a motto:
The Drunkard, 1st hit on Broadway to pass
100 shows, virtue in peril always saved
in the last act, performances every hr.,
stars, and cheap tickets, no booze on sale,
teetotal pledge, no whores in the 3rd tier,
and the upright paid the extra quarter at
the box office.
     When that old lady was born
there were sailors on the Mayflower alive,
in the days of the witch trials, 1st woman
hung black, smallpox, and the colonial wars,
Old Fox, Poor Richard, Long Tom, White Horse,
the taxes, the Boston massacre, 1st man
shot black, the tea party, the revolution,
the blessings of liberty, scouts kicking out
west, killing indians, rough keelboating to
the NW territories, the constitution & bill,
whiskey rebellion, Old Ironsides, the war
of 1812, all those millions of $ going for
the creole land, after the black uprising
and yellow fever, tall orations in congress,
money power, what changes: she was a slave
through 12 administrations; presidents were
nothing more to her than horseflies buzzing.
She toughed it out inside her skinny house:
the wars passed by like summer rains, and 5
generations, like fashions, only the stars
identical, and her, remembering her hymns,
oh and lighting her blessed corncob pipe.
She came out of the yellow store and cried
that what's his name of the Hartford Times
had found her shawl.
     My circulation rose.
Ah, why not out with it? That winter morning
it lit and shut, and they did fire off cannons

as I went free, but the touching service
and the grand march I was behind: it looked
so bold in print, but what are newspapers?
yellow, brittle, blown away, all my essays.
I was a rebel against the old liners, blue
laws, straight hearts, but I lost, I lost;
I had to move the Herald down to Norwalk,
sell it: they hated me, my store? I wanted
to make business fly, and I trusted out
too much, my ledger was red with bad debts,
By failing, in full, lotteries outlawed,
Caroline born, and hungry. Charity had
to leave her weeds, ladyfern, loosestrife,
swampgrass, cattails, black eyed susans,
queen anne's lace, 1 day, and we moved on
to the Big Apple.

gold blvds.: but on the drift: 1st night,
uneasy: and the 7 seas: who caught her:
in other words: free ticket: a mystery: I:
in the slapdash: our voices off the: I was
a shoemaker: fold up the circus: back door

                I was starving for air,
the wind knocked out, by the cold bastard, ah
and squealing:
            I can't breathe:
                          he slugged me
again: I'd shot firecrackers in his parlor,
the landlord slammed me, at the Bull's Head?
where the $ ma had slipped me I spent
on oranges and trouble. That Southbury man
at our poor tavern, looking for a cowboy
to foot it down to Ridgefield and round up
a sight of cattle, and I promoted myself:
I wanted out of that backwater so bad,
I was chasing an ox in the Jan. snow,
Mrs. Brown's horse rolled on my ankle, and
I held my tongue. I was going to York!
with its gold blvds., hotels in clouds.
The lady said 4 pence for the 2 oranges,
which is Conn. by the ½ real, old coin,
for 6 pennies: I talked her down to 5.
I hit the bartender, no! with a stick gun;
he up and walloped me till my head rung.
Not hungry, so downhearted, I went trading,
for an old fashion watch: out / in again,
to swap, 1 thing another, that hard candy,
oh anything for more. After a 1 horse sleigh
to home, my stockings, &c., gone for candy,
ma whipped me solid, but in my room, burning,
I'd seen it: Broadway, the poplars, the docks,
the market, the windmill, and the real prison.
I'd act up, on the road with the 4 man circus,

like in the country store, but on the drift:
we'd blaze in & fade out; I'd leave a horse
at this hotel, a wagon at that, for rent,
high sheriffs chased me with lawsuits, pals
absconded with the money, red men lifted
their bows. I got into a rumpus with a hog
drover:
   whoa! damn it, you horse thieves
have done it now: my pigs are everywhere
you were hogging the road
       apologize, mister,
or I'll make this pistol talk, and blow you
clear through
     I tell you what, let me work
it out back in the wagon with my partner:
I know I can satisfy you
       all right
         you see,
my partner is a shotgun, cocked: you think
life's cheap, well, choose between a load
of shot and a pardon me
       I'm sorry I have
a gun, I ain't that smart
       I'm with you there:
it'd save lives if we were to go unarmed:
       1st evening, uneasy,
        Gardens,

   gaslights
all the way down
    into the barroom, boys

      wisecracks,
  girls going
      organ grinder
the pavement,

     colors hanging,

hotel,

summer

into a country road.
Why did I 1st go through her doors? Oh, for
the hydro oxygen microscope, & a sales talk:
right on Broadway, the American Museum was
losing, oddities from across the country
and the 7 seas, all up for sale: ah, but
I saw it alive! and I approached the owner:
you front the money, I'll run the business,
and if I miss 1 payment, I'll forfeit all:
my references were news editors, show mgrs.,
circus owners; when he asked for security,
I put up Ivy Island.

     Now the woman / fish
I never owned, but hired from Moses, and
I kicked back 1/2 : where did he get her? Ah,
that sea capt. bought her off an infidel
who caught her in his net.

     1 sabbath in
N. Carolina, I sermoned in a pine grove:

       Oh why is it a
cold town, bare benches, down here, when I do a show?
You believe the circus is sinful: but look at how the old
clown's pure trickery tells you stick to the truth, not
appearance; when the acrobat flies through the air, the
Lord protects him; and the minstrel's hit songs are all hal-
lelujah in other words:

     Light applause, it was hopeless;
downplay all that.

     At Boston, the promenade
tickets had squeezed in 1st: they had to roll
the piano man over their heads to the stage.
It was a firebox, what was it? old railroad
depot: they had to bust the windows for air,

and the Nightingale's voice was lost in all
the caterwauling, line bristling outside,
the entrances too skinny, oh and the rumor
the floor was buckling on the tracks under!
At that, the standing room only went crazy,
kicked through a wall: I hallooed calm down,
and exited / came back for Jenny: they rammed
their fists up to me and bawled, money talks!
The blue police did nothing in the hurlyburly;
I smiled: your money back, and a free ticket:
no riot.
            I sold ½ the circus to a rag man,
the tuba player told the barber shaving him
steal away to the free states, and got 6 mos.
in the calaboose, the black singer skipped out,
I went on in blackface and did Old Zip Coon;
hard push, but they encored me. After the show,
in a ruckus outside the tent, I backed my men;
this local boy dragged out a silver 6 shooter
and cocked it:
                    nigger, you don't talk like that
to a white man:
                    Oh, too absurd a way to go;
quick, I rolled up my sleeve:
                            I'm white as you
oh glory:
            He dropped his gun:
                            I beg your pardon:
Ah, poise! I owe my salvation from pistols
and accidents to that and heaven's mercy,
the circus riders and the back street women;
I'd be in the low life if I'd surrendered
to that snake medicine, though I did drink:
I'm just a showman, you're the scientist,
is it a hoax?
                I, I, I don't see how it was
faked, ah, see the fingers?

uh huh
                    not like
any known monkey: the fins?
                    uh huh
                         not like
any known fish
                    so: why say it's a fake?
yes ah, it, it, because I don't believe
in mermaids
                    what logic: you put on airs
of knowledge, but the naked world's a ball
of mystery: well, I do believe in mermaids;
I'll advertise our odds, & they can judge:
Mornings, she'd be in the slapdash kitchen,
that ex pool hall, and Helen baby talking
in her arms, fixing me a corn beef sandwich,
1 handed, to skimp till the new Museum was
paid off: her love's real money.
                         I remember:
1 morning, it had to be summer, I'm riding
around with old Turner, in the white canvas
of the circus wagon, and kind of muddled,
not enough sleep: he's working that old con,
the cups & balls, he called it thimblerig,
and asking me to play, bur for the actual;
green Pennsylvania is sliding by outside,
with a bobwhite flying over the mudflats,
and he screws me up with his mumbo jumbo:
oh, I'm at the stern of a double barrel
steamboat, going, you know, free & easy,
down the low Mississippi, talking politics
with my salt water friend: I hear a boom,
wind blows: storm coming, says the captain;
no, it's a big paddlewheel, says my pal;
it's our voices off the bluffs of Vicksburg,
I say, but the water's squirming, our boat
seesawing, it's skreaking like a waterfall,

the trees walk out and the houses lift up,
ah, folks are going to heaven heels 1st:
it's the Natchez tornado, ribs of our boat
stove in; lucky for us, a streak of lightning
just happens by, I catch it by the fork,
swing on, my pal behind, grease it up with
rattlesnake oil, and we exit the county
in astonishing style
                on the back of the bolt,
that's fabulous: you make it up?
                    no, P. T.,
I read it in Crockett's almanac
                  that so?
out of Nashville, I get it faithfully:
I was hoping to sign that old firebrand
Anne Royal, whirling her green umbrella
at the Capitol, indicted for her black
book & acquitted from the ducking stool,
to the lecture circuit, against the powers:
I ran into old Turner:
              I'm living proof
you can make barrels of money if you wish:
I don't know who on earth I am, or where
I'm from, no schooling: I was a shoemaker:
I learned to write by signing iou's: boy,
I busted my ass: and look at my bankroll!
and that's the secret, Barnum: go ahead,
dream big:
          Our steamboat, the Ceres, who
is the blessing lady: Want shall shun you,
look it up: I'd have no cook after Natchez,
& hired her unsure lover to get her hitched
by the next morning. Down river, this drunk
hurt me with a slingshot, after lying he'd
paid me, and rounded up a gang of keelboat
men, with rifles and sticks, to muscle me.
Was that the time the trumpet? no: it was

outside of Louisville, guns pulled, the mate
and the band fighting, I was breaking it up:
that player slapped me so hard I was starry:
come on, you ape, I said, you're making money:
I got the mayor, on the boat, to go between
the roughs and us: 1 hr. to strike canvas,
fold up the circus, all aboard, and sail,
no help: and they sashayed us, roaring, oh
with pitch pine torches, on our last load,
and as the boat swung out, all yelled hurrah.
At Opelousas I traded the steamboat / circus
in for molasses, and dragged home for good.
I believe I'd gone everywhere in the U.S.A.,
and so I left it all the high pitchmen,
the circuit riders, and the tent shouters:
I'd let it come to me.
                        She'd make me strip
the willows to switch me; I'd hide and seek
in the fields of threat: oh she was always
hissing, but by my skin, she was the wicked,
and not my ma after the 1st hit.
                            Out from
under the rising sun quilt, & up invisible
stairs, I saw her bang out the back door
crazy to whip me, ah, but nothing doing:
she clawed, short of my heels; I laughed
over the withered yard and the red fence;
I walked on air above her: fire on the mountain,
fire on the sea, you can't catch me: old dream.

girls going: the hr. / the bells: from now
on: a feather in: my hat: to live in fire:
the grand hotel: free music: in a circle:
into the air: the local: nonsense, it's
only: like pearls on down: reading the Sun

                        evening, restless,
                              Gardens
             gaslights

                     into the barroom, boys

               nothing happening
     girls going

the pavement,
                   colors hanging,
          hotel,

    summer   organ grinder

into a country road
                The tramp, in black,
all belly, laid a brick down on the sidewalk
at Broadway & Ann St., 1 by Astor House,
1 cattycorner, 1 outside St. Paul's, and 1
last he swapped for the 1 at the crossroad
for the 1 up the block for the 1 cattycorner
for the 1 by the church, no words, repeat,
and on the hr. / the bells clanging, he walked,
with a mob after, into the tolerable dark
wood halls, wide stairs, freaks & phenomenons
of the new Museum, till a blue cop made me
stop blocking the sidewalk with the mystery,
and I paid the tramp off: he'd only come in
to bum a nickel:
              museum or no, Mr. Barnum,

they're St. Paul's poplars, and you can't, ah
it's sacrilegious for you to tie your flags
to them
                    are you English or what? haul down
Old Glory on the 4th of July? hey, deacon,
I'd like to see you dare
                              look, islander,
Barnum is right: you want to save your bones,
you better slope
                        I'm not, ah ha, all right,
I'm going
                    yeah, and you: from now on, clergy
pays full in the American Museum:
                                            Ah late,
bless it: after the fireworks were touched off
& the smoke blown, the sidelong stars all down
and the 4th over, is when I made my entrance,
back in 1810, the year, I don't know what,
in Bethel, Fairfield Co., Conn.; that name
is indian for the river of pines, my cradle.
I was fattened on holy pokes and maple sap,
in the country of the whapperknocker, oh
the Windham bullfrogs and the Moodus noises,
where the humility bird can see the spark
and outfly a gunshot, & the dew mink sings,
and Mrs. Fitch, of Norwalk, stuck a feather
in her bro.'s? cap, & he was Yankee Doodle:
hey Barnum, what piss in the ocean price
for this here jackknife?
                              ah, 4 bits
                                        horseshit,
it ain't worth ½
                    well, I
                              excuse me, sir,
but I'm afraid it's my duty to fine you
$1 for cursing
                    ha! I'm a Knickerbocker,

and I don't give a turd for your Conn.
blue laws
            that'll be $2
                        excuse me, sir,
but who the hell are you?
                        I'm Seelye, justice
of the peace, $3
                you're kidding: oh my jesus,
what an asshole! oh shit, I swore again:
my hat! what's that, a quarter? holy gee!
what am I doing in this jerk off town?
get fined by a little bastard, ah piss
on you! I'm obstropulous? son of a bitch,
I don't believe you god damn yahoos
                        $11
what? oh for crap's sake, I'm about to blow
my top and swear! you blue skin, limp dick,
ass kissing, what am I up to?
                ah, $15
here's 20, you old fart, & keep the change:
I think I'll be cursing it off damn quick:
I had old Lyman walk on in a false beard:
Ladies & businessmen, boys & playgirls, hello, salaam,
and welcome to the opera house: I am Dr. J. Griffin, of
Pernambuco, agt. for a museum of natural, I don't know
what, in the old country, and I'm here on Broadway to
exhibit, not for gain but your gratification, items bagged
in the blank regions of the terrestrial globe, all speci-
mens which are double in anatomy, the missing links in
the chain of species. Ah! look on in wonder at the mud
iguana, from the mountains of the moon, the platypus, ½
seal, ½ duck, I captured down under among the aborig-
ines, in a long battle, the salamander, able to live in fire,
caught in a blue grotto, and the paddle tail snake I invei-
gled from the hokey pokey tribe along the king of rivers,
at a considerable risk, oh and the flying fish, from the gulf
stream. And last, the star of the bizarre collection, taken

in the nets of a heathen chinee fisherman in the southern
seas, and worshipped as a god in the celestial empire: gee
whillikers, it's ugly! the only mermaid!
We saw Vivalla, the prof. of equilibrium
and plate dancing, paralyzed on the left,
with a smart dog that ran a spinning wheel:
we gossiped about old tours, and gave him
$500 and a ticket home; she sang to him.
He died, in the Herald, later, thanking us:
sir, I don't mind you hissing Sr. Vivalla,
that's all behind us, I'm glad you answered
the $1000 challenge, it was to you: ah, now
the point is you lose if you don't match all
his tricks, like it says in the newspaper:
you can spin plates, but 10 at once? or balance
a broomstick, ah on the tip of your nose?
can you stiltwalk, and aim & shoot a musket?
you can toss balls, but he's a hocus pocus:
it's not a Yankee trick, you read the ad:
don't get your back up, I can be a friend:
ah, Green's circus is closed now, right?
you can lose a grand, or make $30 / night:
go on stage vs. Vivalla, make it look real,
play beat, then challenge him to juggle
next night: is it a deal? sign right here:
and our recpts. jumped through the roof.

1st evening, restless,

no reason, I walked from the   Gardens,
gaslights like pearls on down,

into the barroom, wise

ass boys
     full of cocktails, nothing happening,
    girls going by
loud wheels

on the pavement,
    tall flagpole   colors hanging,

and past the grand hotel,

     summer   a poor organ grinder
with his   monkey, out where
     country road
4 stories, and at the tip top, calcium lights
showered Broadway, ice cream was served up
in the aerial garden, the stars & stripes /
banners flying by the mystery windows, images
of all birds & beasts in creation, balcony
with free music, an out of tune brass band
doing bad marches to drive the citizens of
the city of fools inside: and I'd skyrocket:
                      The American Museum
                      open at sunrise
          admittance 1 quarter, children ½ price:
                under this roof you'll see
     arithmetic horses, educated dogs, trained fleas
             wild cranes, flamingos
         anacondas, yaks, camelopards
          white tigers, old baboons
          gypsies, dwarfs, albinos
            giants, fat boys
     American indians in battle and prayer
           dissolving views
         dioramas of the creations
          and the flood
         storms, waterfalls
       models of cities, live statues
       minstrels, rope dancers, jugglers
     marionettes, pantomimes, ventriloquists
        fortune tellers and Yankees
   glassblowing, mechanical looms, photography, &c.
      and an advertising curtain on a new scale!
She was a pygmy growing out of a salmon,
sea demon in rigor / in agony, her skin
all black, wrinkled, 1 frail hand up to

her cheek, and 1 curled on her flat paps,
lips in a circle, baring her awful teeth,
scales down her hairs, and a frayed tail
twisting back along her.   The wooly horse
was foaled in Ind.?: it was a cross between
a camel for hair, deer legs, elephant tail,
and jumped 12 ft. into the air. The papers
said Col. Fremont, missing so long / lost
in Rocky Mt. snows, was found: I said
he'd captured it, Sen. Benton sued me
for false pretenses, arguing the animal
was nowhere in the explorer's letters,
and the judge threw it out. I let it loose
in my acres: folks riding the local saw
the wooly horse out eating Barnum's grass.
At last, I went on stage:
                                the Nightingale
has told me in secret tonight's gate goes
to the Fire Dept., Musical Fund Society,
Poor Women Home, Colored Orphan Asylum,
and the Underground R. R.: all because,
she says, the tickets are too expensive!
she's blessed America:
                                Their hearts, their wallets:
the songbird, scared and pious, the divine Jenny,
for sale, 10¢: oh bonnets, shawls, gloves, robes,
chairs, couches, pianos, cards, whiskeys, horses,
rags and polkas.
                                I can't seem to say why
I tried all hollow 3 mos. like a jackass
to keep the Crystal Palace World's Fair
from crashing, like building a R. R. to
the moon: 1500 players doing the Messiah
and the crowd of 40000 drowning it out,
mock fire of fireworks outside the dome,
the choir hooting Hay day at the firemen,

the orchestra squalling, the monster concert!
With a bad location, bad mgmt., it was dead,
not to be raised: move it to Boston Common
as a convention center: what are you saying,
Barnum? I sloughed it off, and I made ought.
It burned: fire's warning:
                                    why in tarnation
that flag?
            calm down, Lyman, you old sixpence:
everyone on Broadway knows where to catch
the mermaid
                    well, I have to do the pitch,
and it gets tight with a flag 6 yds. long
for a monster that's 1
                            nonsense, it's only
to draw them in, and they know it: it cost
$70
      Barnum, maybe you can fight under
that flag, not me
                        you win, you win: it's down:
                                1st evening, restless,
no reason, I walked from the Battery Gardens,
on the sidewalk, gaslights like pearls on down,
      dog barking   last block
of ice   into the barroom, wise
ass boys in their turn down collars
      full of cocktails, nothing happening,
          girls going by in blue silk ribbons,
a pair of horses   hack cab, loud wheels
on the pavement, by the market, pineapples
          tall flagpole and the colors hanging,
      past the grand hotel, the bowling alley,
the oyster cellar, the lecture room,
      summer   and a poor organ grinder
with his   monkey, out where
          country road
I'm in the ticket office, reading the Sun,

this buck in old sailor's clothes, loitering,
and a whaling Narrative in his back pocket:
1, please
        all right, sir
                is Mr. Barnum in
the Museum?
            that's him
                that's him?
                      it's me
that's it: I got my money's worth:
                  He threw
his ticket away.

catch buffalo: bald eagle? alive: and bang!
American coins: you spring to it: the grand
moon's only: band blowing: the ocean, flirting:
out the window: like pearls: so early: and ah
prize ponies: world's fair: he's a big fake

Grand Buffalo Hunt
free!
at the Stevens racecourse
near the Hoboken ferry
on Thu., Aug. 31, @ 3 o'clock:
watch Mr. French,
the wild west scout,
with perfect riding & better roping
catch buffalo
by lasso
from the vicious bunch
he captured out in New Mexico.
This true sport of the Great Plains
will present absolutely no danger
to the ladies & gentlemen
because of the double railing
around the field:
music by a brass band.
In case of rain, the event will happen
at the same hr., the 1st fair day.

Dear Moses,
          I avgd. $70 / day last wk.,
     sorry you   do less.
The ourangoutang's sick,   indians contrary,
& the prop man wiffling   I was greedy,
     Thumb south, but you advanced the bitch
          and put her on as enchantress,
     ah well, some pork will boil that way,
     bear it   in the knitting machine
   dog power   more poetry than reality.
50 / mo. is too high, get the fat boy down,

what is that monster, and I mean yesterday,
and not the Chinese juggler, or can he work
on a short stage   it for 15 / wk.,
no expenses? Go   whip Miss Darling
    you've a mind to   Forget the seduction,
give her a break,   yours truly.
It was the dr. who leaked the story of her
in the insane asylum to the Times, I think.
The mermaid box   my office, after
the brouhaha in the   the scientifics
& preachers in a   What do I do, fire
all & sundry, and go on the boards myself?
What are you asking for a little horse:
touch me like a Xtian. You want a dead
bald eagle? I bought 2, shot on Long I.
          Dr. Valentine opens Mon.
Yours for ever & a day,

           Barnum

                Fire smudged.
My strategy was plow the 1st yr. profits
back into advertising, but I made things
hum, and the money streaming in so fast,
it was hard to stick to.
              I got big bones
from 10 odd places made into a skeleton,
to bury in Ohio / somewhere, a yr. or so,
dig up by accident, but 1 keen morning
I saw Tom Thumb.
              1 day, in a light pinched
close by winter, I was on the way home
from Albany on business, the grey Hudson
iced over? and the riverboat shut down:
I jumped on the old Housatonic R. R. and
come on to Bridgeport, looked up Philo in
his quiet hotel:
          ah, being as I'm here,
you have an abbreviated boy?

ah, that's
old man Stratton's kid:
He was knee high,
2'1", it's true as you're alive: and bang!
I signed him up, 3 bucks / wk. for 1 mo.,
in case he got to growing. Yrs. later, in
the south, I was approached about a giant
skeleton for 20 grand; I looked into it:
it was my old hoax.
The rain, opening day:
I'd gone in with the wholesale buyers I met
in Mr. Taylor's grimy Brooklyn grocery,
and bought & sold a porterhouse for profit:
I like American coins, not in my fist,
but sliding through my fingers: when I was
over smallpox, I opened the yellow store
in ½ of grandpa's stable? The day before,
in church, I was anxious it might rain:
nobody'd buy oh my cakes, combs, rings,
oysters, & ale.
I love my mixed up house
in all weathers: 2 hrs. from the big city
by the New Haven railway, 4 by steamboat,
in Bridgeport, booming in 46, was the 1st
of many mansions. I told the architect,
like that new pavilion of your old king,
ah, but take the shine off it: you spring
to it, don't show me bills; it'll boost
the Museum. After 2 yrs., I rolled up in
my coach, its motto Love God & Be Merry,
and gazed: the iron fence, bronze deer,
the shipped in timber, and Spanish cocks,
Egyptian geese, Mandarin ducks, English
swans, cows, pigs named for the royalty,
shells, roses, and the shooting fountain,
on 17 acres, ah! Iranistan: ½ Byzantine,
½ Moorish, in red / brown sandstone, 1001

at the warming looked up into the rainbow
dome & the minarets, oh the sharp spires,
28? arcade windows tied to the new patent
burglar alarm, in artificial heat, into
the 4 seasons parlor, 7 arts dining room
with the French porcelain, Russian silver,
Arabesque wood, Indian silk, Chinese maple,
like I had bought the globe, & up the grand
stairs in a curve, by the Italian marbles,
into the lush apartments, in all periods,
with orange satin walls and rosewood tables:
a hurrah's nest, a house of mirrors, gold
leaf patterns, in the gaslight, oh the water
works, the avenues, and a star observatory
in the dome, where I looked out on the grey
mist lifting from Long Island Sound.

                                    Salt tears
at Sandy Hook, with the steamer bells ringing,
last words on the old wharf, her kiss, his slap,
and our ship tugged, and the city brass band
moaning No place like home, my business all
wrapped up, I'm there to float, for 19 days
over the salt Atlantic: ah, you ever hear
about the ghost ship that sailed in the air
above New Haven harbor? the long low swells,
and the grand piano on board, in the chaos
of foam, pure spectacle, and the blue moon
again in a hotel room in that port town,
where the waxworks man said 10 bucks / wk.,
no letters at the desk, no voice I know,
in a strange country, oh starting at 0,
with nothing but Tom Thumb.

                                  Unchanging boy
in his cocked hat and wig, his swagger coat,
britches, silk stockings, pumps and a sword
at his side, oh! singing Yankee Doodle and
dancing, saying? I only get it in snatches:

I am Tom Thumb
                              & don't wear hand me downs:
I climb a ladder to the kitchen table
& breakfast on a strawberry
                        nobody cares:
I live in the world's under, and to me
our rosebush is a big tree
& if it rains, I stand under a horse.
I fall in love with women's knees
            I like to bobsled
on a roof shingle, & ride home on a goose
              I'm a squirt, always, and I go
for dribs & drabs: 1 aria's an opera,
1 kiss a romance, & 1 sky, in clouds,
any day, is a philosophy;
I'm next to nothing, & my words are air,
but the moon's only a little farther away
from me than you:
I saw the citizens of Manhattan up early,
on the Hudson ferry at 10 a.m., the brass
band blowing to divert them, till 3 o'clock,
the scout in feathers & buckskin, in a barn
and jabbing at the little buffaloes to get
them fiery and following them out, where
they just huddled together in the dry grass,
tired out from the drive, till the hubbub
and all swinging their hats and hallooing
spooked them, look out! The buffaloes broke
down the thin fence, crowd every which way,
the animals nowhere / holed up in a swamp;
he lassoed 1 and hauled it out, squalling,
and that was it, the Grand Buffalo Hunt:
oh hurray anyhow, it's free; ah, and I had
the ferry concession.
                        Dear Moses,
                                  I swear
I had to get on the Great Western and

steam back or I'd go crazy, with Charity
howling like all get out as I was gone
when the baby quit breathing, baby born.
She was against my stomping to a fiddle
on grapes, and hitting that cantina by
the ocean, flirting with a dark senorita:
I said, O. K., I won't have a private life.
I wangled 1st refusal on Old Shake's birth
house, to ship to the American Museum: it's
a butcher's! I shook them into saving it.
Under the sign: Is it man or beast? Zip,
the man monkey, the human fly, the pinhead,
barking, eating cigars, making coins vanish:
Ch. Dickens looked in: what is it? I clapped
my hands: that's what it is, a what is it!
I've inscribed Go Ahead! on the blue door
of Tom Thumb's carriage, and with his ponies
he knocked them dead! They didn't survive it:
oh and the merchandising! his lithograph,
life & souvenirs on sale, waltzes & songs,
comedies, dolls, and all Tom Thumb. The salt,
the high steppers, everybody & his bro.
have to see him: pay $30 / day, earn $460,
split ½ with his hold man, $215 in the clear.
I own him, sell him 1000s of times, never
deliver him: not bad for small potatoes;
and nights, I need a cab to lug my silver.

Where's the last page? Cut out that wine
part: it won't go with my teetotaling.
The lease expiring, the owner said he'd turn
the Museum into offices, to scare me up
to higher rent. I said, O. K., I'm expanding
down the block, and scared him into renewing.
Boys were climbing in the windows, and I
was up and after them, Tom Thumb on stage:
I feel as big as anyone: a man in rags

crawled in. I was hauling him out, his hands
at my windpipe, the Genl. making faces
at him. I slugged him with a cane, got him
to the police, slipped back to the hotel.
That afternoon? my daughter had been blowing
bubbles out the window.
                              1st evening, restless,
no reason, I walked from the Battery Gardens,
on the white way, gaslights like pearls on down,
kicking the pigs on the sidewalk, last block
of ice being dragged into the barroom, boys
ah, slouching by the door in their turn down
collars, full of cocktails, nothing happening,
saluting girls going by in pink silk tassels,
a pair of horses and a hack cab, loud wheels
on the worn stones, at the market, pineapples
for sale, tall flagpole and the colors hanging,
and past the grand hotel, the oyster cellar,
the red brick lecture room, the bowling alley,
the summer theater, and a blue organ grinder
with his poor monkey, out where Broadway turns
into a country road.
                              I'm up & doing so
early I bump into myself going to bed,
and, stoking up on chocolate & rolls, &c.,
writing my to do list with my quill pen
in my daily remembrancer, answering mail,
business calls only, ride out at noon,
survey my acres, and back for hamburgers,
alone or with, catnap as good as hrs.,
train into the City, skimming the papers,
cab to the Museum, crackling with ideas
for acts & ballyhoo, check out the books,
across to Astor House for appts., & down
to Wall St. for the whirl of greenbacks, back
home to supper, read Herman Melville's laughs
on me in Yankee Doodle, whist with whoever,

& head for bed at 10, the neighbors yawning:
where's your wife gone to?
                              oh no, I forgot
to put Pick up wife in my blessed daybook!
wake up the coachman, and harness the team!
that minds me of this high tone city man, with a new rig
and ah prize ponies, comes tumbling down our country
road
                    hey bud, how do you get to Ridgefield?
how'd you know my name?
                              what? I guessed it
                                             oh?
guess how
              look, where's this road go?
                                        nowhere, it
stays right there
                    how far to the next town?
                                             never
measured it
              is there a sign?
                              I don't know as I know
don't know much, do you, hayseed
                              ain't lost
                                        tell me:
is this the road to Ridgefield?
                              ah yeah
                                        thank you:
giddap!
              but your horses are going in the wrong
direction:
              Hotels out on the road
paid me to let the Nightingale stay in them,
at my expense! And on April Fool's, I sent
false telegrams to the whole crew, with folks
come cousining, offers from the world's fair,
and news of fires & births, printing the hoax
in the morning paper.

Ah, my ticket taker
didn't know me:
what kind of house last night,
at that big talk?
oh, full up: Barnum draws
good speech?
I don't know: ah it was on his
humbug philosophy:
You say it's flummydiddle? ha:
Promise everything for next to nothing is the world's
way: O. K., if I puff harder, my flags more patriotic, and
my bills gaudy, my ads outdacious, my woodcuts bigger
lies, hinting my falls are tall as the original, nobody said
they were gypped out of a quarter, kids ½ price, at the
American Museum, ever. I am the prince of humbugs,
not liars: I'm out to dazzle.
I was out
in front: they laughed
odd stitch?
I guess
he's up to tricks
oh, you know him?
I what?
not to talk to: his stage door man lets me
in free
he's too tight for such goings on
ah but the old screw's in the dark
that so?
I saw Barnum on the owl train last wk.:
this man, not knowing him, goes on & on
to his face how he's a big fake, Barnum
nodding, allowing it's true, till it dawns
on the sap who the hell he's talking to,
and you, sir, can imagine he felt pretty
damn flat
oh, yes: I, I: oh my, you're
Barnum

the 1 & only:
>   I've always been
in the country store.

well water: you love our country: outside
her window: the Man of Signs: this campaign:
page, missing: into a rainbow: Noble said buy:
was flying: music: any old stories: grand
total: firemen: the odds & ends: all, over

My friends: In the mosaic of a life that is a "strange, event-
ful history," as the bard said, of struggles & triumphs,
whether in a king's castle in the old country or a lean to
in the Americas, I have without fail looked back on the
dear memory of the village of my birth. Why, I can see, as
if yesterday, the hard working
                                              We ate pot luck
of salt pork and potatoes, root vegetables,
onions, now & again: rain waiter, to wash,
well water, to cook: and boiled together
till noon, in the iron pot, up hanging in
the fireplace: if it goes out, take tongs
to the neighbors, at daylight, for a coal
to kindle with: amazing fire, banked up;
in the ashes, red brands: what did we eat?
We had bean swagger, rye bread, applesauce
and hasty pudding on wooden dishes, clams,
and shad in season. And now I'm particular
                                              is all, her
temperance. And now, my friends, it is with pleasure I
offer this fountain to the town of Bethel, in evidence of
the love I bear her, and the honor I have for my forebears,
and the now & future citizens of my native village. Thank
you:
I'm Walter Whitman, from the Daily Eagle,
and ah
          sit down, sit down: what do you want
to cover?
              well, I read your letters to
the Atlas
              and?

        we're both inkslingers, @
1¢ / line
       oh I give it my all, freelance
from wherever I am, on the opening road
what, over there?
           I did rub elbows with
the queen of England, &c., the big noises,
if you
      ah, did you see anything across
the ocean that shifted, or made you love
our country less?
          oh Whitman, in the old days
I was back & forth, across our raw states,
and overseas, it's ice, it's kings & customs:
in America, it's sprawl, and freedom, men
& women in the thick sun
            splendid: I tell you,
that speech, you could work it up into a book:
               Salt tears
at Sandy Hook, with the steamer bells ringing,
last words   her kiss
and our ship tugged, and the city brass band
moaning No place like home
            19 days
over the salt Atlantic

and the grand piano   in the chaos

of foam, pure spectacle, and the blue moon
again in a hotel room in that port town

no letters   no voice
in a strange country, oh starting at 0,
with nothing but Tom Thumb.
      The Nightingale Lights:
       Jenny Lind Arrives

Her ship, the Atlantic, steamed in
on Sunday, and docked at Canal
St. She threw the American flag a
kiss at the old wharf, thronged with
thousands. With a man overboard
and the dock gates splintering, she
disembarked by evergreens hung with
Old Glory, and a welcome arch with
a bald eagle. Daffodils were tossed at
her carriage on West St. where P. T.
Barnum in the high box was his own
advertisement. Later, his Great Asiatic
Caravan, Museum, & Menagerie, with
elephants hooked to chariots, walked
up Broadway, Tom Thumb in charge.
The Musical Fund Society played
Hail Columbia outside her window all
night: red shirt firemen with lanterns
sang. This reporter has learned all this
was not spontaneous but staged by
I know, I know: the humbug. N. Y. had never
seen anything like it, and now all we had
to do was hear her sing.
                        What was my A B C?
I read! on sabbath morning, the folks asleep,
no chores for hrs.: the Weatherwise Almanac,
with the Man of Signs, arrows from his body
to the stars, & the fool stories, I believed,
and Kendall's Travels, down east into words,
across the pine tree and green mt. states,
and Irving's History, off color jokes told
by an imaginary man, and Dexter's Pickle,
with the art of money making, and ma's books,
cast off, and in my room: Homer's Odyssey,
in prose, said the old world & the bronze age
are inside me, and the red Phil. edition
of Wm. Shakespeare showed me what dreams

can coil in language, 1 midsummer night.
This campaign, like none in history, I had
to go national, wild reviews, cheap rags
on nothing but her, & letters keying on
her charities for those innocent of music,
dated 10 days after they were published.
I had her do a contest for an ode to sing,
& most of them weren't fit to feed the pigs:
Bayard Taylor, whose Faust is on my desk,
was the winner, inspired by a fast buck.
Ah, I put on a ticket auction only so it
would be reported: in the downpour, I told
this hatter, next door, you get the 1st,
& tripled his business. It's the 1st time
tickets were scalped: I upped her share
in our contract. No odds in that, or did
she ask me that 1st night? Oh tear it up:
I'd sign anything for her.

     In Sun. school,
I wrote essays 2 yrs. for tickets, and all
for what? a 10¢ book.

     The 1st page missing:
you're holy, Uncle Sol! do me this favor
and be rewarded in this world or the next:
mail all these out to the press, I haven't
read them. Why, even the Savior had John
the Baptist as his advance man, why not
old Sol to light the way to Crescent City?

     Yours truly, P. T. Barnum
P. S. If I'm the whole team and the dog
under the wagon, shouldn't I write my tall
story, like you?

     1st rehearsal, the Battery
guns boomed: gold state, joining the Union.
Oh 1000s! check the number, of the high hats
sat down, as stiff as church: ah the sea air
coming up the Narrows, the bridge, the island,

and the old fort, the by Goddest opera house
in the U.S.A., open on time / early. With
2 police lines; inside, I zoned the Garden
into a rainbow: boys & gaslights that matched
ticket & stub; and outside, rowdies in boats
pig whistling while / before the Nightingale,
the audience on fire to worship themselves
worshipping her.
     In my long fight, I backed
the Fire Annihilator, that could whistle out
blazes, and sold machines & territory, for
big rolls. Apes at the demonstration knocked
the inventor over, and the building burned.
Oh, fakery! it made me more $ than truth:
I was famous for it, and hurt the project.
Any salesman would keep the money down,
but I was a showman, and lost 10 grand.
Noble said buy ½ int. in the 50 acres
he'd come into, and more in more, and we
might slap up a new city, E. Bridgeport:
pour in 1000000 bucks and see, hold back
alternate lots, and unload on easy terms.
It jacked up 10x, and I was voted Pres.
of the Pequonnock Bank: Jenny Lind gazed
at me? across our note!
       To the arpeggios
of a show piece from a light opera, hush
and there she was, on stage, white dress,
the Nightingale. She was shaky at 1st,
but 4 bars in, and she was flying: music
filled up her flesh, and shone, no forcing,
the notes, so high, hammering into glory,
sliding away to nothing, out of her throat,
like offerings, to the top gallery, which
was our poor heaven. It all made us cry:
she was a natural. The last aria over,
we roared her back for curtain calls; I saw,

oh angel! there is a world above mine:
they yelled: where's Barnum? and I thought,
Barnum's nowhere.

Salt tears
at Sandy Hook, with the steamer bells ringing,
her kiss
the city brass band
moaning

over the salt Atlantic

the long low swells
in the chaos
of foam, pure spectacle
hotel room in that port town

strange   oh starting at 0,
with nothing but Tom Thumb.
Each time, I lose
details:
where are my specs? Barnum, any old
stories for this wk.'s column?
I don't know:
Leland, it ain't Illustrated News, but would
you stick this in?
ah son, did you wet down
the tobacco?
yes, pa
and water the rum?
yes, pa
mix sand in the sugar?
yes, pa
chicory in the coffee?
yes, pa
all right,
come up to prayers

I just set the type:
Count up all the 95 concerts: money talks:

Big Apple	286
Beantown	70
Bee Hive	6
Quaker City	48
Mobtown	32
Capital City	15
Queen City	12
Earthquake City	10
Crawfish Town	87
Bluff City	5
Blue City	4
Solid City	30
Rock City	12
Fall City	19
4 Lake City	3
Ragtown	44
Nail City	5
Big Smoke	7
grand total	712

gross 535000; 1st national tour, & Lindomania:
Americans are all firemen: she said.
                              Our circus
in the sandhills: they jammed in by the 100,
poor, and rawboned, in Saturday clothes, after
prayer meeting, spit on their jaws, drawling
rough jokes: at the clown's tricks, they said
he was in league with the devil; they howled
at the minstrel with his bones & banjo; and
the big hand was the acrobat spinning dishes.
Old clown:
                    dear patrons, our amusements and
diversions are at an end for the evening,
our wish, your satisfaction:
                              Nobody moved,
waiting for the next act; and the acrobat:

ah ha, signor, you no speak English: I go,
Barnum
        all right, Vivalla:
                     He went on stage:
ladies & people, it's ah, finish:
                 Nothing:
he rung down ½? the curtain:
                    oh, all right!
it's the next number: I bet they're toting
that plunder off to make room for a dance:
and I walked on:
                the show is over, it's done,
stop, through, period, the tents are folded,
that's all, no more, the end, we're closed!
They wavered toward the exit; oh my audience,
face it, we're clodpoles! and 3 boys came up:
our gals would like a tune on the big drum:
The old clown remembered we had a bass drum
from when our band quit, and slammed on it:
oh, jim dandy! & it was the top of the show!
Oh I'd had it with the travelling circus,
& sold the Illustrated Bible door to door
till bad agts. ate up all of my profits.
I read Whitman? in the Post saying, though
her voice did somersaults, her head was empty:
I was anxious in the air of her bad lawyers,
after the money, all tour, and at the last,
they warped her, I let her out of the contract,
into their swindles. She married, she began
to snarl in concerts, the numbers dropped off,
and she left America in the rain, with only
the firemen there to sing to her.
                           Salt tears
at Sandy Hook   ringing

moaning

the salt Atlantic

                                   in the chaos

of foam
        hotel room

                                        0

  nothing   Tom Thumb
                           Ah well,
the pages will remember: best I can do,
in days on fire. Oh if I've made a fortune,
my stars! it's not out of my fabrications,
but that I don't ½ do: I do with all I am.
1st, sign it To the universal Yankee nation:
mail out announcements to the papers, 57
publishers want it, not that I shook hands
with Redfield, $1.25/copy and a 30% cut,
give talks on humbug, get the mermaid back
into the Museum, to promote it.
                              What is
the book? the Life: out of a bag of scraps,
my old high feathers, I stitched the odds
& ends of all I've worn, in my born days,
into a memory quilt to hold on to after
I'm gone.
            The saloons were tight, roof
crowded, customers in the st., coin out,
in line: it soured my capitalistic belly.
I had my carpenters go through the wall,
bang up temporary stairs for a back exit
to create flow, but they kept on circling,
because they loved it all, over & over;
I had my painter do a hand pointing, To
the Egress, and thinking it was another
new animal, they poured out & discovered
it was the world:

1855

1 Jan   review of the Life with Henry Thoreau's
Walden in the Knickerbocker Town &
Country Humbugs he lived in a shack &c
economy

30 Jan   need boost for E Bridgeport & Mon
approached by citizen suggests I get Jerome
Clock Co to move to the new city & merge
with Terry & Barnum Mfg

5 Feb   cheap all brass 1 day mvmt clocks sold
around the world in China wheels taken out
& case used as local god's shrine proving
there is faith without works

18 Mar   Sun Mr Jerome @ Iranistan asks I float him
through bad season stop layoffs & he'll
agree to move Imagine 1000 workmen

2 Apr   Jerome total assets $40000 capital $187000
surplus biggest in the state Letters from
banks say he's sound &c donated big clock
to Bridgeport church

7 May   loan Jerome Clock Co $50000 in notes
renewable & accept drafts $60000 more
total liability outstanding in 3 mos temporary
security + exchange of stock

14 May   old notes cancelled & returned new notes
signed some without dates day in day out

4 Jun   agt says banks hold Jerome's notes &
worried about them said otherwise to make
sure I'd loan him $ but it doesn't look
unsteady His secy says he'll snap his fingers
at them

17 Jul   xfer Museum prop lease to mgr Greenwood
$1

18 Jul   sell it to Charity same consideration

20 Jul   sell Museum coll to Greenwood for notes
secured by chattel mortgage He hires bldg
from Charity @ $19000 / yr 23 yrs + $10000

lease to owner's heirs

10 Oct note for $13000 to Beach here for business
venture falling due & not a $ to pay it He
keeps his word or the note will be protested

30 Oct cousin Nichols forging my signature to the
tune of $40000 for gambling debts
Cleveland brokers with the paper say I
authorized it Judge sentences him for now
may pardon

2 Nov Bateman opening theater St. Louis owes
$4000 of that $1500 is back by garnisheeing
bank of dep Write Sol private & confidential
for lawyer to get bal he's hard to catch
napping

31 Nov N Haven bank slow to discount my notes
Are they taken up as they expire

6 Dec check how much clock co loan is still out I
disremember If he's trying to come it over
me he's got another thing coming

1856

4 Jan agt says it's a swindle & I'm ruined
Refreshing news I don't believe it credit
stretched to ½ a 1000000 Notes used over &
over That's life

12 Jan leave Iranistan & outbldgs to Philo Sat Hope
protection Not liable on the original terms

14 Jan pay $40000 personal claims @ my banks &
stores & fail

15 Jan I am bankrupt

31 Jan mortgaged Iranistan 3x in 2 wks for $102000
Appoint Johnson trustee good man
Negotiate notes down to 15-25%

2 Feb I've been wound up the clocks & in my skull
there's a ticking

4 Feb all my show money for their old debts
Jerome Mfg Co never moved to E Bridgeport
only reason I advanced the snakes $1

Insolvent 15¢ on the $
11 Feb   I offer $150000 to let me up creditors want
nothing less than par & int after sale of prop
every ¢ think I'm hoaxing hiding money
3 Mar   hauled in day after day They can't nail me in
cross Do you own a gold watch Counsel am
I bound to answer Yes Yes sir What did it
cost About $250 Where is it I believe it's in
my pocket Court rules against the 2 penny
lawyers
10 Mar   old clock bldg bought by sewing machine co
17 Mar   I bet some clock co paper was sold short to
note shavers @ high int Claims made that
were paid off Fraud & the Judge will see it
7 Apr   sewing machine loans me $ to buy
Bridgeport prop back from my creditors at
auction in Charity's name Trees money @
int & real estate all go on working @ night &
on Sun
14 Apr   refuse all money offers It's not enough Oh
what a tangle
17 Apr   quit smoking 10 cigars / day too high
21 Apr   damn Tribune prints Jerome's lies 1 I
merged to unload my clock co's debts 2 I'd
endorse notes to any extent 3 He never met
me before the fall 4 His son negotiated it
without consent How innocent Reply
tomorrow
25 Apr   idiot papers exulting All tearing me up The
deceiver self deceived The great clock
bubble Ingratitude Bridgeport people in
sympathy rally in Wash Hall praise me back
me biggest town meeting ever
1 May   what did I do Not do I lost my edge
5 May   out of the whirl I give up business & care
walk in the Long Island sea air away from
the war for the almighty $

6 May   Helen who throws money away @ 15 writes
            Take me out of fancy school I can teach
            piano help out Dear daughter

11 May I found a dead whale on beach Ship to
            Museum & exhibit on ice

26 May whale profits pay board @ Westhampton
            farm

1 Dec   sail to London in secret starting at 0 with
            nothing but Tom Thumb & a child actress I'm
            still alive

old notebooks / blue scrawls / rough cuttings / lay
down / & the stories dovetailed / only a fraction /
a crescent / of who I am / my eyes are burning /
old eyes / children / these bones going rise again /
in the twinkling of an eye / at the last trump /
mammy / I've got to face the music / the angel /
is that the whistle tooter / well strike it up /
oh the steam fiddle / and the big tubs / play
full blast / with fal de ral &c / mount bugle /
the windjammers blow brass / in the grand march /
& make parade / kick them / the ballyhoo wagons
go by like days / all the clowns do cartwheels /
and business / at the come in / the kid in me
goes hoopla / it's a holiday / in that tank
on wheels / 1st hippopotamus / the behemoth
of scripture / sharks / dolphins / sting rays /
fat seals / sea horses / & the mermaid making
prophecies / in an iron cage / the monster
gorilla roaring up Broadway / ah the bars are
bending / back of him the animals / for miles /
wild antelope / still buffalo / foul camel /
fine donkey / holy elephant / little fox /
frail giraffe / dark hyena / slow inchworm /
true jaybird / tame kangaroo / familiar lion /
old monkey / hard nautilus / quick ostrich /
dream pony / young quail / tough rhinoceros /
bad sidewinder / sudden tiger / hoax unicorn /
thin vulture / real warthog / unknown x /

big yak / bright zebra / &c / into the light /
cages open / that snake / oh Adam / ladies
with heart in there / dare anything keepers /
animal men / from the back yard / the poster
brigade / the hammer gang / the roustabouts /
top men / outside talkers / the colossal wagon /
the Amazon woman / above / with 1 breast bare /
the what is it inside / 6 black horses walking

all these side shows / go in / oh male & female
white whales are spouting in the St. Lawrence /
trap them by splashing till the tide is out /
drag them in slip knots / to boxes of water
& seaweed / railroad them 700 miles / flash
wires / what a come on / to our Museum's big
pools filled by iron pipes under the avenue /
steam pumps down at the docks / with NY Bay
salt water / people who believe in the fake
angel fish won't fall for the real white whale
and so without faith fool themselves and miss
the amazing / Old Neptune / sea lion lolling
in the grand aquarial garden / in water hauled
up from the Sound by Fall River steamboats /
and he that believeth not shall be damned /
she holds the lease / without Charity I am
nothing / I buy it back / and Barnum's on
his feet again / big hand / I'm crying / on
the road / we show our knives / to indians /

on their back legs / on streets of gold /
everybody but himself / the tattooed man /
look at his skin / all the strange people /
the albino family / the blind black piano
player / the hip dancer / the no head man /
the snake charmer / the living skeleton /
the fortune teller / the bearded lady and
the hairy boy / the lightning calculator /

the acrobat bragging about the redskins /
he slips into the woods / to take a crap /
in feathers & makeup / we chase him whooping /
he stretches his story and we let him down /
I hire the braves away from a 2 bit war
on the western plains / oh indians draw /
I can't get make believe into their heads /
they hide in back of the flat bushes / on
stage / on the lookout for actual enemies /
the woman dies / they lay a basket of food
up on the roof / for her spirit / go home
to their wilderness / Hand in the Water and
White Bull before Big Horn / I lead around
the city / into the sold out Lecture Hall /
mock in our tongue / till they catch on
I'm sticking them for quarters at the door /
and exit / with flashing eyes / oh I'm wide
awake / and send 3 substitutes to the field
for the Union / they hang the white flag over

the weight guesser / the quick change artist /
the giant lady & giant / General Tom Thumb /
Commodore Nutt / Admiral Dot / Major Atom /
you / in a contortion mirror / the whiteface /
in dots / & paint on smile / oh & the troupe /
all aces / strong man / pole balancer / back
bender / leaper / understander / high man /
woman / the human cannonball / caught by

Old Glory / troops / the millionaire & I
ride into a quote peace meeting / when they
see us loyalists they bolt into a cornfield /
gunfire / and on the shoulders of the boys
in blue / speech speech / I sing the star
spangled banner / & haul theirs in the mud
behind our omnibus / I'm sorry it gets out
of hand / & they bust up the Farmer's press /
no more meetings / will my house be burned /
ah bombs blow off in the American Museum /
confederate spies / and the fire brigade
saves it / oh he floats through the air
with the greatest / ship dead animals to
the Smithsonian / swap for anything rare /
Tom Thumb / love at 1st sight / a girl
his size / his rival dwarf knocks him over /
but he won't hold off for $ / Grace Church /
and the 400 / in the hard pews / to watch
the man in miniature & the queen of beauty /

the trapeze flyer / the wire rope walker /
woman with iron jaws / no net / spec girls /
death defying aerialists / cloud swinging /
muscle grinding / jugglers / tumblers / I hold
my breath / new music from the horse piano /
who's this / in the street pageant / grandpa /
oh gracious / squire selling us his tales /
pa's dream / ma's switch / my old mud show /

around the world west for 3 years / jig band /
1500 tricks / Tom Thumb / at the state fair /
the damn fools charge me $25 for a license /
it says I can give exhibitions for cash /
I sell licenses for $10 to everyone there /
my cow / she rubs her nose on the yard man /
outside my window / I don't see Jenny Lind /
he says keep off the grass / do you know who
I am / ah no / but you ain't Barnum's cow /
I yell / what is it / she need milking / no /
she shrills / the next boat home / she says
what I say goes / oh ma / is that why you
had me / to hit me / she goes and leaves me
9 acres / I run for the state house / to vote
for abolition / and win / you copperheads /
majority rule is in my blood / cut white
out of the constitution / let moral men
who can read cast ballots / sirs / will you
let octaroons vote in only 7 of 8 elections /

Old Turner ragging anyone / old Hawley and
his frauds / Vivalla spinning plates / Lyman
pitching in blowhard style / Greenwood good
man / Moses / with an answer to my letter /
the Nightingale in voice / ghosts waving /
oh / heralds / and the Congress of Nations /
all flags & hats / soldiers in helmets /
bishops mitres / kings crowns / in America /

my minstrel show singer takes off / all I
can get is a black boy / I can't show him
in the big city / so I black & wig him to
look like a white boy in blackface / Lord /
negroes are in God's image / let them go /
grandma dying / from what / they say a nail /
read your Bible Taylor / love God by loving
people / her stiff fingers / do I remember
all that / or the story told me / in tears /
is that after / I can't mind her / forget /
the Cleveland kid too sick to come I parade
the camels & elephants / under his window /
and do the show / ah fire / is a good slave /
bad master / the railroads jacking up fares /
I'm for cheap tickets / expansion / bust
the monopoly / by Yankee sticktoitiveness /
the American Museum is in flames / lay down
the wire / I'm for the people / let women
work for money / buy that slave girl / Star

liberty goddess / the father of his country /
live eagle / the rail splitter with a dwarf /
the image of me / the balloons / the flying
machine diving off a sky scraper / the stars
& stripes / Zulu chiefs / Nubian warriors /
oh no / who cued the damn Allegoric March
of the new Congress of Savages / wild men
of Borneo / harsh Afghan nomads / sinuous

of the East / don't free her / drop what /
hey / it's for kids / electrify yourself /
get more from everywhere / to make it pay
put it on wheels / 3 locomotives / 76 cars /
do 100 miles a night / move the rubes in /
bewilder them / make it 3 rings / 3 shows
a day / open in spring / to universal love
and 1 million dollars / and out in front

oh the big top / look up / sky blue / the silver
stars and below / the acts whirl through the void /
and then bow out / the wonder / temporary hills
on the red horizon / clouds / white canvas / and
the Sound / in my grey eyes / faint Long Island
across / what river / oblivion / and I look back /
my guts / the stroke / heart's worn / they say
it's nothing / charades / shots mask the pain /

Indian dancing girls / vanishing Mayans /
Arab giants / shuddering Mongols / and lost
Incas / ½ naked / from all over the globe /
and thanks for the adjectives / Hamilton /
the 2 voice woman / marimba / steel drums /
4 brass bands / cymbals / calliope / chime
of bells / bagpipes / black jubilee singers /
all showboating by / in a glory of electric

old Grizzly Adams / white beard / with wolf's
head hat / and a cracked skull / big bears /
mountain lions / he's tamed / around the Horn
from California / like the happy family / monkey
dove hoot owl quill pig &c in 1 cage / I loan
him the suit he's buried in / oh his last words /
that's fine / I don't need you / Reverend / your
last rites / I'm a pretty rough customer / but

is that the 3 masted schooner / P. T. Barnum /
in the dark / riding at anchor / salt tears
at Sandy Hook / home from her maiden voyage /
what is it / April / when I go to remember
I look up / old / I want to do big things /
I'm saving the sky rockets and the grand
transformation for last / Mister Vanderbilt /
our ship / the North America / made it around /

& calcium light / playing 1 for the money /
our expenses more than the gross box office
of any outfit / 10 grand says so / close up
the schools / the works / it's Barnum day /
oh hurry on out / to the sawdust land / in
the new season / & play / in the biggest rag
of our gypsy camp / no short changers / only
great kinkers / in the best show this side

my heart / right place / I've heard preaching
every blessed day / not just on the sabbath /
it might be an old grizzly give the sermon /
my church / wild daisies / and a rainbow trout
bucking out of the creek / led me in prayer /
the stars at night / or the skittering rain
in the high Sierras / you know / whoever cut
them canyons / in the back country / loves me

you have a statement / all the greenbacks to
charities & the Barnum Institute / I'm worth
4 million & change / I can't buy the Cardiff /
I bankroll the Colorado giant / bury it near
that real estate I can't unload / that hoax
of a hoax / outdraws it / silk flag / blue
monogram / on the glass cupola / I'm home /
old depot I turn into Madison Square Garden /

of paradise / from Bay City to Galveston
& Bangor to Omaha / it's P. T. Barnum's
Great Travelling Exposition & World's Fair
Museum Menagerie Grand International Zoo
Polytechnic Institute Caravan Hippodrome
& Huge Circus / the Greatest Show on Earth:
Fish: what was the take at the Garden?
                                        more
than 14 horses
                good:

and so no thanks / I'm a snow goose / and on
my way / get the money to my old woman / ain't
she something / I'd like to rest / I never
done it on earth / oh Adams / what a trouper /
the Siamese Twins / tied by an arm of flesh /
at the belly / 1 sweet / on wine & women /
1 sour / on books & women / ah Chang & Eng /
fist fighting / 2 for the show / they marry

ground acts / in the center ring / why is
the ring 42 feet wide / the horses remember /
1st night / uneasy / no reason / I write
my voice / on Edison's new talking machine /
yeah I blow my own horn / in America noise
is power / I ballyhoo you in with language /
but I deliver / not like these thin spirits /
advertisers / Lord / am I the father of lies /

2 Tarheel sisters / have 21 count them babies /
the arm waver says / I move we cut the number
of members / smooth things / but table it till
it's a full house / I say by your own thinking
we should vote now / laughter / by a landslide /
that seat in Congress / I lose to my cousin /
oh I can't shake my image / if I can amuse
the country I don't care who makes the laws /
160 million hard tickets / bless advertising /
ah 2 faced words / my twin / the Reverend /
I'm Chapin at the bit / well and who better
to get the show an angel / I'm in the wings /
I ham it up & make my eggs it / ooh / and
the masses / them asses / if I corral them /
I'll Barnum / ha / free passes / look it up
in Numbers / thou shalt not pass / I sneak
out of the Cary know it all salon / Phoebe
catches me / hey I won't carry anything off /
she opens her arms / I wish you would / mayor

Snap the Whip / that painting / wild boys /
& girls with hoops / glory it takes me back /
3 to get ready / oh summer / by Winslow Homer /
buy it / I cheat my heirs & the sea / stones /
salt meadows / hard farmers / till I put in
the music stand / war monument / horse drive
along the shore / & when the harbor's choked /
and the woods swallowed / come to Seaside Park /

in 75 / close saloons on Sunday / suspend
cops who drink beer with their stars on /
sue my own gas & water company / cut city
hall salaries / put the baseball players
to work / and get rid of the whores down
at the post office / I'm no politician /
my idea fly the red white & blue / fire
a 13 gun salute / ring Bridgeport bells /
the centennial / after a term / step down /
and 4 to go / on the world is what you
make it lecture tour / out west / do I
look over my left shoulder at the new moon /
room #13 / every hotel / but no bad luck /
get there on time / back on the Cannonball /
I get a letter / 4 postmarks / addressed
P. T. Barnum / America / and I count ties /
I see the elephant / and point out sights /
big river / the plains / like it's my show /
on the Union Pacific / the great divide

where Ball's bronze statue of me is going /
after I catch a ride on that comet Clemens
has us go sailing in / in his Sun sketch /
on a grand tour / and back in the 1990s /
come over Sam & bring the family / for ozone
and clambakes / what am I / 81 / my book
on sale at the gate / new chapter each year /
people trying to get into the next edition /

and back through rainbows & the big trees /
to where / the foreign words / I'm overseas /
Charity dies in a telegram / sick years /
was she faking / or was I too razzle dazzle
for that country girl / praying to the angel
of mercy / take me home / I don't leave this
black room / but I'm at the Mountain Grove
burying ground / ah Charity / where did
it go / I remember you / that 1st night /
in the heaven of rain / she's 8 & English
when I meet her / I love her letters before
I touch / Fish's daughter / 40 years younger /
after our honeymoon in the White Mountains /
my daughters on the porch in black / the world
is big / our hearts should be / our children /
grandchildren / baby double grands / & Jumbo
the elephant / 12 feet to the top of his spine
and the gold howdah / where anyone can ride /
7 tons / loves music & kids / now big is jumbo /

1 July morning / relaxing / carpenter smokes /
Iranistan burns / pump sparks / the American
Museum burns / a sign / says Horace Greeley /
go fishing / bad chimney / New Museum burns /
circus / the winter quarters burn / this trial
by fire / the show must go on / and I give it
a whirl / for a flyer / Longfellow your Comedy
is on my desk / is there a poetry of motion /

on a railway spur / he's hit by a freight /
we show his widow next to his bones & hide /
only 4 seasons / oh the all time bull act /
this rainy afternoon / I hope the elephants
don't scare / ah with the rat sheets matching
circus against banner / our tin star catching
pickpockets / and canvas men working over
the local roughs / it's getaway day / time
to pull up stakes at this old circus / blow
on to the next stand / is it in your blood /
want to get with it / well put on spangles /
you've got a spot / 6 minutes / for love
or money / & hey / 1st of May / for luck /
don't eat peanuts in the dress top / or put
your costume on backwards / and always step
into the ring right foot 1st / you're in
the horse opera / what's Paper Collar Joe /
that Broadway confidence man / like to say /
there's a sucker born every minute / oh

look at my horses dance / no hurry / Bailey /
our contract is for 50 years / they think
I'm sharp / & all I know's I don't / I just
work hard and let them think / you shadow /
ah what logistics / under that derby hat
on your bald head / in spectacles / no sleep /
you think too much / chewing on rubber bands /
twirling a silver dollar / you manage it all /

I'm in big operations / for red or blue /
agents chance their lives to get the sacred
white elephant / not white / but very sacred /
God made that animal / Bailey and I would
have made it whiter / 6 grand / ah well /
you pays your money & you takes your choice /
where is that page / on my grand entrance /
if I had the elephant's memory / oh Marina /
ah here / in 89 / it's the Olympia / trumpet /
bareback riders get down / & the clowns stop /
acrobats fold their arms / and trapeze artists
sit on their bars / lift my top hat / you come
to see Barnum / well / I'm Barnum / & the band
playing Hail to the / what / the self made man /
pile it all up / spirits saying:

                       put these
scrapbooks down cellar: in a fireproof box:
last thoughts: of you, Miss Fish:

                           it's Nancy:

as a full partner / I wanted her / so hard /
the Danbury concert / that kid / Charles Ives /
he does Variations on America / the future /
that pretty country / I dreamed this line /
oh centuries in minutes / I say bright side it /
absorb rivals / get all cheaper / 2 circuses
crisscross / money rolls in / this carnival /
no end / as long as they make babies / my stars

I come it over that news man / 1st elephant
born in captivity / that's good / not really /
at another circus / that's bad / not really /
in a telegram I offer 100 grand / that's good /
not really / they blow it up into a poster /
and day & date me / rake it in / that's bad /
not really / I'm so knocked out / by his savvy /
I say let's do united shows / for 1 season /
that's what / yeah / that's Barnum & Bailey /
the big combination / what time is it / 6:30 /
the Evening Sun is good enough / to print
my obit / early / for me / ah the last pitch /
at Kansas City / afternoon / with the kids /
I wish my body was burned / and not gawked at
by each & every / man / with his wife's ashes
in a bronze jar / remarries / sprinkles them
on the ice on his steps / so his new bride
won't slip / call off the cops / I'm running
the show / no matter what your Society says /
no danger to Salamander / the horse / sir /
I mean business / look here / I stick my hand
into the flames / it's O. K. / I'll jump through
this hoop of fire / and the clowns after me /
fanfare:
          sweetheart, I hear a brass band up
in heaven
          you what? are you fooling, Barnum?
Barnum?

          and that's the size of it, of his
long rigmarole. I'm sorry there wasn't more
absurd philosophy. . . okay, I'm not sorry.
What really happened, I wonder? We can't
ask him; at last, when there was only one
old man who'd been to the original circus,
what images died with him? And the book,
the Life, is full of holes: at the 1st show,

in what, Brooklyn, I think, in April of 71,
after the clowns had done their walkaround,
before the wild horses had been let loose,
how did the sawdust smell? etc., not in
his book; what is, is slanted: half lost,
invented, more than remembered, one sided,
in two talking language, so I've got all
this stuff from ah, I figured I was free
to add yarns out of Botkin's treasuries
of American folklore, dreams, proposals,
& so on, out of my own past, and slanted,
of course—whatever we do, our days go up
in smoke, untangling into fiction. If it
never happened, so what? It's good to go
over, if nothing else, for the spectacle,
one afternoon, in the city of roses, with
the crazy weather, don't you love it? All
this blank verse and I'm thirsty. . . That's
the wine; hey Laura, got a glass of water?

Amelia Earhart

relative peace in the Asia-Pacific region
but the chairman had concerns over ongoing
conflicts elsewhere. He urged the foreign
ministers, in Jakarta, yesterday, to sign
the nuclear test ban treaty before winter.
This is Radio Hong Kong, broadcasting on
short wave frequency 6210 mhz. It is now

blue midnight, and the Royal Observatory
reports 28° Celsius, and occasional gusts
offshore. The tropical blue storm Gloria,
over the western ocean, now moving north-
west, at 15 km/hr, is approaching blue
landfall. The blue weather's mainly fine,
apart blue from a few isolated showers.

Oh listen, the blue flight had no landing,
the worlds are out of balance, and because
the airplane vanished, I, never arriving,
now haunt the raw newspaper, and in words
I hate. Do you read me? in the white noise
tonight, unknown! in air, history, lost,
down here with the legends, sea serpent,

mermaid, I sprawl, unburied, by the wreck
Electra, withering in the salt, -3 miles
altitude, no navigator, as the fish knock
my ribs, and coral grows on my white bones,
unsleeping, in the lurid current, clouds
foam, in seaweed, in deep; in life, I flew
2 oceans, but ghosts can't cross water: oh

for the love of pity, listen, till morning
is here, and I go dead. Where on earth did
I end up, they wonder, on the next-to-last
jump of the '37 world flight? That question
leads to a cheap mythology. . . Cue violins,
as usual, for the Hollywood movie, in black-
and-white, romance, suspense, courage, in

this Pacific mystery, starring the glamour
girl aviator, torn between the navigator,
the love interest, and the good old U.S.A.,
in the dynamite story officials didn't dare
reveal before Pearl Harbor: she didn't fly
east, as announced, but north on a mission
for the military, diverted to the islands

mandated to the Rising Sun, and reporting
false positions to cover, overflying Truk
lagoon, low pass, by landing lights, air-
fields and shipyards, illegal, for a war.
The code word cloudy in her radio traffic
told Navy intelligence, surveillance had
the American fleet in danger of assault

by zeros. She hit bad weather; not able
to see Howland Island, in the salt haze,
with an off chart, and the voice channel
jammed, by the sabotage? of her own Coast
Guard, no directions, the other plan, fly
back and ditch in the forbidden islands,
the air-sea search giving the Navy, in

combing the ocean, reconnaissance, in 4
quadrants, by cutter, minesweeper, battle-
ship, 4 destroyers, aircraft carrier, and
all its airplanes, criss-crossing. Coming
in on empty, she crashed on an outlying

reef, across blue water from a low atoll,
her lover banging his head, oh but alive.

She was in the Red Cross, and bandaged him,
in the lifeboat, rowing over shallows, to
the beach, in no man's land, and burying
her maps and instruments under a palm tree;
fishermen, hiding in the jungle, caught
her eye, and motioning to them, she saw,
out of the grass huts, soldiers, hustling,

dark looks at the down airplane, questions
in bad English:—American spy girl? and her
man laughed, was slapped, she cried out hurt,
was waved at gunpoint to a seaplane. . . Cross
fade, to a long shot, caption, Garapan City,
Saipan; military police, cracking a joke:
—The U.S. has to use a woman under cover,

their men are cowards. . . They dragged him
away, hands tied, walked her, arms black
and blue, to a rain-streaked prison hotel,
iron bars in the useless windows, snails
crawling, her thumbs hung in metal rings
above her as she sagged against the wall.
The dysentery she caught in Java flared

up; they changed her out of her trousers
into a blue shift. The girl, looking after
her, smiled, handing her an apple, touched
her breast:—Consolacion; and she winced,
thanking her with a pearl ring. They shot
3 endings, and showed them to avg. people
to see what would go over at the box office.

Oh the crackpots who cash in on my enigma
and ride my name like a ghost automobile
down easy to the bank, hack into steaming
jungles, hunting for wreckage, interview
old South Sea islanders who squint at my
photo and nod, and who see in documents
declassified by the Navy, conspiracies:

like the suspicious Air Force major, retd.,
whose obsessions led him to Long Island,
the Sea Spray Inn, in '64, a meeting of
the Early Flyers, cocktails and memories,
and the mystery woman:—Ah, you knew AE?
Her eyes glimmering, she said very well,
no photographs, please; she had on her oak

leaf decoration and the red-white-and-blue
ribbon for the Atlantic flight:—You think
she's dead? She said she was alive as long
as we remember her. With his voice shaking:
—I know it's you, Amelia: you say you're
married, but if I write the Phoenix Islands
into a column, Gardner, Enderbury, Sydney,

Birnie, Phoenix, Hull, Canton, and McKean,
I can draw a circle through the letters
of your so-called husband's name, oh and
its positions, 1st, 7th, 2nd, etc., mean
172 ° 13' W longitude, 4° 21' S latitude,
at the very lagoon on Hull Island where
your plane went down: I cracked the code!

I know everything: that morning, you had
company: fighters off the Japanese carrier
looming in Jaluit harbor; the machine guns
rattled, and you tried to veer, your thin
aluminum belly ripped, black smoke blowing
out of you, bawled your line of position,
last message, and crash-landed on the edge

of the closest atoll, all the birds, foam
hissing, and the plane burning. You looked
at the buzzing sky, and the American flyer
on patrol, and waved to him, oh but before
your rescue, this landing boat shoved into
the blue lagoon, leaving the red sun flag;
they took you to jail in Saipan, questions,

to the Imperial Palace, in Tokyo: kept in
that luxury prison, U.S. hero under wraps,
in a kimono, you learned the tea ceremony,
under a master, taught language, and were
allowed to fly their sister to your world-
flight plane. 7 springs, and 7 blossomings
of the cherries. . . One night, in June '44,

you filled in on radio for demoralizing
Tokyo Rose, and not knowing it was to air
your voice as blackmail in a treaty, you
started out:—Ah, hello, all-forgetting
and forgotten blue Yankee veterans out
in the South Pacific, it's the Zero Hour,
for boys with time to kill. Okay, on old

timer's night, it's—hold on, flash: After
4 days of bombing and off-shore shelling,
a U.S. force has now gained the beachhead
at Saipan—hurrah for Main St., brass bands
on Independence Day! And you played Stars

and Stripes Forever, till the secret police
raided the station, cut off the broadcast,

and put you under arrest in a blind house.
It had backfired; America abandoned you
under the rose of secrecy. Surrender day,
on 1 condition, the emperor not be given
to the Allies and hung, they let you go.
1st woman ashore, off of a B-29, to pick
up pows, your old comrade, Jackie Cochran:

she'd come to spirit you, older, heavier,
incognito in a nun's white veil, not back
to that publicity inferno, your ballyhoo
husband, and his 1-upmanship, but to a new
life, and in the perfect disguise, a dress,
and makeup, with your hair done, legally
dead, and living on in Bedford Hills. Etc.

Ah, the dead are vulnerable, who can't
impeach the forgeries of the definitive
bio, which won't come out till publishers
hear what new slant the author can give
to the old life to sell it again, whether
I was my husband's act, or a bad flyer,
by word of them I let down or beat out,

and add acknowledgements, prologue, cold
facts, photographs, epilogue, appendices,
glossary, notes, reading, index, and maps
on the end papers, quotes from the reviews
on the slick jacket. She had to time it,
drop her ailerons, slide over the blank
ocean, guess altitude or else, and stall:

after the roar all night, oh grace, if only
a minute, and silence, bang down on the hard
water, pitching forward, white wash, cockpit
hauled under by the engines, and no way out
by hatch, the zero tanks floating the tail,
and the listing airplane, lifting, sagging,
in the rough waves,—Ah Christ, she saw,

we're sinking; the sea poured into vents,
flooding across her feet, no time, and no
Jacob's ladder, she had to climb on out,
up the catwalk, hand hold, on the radio,
jam boots against gas tanks, backsliding,
but she got to the navigator, blood down
his face, he'd hit the table, star-crossed,

with 2 highway smash-ups before the flight,
and his new bride, no answer, he was knocked
out, and working to the life raft, she yanked
it, looked out the window at the deep ocean,
right there, inflating it to 1/2, she sighed
and then leaned out, lugging it out the door,
the day so bright, wrestling the man into it,

pumping it full, and tethering it, she
went back for compass, matches, canteen,
kite, ax, no flares, left back, and to
the awful door, he was slipping under
the water, no hope, the raft sinking, oh
and his loose arm flying out as a shark
rammed him, more following, all failing,

no way to swim, this hit parade song going
in her head, she felt—I don't want to be
Ophelia, pulled beneath "from her melodious
lay to muddy death;" no warning, and over-
whelmed by water, the airplane went down
and her with it, chaos swallowing, waves
closing above her, she held her breath

and breathed, salt water cut her throat,
life flashed: daddy's fish story the 1st
airplane state fair that peach basket hat
bound for the port of nowhere yearbook
the curse at Kalamazoo River no swimming
and she fly by feel and I you mean seat
of the pants the rudder vibrating I'm

the organ grinder is my lost jackknife in
the moon and tall headline Boston woman
flies into morning on surprise Horseshoe
Bend big train I'm dancing on the firebox
in dirty overalls Lucky Strike ad and I

don't smoke fast woman they hiss no hats
Gyp says out the strange door into this

green sea publicity dive and I fly in as
maid of honor canaries 1 ocean I hate
to get my hair wet the showgirls cancan
on the wings movie the mansion on fire
2 oceans the bear went over the mountain
to gulf dear cowboys point cheap lawyer
pilots are always dreaming to California

by the long way the code keys and trailing
antenna useless morning sick am I pregnant
lost star Electra of the Pleiades and there
are always islands, drowning, hand, air—Oh,
ball up the pages of those phantom stories,
and throw them out; all wrong: they hurt
my ghost. And I go back to my transmission.

The summer is harsh, this island morning,
the load heavy in our Lockheed: I cock
to the engine's rhythm, keep wondering
if the fuel flow is okay, flight check,
lift finger Ready, gun and idle, stick
under my palm, I sigh and grin, wave at
the colonists and natives, and roll out

of the aerodrome, swing, taxi, gun twice,
open her, 1000 yards, all dirt, and rough,
she won't pull up, 50 to the cliff, cross-
road bounces me, into the air, and off,
green ocean, as I sink down, light surf,
see bottom, at my shadow, the fish scatter
like fireworks, 6 feet, I spray up water

and start to climb, the clouds, 100 feet,
ah! goodbye, New Guinea. . . Dreams call
to me. Noonan, in back; we're on our next-
to-last leg, to the coral island, middle
of nowhere, by dead reckoning, radio coil,
star sextant. . . over a rose-color sea. . .
How many fathoms down does our mother go?

As little sister, who I call blue pigeon,
after the song, and I'd say, oh thousands
of years ago, when mama was young, June,
1890, her presentation ball, pine boards
in a back yard pavilion, Japanese lanterns
in the garden, dusk, St. Joe men playing
slow waltzes and reels, she was greeting

and in walked daddy: she liked him and saw
he liked her. 7 years after, ah thousands
of years ago, in summer, I was born, Amelia,
her mama, Mary, his, Earhart, the judge's
granddaughter, in Atchison; but daddy was
a railroad man: I'm from there, Kansas City,
Des Moines, St. Paul, Springfield, Chicago,

and down the line. . . in a gold rush water
hole, on Quality Hill, in grandma's house:
her ma saw George Washington riding a mare,
and she her daughter in an airplane: this
flying country. My birthdays, all picnics,
no party, no dress, and I can whoop it up
in the green woods, go wild, and only slip

home for July 24 ice cream, in the mixer. . .
I'm a jayhawk and go stilt walking, I whiz
till the swing jumps, go for a whirl on our
flying dutchman, and ride it till she dies,
upside down, the tomboy, and so mama folds
our frills away; skirts are fragile, and you
are dressed in caution; Aunt Maggie sews blue

bloomers, tucked at the knee, invented by
Amelia Bloomer, for freedom of legs: the 1st
in town, I go, loose and outcast, Saturday
indian, in disguise, with daddy, who taught
me to waltz, that wonder, and then I put
on Alexander's Ragtime Band and dance, la!
to the Red Wing on the wind-up Victrola.

Our big dog has the tease boys on the roof,
and turns on me, roiling: I remember daddy:
—Don't ever run;—Oh James Ferocious you've
tipped your water again; I out my hand to
his hackles, lead him in the kitchen. Daddy:

—You were brave with him.—Oh I never had
time to be scared. He kissed my forehead.

St. Louis, World's Fair, 1904, I pleaded
to go on sky cars, mama said no; I rode
the elephant, the ferris wheel, and tried
to make a roller coaster in our back yard.
Uncle Nicey anchors wood to the roof stud,
long nails, 8 feet high, slaps it:—Good;
I shin up with a skate wheel board I made:

—Let me go; I slide down, track greased,
and bang a trestle, crack up; shirt torn,
and my lip bloody:—Oh Pidge, it's just
like flying! Mama had Sadie tear it down,
but daddy, who let us stay up to gaze on
the comet, Xmas gave me a boy's sled that
I could bellyflop on, would've okayed it.

I see the water rising, Missouri in flood,
on the way home, slopping over the tracks,
logs slamming the coach, oil lamps dead,
river snarling, train inching, bad leaks:
—As long as the fire's going, it works,
says daddy. Pigeon:—You afraid, Meelie?
—Course not. . . Exploring, we go through

our orchard, of apples, peaches, and plums,
under a ditch at the back fence, to danger,
in the thorns, with badgers for buffaloes,
the outlaw cave, ashes, bottles, old paper,
for treasure, big whirls in the yellow river,
the banks washing out, the climb back hard,
late for supper, and the bluff is outlawed.

That summer night, crickets going, locusts
saying It's hot, the bluejays quiet, bats

skittering, at dusk, the sun a ball of peace
under off-color clouds, above the tall grass,
fireflies, odors out of the white hollyhocks,
rose geraniums, dark heliotropes; we traipse
out of the arbor, holding a snatch of grapes:

grandma:—Quit that racing in the garden;
I'm hot just looking: on the verandah, girls.
I, on imagination's horse:—Whoa, Saladin;
but grandma, when we go quick the air blows
on us, to cool; and she throws up her hands.
Toot and Katch call from next door:—Cousins!
and she nods:—Go through the gate, ladies.

I jump the fence, as always. She drawls:—I
never used to do all that, only roll hoops. . .
The 2nd St. arc light comes on, and Charlie
carries a taper to our soft North Terrace
gas light; time to go in, for boys' success
stories: Onward & Upward, Through by Day,
The Starry Flag; no dolls, only my donkey,

Donk, who walks in puddles, hammers nails,
and comes to bed. It was going to last
for honeymoons to come; one morning it was
all whisked away. Good night, gas light,
horse & carriage, old century, good night,
grandma's house, good night, childhood.
It's quarter to, time to radio the ground.

KHAQQ TO LAE AT 8000 FEET SIGNS OF STRONGER-THAN-FORECAST HEADWINDS

Because daddy, my 1st word, who made days
adventures, in big vocabulary, with his
mystery inventions, challenges, our arias
at the upright piano, riding to parties,
1 dance and back at midnight, one fall was
off the streetcar, and balance, no spring
in his walk, no larking, and saying nothing

to mama's ice look; he was in the hotel bar
with railroad men, and couldn't hold booze.
And it was letdowns, black moods, the cure,
firings, other cities. I was packing his
bag for a Great Northern run, and there's
a flask; I empty it in the sink; he barks
and is about to slap me, when mama stops

his arm. He never. . . Because I was hissed
weak sister at high school, for not fooling
around behind the deaf teacher, atheist
at boarding school, for not bible pounding
that indian poet; why have you-be-damning
girls' clubs, and why must Ghosts be taboo?
and the headmistress blazed. In chemistry,

on a hard question, I just quote poetry:
"autour de premier aeroplane," circles
Apollinaire, in air. . . In carriage, ah,
I'm a hockey star, and I hate the graces:
walk so, bow so, my law! the exercises:

big room, with a little chair, you aim
your behind and climb on; it's a scream. . .

What animal display is it that a woman old
enough to breed must be glamorized? Hair
only to comb and curl, eyebrows pluck and
pencil, eyes shadow, line, lashes mascara,
skin, pancake, cheeks, rouge, nose, powder,
lips, red grease, ears hole, hoop, throat
circle, perfume, breasts bra, waist corset,

wrists bracelet, ring finger ring, nails
gloss, hips girdle, legs shave, hose, heels
high, rig out in silks, frills, feathers,
chains, and never age, your image? I was
made by god, good to the world's 7 seas,
and I don't need makeup: oh my bare body
is actual divinity. Amen; it's in the eye.

I went after the pigeon to Canada, lolling
by the glass lake, trying to play the New
World Symphony on the banjo, and studying
auto mechanics with boys. . . Because I saw
3 one-legged men, King St., at Xmas, who
were back from the Great War, which wasn't
brass bands, dancing with uniforms; I quit

school for the Red Cross: 12 on, 2 off, at
the new Military Hospital, cooking, washing,
for the paralyzed g.i.s, oh the shell shocked;
when it's a fire alarm, I hear them howling,
begging. At the Armistice, whistles blowing,
inaudible speeches, music, streamers flying,
hullabaloo, and not 1 word of thanksgiving.

It's a man's game, but let's open up honor:
draft women, so they can blind, burn, gun

down, murder, suffer, shovel the dead under,
die in headlines; don't give me that line
about chivalry, their frailty; bull: women
do so much of the dirt work in the world,
nobody looks. Let them in the foxhole, and

men will clear out; we'll be done with wars,
I told the Daughters of the American Rev.
Ah! "Damned spirits all, that in crossways
and floods have burial." Crossroad, ocean.
—I'll go west, keep mama married, Pigeon:
after, it's my life. You wait on the shore.
Look at those clouds. . . Oh the one I adore.

I'm coming into them, in the forecast,
Pearl Harbor wireless, but I can go
over the rain squalls, 250 miles east
of the island, it's a pleasure, to 10K
for now. Stick back, ease into it, on my
own, give her throttle: how many horses
under the cowling? I rode on Saturdays

at the Toronto stables, and saw that big
and rawboned dapple gray.—Hey March, ah can
I ride him?—That outlaw? Can you get a leg
over him? I guess his old cavalry man
was mean: Dynamite, bucking for the moon,
throwed 2 boys lately, kicking like hell.
I split my apple, and step to his stall:

his ears go back, he shows his teeth—Ts, ts;
I lay the green crescents in with his feed,
and palm his neck: like when I had to balance
on a wood crate, at the tiny window, the shed
next door, the pretty mare, all cramped inside,
heat, flies; she'd bang her hoofs, and the man
would whip her, hard to break her; I'd reach in

grass and caresses, and she'd calm. That black
beauty, one day, spooks at a newspaper blowing
and shies, he lashes her, she flinches, her tack
comes loose, and Nellie bolts, her traces flying,
down the drive, and—Runaway! he's yelling;
did the angel of the wild say jump? and she
is off the bridge, oh, if only she could fly,

and cracks into the thin waters, Kaw River.
—Mr. Oldham twisted his ankle, dear, would
you take a piece of Sadie's cake on over.
I move my hands behind my back; I stand,
shaking my head: no. I was all of 7, and
till then I'd never disobeyed my mama. Oh
to get my heels off of the ground: I'd go

from curb to shafts, and crawl up on the fat
heavy-footed sorrel at the butcher's wagon,
who'd warp his backbone for nothing.—Lift
me down, mama. . . Give me a horse of my own,
grandma!—Don't want you riding, little woman.
—Why?—Because I say so. It's the same hiss
as for mama, who did tricks on a circus horse

behind her back. We'd go live with the post-
man at, what was it, Minnesota lake, summers,
help with haying; I'd get to take Prince out,
indian pony, with a white star on his nose,
who got away with dawdling, and my bare heels
on his big flanks won't urge him. In hopes,
I flirt his reins, lope to a fence, he leaps

over and down, spraying up mud: ah love,
he's snickering from hunger; no saddle,
and I walk back, after. We were both 12;
I'd brush him out, and he'd nuzzle my little
shoulder, spirit him sugar, and he'd gentle.
Like with Dynamite, who I fed every night
on my way home, and in a month, he'd hit

a canter; I handled him, with an easy bit
and my light hands.—March, what do I owe?
—Nothing; you saved him, Amelia. Pilot,
the Royal Flying Corps:—Hey, I like how
you ride him, in reflex; you have to play

it, like my aeroplane; it goes like silk;
and if it's contrary, you have a comeback.

Come out to Armour Heights next week and see.
He's like the Hospital boys:—It's flying, is
all; if you crash, you crash: I ain't a hero.
—Okay; can I go up, etc.?—Ah, no civilians.
His snow lashes me; he clears the evergreens,
circles over the fair grounds: in my 20 eye,
the little plane, dark against the winter sky,

harsh sun, red wings, the ace: and he dives at
my sister and I, watching on a grassy clearing,
jazzing us because we're girls: if he loses it,
we're goners, and she lights out; daddy's strong
—Don't ever run; I stand: what is it saying,
that red aeroplane, as it rushes over my head?
All my free hours after are at the airfield:

airspeed down, foot the right rudder, holding
against the torque, I jump it up, heels, oh!
in the air, on the cloud's bare back, riding,
rain slanting into the archipelago below,
on the landlubbers, under the gray sky, who
don't remember: above that ceiling of mist,
in this blue world, the sun is always out.

I can straight-and-level at this altitude,
stick force on my hand zero, and it flies
itself, better than I, when there's no need;
steady it, and not by the cant of the nose,
but by wings and horizon: counterclockwise
around the world, nothing to do but conjure. . .
I stuck a feather from the turkey duster

into the turned up brim of my straw hat
like a rough rider for my easter bonnet
as I made do, when daddy, off a street-
car, drunk, was in a St. Paul accident,
our last $10 going to stitch up his cut.
Oh and the electric streetcar rides I had
in L.A., early 20s, 4th St. to the end

of the line, by the ho-hum buildings,
to my flying lessons, where I can sit
in a sphere of air, freedom, all vectors
open to me: and in my pilot's helmet,
leather jacket I sleep in to age it,
breeches and boots, ah! the looks I get:
am I a freak? I hide in the Rubaiyat,

"And naked on the Air of Heaven ride."
I was behind the ropes, at the air show:
—Is he the host, daddy, ask him what kind
of money to learn; I'd sneak under, but I
can't have him laughing at outlandish me.
—$100/hr, 10 hrs. Why are you so curious?
—I want to fly. And I went up with Hawks,

that barnstormer, 1 buck for 10 minutes,
in his old war surplus crate, and I mean
it's wired together.—My $. Who's this?
—He's flying with us.—Ah; why? They grin
till I catch on: they think I'm a woman
and frail, I might crack up, into hysteria,
jump, oh and the man's there to be my hero:

—I've been around aeroplanes, and I'm cool;
—Sorry, lady, if he don't go, you don't.
1st flight, white morning, and this fool
man babysitting me, crammed in the front
cockpit; air clear, the motor loud, we lift
over the oil derricks, the orange groves,
downtown, to where the Hollywood Hills

and the blue Pacific, strangers, now are
side-by-side in my eye; I see an island
shining out there; he idles, smooth air,
mocking me,—20000 feet! we're at 300;
my soul and body, lilting to fly, oh and
over the world's edge. At supper,—Holy
smoke, ah you're not daydreaming, Millie?

I can't afford that. I worked, for $1/hr,
horsed with the mail room boys, was snubbed
by the society girls, squeal! this is where
I get off and walk, down Long Beach Blvd.
Men run the show, join the service, get paid
to learn; the controls, even the parachute,
fit their bodies, and we have to make shift,

and I paid Neta, that he-woman, red hair,
black flying coat, $1/minute with inherited
Liberty bonds, because she wouldn't sneer,
or scare me off. 1st, lectures on the ground,
in the tool shack, tin roof, santanna wind,

the day electric:—Air speed, gyro horizon,
altimeter, turn & bank. Go over the biplane.

—Okay: the cockpit, fuselage, wheel, strut,
static opening, engine, propeller, cool holes,
carb intake screen, oil radiator, wheel, strut,
wing, ailerons, flaps, stabilizers, elevators,
rudder, tail skid, and wing.—The aeroplane's
awkward on the ground: it lurches, and it
lags; but in the air, it's in its element.

By the oil wells, I hitch in a tin lizzy;
the little girl:—Why're you in those togs?
—I'm a flyer.—Oh that's dreamy, but you
don't look it, in braids. They cut mama's
long fox hair, 16: typhoid, superstitions
it weakened her; I pin mine up and back
so she can't tell I bob inches off week

by week: if I look female, they won't rag
at my aviating. I'm at Tweedy Road; today
I solo. In trousers, it's easier to leg
up into the aeroplane. I taxi, and blow
dust clouds; the left wing sags, and I
get out, fix the shock absorber, take off
and coil up over South Gate in the rough

air of beauty, to 5K, and so what, fooling,
loop, roll, and for the fun of it, like mama,
1st woman to go up Pike's Peak, sun breaking
down the gray sky, that morning, my soul, oh
flying, without a sex, alone, no saying no,
off earth, "can fling the Dust," and glory
with doves and swallows. I sideslip down to

telegraph poles, can I split them? I was 10,
coasting a hill, lying on that sled too tough

for girls, and out of nowhere, the junk man,
his horse, in front: too icy to turn, and deaf
to hear; I make up my mind, and slide in safe,
between the legs, under the horse, good thing
I was riding like a boy, and I whiz and bang,

bad landing, tail high, on the dry field.
This cornhusker takes a snapshot; the boys:
—Were you scared?—I sang, 1st time, loud
as I could.—Only thing you did right was
land it wrong; how was it? Neta:—Congrats,
AE!—Oh, nothing special, I say; but I'm
mile high, and I vow to save every dime

for that aeroplane; I overhear them call me
a natural, whoa! I'm sorry, Noonan, not here,
but daydreaming, wing low, the weight of my
arm on the stick, and so holding left rudder,
not thinking, going down, with back pressure,
right aileron, up elevator, when I should be
doing nothing, only feel it, and let her fly.

Oh I adore that moment, I launch into
the blue: 1 of 12 women flyers on earth, I
rounded up all my savings, help from mama
and even the pigeon, top $, for that new
air-cooled 3-cylinder 60-hp loud yellow
Canary, light and simple, and my 1st love,
out there on the apron, on my birthday 25.

They all call it a kite, but it's my own
sweet property, to air or crash, and I
can haul it by the tail, without a man.
It's a sandpiper, and it loves to fly:
mornings, I taxi it to the dirt runway,
and 3 points down, I eye an orange tree
at the other end; I throttle it up slow

to full, right rudder, to counter the torque,
go for that tree, the tail will come up when
it's good and ready, lift forward, don't walk
it, as the nose sways, tail up, I'm airborne,
controls go firm, stick back, ah ah, come on,
it gets light and skips, give it more angle
of attack, oh up, and I lark, wings level,

rev it, that roar an anthem, the arrow
to climb, I relax back, in this machine,
over the orange tree, in the open sky,
and do the impossible: I sit in heaven,
alive! tilting my wings. October, in
indirect sun, at the field, to advertise
the plane, I spiralled up, 1 hr, high as

she'll go; at 12K, she starts in knocking,
ah shoot, I'm climbing at a ft/sec, better
pull out. I land, saying,—What's wrong?
to the grease boys:—Spark control lever;
but look at this: the world's record for
ah, woman's altitude! 14K. I worked my way
up. Neta got hitched, and kissed it off; I

signed up with a joyrider, this army pilot,
after the war, never drifted out of flying,
the industry's backbone. I learned to stunt:
bank, skid, slip, spin, get out of anything,
loop, barrel roll, dare, in the beginning,
when the teacher had a crowbar to whack
you loose if your hand froze on the stick.

Ah, bless Bernouilli's principle: I fly
when lift = gravity, thrust drag; I rock
in the slipstream, and the propellers go
clockwise; I yaw and rudder, wind wake
scalloping clouds; and, power up, I break
into a characteristic stall, like a wave
falling, let go all controls: it'll dive

and recover to level, by itself—made, oh
to fly! ". . . Dorothy found she was riding"
a cyclone. That Kansas girl: this is my way
to Oz. I walk into the hangar, whistling,
blue salesman, for space, and interrupting
off-color jokes; I like to get all dirty,
studying with men, not in the air, wary

of inviting them, and their misgivings. At
the Air Rodeo:—You race?—I guess I can. . .
—Oh, he'll do the flying, you just ghost it,
and land, the lady winner.—No. Clouds blown,
jagging, in the blue grace, the coiling plane

over the congregation. I see the Milky Way,
wish I had time to make words dance for me;

I write, sign it Emil A. Harte: The hills
can't see the sun go down steeping the lake
they hold like I, from an airplane. Nichols
topped me, so I greased up my face and took
off, in my ship: the mackerel clouds prick
me, blank my goggles, no direction, sleet
on the light cotton wings, nothing for it

but to spin out of the snow, at 12K, shoot,
and quick—am I upside down? in a circle?
so long, break cloud, oh god, kick out
of it, landing, scared:—This vertical:
you go to sleep, sweetheart?—Ah no, I tail-
spun out, to get under the weather.—What
if it had lasted all the way?—Well, Hamlet

would make a bad pilot, with 2nd thoughts. . .
Landing is a power-off stall, all looking
for the gravity outlaw, in over the roofs,
low, on the approach, to get what's coming.
I scan out ahead, wing on line with wing,
holding out till no play in the elevators,
or travel in the stick, and touch 3 wheels

to earth. 1 bounce and they call it a crash:
I practise in secret. Mama left daddy, moving
back east, and I had to let it go for cash,
my Canary, to that air force kid, showboating
from the gas station to the light pole, doing
eights in a vertical bank, and oh sickening
look, slips off, down sideways, crumpling

into his graveyard. . . I was in the N.Y. Times
in my flying suit; cousins:—It's beneath us:

a lady's in print when she's born, marries,
and is buried. Oh fiddlesticks! They're ghosts
and don't know it. Cloud billows, tall banks,
I'm in the thick, better slide under, turn on
carb heat, and idle, and here she goes, down.

KHAQQ TO LAE AT 10000 FEET BUT REDUCING
ALTITUDE BECAUSE OF BANKS OF CUMULUS

I bought a car, the Yellow Peril, common
in L.A., bold in Boston, and drove across
the great divide. I had the old infection
that hurt flying, 24-hr sinus headaches;
they operated, and I took a pre-med course,
no doctor, but it woke up 5 years' memory,
green walks, and actual days, at Columbia:

I went everywhere forbidden, after class,
labyrinth of tunnels, the golden statue's
lap, and the library dome: I looked across
at the angel trumpeting above St. John's.
—Louise, the camera! In my button shoes,
long skirt, and black straw hat.—The pass-
key, Amelia, how'd you—I told him it's

in the name of science. He tried to razz
me, about a suicide jump. Look around us,
oh la! 100 cities in 1, electricity, jazz,
you'd have to be out of your mind to kiss
it off, in the daffodil spring, all this.
I knew that girl, with everything, once,
who cut her wrists out of a bad romance;

I sure enough don't know a man I'd die for.
—Well, last night, he proposed. —Ah Louise!
—Should I, I still have this year, 4 more
till my medical degree.—He has good eyes,
but why let your life go while he keeps his?
Your life.—Everyone is having babies but
me, and I, ah, maybe nobody else—So what?

It's worse to be on reins. Says I, who's not
in love. . . Let's go ride horses in the Park.
In 1920, when women in America got to vote.
Today, she's a doctor. Old roaring New York. . .
Years later, Sam asked me at a Boston quick-
lunch stand:—We have the fair play meetings,
swimming and tennis, the theater and kisses,

in common; honey, you ought to settle down
with me, come live in the Marblehead mansion.
—I love you, but no.—Why? my job at Edison,
my hours? I'll change companies, profession,
whatever.—You don't get it. I'm moving in
the House to work with kids, and I'm going
ahead, married or not: I might go flying.

—It's absurd; I'm the money maker.—I won't
be a housewife, okay? Stay in the kitchen
till I'm no good for anything outside it,
while the man dreams big. What is a woman?
Not second, out of Adam's rib: I have my own
backbone. You write a part that I won't play:
to be and not to do; I write myself. . . You

know what tore it?—No, what.—You were glad
I sold my airplane. All afternoon, the rains.
At the settlement house, in the back yard,
that April day, I was rehearsing the kids,
Through the Looking Glass, where Alice goes;
out of the blue, it's the telephone, for me:
—Miss Earhart, we wonder if you would do

something aeronautical and, well, dangerous?
—Is this a joke?—It's hush-hush.—Are you
a bootlegger?—You have a pilot's license?
Will you promise not to repeat what I—Okay.
—Would you like to fly the Atlantic?—Yeah.

At the interview, not 1 question on flying,
just the 3 men looking at my image, judging

my walk, my words. . . Mrs. Guest was the angel:
she bought the 3-motor monoplane from Byrd.
Her boy:—If you go, mother, I'll quit school;
—Get an American woman to do it, she said.
I wasn't too interesting to drown, was made
commander, and I'd pilot if the weather was
fair. I practised over the Lynn salt marshes,

and over Nahant beach, imagining that sharp
publisher, George Putnam. I wrote my popping
off letter and sealed it, to be opened up
if. . .: Dear Dad, Hooray for the last shining
adventure. I wish I'd made it, but no crying:
it was worth it. I have no hope we'll hook
up later; if only we could. Goodbye, luck,

love, your daughter. Summer, in Newfoundland,
the Atlantic's graveyard, waiting, gray water
and silverware washing up on shore, I read
a book about the Titanic, played draw poker
with the men, winning big, till the weather
lightened: was Bill too whiskeyed up to fly?
Cold shower, hot java; I give the word: go.

They gas it up, by my orders, heavy, so much
to get that seaplane to lumber out of the bay;
wing dips, and I slide toward the open hatch,
Slim catches me. At my log book, faithfully,
oil barrel, my table: It's the true rainbow,
the famous circle, in yellow: in the center's
our shadow? Long grind, the sea in wrinkles

like an elephant's back. Too rough & opaque
for me to take controls. I'm getting maid's

knee, kneeling at the window, where I soak
up beauty. Haze follows us, up in the stars.
So cold: N, horizon; S, smudge. Oh, sparkles
out the exhaust. The machine a marvel, & so
the mind. Instrument flying. 5000 now. Radio

dead, gas vanishing, engine missing. In mist,
blue shadow: is it real? Land! Stick back;
ride to the wharf in a Wales fisherman's boat.
Bill flies blind 2000 mi., is off by 1; look
in the papers: it's "Girl Crosses Atlantic."
I was 31. They can handle girl, get anxious
at woman. In 20 hrs. 40 min. I'm world famous,

and for what? I was a sack of potatoes. I
swear, next flight is on my lonesome. Absurd
parade, up Wall, in ticker tape: oh U.S.A.,
I'm a fake hero. And aviation? They grind
only 2 questions:—Were you afraid? What did
you wear? They insult me with "Lady Lindy."
Newspapers. All I want to do is air-gypsy

cross-country, zoom New York Pennsylvania
Indiana Ohio Missouri Oklahoma Texas New
Mexico Arizona California, do a 180. GP:
—32 cities have asked to see you. 1st solo
from sea to shining sea and back.—Really?
I pasted that story in my old scrapbook
of women's 1sts. I'm due, it's 5 o'clock:

KHAQQ TO LAE AT 7000 FEET AND MAKING 150 MPH

This watch, gold, waterproof, sure tick
of its movement, worn by that motorboat
pilot who disappeared into a big lake,
oh like his name, Seagrave, was fished
out and it given to me, around my wrist. . .

Our courting, all in minutes stolen, before
takeoff, coffee break at the office, after-

lecture taxi ride; that afternoon, flirting,
Chicago hotel, dozing on the one bed, waking
at dusk, stars in the skylight, his skimming,
licking, show me my body's love, uncovering
blue eyes open mouth tough nipples shivering
belly wet crack. . . Oh GP had grit, asking,
one winter; I said no, I don't want anything

all the time; and he kept on; proposal #6,
in a Lockheed hangar, in the engine's heat:
I nod, and pat his arm, climb in, and gas
her, roaring, wave my scarf, fly off, in late
October. The day I was a bride, I wore what
I always—school yearbook, under my picture,
"The girl in brown, who walks alone." Unsure,

I pick up a pencil, heart banging, early
morning: Dear Gyp, we've talked this over;
I have to write it down before we marry,
which I'm a fool to do, as it will shatter
my chance to work. It means so much, I waver,
and I don't have the heart to look ahead.
Don't be faithful, or ask me to, that's old

hat; be honest. Out of my way, and I yours;
and out of the world's eyes, we'll couple.
I need my own address, for sanctuary: this
is so attractive, but it's still a bridle,
and only love can make me stand. One final,

cold promise: if in a year it's not so rosy,
let me go. I'll do my best in all, give you

my skin, and secret, I guess you want. AE.
I shove the letter at him, in hopes, biting
my lips, like a schoolgirl, ah not to cry;
he nods at me, with a 1-sided smile, taking
my hand for the ceremony, fire crackling:
the civil wedding, without the word obey,
the judge reciting, that hard winter day,

in a fishing town, Connecticut, no bouquet,
ring borrowed from his ma, till death do us
part. My sister wires a gypsy blessing: May
the floods never rise to your cooking pots. . .
Over the broomstick, at 33. After the kiss,
to the judge's son:—I was saying, the army
won't back the autogyro, and so the navy—

the judge breaks in:—My best to you, Mrs.
Putnam.—I'm sticking with my name. When
my dream boat, comes home. . . Ah, it's news
on the bamboo fishing pole, our position:
he got himself a star sight, check it on
the flight chart; great: my dreams no more
will roam. On course: radio back to shore.

KHAQQ TO LAE POSITION LATITUDE 4° 33.5'
SOUTH LONGITUDE 159° 7' EAST

If she offers her body, and he his money,
is that a marriage of spirits? Man, look
at a woman and see her, human; if she
says I, it's better; she blooms at work.
I was exalted the day the go-for-broke
Ruth Nichols, in her stripped down Vega
and her long johns, out of Jersey City,

went for altitude at the end of winter;
and she, who'd told her big $ family
forget society girl, she was a flyer,
had no money for a real oxygen supply;
with a hose and tank, she whirls away
in the sky going dark and darker blue,
over 5 miles, and breathing below zero

air into her mouth, till her last gallons
are out, she plunges, her eardrums in pain,
down to the airport; they ask how it was:
at 1st, she can't, her tongue is frozen. . .

I live in a shifting world, and so soon
I pack it up and go, wherever, and those
old snapshots kind of hold it in my eyes.

Like the Steichen, of the glass mural, at
Radio City, New Roxy Theater, 9 windows:
at left, dark column, cut by sprays, next
to curtains, all curling, in step designs,
and open, a stage? a woman, in her arms,
a shawl, pouring, her back to us, the sky
in ribbons, above her, lit by electricity

and mirrors; pearl light, out the window,
hint of snow, when I, mysterious, lowered
the paper, saying,—Okay with you if I fly
the Atlantic solo, in spring? He called
Balchen, with Amundsen at the north, Byrd
at the south, pole, ice seas, blue eyes:
—You're ready, with a log over 1000 hrs;

we'll fix the ship up with a 500 hp super-
charged engine. She looks over the thick
skyscrapers, at the wind in strips of air
laced by energy lines, white rainbow in back
of the airplane, as if thinking—I'm stuck
in an office, grime windows, a crack of sky:
you fly for me, Amelia. She sees the Vega,

star bright, over the waves, blue curving,
green straight, double; propeller whirls,
energy circles; black sections, looming
rain; in the off geometry, hard showers.

We'd asked what's it like out, what does
Doc Kimball say? Earth turns, the weather
blows east across it, like water counter-

clockwise, haunting him, inside his bureau,
in thin telegrams, at his desk, building
a map of isobars, and the mid-Atlantic low.
One last look at the dogwoods, blossoming,
and out to Harbour Grace; the man pumping
gas:—Good luck, Miss Earhart.—I can use
it; 7 women have died trying.—You choose

this anniversary of Lindbergh?—Oh, I did;
5 years: the tide comes in and out, and we
edge into the miraculous, so maybe your kid
can walk on the moon, Major Aldrin. I eye
old Balchen, with a little smile:—Think I
can make it?—Yeah, sure. I sit in the red
airplane, rev it, check the mags, and nod.

KHAQQ TO LAE ON COURSE FOR HOWLAND ISLAND
ALTITUDE 12000 FEET CHANGING FROM 6210 TO 3105

LAE TO KHAQQ STAY ON THIS FREQUENCY SIGNAL WEAK
HEAVY STATIC

KHAQQ TO LAE WISH TO CONTACT AMERICAN CUTTER
ON THE NIGHT BAND

Into the wind, and the long sundown, so I
won't arrive at dusk on an unknown coast,
with my lucky elephant bracelet and a saw-
buck, oh out to sea, beauty, action, just
for that, and to show a woman can, I start;
between the private takeoff and the shock
of landing, there's no witness to my work.

4 hrs out, lightning, and I see the moon
blink, the altimeter, hands swinging, ah!
out of commission, the rain blowing down,
and I see fire, in the manifold ring—why
did I look? Wasn't the storm south; am I
off course? That crack is worse; the weld
is broken; if it splits . . . Well, should

I go back? Night landing, Newfoundland,
heavy fuel; in 4 hrs I'll be half-way . . .
Zero visibility, no horizon, burning, and
I shove on, climb over the clouds, now
I ice up, I'm spinning, dirty window,
god! but Lindbergh, same trouble, and he
made it: I go down to melt, till I see

whitecaps breaking, on the black tide,
glad it's not a smooth sea, wave salts
under my nose, manifold shaking; I hold
under ice, over water, sip tomato juice,
in steady mist, too low, no instruments,
where is the plane, in space? The gyro
compass, a life-saver. 1st light, I fly

white clouds, foam blowing, north, west,
ice on the wing's edge, the sun dazzling,
dark glasses, did I drift south? East,
skim water, to a boat, manifold rattling,
I switch to reserve tanks, gauge leaking
on me, and what if the fumes catch fire?
Don't miss the island; I can't see far . . .

KHAQQ TO ITASCA DO YOU READ ME A SHIP
IN SIGHT AHEAD

It's Ireland, turn right, into the high
hills, thunder, and no altimeter, I 180,

up a railroad, hope for a city, no, only
a sloping farm, cows scare, I light, oh
in the grass, the manifold in flames, so
tired, the engine, unfailing, the heart,
and I sit in the cockpit: I've done it.

—Where am I?—In Gallagher's pasture.
Come far?—From America.—Are you man
or woman?—Could I have a sip of water?
GP, on the phone:—Oh, your voice again,
AE, you are the world's greatest woman.
—I was on fire, and I figured, you know,
I'd rather drown than burn, so I flew low.

Our trans-Atlantic talk, green headland,
lighthouse, shamrock, leaves in a fan
with a crazy flower, and water, down and
into a blue pool signed: Maurice Heaton;
under the mural, with my legs up, I lean
on my hand, natural smile, eyes, not shy,
downcast: I look straight into the camera.

The Irish taxed me, for importing gas,
the Lindberghs, in mourning, telegraphed,
Smith, who I beat to it, was gracious,
the mobs . . . I will meet you, I will greet
you, London Paris Rome Washington, out
to touch me; newspapers:—It's unwomanly.
—There is no woman, but women, and we

are what we do. All the aeronautical prizes:
the Distinguished Flying Cross, 1st woman,
from Congress, and I don't know, silver wings
of the 381st National Observation Squadron,
American Society British Guild French Legion;
I stuck songs and praise in a folder, Bunk;
with Eleanor Roosevelt, I did the cakewalk,

we went flying. I met Orville:—Well, did
you know there was a Wright sister? Back
when, she was a schoolteacher; her hard
money it was that let Wilbur and I work;
she sewed the wings for us at Kitty Hawk.
And I saw Babe Didrikson air the javelin
and win, at the Olympics, and took off in

my little red bus, non-stop record 19 hrs,
only 1 minute over Hawks, cross-country.

One winter day, kicking Hollywood ideas
around:—I like Kate Hepburn cast as me,
but I still want to solo the Pacific; oh
I know it's killed 10. Hawaii businessmen
backed me, to advertise their island sun.

The navy said no till we upped the radio's
range, and the Star Bulletin was uneasy I'd
sold out for 10 grand, to sugar and hotels:
the boys were about to fold; I up and said:
—I smell cowardice in here. I'll go ahead
with or without your bankroll. They clapped.
I gave Gyp a popping off letter:—I'll lift

that heavy load, off a rough field, as best
I can, and if I don't shine this time, it
won't be because the engine isn't excellent
or women can't fly. All night, breaking out
the window, the waves, lagging and constant,
not sleeping, I was thinking of the captain
last November, who went down in that ocean:

1 weak sos, and he was gone; and dreaming
of Ruth Law, and that day in 1916 Chicago
she was out to top a man: she's shimmying
through the Loop, and out to open country,
with a clock and compass, in a wheelbarrow
with wings, the end, rocking the last drops
into the carb, and gliding to a distance

record; down in the barnyard, she answers
—What? Oh I did it for nothing, just to

do it. The tropic rain, all morning, is
slackening at last: that field is muddy,
wind against me, but, storms on the way,
it's this afternoon or never. I see news-
reels, ambulances, fire trucks, and ladies

with handkerchiefs, ready for an emergency:
I roll, wheels in mud, spraying, get light,
and look, my old mechanic, running with me;
I side-to-side, and into the air, I jolt,
all of a sudden, drop, don't crash, ignite
the extra fuel, full power and she catches,
oh I'm this machine. Over the cane fields,

I swing out toward Diamond Head, and round
the point, gray sky; they going to shoot
at me, too low over the navy yard? in scud
to 6K and above, stars, my god, rising out
of the ocean, hang outside of the cockpit:
I fly out of the Magellanic Clouds, slide
under Polaris toward morning, the mainland.

14 changes in course, by my little chart,
the big ocean: will I see, ah searchlight;
I blink my lights 3 times; like buckshot,
their code, crackling. I radio back, not
my position, but the filmy clouds, washed
out moon, the black water, in come-and-go
drizzle blowing in through the port window.

I drink hot chocolate, and interview live
on the all-night talk show, stand still,
in rapture, at the river of stars: I give
up the day-to-day for this holy dazzle.
Light at the horizon, and the lights fail
in the overwhelming sun; and what is it,
coming up too far south, by my fool chart.

No earth, white mist, I'm in my own world,
with opera in waves on the radio, crashing;
oh the last hour's hard, looking the cloud
shadows into islands, shores, dissolving;
through holes, I see blue water, rippling,
dive down, and it's a $ Liner; I can follow
her wake a ways, to the hills of California.

After Atlantic war, Pacific peace: the 1st
person to cross that ocean, and at Oakland:
—Your transmission: I'm tired?—You missed
my meaning in static: of the fog, I said.
10000 hurrah, crying, by the armed guard,
shove American Beauty roses at my breast.
That landing is in the diary of my heart.

I saw a little white horse at the circus,
and here I am, jumping through this hoop:
I record, and lecture, circle for the box
office, women in flying, till I can loop
back up. After the newsreel smiles, I slip
off to the whatever hotel, where I have
to type up the big money Times exclusive,

then out on tour, booked by my P. T. Bar-
num impresario, manager and shadow, down-
to-earth man and high-flying woman, star
of this sideshow, I blow in, 1 hr alone,
and face-to-face with that old question:
What did I wear? Come on; my flying clothes:
high laced boots, brown broadcloth britches,

white silk shirt, wild tie, drab sweater,
long leather coat, with pockets, collar,
cream silk scarf, goggles, thin leather
flying helmet; on routine flights I wear
my everydays. I'm tall as you in the air,
as light, as strong; on earth, 5'8, 117.
My hair is combed by wind, and my skin sun-

freckled; I go for the simple, clothes
that last, in grace: I design long-line
plain get-ups, not for the stay-at-home,
but the woman in motion. I go around in
pants, like nobody, ha! I'm a man woman:
I might put on overalls and carry roses,
and I'm a pilot with a string of pearls.

Ah well, not too much profit in a shirt
made of a parachute. . . Next: Was I scared?
I looked at the chance of dying, straight
on, and then put it out of my hard head.
If you want brave, those '29 flyers had
insides, 1st woman's air race, California
to the Ohio finish line, and the mockery

we faced: Will Rogers called it the Powder
Puff Derby, and us Sweethearts of the Air,
anything but pilots. The NAA didn't dare
let us cross the Rockies, were asking for
men as navigators, and I wouldn't enter
till they backed down. We had Ruth Elder,
ocean fighter, Phoebe Omlie, sky diver

and flying teacher, Pancho Barnes, stunt
pilot, Ruth Nichols, distance, Gladys O'
Donnell, circuit racer, and Bobbi Trout,
endurance champ, and Louise Thaden, who
held the records. Women are weak, they say,
but look at Maggie Perry, able to fly 48
hrs with typhoid; they say hysterical, but

look at Blanche Noyes, down in the mesquite,
on fire, with handfuls of sand, and at it
in the air again; they say frivolous, but
oh, look at Marvel Crosson, who bailed out
in the Gila River hills, and died wrapped
in her parachute silk, for love of flight. . .
Okay, I'll ask you: Who's Lady Lindy? Not

me: no lady, not Lindbergh. Newspapermen
are fish for the old lure of alliteration
and hook of categories. I crossed my own
Atlantic, and my name is Earhart.—Anne,
I said,—I'm sorry; at our Rye mansion,

under the dogwoods, and she with her blue
questioning eyes, possible smile,—You

are tall and slim, true face, cool eyes,
clear mind, in balance, and bolt across
oceans. . . Ah, but the country headlines
my act, margins it, and back to business.
Aviation pays women 38¢/hr, and men 70¢,
for the same job; I asked a manager why:
—They work for less; my costs are high. . .

Because of the accident of sex, a woman
has to do it better, for the same credit.
They don't trust us with a real airplane,
think our periods make us crazy; I asked
a circus lady if she excused her tight-
rope walkers:—Oh no, for heaven's sakes!
I campaigned for 2 years, at Air Commerce;

at last, they hired 1 woman, as a token.
I'm afraid all my 1sts add up to zero,
women pilots, blackballed, by power men:
I opened the door for the stewardess. Oh,
I say go ahead, against the odds, fly;
I'm here to sway girls: you can do it
if, like grandma said, you have spirit;

I'm proof: ignore old boys, don't take no
for an answer; how can you earn your spurs
if you don't ride? make it happen. The day
we're equals in the sun will be centuries
in coming. Good night. I walk in applause,
to the loose reception, and sign my little
autograph, talk to the local paper, till

midnight, I'm on the road, to Sioux City,
300 miles. I stack the money up from books

like The Fun of It: Random Records of My
Own Flying and Women in Aviation, stamps,
advertising, handouts, whatever it takes
for the next flight. And go to sleep: hold
you closely, my own. . . I'm looking to land

on an atoll in the lonesome Pacific: ah
women, what is harder? Well, it's after
12, in the crescent moon, and no radio
from the navy cutter, flying over water
in the dark, again. I wish I could hear
sign on, swing music, and any old shows,
human voices, chattering, over the noise

of engines, but no contact yet, too far.

After the 2nd ocean, FDR:—You're a woman
from pioneer America, out on the frontier
of air, and showed flying isn't for men
only. I founded the 99s, for all women
pilots and aerial experience. . . Invited
to Mexico: Wiley Post, around-the-world

air man, with the eye patch:—What route?
—Straight as I can.—Across the Gulf?
—Yeah.—Kind of far; how much time cut?
—1 hr.—Amelia, don't; it isn't safe.
—Hah, I can hardly wait: I had to laugh.
I go by midnight, in the generous moon,
over Baja, white haze, white water, on

1 engine, overheating, over the sierra,
to the high mesa; I'd drift out of line,
they said, last leg: I find Guadalajara,
this unknown railroad, grain of sand in
my eye and the maps blurred, and I sit down,
dry lake, sign language with the vaqueros,
who know me; they motion south, and I rise.

Why am I a chalkboard on which they love
to scrawl adjectives? They call me simple,
complex, thorough, grand, pioneer, above
my age, ahead of my time, unique, immortal,
restless, rebelling, strong, original,
calm, invulnerable, open-air, slow-moving,
speed-crazy, on wings, upward, dazzling,

unexpectedly feminine, quiet, music- and

book-loving, intellectual, fire-eating,
quick, honest, fascinating, fascinated,
valid, dreaming, down-to-earth, searching,
foresighted, illegible, mysterious, caring,
misunderstood, misunderstanding, graceful,
steady, in style, inspiring, practical,

excellent, imperfect, lucky, many-sided,
equal, skilled, in charge, free-spirited,
supporting, rival, devoted, open-handed,
flush, hard up, moving, tender-hearted,
cool, poised, light, fun, high-minded,
scared, brave, daring, elegant, comely,
arrogant, famous, solitary, friendly,

loved, gold-digging, gracious, well-bred,
rude, praiseworthy, praised, human, humane,
pure, home-wrecking, sacrificing, tousled,
legendary, childless, magical, uncertain,
unorthodox, undaunted, undefeated, uncommon,
undomestic, unfailing, ungracious, unfaithful,
unbound, unsentimental, untiring, unusual,

tomboy, golden girl, true daughter, dear
sister, nurse, pacifist, horseback rider,
student, clerk, photographer, truck driver,
social worker, pilot, wife, loner, author,
talker, feminist, designer, record holder,
hero, the 1st lady of the American sky:
a cloud of language, through which I fly.

Oh the horses of Mexico, and hat dancing
with the charros, and women will be free
as men are, whatever country, I'm hoping;
the army boys lay out a 3-mile runway
on the Lake Texcoco mud flats, warn me
she won't go up in the rare air; I'm in,

575

check by headlights, and the young moon.

I push her past 100 mph, and in 1 mile she
rises, up over the bull ring, the mud
ranchos, the floating gardens, Xochimilco,
the snows of Popocatapetl, and the divide,
clouds down. . . Moon and water—I go around
thunderheads—will sing. . . lit up by pure
lightning; my ship's handsome, nobody here

to see. Blue gulf, last flight in a single
engine, on to New Orleans, I pick up radio,
slide home on that party line, to Mobile;
my partner in the east coast shuttle:—Hey,
that's enough, Amelia; better land; and I,
—No thanks, I'm going on; at the hangar,
in the mob, cops yank me in a tug-of-war.

KHAQQ TO ITASCA 14 HOURS OUT CLOUDY AND
OVERCAST DO YOU READ ME

I wonder if they'll pick that up in static.
This flight got under way at a forum: Women
and the Changing World, for the Herald, N.Y.,
Wiley's airplane down with Will:—I'm not in
the lost generation; it's okay to rally on
peace, dance to low-down jazz, look cubist,
fly if it's in their hearts. This president

invited me to work his coeds up toward
careers, and that Indiana research outfit
poured in 40 grand to get me a Lockheed
Electra, S3H-1 Wasp engines, 1100 hp at
full, on my birthday 39; shakedown flight,
I thought, "I'll put a girdle round about
the earth:" Shakespeare, dreaming; and not

at high latitude, in the short cut, but
at the world's waist, across the 7 heavens
in my own Golden Hind, 1 more long flight
in me. Oh charts are fine: the compass rose,
the courses, changes, the prevailing winds,
distances, notes on local weather, main
altitudes, crisis landings. . . white ocean.

Call it world flight, and I have 5 chapters
and 1001 details to Scheherezade through:
get money, lay out headings, arrange visas,
line up fuel drums, mortgage my future, ah
but what are futures for? I study zero

visibility flying, fish for a star navigator,
and reel him in, off of a South Seas clipper,

Fred Noonan, old hand, 1-time hard drinker,
to handle the chronometers, bubble sextant,
pelorus, aperiodic compass, drift indicator,
and back over the catwalk from this cockpit.
Jackie Cochran, ace flyer, and I heart-
to-heart over aviation all Xmas, and she
opens me up to the 6th sense, telepathy:

United Airlines flight was missing,—Here,
I prophesy, and touch the map's pale color,
telephone, and the wreck's under my finger.
She sees I'm crossing over uncharted water,
and worries; we promise to esp each other.
In the blue winter dusk, the traffic light,
I see this old man, going hungry, and not

begging: I tell Gyp, so hard, I'd hate it,
I don't think I'll live to be old. . . I fly
off on St. Patrick's, dip under the almost
done Golden Gate, and sight a plane at sea,
right engine in and out, ice in carb, I
leaned it too much, rainbow, gold nothing
sun down, copilot on, and Venus setting.

KHAQQ TO ITASCA BROADCAST ON 3105 KCS ON
HOUR AND HALF OVERCAST

I'm back on instruments, the moon's a life-
saver, giving us horizon; they're shooting
star sights out of the hatch, through brief
holes in the clouds; at last, stars fading,
I throttle down to arrive in the morning,
keeping it at 10° to the starboard bow,
and set a trans-Pacific record anyhow.

After a test flight, right propellers had
conked out, I taxi down the even pavement
at Oahu, our destination, Howland Island,
into a slight crosswind, 1000 ft, the right
wing sags, shocks gone? power down left,
it's swerving, no control, ground loop, ah
slam down, white sparks up from the belly,

our ship, dripping with fuel, time slows
to a still point, the airfield sliding,
fingers uncurling, I—remember wheels
stuck in the mud, tall grass, she noses
over, the safety belt breaks, my body's
sailing, to the dry weeds, the airplane
on its back; that morning, in a bad spin,

I hit the brakes, leaning, the door opens
and knocks me in, and my skull's cut; okay,
I crash, like anybody: the vulgar papers
and movies are bored to death, can't do
without crack-ups and lost flyers, but ah,
that isn't aviation. If I don't come back,
I'll go down a legend my ghost will mock:

yeah, it was a woman who died, not a man—
so what? 1st time, I was flying back
from the Goodyear field: if I go in low,
I'll hit the eucalyptus trees that flank
the runway, so I pull up, stall, pancake
into a cabbage patch, bite tongue, fingers,
like now, uncurling, I—cut the switches:

if I don't burn up, I'm trying it again.
It's a miracle; heaven, it hurts to see,
out of my daze, that fabulous airplane
broken. . . of the tender love I bring. I

sigh:—We'll go on around the other way.
4 a.m., when the birds tweet, and I radio
my waves ahead, toward the light of day.

KHAQQ TO ITASCA CAN'T HEAR YOU ON 3105 KCS
PARTLY CLOUDY

Questions come up:—Why on earth are you
going ahead?—Oh, are you saying my luck
will run out, like front money, that how
it works? I'm just this way; I jaywalk
where my heart leans, and risk is music.
It's useless, like poetry, this gesture:
I light out into the wilderness of air,

and to validate a dream in a woman's eye.
All my pals at the airfield say pull out;
Louise, on that last night:—You're crazy;
you're tops, now and always, nothing to get
and all to lose, why open up to a knock-out?
I shake my head as we sit on the life raft:
—Ha, you should talk; didn't you fly that

air race with a gas tank around your neck?
I've gone all out, and so this is my fling.
Ah, my date's already in the doomsday book,
when I'm done; if I go down, it's doing
what I love. The off-shore breeze blowing
in my hair:—I never run. My one regret,
no time to have a kid, like yours; just

tell her to ride that iron horse, ah build
harbor bridges, and go after the bad guys.
That sugar daddy, Baruch, gave 25 grand:
—I like your everlasting guts. . . I buzz
5th Ave. at noon, to advertise, tip wings
at 42nd St.; and I sprawl, grease monkey,
watching it get better, navigation, radio,

load. . . Kind of tired: pull out that can,
tomato juice, ice pick. We pack by stars,
land compass, matchbox, little ax, canteen,
life boat, flare pistol, orange kite, rags,
good night, dear pony, and I rub her nose.
Dark out, in the a.m., and the human city
asleep, crew yawning, and the air heavy

with dew, so fine for wings to cut into,
the engines idling, and the quick goodbyes,
coffee, and into the tight cockpit, stow
bag and bottle, oh the feeling, 50 dials,
green magic, flight plan, it's in my hands,
I'm up to getaway speed, without a word,
we're in the air, May 20, out of Oakland.

It's all a whirl, the country abstracting,
actual oaks, and shadow trees, I sky down
to Burbank, Tucson, saguaros, sand blowing,
New Orleans, old night, riverboat, jazz in
the air, Miami, lunch at the greasy spoon
across the coast highway, oh the buttermilk,
the lighthouse, over the shoals, the Tropic,

San Juan, white church, in the Gulf Stream,
Caripito, red roofs, oil tanks, orchids,
grapes, Paramaribo, at the edge, steam
on the river, jungle, leopard, Fortaleza,
tidal flats, modern towers, catamarans,
baskets of fish, Natal, red dirt, ibis,
shipwreck under ribbons of surf, across

the Atlantic rains, to St. Louis, thick
cloud, oasis of palms, simple huts, Dakar,
peninsula, rose city, human smells, mosaic,
Gao, queen, pyramid in ruins, mosque, poor
barrens, Ft. Lamy, blank space, El Fasher,

thorn hedge, sultan's palace, rush baskets,
Khartoum, heat waves, squares and streets

the imperial flag, camel rider, old Nile,
Massawa, sailboat on the Red Sea, salt
piles, Assab, empty coast, bone dry well,
forbidden Arabia, border, Karachi, desert
ship, Calcutta, aerodrome, black eagles,
crowded harbor, city, elephant and howdah,
Akyab, banyan, solid monsoon, mud volcano,

Rangoon, flying fish, gold pagoda, quick
rickshaws, Bangkok, temples, junks, dream
waters, Singapore, island, theater music,
Bandoeng, rice terraces, shadow drama,
Surabaya, dog cart, Koepang, pleasure dome,
dry grass, cliffs, last outpost, merchant,
green seas, Port Darwin, kangaroo, forest,

pearl diver, Lae, village in river, monkey,
oh, hallelujah motion, around the world.
Backfire and fire, cross the equator, no
Neptune to douse me, wrong turn, long ride,
back track; and now, over the dateline, led
on by the horizon, to yesterday, skywriting. . .
Air speed, time, distance, the true heading:

KHAQQ TO ITASCA WANT BEARING ON 3105 ON HOUR
WILL WHISTLE IN MIKE ABOUT 200 MILES OUT
APPROXIMATELY WHISTLING NOW

Whoo; wait for answer. . . And in this other
world all the way, this melting geography:
through the rain maker, low sheet, thunder-
head, fair-weather, snail clouds, and into
the mackerel sky, white veil, sun's halo,
up to ice crystals, mare's tail, anvil;

I rode Antony's horse, and Hamlet's whale,

slammed into hills, into oceans of haze,
invisible stream, no map, no buoy, flows
from high to low, and easterly, over waves
of heat, slow rocking, updrafts like sprays,
rough air, or easy sailing, and heaven is
the troposphere. . . We'll be sweethearts, oh
forever. . . Old earth lies in squares below,

like stanzas. . . I can't raise them, no
receiver, dynamo working under the seat;
I'll relay it to him, in back: bad radio. . .

The east is lightening, and with no rest,
morning is close; this signal, this ghost
transmission, will fade out; I'll sag into
black ocean, abide, swaying in the agony

of the tides, which won't give up the dead.
Ah quick, little to tell; after this wave,
last words, grace me, now and then, rolled
in the mystery, with a moment of your love. . .
Time's flying, quarter to 7; if I can give
them my voice to follow, and get a bearing,
we'll close on that island in not too long,

by his star fix, out of the all night rack,
and the sun glaring on the colossal water.

KHAQQ TO ITASCA PLEASE TAKE BEARING ON US
AND REPORT IN 1/2 HOUR I WILL MAKE NOISE
IN MIKE ABOUT 100 MILES OUT

Day off, we forded the river in a truck
to a cocoanut grove, huts on stilts, fire
of the women, oh the jungle to explore,
and back to cable a chapter to the Herald:
We won't be home by 4th of July as hoped.

I was looking west, over Pacific breakers,
and this last evening, east; in a few days,
the world's river's run under us, the end's
this ocean; I'll be glad, its blue hazards
behind me. But in my old poem, "Courage is
the price that life exacts for granting peace.

585

The soul that knows it not knows no release. . ."

At every landing, passports, visas, all
those countries, and 1 sky: and America
ahead, good times, hard times, dust bowl,
new deal, steel strikes, gun men, jumbo
circus, and coast-to-coast flights daily,
sliding toward war. . . Why is that island
How Land? Low reef, mile long, 1/2 wide;

but I'm Air Heart. I let her down, don't
see the cutter, ah, only acres of water,
the dazzle at the equator, did we drift
north, arrow to the left, on the gas meter,
from head winds, carb, the sun line's where?

KHAQQ CALLING ITASCA WE MUST BE ON YOU BUT
CAN'T SEE YOU GAS IS RUNNING LOW BEEN UNABLE
TO REACH YOU BY RADIO FLYING AT 1000 FEET

I ain't lost but I don't know where I'm at,
as the old barnstormer said: what was it,

his fixes, or the charts, not enough fuel
for other islands, we need to stretch it,
maximum cruise, go down to 1 1/2 stall,
on the back side of the power curve, point
up, overshoot, turn south on the current
line of position run forward from the last
star, and circle, in hopes we make it out.

KHAQQ CALLING ITASCA WE ARE CIRCLING BUT
CAN'T HEAR YOU GO AHEAD ON 7500 WITH A
LONG COUNT NOW OR ON THE SCHEDULED TIME
ON THE 1/2 HOUR

Come on, give me the letter A, like you. . .

DOT DASH DOT DASH DOT DASH DOT DASH DOT DASH
GO AHEAD ON 3105

Oh, the coast guard! if the direction loop
homes on that frequency, we'll read them now:

KHAQQ CALLING ITASCA WE RECEIVED YOUR SIGNALS
BUT CAN'T GET A MINIMUM PLEASE TAKE BEARING
ON US AND ANSWER ON 3105 WITH VOICE
DOT DASH DOT DASH DOT DASH DOT DASH DOT DASH

Around the circle, bad omens, as I slip:
this route never flown; and on her lit up
globe, mama couldn't see the island; for
weight I left my lucky bracelet back there;

I didn't wear my wings, on this one flight.
Smooth air, sure of our longitude, ceiling
unlimited, ah but no position, poor contact:
if we go in. . . oh Gyp! I was a kid, reading
in our library, and in all the showboating
adventure books, they had none with girl
heroes, and I—well, maybe now they will.

KHAQQ TO ITASCA WE ARE ON THE LINE 157 337
NORTH AND SOUTH WILL REPEAT MESSAGE WE WILL
REPEAT THIS ON 6210 KCS WAIT 3105 WE ARE
RUNNING ON LINE LISTEN 6210 KCS

It's a dead stick landing, and the tail's
down, lessen the blow. When my dream boat
comes home. . . Ditch in the 6 foot waves.
We've come 24000 miles. Oh, that was it,
I was thinking, yesterday, on my way out
to the aerodrome: Charlie let us play in
the old 2-seat carriage in grandma's barn,

with an invisible horse, the blue pigeon,
the girls, and I, whooping at dangers in
the clouds of dust, imaginary country, on
the way to Cherryville, never arriving. In
the salty morning, I know what's on the line,
but la-de-da; in the come what may sun,
I go on walking out to the lovely airplane.

Blue Ridge

Nothing, only white froth, on the surface,
in the current; it fizzles and gives back
sky, wharf, our images, but in an unsure
mirror, the shallows; it shifts, look: all
our yesterdays, under, in the sea tangle,
in the green obscure, where the hours warp
and the years writhe. I cup the salt water
and it slides off; oh can we dive? How do
I take you back, to the mermaid songs, days
of hallucination, and circuit riding into
the south, if it's only conjured? that time,
in the mountains like smoke, a woman, from
the last century, a photograph, her eyes,
and what her life was, I could only wonder.

Undeclared war, the number 2 song Rainy
Day Women #12 and 35, the hidden meaning,
marijuana cigarette, American Tobacco Co.,
last word in smoking, Surgeon General's
warning, Motion Picture Code okays blue
language, the top moneymaker, Thunderball,
Rose Bowl, doves vs. hawks, the in crowd,
American Heritage, 1/2 price, in stereo,
General Motors detectives tail consumer
advocate, heart fund, underground radio.

Great Society programs, war on poverty, cut
back to bankroll Southeast Asian war, ooh
take it all off, she drawls, to The Stripper,
shaving cream, more troops, long hair, Supreme
Court, inform suspect of rights, to silence,
old vaudeville and silent movie star dies,
her miniskirt rides up, shows stocking tops
and thighs, Gemini docking, whirls, rapture
of the deep, power steering, power brakes,
hippies, vote march, sheriff lets gunman go.

B-52 bomber, 3rd world, can't hear it coming,
He's a real nowhere man, collides in mid-air,
Gulf & Western corporate takeover, soft moon
landing, National Organization, wet and wild,
of Women says false image in the mass media,
go go dancers, 13th broken arrow, hydrogen
bombs fall on the Spanish coast, speed stick
deodorant, Playboy centerfold, integrated
circuit, whites excluded, black power, and
the president gives go-ahead for air strikes.

Free love, soul music, drought of century,
new moon drops under-makeup moisture film,
Ford Mustang, Bronco, Falcon, Thunderbird,
charge it, American Express, it's our time

machine, jet, generation gap, When a man
loves a woman, antiwar rally, sleep out
in the rain, eye shadow, Metropolitan Life
Insurance, transit strike, New York, cars
lock, lose your heart to the 1966 Cadillac,
and things go better with Coke, trade-mark.

In the anonymous night, the sultry air,
no rain, the naked man, cock under wraps,
the god of messages? on his roost, time,
12 numbers, a circle, through the facade,
on my lonesome, I go into the tabernacle

of motion, on the ceiling the zodiac, and
after money changes, my prayer's holding
a blue ticket to the back country, love
gone cold or in its early fire, twanging
on the salvation radios, without a body.

All strangers, but we're strands in a cord,
one direction, for now, out of the belly,
under the black river, to the ghost whinny
of the iron horse, pitiful lights, the rough
city, go sliding past, I south, oh rocking

in the rails' arms, a pilgrim, with faith
in nothing, with a tale, a blue-eyed girl
by me, it happens, ah talk to her, make
up for the old days, lifting their arms,
as we highball, the American dark, opening.

Ah, you're into Hawthorne; I have a hard
time with his shadow, like the Puritan
black he wrestled with got into him, his
black novels. I don't mean to

                           What you got
against the black novel?

                      I, ha, well, I'm
from California, and we don't feel guilt.
I mean

         I'm from Santa Monica.

                    Venice: I
must live a mile from you by the palm trees
on Ocean Blvd.

           I'm Leah.

                offers her hand:
first touch: I intro and she

                You ever read
his short stories?

            holds up the book, and I
shake no

        In this skyscraper country, we
look down on lean-to art. Oh, but that's
Hawthorne, and our first light.

                The Twice-
Told Tales.

        Yeah, like in that wild Vision
of the Fountain: a girl, a beauty, is in
the water, and vanishes; back of a rainbow,
and gone; at night, where he's staying, he
thrills to a voice, of memory and promise:
in the firelight, he sees she's in the room.
It's love on the level of skin, and coming
in through the eye.

         Oh, fantastic.

              Where you
headed?

       Blowing Rock, North Carolina. I

get off at Roanoke.
I'm getting off there
to see my sister.
Is that named after
Yeah,
the lost colony, on the green island: they
sailed out of Shakespeare's world. No sign
of trouble but all gone, and the first born
American child, missing.
I remember: first
mystery.
train follows a curve: she leans
into me delicious and she
We're together
till morning and I, is it crazy, I'm not
into the book or dreaming, I wonder if
you could tell a story, oh just to blow
away the hours?
Ah sure, this summer—I'm
still wet, and from a rain of wonder.
It's
okay with you?
Yeah, I'm overflowing with
my strange July; one sec.
I out with my
new flask
Ah good; one sip of this here
southern whiskey, I'll feel it again. It
was, well, last week for you, long time
back for me, living in the Village, on
the edge
oil refinery lights drifting by

All I see is the skin, that conjunction
of roses, of the angels waiting
tables, dirty glasses
from their hands' heaven
to this invisible man
as dollars whoop it up,
my fingers sting with cuts from love
songs cracked under the water:
oh they have eyes, but for the star
next season will blow out.

At last, the hungers
go home, to actual arms,
and the imagination has to lug
the greasy cans
to the blue street, moon down,
lock up the night and slide down West
Broadway over the rose grey cobble-
stones half asleep,
iron bars, the gate and windows
of the brownstone lost in memory

of its poor vines, the locust tree
down-hearted in a square of dirt,
the thief under the news
and the derelict wine,
to a breakfast joint, sour bread
under syrup, and up
Canal St. to the abandoned loft,
as trucks, slamming, on circle routes,
haul daybreak out of the East River
into the brown sky.

I wake up in the accidental room, horns,
sirens, the afternoon blurring. So long,
hustler, who last night in the bone bang
snake charm acid rock at the light show
told lies at 2 am, and screwed two girls;

so long, crazy, who stacking up confusion
pamphlets, is anxious, Noah's on the run,
the ark not finished, and the blue police
are closing in. Hungry, but I can't cook
in this brown water. I slouch at the old

desk, and under the belly dancer, I count,
catalog, commentary, after what syllable
the bard sets a caesura, how that silence
works in "Like as the waves make towards
the pebbled shore," in his sea rhythm. I

go back, to the first satellite, the cold
war scare money to schools, the military
hand on my thin shoulder, ah to guide me
like a missile into physics, its algebra
so clear, when I daydreamed into poetry

howling, in a street music, the dynamo
language, into my eye, out of my fingers,
its figures so unsure. Sputnik, beatnik:
sky rocket, underground poem: I waver.
Oh my true love, sing Down in the valley,

skimmed off her clothes, valley so low,
laid on the bed, hang your head over, I
was frozen, hear the wind blow, not long
till the break-up: oh my country, thanks
for nothing, and my forefather, who was

a board, for punishment, mother, no voice.

No home, no girl, no school, no job, no face,
sex hymns and mystery songs outside; kids
used to call me Einstein: wish I could go
read the equations on his last chalkboard.

I was wondering, ah if you could show me
where Einstein worked.
                              the old man's eyes
startle, and then light
                        You are a tourist
and I'm your guide?
                      ah no, I'm bothering
a genius
            Oh, I thought
                        I'm an attendant?
his own apple and tea
                        I've been here off
and on since 33.
                      I don't want to break in
On what? I have a free hand to do nothing,
if l like. I listen to your young radio;
you'll know that song, Mr. Tambourine Man:
he talks of driving memory and fate deep
beneath the waves, forget today, denying
all time?
            It might be in the night after
a break-up.
              Ah! a love song, from which
the beloved's been erased. It's Room 115,
in back; no, come with me.
                            he hitches on
his black winter coat and hat, in July:
we cross the open field, the Institute
for Advanced Study
                      Once, he was alive,
and I would talk with Einstein in the sun
on the sidewalk to work.
                          You knew him? Who
are you?
          Godel.
              The Incompleteness Theorem
Godel?

Ah, my fame is unbounded.

What are
you working on?

Proof no infinity exists
between the natural and the real numbers,
is what I tell them. In here.

Historical
Studies Library

What have I done in life
but uncover a paradox? And I'm getting
nowhere fast on the continuum hypothesis.
his office: back wall, a window: a pool,
and woods: lights off, desk empty, one
glass, empty: he smiles, and motions me
into an easy chair

Light, quicksilvering,
takes time: the Milky Way is thousands
of years ago, the sun eight minutes, in
the moment, lightning thunder, my image
crosses to you, I have moved on, unknown:
all you see is the past. . . What would
you say if I told you how to walk into
the world that was?

Well, I read science
fiction, but you, what

Did I discover?
In the library, Albert and I'd talked
over his field equation: let R sub ik
be the curvature tensor, R its scalar,
g sub ik gravitational potential, kappa
the gravitational constant, T sub ik
dust, and the energy tensor of matter;
then R sub ik minus one-half g sub ik R
plus kappa T sub ik equals zero. Hard
to fathom: each of the exact solutions
lights up a universe. I was after proof
time can't pass, to uphold Kant's dream

with formulas. You can image spacetime
by subtracting one dimension: a sphere,
finite, unbounded, its surface now, its
inside, the past, and its swelling, time,
and all you've ever been is a world line
through it. If it rotates, like atoms and
galaxies, lines twist, strands in a cord,
and can't be cut across: no now, and time
is ideal. I found a solution, then I saw,
in the linear element, a world line as
a backwards winding helix: there existed
null lines which circled the origin and
came back below the surface, or earlier
in time. Any one world line has a before
and after, but not the whole universe:
I showed Einstein; he nodded, said he'd
always thought time local, not global.
It had no red shift, so it wasn't real;
my logic had holes, time passes, but
wrong turns can get you places, ah?
I went ahead, in secret, because when
Einstein gave us energy equals matter,
this country gave the world Hiroshima.
I found other solutions, in the general
theory of relativity, with time travel,
and one with closed timelike geodesics:
back roads. You go along a curve, no need
of force, into your own future but into
the world's past, and back to the point
of origin. Events come before themselves,
and there's no now, no time to travel in:
we live in Einstein space and Godel time,
space is warped, time complex. I'd like
you to library, and meditate on it,
meet me in a day or so with questions,
and, in a miracle of number, go back.

Outside, in the wave, watches
dazzle, and fury ahead
to the next hour:
but in the grind, the mortal man
ages without a future.
In this congregation of voices,
I'm free floating,
go from journal to old edition:
down my backbone
insight shivers.

Okay: are you saying the past, once real,
exists?
      Oh yes; the snows of yesteryear
are all still there.
             Time travel isn't
like in The Time Machine?
                  In his romance,
if a traveller at A goes back in time
to B, then lives forward, it's as if two
travellers materialized at B, one living
backward, colliding with a third at A,
and both vanish? No, all this violates
physics. In Wells, the singularity is
in the world line; in Godel, it is in
spacetime.
        And it's a back road?
                     It is
a natural time machine, invisible door
in the summer day.
           It's dangerous?
                     No
more than living.
        his hair: the right
is black, and the left silver
              Where would
I go? The world, sun, and galaxy all move:
one year ago is space.
           Ah, this is good:
the back road's out of the atoms of where
you are on earth; only time slips, a set
number of moments, on your road.
                It's mine?
Your set of roads is just for you, but may
let others through.
        I stay how long?
                    It is
indeterminate.

And I come back
                    Through
another door, helplessly, back to where
you started, same world, the very minute,
only older.
              Can I go back through?
                              Only
so many world lines fit into a back road:
it gets used up, but it is unknown when.
Will I change history?
                        If you are going
to go, then you have gone: it's history.
Agathon said it first: the only thing
God can't do is to undo what's been done.
Ah, do I have a choice?
                          You feel that way.
What if, in the famous paradox, I go back
and quote kill my grandfather, so I'm not
born, and I don't go back, and he lives,
I'm born, go back, etc.
                          It's determinism
biting its own tail. As to time travel,
ah, how is its impossibility so proved?
Physical? It's compatible with the field
equation. Mathematical? It derives from
its solution. Conceptual? In the physics
of old causality, we find new laws, which
are consistency constraints on all action
in this chronology-violating environment.
Philosophical? By invalidating free will:
physics does already, and it's a puzzle.
The answer is you can't do the impossible:
the past is a priori, eh? There are only
back roads to what has happened.
                                    What if
my grandmother gives me a watch, and I
go back and give it to her; then who made

the watch?
The watchmaker: the answer is,
etc. Time is strange, but there are always
two watches.
The invisible doors: is
there record of anyone
Oh yes, the women,
Moberly and Jourdain, in a book, Adventure,
it's true, holidaying in Versailles, walked
in the Trianon garden, from 1901 to 1789,
on a back road. Einstein was able to solve
that mystery, Mercury's perihelion, with
relativity; all my findings are abstract,
ghosts in this world. I want you to send
a signal from the past, a story, tell me,
what will it be?
I, huh? Oh I don't know,
ah, how the sun created strawberries.
I make up a story, old man's eyes closed
I want you to add it to Cherokee myth.
And if I go, that'll be recorded in
a book?
Yes, let me look it up in Mooney:
ah! here: V. 12: Origin of Strawberries.
Our experiment has worked.
And what if I
don't go?
As you like it: I measured you
day before yesterday and discovered one
of your back roads by 82° longitude and
36° latitude: you just stay on the Blue
Ridge Parkway, to Blowing Rock, North
Carolina.
looks at me like I've caught
him in his hideout: I go

Independence Day, light traffic, and
I hitchhike out on Highway 1, south:
time stalls under the sun, big rig,
no markings, brakes, whooshing, ahead,
and I climb up into the gypsy's cab.

How far you going? Blowing Rock. Well, I
can get you close; I got to cut over on
421 to Wilkesboro; you can walk in from
there. Long haul: how bout you keep me
on the ball with a story. Okay, thanks.

We shift out of the real city, grime,
poverty streets, cops in armor, kids
shooting up, cursing, gunshots, cars
on fire, banks like churches, schizos
yacking, news bulletins, chaos, smoke.

I tell Lost Horizon, that I first heard
on old records: the usual war, the hero
skyjacked out, crash in the Himalayas,
strange monastery, sanctuary of peace
and the arts, but no leaving the Valley

of the Blue Moon, high lama, You are
still alive, Father, and of impossible
years, time slows up here, the break out,
and the girl dying of old age, and he
at last climbing back toward Shangri-La.

I dream the past: pioneers, slam-banging
on riverboats and prairie schooners, into
barn dances, and in between reels, tall
tales under the stars, good night, ladies,
and the last waltz: oh, wasn't it better?

From the capitol south, it's solid green;

606

we stop at a roadside diner, for fried
chicken and gravy, firecrackers outside,
becoming pals, against the nation's rips,
the jukebox six months behind the times.

Into the back country: gas stations, run-
down general stores, nothing but telephone
poles, shacks, nothing, the highway runs
out, unfinished, I'm walking a dirt road,
hawks are shrilling in the overcast sky.

The vague directions, was this all wrong?
the unfamiliar mountain, in a cold rain,
deep bushes, at dusk. Why did I believe
that story, let myself go into this wild?
I better look for light or chimney smoke.

Airplane up there, braying, and sudden all
is still, no crows, the pines look flat,
no light and shadow, and unreal, no air,
and I feel bleak, under oppression, dream,
sleepwalking, lonesome. Ah, I can't hear

my shoes, the trees are watery, can I
see through them? It's all a backdrop
on stage, and gives a shiver; I make up
my mind, go back to the road, and won't
turn around, nothing can make me. Oh,

the branches moan, at last, I up a crest,
and come around a black spruce bang into
the burning eyes! a mountain lion, moving
on the hump of a boulder, green blotches,
I bellow, back up, and he writhes away,

but I lose balance, over the, too steep
to catch, ridge, down slope, at bottom
crack leg on a river rock and pitch into
ice water, breathless, in the white rush,
head under, out, whirling, oh too deep,

when I lift into the air and light down

on the creek bank: who hoisted me? I look
back, ah! man beast, with a wildcat head
and naked body, laughing; I bawl, he offs
the mask, wild man, and with big hands.

Ah ha ha! Higinahi. Ah ha. Asiyu, utsuti,
ah ha ha!
      Ah! You saved me from drowning.
Wadan? Ha yu.
         in a loin cloth: slant eyes
Nayehi digwadaita.
           hand against his chest
Tugaluna ditsadaita. Ha!
            flicking at me:
I shrug
   Thank you.
      he walks away
          Tadeya
statakuhl.
    with a wave
      Wait! I'm lost, I
still raining
    Gatsu?
      he turns, hand out
Nowhere to go.
      lifting my arms
        Ha yu.
with his big hand on my back we go down-
stream, into the thickets, into the mist

Stiff hides, stitched up, in a lean-to,
a fire, sizzling, man smoking, stone pipe,
man reading a newspaper in two alphabets,
one with strange letters, boy eating blue-
berries; we squeeze in under: he talks.

Tsiwanihu, hatuganiga. Tluntutsi:

detsi kana; hana gwadina hukikahuna,
kala asunyi, amayastun. Tugaluna,
ah ha ha! Guhi. Ehinugai! Tsiwanihu:
higinahi. Tadeya statakuhl. Astai.

That paper, the Cherokee Phoenix, 1834:
dried fish and chestnut bread, and I
lie down, beat, unknown on earth, crying.
Daksawaihu. Hilunnu: and he lays his arm
over my shoulder: hilunnu. The indians.

I'm Detsistayahihu, I Shoot Lightning, and
I talk your talk. Where were you swimming,
when the fisherman caught you?
                        his eyes
shining, and a half smile
                    Ah, Blowing Rock.
I'm lost. Who hauled me out?
                    Nayehi, I Live
Anywhere: it's the name of the invisible
spirits, up on the bald mountains, who love
music, and who care for lost travellers:
it's his mama's house.
                bark roof, dry grass
in the clay walls
         What year is it?
                  You are
lost: 37.
     he smiles: joking?
              Your shoes,
no good up here, on the slick creek rocks:
you take these moccasins.
             Oh I—thank you,
I Shoot Lightning.
        eyes light
            Too tense
for you to stay in a red town. I'll take
you back to your people this afternoon.
Anything else?
        You're Cherokee?
              No, not
Tsalagi, outsider's name; we're Yunwiya:
real people.
      I want to tell him thanks.
What is the word?
        Wadan.
          Why's he call
me Tugaluna?

Little fish in a big stream.
Let's go see him.

Ah, breakfast, today, from the sure hands
of the big old woman: corn cakes fried in
bear grease, speckled trout, in the circle
fireplace, apricot juice, wide bench, white
oak and river cane baskets. This must be

the past: good country, too many indians.
Outside, a kid shooting his blowpipe at
a grasshopper; it turns out he's a tale
collector. I haven't yet sent the signal:
was I invulnerable to wildcat and river?

Will I be mortal now if I tell a story?
I talk, and I Shoot Lightning gives it word
for word, breath white, in the cold morning.
The first man and woman were quarreling;
she walks out, toward the sun's country.

He's sorry and follows her, she keeps on,
till the one sun, that shares its light on
all equally, in pity asks him, You still
mad? No. You want her back? Yes. He makes
the first huckleberries, in her path, but

she passes them by. A bush of blackberries;
she passes them by. A tree, serviceberries,
so tempting; she passes them by. The first
strawberries, all ripe: she stoops to pick
a few, faces the west, and memory, her man;

she can't walk on. The longer, the more. She
picks the best of the berries, walks back;
they meet, he's good to her, and they go home.
We walk upstream; in a tilting field, girls
are picking strawberries, down in the grass,

short skirts, legs bare, short vests, silver

broaches, arms, belly bare, open, and breasts
flashing, in the light breeze, as they wade
in and out of the creek, thighs shining, and
one above all, who's I Live Anywhere's hope.

She gives me strawberry: on my tongue,
slow dazzle, and welcome rain. In a bare
space, he crouches, painting white streaks
with a thick finger on his dark cheeks,
chanting: Ku! Sge! Alahiyi tsuldahisti,

higeya tsuldiyi, hatuganiga. Elahiyi iyuta
ditsuldahisti, higeya Tsunega. Tsisati
nigesuna. Tsaduhiyi. Nagwaskini usinuliyu
huskwaneluyu tsisgaya aginega. What is
he saying? It's a spell to get her love.

Listen! In the southern earth you lie,
oh you god woman, come so close to hear.
In the southern earth, you rest, oh
white woman. No one's lonesome with you.
You are beauty. In a moment you make
me white. No one's lonesome with me.
You make my road white. It will never
be dark. You set me on it. It will never
be blue. You bring down to me from
above the white road, into the middle.

I will stand up on the earth. No one's
lonesome with me. I'm good looking. You
put me into the white house; it moves;
no one's lonesome with me. I will never
be blue. In a moment you make it happen.
Now make the woman blue. Oh make her road
blue. Cover her in veils of loneliness.
Set her down on the blue road. Bring
her down, into the middle, and where
her feet are now, wherever she goes,

let her be lonesome, as if marked for it.
Hey, I'm in the twister clan, the only
for her. No one's lonesome with me.
I'm good looking. Let her soul come into
the center of my soul, never to turn
away. In the middle of men, let her not
think of them. I'm in the only for her,
of the seven clans. Others are lonesome,
the men, bad looking, only fit to run
with polecat, possum, and the rain crow.

In all the seven clans, you can be lonesome.
They're not even good looking, go around
in trash, in dung. But I, oh I was born to
be white. I stand, facing the sun's country.

No one's lonesome with me. I'm good looking.
It's certain, I will never be blue. I'm in
the everlasting white house, wherever I go.
No one's lonesome with me. Her soul has come
into the center of my soul, never to turn
away. I, I Live Anywhere, take it. Listen.

In the cold afternoon, summer gives fire,
the heights lose it. I shake his big hand,
and we set out, northeast; over the first
crest, I see where I am, pines, and beyond,
oh the blue ranges, the waves of earth,

pale and paler, is the last line clouds,
and in the dark hollows between, mystery.
I turn to I Shoot Lightning, looking for
words and release: What are these mountains?
We call them the unending. Mile and miles

I walk, in my rough moccasins, breathing
hard, by the red man, down ledges and ribs,
across creeks on down timber, and up hill
through thick unbelievable bushes, till
whippoorwill's calling, and it hits me.

Wait; wait a second: if this is 1837, it's
before that big removal; oh man, go into
hiding or the whites are going to drag you
out of these hills.
                    Ah, that treaty isn't
binding, not voted on by the Nation. . .
                                        No.
I know: all that treatying's a double cross:
they are coming to force you out of this
mountain glory into the worst shit American
desert.
          Are you a prophet? How do you know
it will happen?
                I, yes, where I come from
it's already over. Ah god, god! the trail
of tears.
          No, let me tell you, one time
our ancestors heard voices hanging in air
for days, spirits, warning, wars and exile,
said fast a week, in quiet, and we'll take

you under the river. They all voted to go,
praying, fasting, and scared by thunder
and the earth quivering, were taken under.
And on summer days, when the wind ripples
the water, you can hear them talking; when
we drag the river for fish and it catches,
it's our kin, as if to say, remember us:
and this is why we will never leave this
white river, this country.

                              his eyes water
I promise this disaster. Our soldiers will
circle your houses, and at gun gather you
into concentration camps, then steamboats,
down southern roads into the Oklahoma dust:
on the long way, by frozen rivers, starving,
sick, heartbroken in the winter air, one
out of three, man, woman, child, will die.
It's black and blue on our history's skin,
and nothing, no bravado to come, not flying
the Atlantic Ocean, not walking on the moon,
will heal it.

            Well, there is that wild bunch,
going back into the caves, to live on roots,
berries, and by short hunts, till it's over.
But all of the clans, what can I say to make
them believe? You have old prophecies that
came true?
            No, but
                        You can foretell the day
after tomorrow?
                  No. I want to touch you
across a century: my arm's not that long.

After that, nothing to say, and we go up,
high ridge, dog charging out, man hushing it
from inside a dark cabin; I turn, the red
man's gone, no motion, the bushes, no trace.
I know where I am: I can smell the smoke.

Come in, stranger.
                    Thanks, I
                                    What brings you up
this way off branch?
                        Well I, I'm lost.
                                        And whar
you from?
                It's a long story.
                                    You been livin
with the indians.
                    How'd you
                                    Your shoes. Shame
all this carryin on over thar land.
                                    They were
real fine to me.
                    Oh well, everhow you come,
you're welcome to what all I got.
                                    It's so—
I'm very grateful.
                    It's nothin. It's how we do
up here.
            It's getting dark.
                                It's comin on to
candle lightin.
                    his language: he gets a coal
on fire, to start the kerosene lamp, no glass
Air you belly empty?
                        I am.
                                    You take a cheer,
and I'll, for heaven's sakes, I'm Tom Walker,
but they call me Old Man.
                                we shake
                                        Who mought
you be?
            Stranger's as good as any.
                                        How old
be you?

what year, minus
                        What do you do?
I've been divided.
                    Whar's your woman?
                                    I don't
have a
            Whar you aimin to go?
                                I don't know.
Well, here's some spring water.
                                gourd dipper
You can take up with me till you can answer
a question.
                    the water: cold, clear
                                    Oh, god,
it's just like wine!

Out of the quiet, all I want for good night
prayer, under a sun and moon quilt, thin
sheet, on a goose feather mattress and corn
shuck sack on ropes and a white pine bed,
I wake in the Blue Ridge, with the old man

in the cockloft, or no, long up and out,
down the crude ladder, and the sap singing
in the birch logs burning in the fit stone
fireplace, on the mantel, pipes and a twig,
on the old puncheon floor, couple of green

maple chairs, split bottom seats, plain table
with wood bowls from last night's supper, pork
ribs swimming in grease, half fried cabbage,
grit corn bread, pure water, big hickory
slip, little broom corn baskets, tin trunk,

from the roof beams, strings of dried apples,
tobacco, seed gourds, hunting pouch, the wall,
old guitar, and a woodcut, a girl, torn out of
the almanac, on the window sill, in this cabin,
stone piers, and logs, rough-hewn and chinked

with clay, and daubed with mud, half dove-
tailed at the corners, ends cut off flush
to keep out rain, but full of warps and sags,
cracks and cat holes, oak shakes for roof,
over the always open door, buck antlers,

across them, flintlock rifle, hanging down,
powder horn, and on the porch, under eaves,
morning glory, and the wild mountain ivy,
wash tub, hand loom full of spider webs,
pure air, and mist roiling out of the gap.

Mornin.
                Mornin, Old Man.
                                Air you stoppin?
Well, if I might: I got
                        I know: nowhere
to go.
        Where am I?
                        Up on Lonesome Ridge.
It close to Blowing Rock?
                        The general store
that Dinah runs. Look south, Hanging Rock
and the Green Knob, and it's Bull Mountain,
to the right's Sugar Mountain; over Hemlock
Ridge, over all of them is the Grandfather
Mountain; and off, past Hump and Big Yellow
and Grassy Ridge, is Roan Mountain and its
round rainbow; way off, the Black Mountains,
the Smoky Mountains.
                        Any neighbors?
                                You got,
the southern side, you got the, better keep
clear of, the Johnson boys, Wild Bill and all,
you see yonder, across Light a Rag Creek,
white corn tassels wavin, that's Uncle Joe
Harmon, he musics on the fiddle, Aunt Sal,
all their paradise of girls, Rachel, Rebecca,
Sarah, Judith, and all the boys, over thar
on Redbird Hill, and on the yonder side's
Rob Campbell and Mag, their daughters, Emily,
Lily, and May. I plumb forgot Grandma Liza,
and she's the man-whuppinest old lady ever
I seen. An at's is cove.
                        his hair so white:
in his eyes, fire
                I'll get you biscuit bread,
buttermilk, and honey in the comb: you can
hep at the still.

Are you moonshining?
Yes.
You go against the law?
How's at?
By not
paying the revenue tax.
What, no, why that
whiskey tax the crack old Washington had,
Jefferson undid hisself, at century's turn.
Twant fair nohow, caint get the craps out
of this rough country, the markets so far,
what can we do but still it, and do without
income. I's in with the boys at stood agin
the govment, and march on Pittsburgh in
the whiskey rebellion, ah torches to burn
em down, the citizens brung us old corn
in buckets, and we laid our rifles away,
and dance all night. Good lord, them was
the days. Agin the law? Ha! let em try.

In the Irish hills, down generations,
in the Scottish highlands, over oceans,
in the American mountains, whiskey:
get corn, one bushel,
shuck it, strip it, into a bucket,
warm water, and cover:
oh the cold moon coils into the sky,
pines lean
away from wind, and water
in the blue river gives rise to ballads.

Green inches,
dry it, grind it, in a tub mill,
boiling water, three times the sun
for the sweet mash, nine sour, pour beer
in a copper kettle, with a worm, through
spring water, and under, a fire:
oh the cold river coils into the pines,
wind leans
away from blue ballads, and the sky
in the water gives rise to the moon.

Spirit beads in the cold worm,
slips into singlings, weak and oily;
run them back, into doublings,
too quick, is rank, or long, too pure,
pour it, see bubbles, down through charcoal,
two gallons, white lightning:
oh the cold ballads coil into the sky,
moon leans
away from the water, and wind
in the blue pines gives rise to a river.

As the ends burn, you ease em in.
                              oak poles
smoldering
          Like this?
                        Yeah, and keep her goin;
I'm lookin at the bead.
                          the bubbles rising
It's might nigh done.
                     with a swallow
                              Bald face.
You want to chase it with water.
                              on my tongue
smoke, in my throat fire
                        Ha, here, whooee,
ain't nothin better.
                      the whiskey hits my belly
and joy spreads out
                    It's heating up my insides.
cold afternoon
              I'll go again, if it's all right.
Well, I's thinkin you was a goin to drap dead
or go wild, one, but go ahead, it'll man you.

The wavering hills go dark, and the Old Man,
in a coonskin cap, a hunting shirt, and dusty
jeans, barefoot, thumb in pocket, tilting back
whiskey, sky rose over the last ridge, listens,
a girl, or is it the blue mountains, singing?

Come all you fair and tender ladies,
be careful how you court young men:
look at the stars on a summer mornin,
first appear and then they're gone.

He'll tell to you some lovin story
ain't nothin but a far-flung lie:
straightway he'll go and court another
and when he sees you pass you by.

Don't he recall our days of heaven
when his head lay on my breast:
he'd make me believe by his arm fallin
that the sun rose in the west.

I wish I was a little sparrow
and I had wings and I could fly:
I'd fly away to my false true lover
and when he'd speak I would deny.

If I'd a knowed afore I courted
love would fade the way it done
I'd a locked my heart in a box of hickory
and kept it from the common sun.

Come all you fair and tender ladies,
take warnin how you court young men:
look at the stars on a summer mornin,
first appear and then they're gone.

Go over to Redbird Hill, the Old Man said,
I'm porely; get the old woman to fetch me
yerbs for the cold. Will the mountain lions.
Hell no, they hide; they's plenty to eat
beside of you. I follow the near dry creek,

in the tangle, where the green under works
to get at sun, birches, buckeyes, hemlocks
wrestling, leaves slant, laurels blossom
sharp and bitter, till I come to the water,
a solid log crossing from weathered rocks

over its curves and purling, I shove into
wet ferns feather into the little trail,
white tassels floating off of the sourwood,
branches in mist, lilies over my head, red
berries waiting, the cabin, under a willow,

by a cold spring, and in the dooryard, roses:
green moss on a shake roof, and all the chairs
on the porch different, the house, of what's
at hand, true wood, the lines natural, slim
girl? sliding, graceful, into the dark room.

You'll be the stranger over at the Old Man's.
I am, how do you know?
                          she's worn and faded
Oh we be knowin.
                 Who was it I heard singing
so pretty?
        she motions me in the front door,
and the girl's out the back: so wild
                         Rachel,
you sashay in here, he's a payin you, hey!
girl laughs, or a bird coos, unseen, and gone
I've come for ah, medicine; Tom's got a cold.
You want the mother woman.
                     not her? so old
Come on out back.
              big table, piles of wool
I reckon you are from a whoop and holler.
From ah, the big city.
            I's borned in this
country, ain't never been out of it. You
like it up here?
            Well, the water is amazing.
You all in the city must have fine springs.
God, no; so dirty, you can't call it water.
Is that right?
        she talks so slow, in her
eyes, questions
          Liza, it's the stranger.
Old Man's on the down go.
             Ah well, what is
to be will be, and what ain't might. Is he
bed fast? What did he do, spin a chair on
one leg?
       You the doctor?
            I am the seventh
sister, nor saw my daddy's face, I married
and kept my name, and I can heal, by leaf

in the shape of what is to cure, with sang
and galax, cherry bark, honey and flax, oh
and carry this buckeye seed in your pocket
for luck. What's his misery?

                            grey hair all
crazy: into the day dark cabin

                                 It's a cold.
Well here's a race of ginger for tea, sage,
and is he coughin?

                  No, ah with a high fever.
You take this poke of boneset now and come
back for fern fronds.

                    Won't you come acrost
Aunt Sal touches my arm

                     tonight for supper?
Sure: thanks.

           as I go back, over and over:
that girl, who slipped away

Rain showers blow through the afternoon, dusk
early in the hollow; with sourwood walking
stick from the Old Man, I go down and up
through the hush, music, in the white pines:
old timber, old mountains go so far back.

Two cabins, space between roofed, a table,
the men and boys sit, women and girls wait,
by light of candles, the human faces, here
the younger sisters, then Rachel, driving
in cows, in the dust, barefoot, dancing.

Over cornbread and sowbelly, green snaps,
tea, whiskey, Liza, with a corn cob pipe,
Get the almanac and see when he'll full,
like I'm the moon; Uncle Joe, Where do
you live at; California, unknown to him.

Air you likin our roads? from Sal. I say,
Where I come from, we got ah sleds that go
all by themselves. Oh that's tall talk.
Rachel, her hair over one eye, and holding
back smile: Oh, you are from far lands away.

Her voice, low, sweet, she must be sixteen,
dreamy-eyed, love in my eye, first sight,
I can't follow it all, as her daddy nods
off on the porch chair, her mama goes in,
does dishes, whistling, fragments of hymns?

Out of the ashes, sweet potatoes, dusted with
a turkey feather, he wakes and holds a fiddle
at his chest, the bow by the middle, reels out
Don't mind the weather when the wind don't blow,
the Harmon girls in harmony, That ding-dang fool,

he don't know how to court, her ma twines oak

leaves, flowers and fern, a garland, in Rachel's
dark hair, I love the ground whereon she stands,
to Oh the cuckoo, she's a pretty, she hikes up
her homespun dress, to the tops of her white

thighs, and dances, loose and natural, as
the music fires her, her hips shaking say
the body's good, I whirl inside, I can't
resist, this girl. After the last Shady
Grove, my darlin, over too early, just

out of the light, old airs are running, I
couldn't get back with a lantern, better
ask, but they're all in bed, but I have to,
I look up into the sky I had forgotten,
oh its long black hair is thick with stars.

You lost?

       It's her: steps out of a pine tree

Too dark for me.

          You're welcome to stay on,

in the extry bed.

        my heart

           Oh the Old Man

would worry, and I got to give him the fern.

her voice, light of the moon

            I'll get you

 acrost.

     You'll be okay?

         Okay?

            new word to her

All right?

     I'll fetch a light.

          unknown to me

song: river running where the sun can't see:

she's back with a lantern

        I love American

songs: in these mountains, I feel like I'm

in their high cradle.

        It's all I got, as I

caint read.

    Man named Sharp came up here,

and wrote them down.

       Did he cut anything,

that Sharp man?

      Yeah, all the bawdy verses.

light sliding down her arm, grazing her hip

What kind of songs in your country?

           Number

one's Strangers in the Night, but I don't,

ah

  Well, this is it. What's number one,

you give em numbers?

      We catch music out

of the air and hold it, ghost of the voice
is there, but the musician you don't meet.
It's sold, like an ad for more, and, and
I don't like to say it, but the big money
is number one.
                Well, I sing as I'm here,
for nothin.
           her light quivers and is lost
in the black timber

Next stop, Front Royal, 2 minutes.

                                          invisible

conductor, in the almost dark

                               That's us.

You only have that bag?

                          I've got it.

                                woman

ahead of us, with Amelia Earhart luggage

What track?

                Look: Norfolk and Western line,

Track 2.

            It'll be awhile if it's on time;

we can wait here.

                  You been time travelling

this summer, huh? In the Hawthorne story,

her name was Rachel: maybe all of this is

only spun out of nothing.

                    It's a mystery,

stretching between nothing and nothing,

but blessed with music.

                     Well, you just go on:

she ah, had left you back at Lonesome Ridge

that night.

                  Yeah; well, women ask me how I

can love their eyes before their history;

don't know: I look into them, can't think

straight, and I fall into their blue grace.

All night, the air blowing, and swaying
the limbs, desire, in drops, comes down,
in the hiss of dreams, half dreams, it
shivers, hammers on the roof, marks time
in the rain barrel, and in the red-eyed

morning, the sky is streaked with fire.
I won't touch food, belly too restless,
I circle the room, go from bed to burning
branches, to the iron-cinched bucket, to
the stack of quilts, and to the window:

no man, if I don't take her? So young,
but she knows it, deep? She doesn't care?
I open the almanac, but now she won't,
is how I pick the absurd she loves me
loves me not daisy, as it grows back.

I burn questions, to thin smoke, silent
heaven, make up poor superstitions I drop
into faith's hole. I'm paralyzed, all to
be done, nothing to do; outside, doves
call mates out of their natural throats.

Hi, what's your name?
                        kid in shirt-tail,
stains out of the red clay, riding a pig
Caleb.
        Is Rachel around?
                        She's goin down
to the lake with ah Clay.
                        god don't let her
We ain't talkin to you.
                        sores on his face
What? What is the
                Granny says you're lyin:
it ain't nobody in California but only
Mexicans.
        Rachel, in the dim door, and I
forget all words I had worked out to say
I can explain what I, if you, hold on,
where are you going?
                        I heared the wind blow
before. We tell the truth, up here. Why do
you look at me that way?
                        she whirls, into

the pines

Old Man
   You wonderin why I brung you here.
white cascade into a blue pool, morning
Yeah, I
  Catch trout.
      Oh, fishing's fine,
but I'm squeamish about
       It don't matter,
you caint catch trout: too hard.
       And you
ain't got a pole.
   talking like him
      I seen
you down and out: what ails you? Air you
drooped up?
   What?
    Lovesick.
      no answer
       Well,
you don't waste no time: one supper acrost
the gap, you're sighin. Ah, what daughter,
not that wild un?
     no answer: all our words
to the waterfall
    You see them brook trout?
clear water, dead trunk, boulders, algae
       No.
Go on lookin.
   I can't make out
      Its back
is sun ripples on grey rocks, its belly
the pale surface, it can chameleon.
      I saw
it flash!
   Invisible till it moves, flows
out to whar it's goin and back.
     Like water

637

in water.

        Now you're catchin trout. Its sides
are all red stars and light of day. Ain't much
prettier. You got it good?

               looks over into
my eyes

      I think about her morning to night:
can't stop.

        almost crying

            If only I: I can't
make her love me.

          Or tell the water what
way to run, but you can let her. You can
go easy.

      Why, if I open up out of a true
passion?

      Keerful you don't cast your shadder
on the water.

        step back

           Or those wild fish
will fly.

      creek slides

         Them trout are stream-
line; they jest set in a still, face thin
and hold agin the current.

            he shows me:
flat hand

      I thought they swam.

           Use few
motions as can, let the water swim by,
carry air and food to em.

        How do they
know where they are?

         Oh they got eyes,
know mornin, evenin, by the sun's slant,
good eyes. What do you do?

         Study laws of

nature, and I make songs.
                                    I wouldn't lose
no sleep over it, your sap's risin, and
you're a good man. Why not sing her your
laws of nature?
                        Down at the creek, maybe
she'll hear?
                    Ain't no hurry: we go it slow
up here.
                Hey look, one chased out the other.
Yeah, it's holdin on to like a yard wide,
for spawnin, at's its way.
                                    How in the world
you figure all of this out?
                                    Oh I jest set.
trout shimmering
                            You got to court her. When
this here fish wants it better, oh he bucks
real fast, and swims up into the waterfall.

My girl, my girl,
don't you lie to me:
tell me where
did you sleep last night?

In the pines, in the pines,
where the sun never shines:
I shivered
the whole night through.

Betrayed, betrayed:
in a stranger's arms;
darlin, where
is there mercy in me?

No night, no night
is oh so long
but it ends
in the light of day.

At's a hard song.
                    out of white corn tassels
Hey, Rachel: you're talkin to me.
                              Ah that
old lady, all the time pushin: the heck
with her.
              on the bridge, straddle
                              I don't
member em last two verses.
                        I made them up.
she tilts her head, dark hair over her eye
Tell me bout your come from.
                              doves rippling
You know the day after tomorrow?
                              It ain't
here yet.
          That's my country. I was born, ah
it's strange, over a hundred years on, and
I walked back here.
                  her eyes far off
                              Go on.
Well, in that world to come, if I have money,
I can fly in a bird of metal, miles high,
from the ocean over America, all the smoke
cities and the old farms, down into an ocean
of lights all night, get whirled away into
ten thousand houses stacked to the sky, ride
a climbing room, to a temporary home, turn
a stream of pictures and stories on, from
other where and when.
                        Miracles: yall must
live in a haze of wonder.
                        Ah, we complain
if the flight's late, or the show's no good.
Can I get to thar?
                  And leave this paradise?
The water, music for free, pure air, time,

the peace?

       Because of I'm a woman, I caint
go out without askin. I sow, I bend over
the hoe, I milk and chase the cows, and hack
up firewood when the men folks fail to, out
pitchin horseshoes. I shear, wash, card, reel,
spin, dye, weave sheets and quilts, smoke
meat, make soap, haul water, cook everthing.
Like ma, I'll grow old afore my day, and if
I say anything, I get shet up. I caint write,
read, figure, caint even pray, ain't nobody
to learn me: I want to see town, ain't been
one step further nor Blowin Rock. Now whar's
your paradise?

         her voice cracking

             Ah Rachel,
it ain't right, and I'd company you anywhere.
Just keep talkin, Mr. Day After Tomorrow.
that night, I whisper and slide into sleep

All wondering if I have twelve, I don't
know, as the fiddle starts,
I climb on the unsteady raft, the flood,
with my ex-love, her and not her,
that swell, the pines jutting
out of the prodigious waters,
unknown if fresh or salt, the south,
how will you steer, she says,
and I lean in,
peace! I will stop your mouth.

Her kid sister, sallow, listless, says Heart
Lake, and I follow the water talking, books
in the running brooks, if I can't read I'll
go crazy, only that almanac, I guess I am
in its lost year, with her swimming, why do

I always. . . She opened the blind date door,
after letters, her shoulders so slender,
close to the ocean eyes, and I loved her.
And in first grade, first morning, before
the bell, on swings, not swinging, first

sight, sun blonde, but who is romantic
at five, oh she and I, was out of touch
at home. . . In the laurel, brown ripples,
more like a hole, she comes up naked out
of water, shivering off her long hair,

bare neck, dripping off her brown nipples,
rivering into her groin, holding a white
sheet, wings, open, till I see she sees
I see, closing, and she slips away, into
the, her beauty, oh, no words, just now.

All in a whirl, all going to Redbird Hill,
the guitar night, the sliding fiddle, cock-
a-doodle banjo, and Sourwood Mountain goes
on, Oh my true love lives over the river,
Couple of jumps and I'll be with her, in

between the lines of love, Hey ho diddle
um day, she knows all of the steps and calls,
didn't invite me, Old Man got wind and had
me led across the gap, Why's she blow hot
and cold, If you discover it, let on to me,

whiskey makes it lighter, First couple cage
you as you spin, Bird hop out and hoot owl
in, Arms round and hootin again, I go to her,
Ah, show me the motions, Rachel, and she,
It don't make no differ long as the music's

in you, I recollect the high school dances,
I'd circle without the nerve to ask a girl,
and now I swing partner to hand to hand
partner, at Gamblin Man, I see her smiling
over, oh Blue Ridge, I love your daughter.

after Fox Chase, all spreading out
                              You walk
me back?
              Ah, Rachel; what if your folks see?
I told mama your tale, she told the granny,
and she just thinks you're bereft.
                                    You were
so fine calling the dance and dancing, I wish
I had a picture.
                    A woodcut?
                                A photograph.
A what?
              Light writing: we catch an image
out of the air, hold it, ghost of the body.
In the future?
                    Yeah. Your old man can sure
fiddle.
          Oh he's a fool for it.
                                I'd like
to fool with you.
                    At all the frolics—what?
Fiddle around with you.
                              Oh you're so bad!
she laughs, slapping my shoulder
                                    Hey, peace!
I catch her arm: she relaxes
                              That's what
I want to do.
              What?
                        That light writin.
                                          Well,
you get paper and dip it in washes of salt
and silver, hang it up wet in a dark room
with a little hole, and the world outside
will be saved on the page: you rinse it in
soda, sit it right next to another paper
in a frame, in the sun, and what was up-

side down, left right, and black for white,
will come out true.
                              I want to try it out.
Hey, any books in your cabin?
                                        No, nary
a one, but grandma's book o trompins.
                                        What?
When I'm at the loom, with the warp green
from willow bark, and the woof ruddy from
hickory, criss cross, the dots and dashes
say when to tromp the treadles, weaving
the winter sheets into the wheels of time,
snail's trail, rose in the wilderness.
                                        Oh,
I meant stories.
                    Old Man reads us tales
out the almanac.
                    Out—oh, it has writing.

Go ahead! Davy Crockett's 18 Almanack 37
of Wild Sports in the West, Life in the Back-
woods, & Sketches of Texas. Is it by him?
Month, with a quatrain, old country verse,
sun's declinations? moon's phases, days,

rising and setting, sun slow, moon south,
highwater, aspects, weather prophecies,
death, birth years, in, out of history,
deer begin to fat, girls kissing, corn
ripens, animal essays in standard 19th C.

eloquence, raw woodcuts, oh glory the all-
American crack of lightning language: I can
whoop to a corncracker, jump Mississippi,
dive down, and come up salty, play on a corn-
stalk fiddle, and beat all holler; I yell

and the bears walk backwards; when I dance,
the stars go shooting, the girls open arms
and say come on, and we hitch a ride on
a thunderbolt and roll away home. Why
has no pine shot up out of this dream soil?

Old Man, you don't ever say nothin, but
what you have to.
     And why should I?
         Well I
talk all the time.
      Don't nobody care to
hear what I'm thinkin.
        With all you know?
What I know is what I don't know, and that's
too rare.
   Where is it?
        Over this hogback.
How's it goin with that girl yonder?
          Oh I
don't know: we're friends; she's a cold fish.
Ah huh.
    But I go on talkin with her. Who's
that on the porch?
       Old Sam; his brother's son
Long John, whose wives are sisters; Luke,
their uncle, whose wife's Long John's sister
and Old Sam's daddy's sister.
         Mornin, Walker!
Who's 'at with you?
       He's kin to me, leave it
at that. In here.
      the general store, shelves
almost bare, man with moustache, fast talking
the territory. And I do.
        And that makes you
Better drummer.
      Whar's Dinah?
          Old Man Walker
She got a hurtin in her breast, and nobody
She see Liza?
     Nobody can hep her.
         I can

prove it.
       moustache
            How's at?
                   I can name all
the trees in this country as you go walkin
down hill.
       I'll lay you a flask of whiskey
to nothin you caint.

Look here,
in the sheer mountains,
at the top, wild
cherry, aspen shivering,
maple in stripes, red, black
spruce in mystery, dark balsam fir,
up high,
mountain oak, beech, branches
circling, yellow birch, buckeye, light
pouring off blossoms, chestnut, cream,

on the lower slopes,
white oak, so tall, tough hickory,
pitch pine, everwhere, evergreen,
locust, shadow, dogwood, glimmer,
and lower,
basswood, bare trunk, sugar maple,
sweet inside, that smell,
magnolia, red seeds, white blooms,
holly, in the creek, holding
berries, sprays, sourwood, best honey,

butternut, box
elder, ash, like fern, poplar, roots
in the water, crown sky, old hemlock,
and low, shallow root elm,
sycamore, ball shape and seed,
persimmon, blue
flowers, gum, hollow, willow, hanging,
mist in between, blue ridges,
and from dome to bottom, you go by parallels
down America.

Well, old hoss, you lose: you done left out
the redbud.
    Go to hell.
       These boys will quit
yammerin
   Old Man
     by day down I hope.
         Where
is everything?
    Hah?
      Well I see shelves but
no flour, no salt, no sugar, no coffee, no
tobacco.
    Yeah, and they're out of fiddles.
This is the country of do without.
        And when
nothing's in, what do you do?
       Get by. I
need it, I aks a neighbor.
      And he has more?
No rich, no poor, up here.
       You take my cash?
I ain't never took no payment from company,
and this no time to start. Besides, I ain't
seed nothin but coins. We don't use money.
What do you pay in?
      Oh, beeswax, eggs, honey,
a turn of corn, hog's backbones, coonskins,
roots, whiskey. Old fashion: ain't no inroads
up here, no progress.
     Where I'm from, we're
all the time counting dollars.
      We caint add
anyhow. Hey Gamblin Man, can we do business?
What all you want?
    Go ahead.
      Common salt.

Yeah.
>   Silver nitrate.
>   >   What?
>   >   >   Nitrate of silver.
fast talker
>   Potassium iodide.
>   >   >   I'm writin it.
Black paint.
>   What for?
>   >   Some wax.
>   >   >   Got that.
A tin.
>   Of what?
>   >   Nothing.
>   >   >   I caint get you
a tin of nothin.
>   >   All right, then crackers.
You mixin love potions on Lonesome Ridge?
A nail.
>   You can get this?
>   >   Old Man
>   >   >   All but
them fancy words.
>   >   I can.
>   >   >   moustache, smiling
I have sources.
>   >   What will you take for it
and not back out?
>   >   >   A bear, and I mean steaks,
oil, skin and all.
>   >   >   See you at the full moon,
by a couple of days. Let's go. Well, kin,
would you be wantin to sally on out with
us on the hunt?
>   >   >   It ain't for me. I can't
ah kill animals.
>   >   >   You will eat em though?

Old Man, you're going to all this trouble
for me.

Oh, I's a goin anyhow. That frost
gets into the air, and the woodbine's red,
I got to go, collect up my boots, gun, dog,
tobacco, traipse into the hills, if only
to listen for the whir of grouse, skimmin
around the slope, the color of dirt, under
the laurel bushes. Look atter the cabin.

Old Man leaving: Corn's in, not shucked,
few potatoes, firewood enough, bunch beans,
onions, hog meat, snaps, milk in the spring
house, lots of honey, blackberries, water,
and all the pine top whiskey you can handle:

that apple tree can take care of itself,
chickens go wild and scratch for feed,
razorback pigs go loose, through thickets,
snuff and uproot, turkeys go after mast,
and sheep pea vines, and cows crap grass;

don't need to do nothin, only salt em
if you've a mind to, and knock flint steel
to spark and kindle, so time don't matter.
Leave the door open: ain't no sneak thieves
up here, we don't worry, get on by little;

I don't need no slicker, blanket and tent:
I got me a fryin pan, a cup, corn pone,
salt pork, coffee, in a sack on my back,
and I sleep out under the sky: I am this
country, it can rain on me all it likes.

You done sweat it out in that tub?
                              Ah Rachel,
thanks for comin.
                    Here, swig more water. She
said you want much.
                    Not sick, but sick, way
too much whiskey. It would brighten me, but
I'm drunk all of the time and it don't work,
I can't ah sleep, too weary, oh I'm scared
to go to sleep.
                    You just lay down, listen
to a way back tale.
                    I'm sorry I'm so
                              Sh sh.
Ah, it goes, long time ago this old king,
three daughters, one day he aks em what
he could fotch em out of the general store,
they's fixin to go to a frolic that night,
and so the first gal she told him she wish
for a green dress, flashin, and the next,
all red, and the least, he love her best,
said only, white. The old king saddled up
his beast to town for all the frocks and on
the way back hit his head on a pine bough
and the bough broke and when he look oh la,
twas full of white roses. He come on home,
on his throne he's a smilin, Girls, how much
do you love me? Oh, says the first, why more
n I can say, and he give her a white rose
on her green dress, and the next, Oh more
n life, and he give her a white rose on her
red dress, and last, How much you love your
old daddy? She thought a spell: I love you
like meat loves salt. Well, it contraried him:
Is that your answer? Yes, the dyin truth.
That crazied him, he hid her dress and lock
her in a high tower out on the bare prairies,

nor let her see nobody but one old woman
to get her bread and water. And come a time
in the winder she's combin her hair, cryin,
the duke of England he rid up and seen her,
clomb up a vine and carried that girl down
over the ocean sea, and married her. Them two
other sisters got hitch, and the old king
was sad one day, move in with his daughter.
She welcome him but atter a couple days
said, Ain't no room for all your sarvants,
and sent em off. He move on to the tother
daughter and she done put him in the stable
to sleep, so he move on all on his lonesome.
And now them gals' men's a makin war agin
the duke of England, who come back acrost
the waters, and all started in to fightin,
and the least girl she sail along, and one
mornin they's out a walkin in the country
and chance on the old king, out of his head,
with a crown of briars, oh and he don't know
his little girl, but they took keer on him.
His sisters was caught up in a thorn bush
and just a hollerin. She says, What you doin
in thar? Our men they put us here, and Oh
you have as I do remember done me wrong,
says the old king, and he just let em be.
When the war's over and done with the duke
took the old man over the sea, and one day
the girl says, Cook, leave out the salt on
that meat, and the old king, Ah, this here meat
it don't eat right. His daughter brung a dish
of salt, not sayin a word, only standin there,
and the old king knowed her, and got his mind
back again. He sent his man acrost the waters
to get that white dress what he'd hid and when
he give it to her, it had a branch of white
roses, in all that time it didn't wither,

657

I don't know how, but la, like it was picked
that very day.
           Where'd you hear that?
                        I don't
memorize who told me.
               It's King Lear in with
the Cap o Rushes: if it's oral transmission,
my god, it's from the days—you ever hear
of Shakespeare?
           In them almanacs.
                    "And time
that gave doth now his gift confound." Oh I'm
in wild love with his language.
              Hey, you're
yet wakin: you get dreamy, and I'll tell you
another. Ah, Crockett's riding to the Washita,
only him talkin, and the horse cloppin, and
he hears a fiddle, Hail Columbia, windin out
of the river, first rate, and fine as silk,
it goes into Over the Water to
                    wake up, dusk,
sweating, good sleep, her at my side

old kids, from the near hollows: tall stack
of unshucked corn, by the ramshackle pen
If Old Man's gone, is they a jug of whiskey
under the pile?
          Don't worry, bud, we buried
it there.
       Cat's got its tail toward the fire:
cold weather, sure.
            Don't feel like shuckin:
I believe I'll jest tilt back agin the crib
and play banjo.
          Druther play checkers.
                      Oh
you hush. It's a good time.
               Do Kiss the one
that you love best, kiss her afore she goes
to rest.
       Log's shakin off light.
                 Ah, three
swallows, whoever gets it, and pass it on
for one?
        Who keers, I want the red ear for
a kiss from pick the girl.
               You getting this,
stranger?
       You mean, like indian corn?
                    It's
all
   Some come here to fiddle and dance, I
come here to marry.
            she sits by me
                Know how
it's done?
       Oh, we have corn. What is that
loud bangin I hear at night, on the roof?
Acorns fallin.
        so fine?

If you seed corn
when the dogwoods whiten, in the new moon,
it'll be straight and tall.
                    That so?
                            You
find mold or bug on it, just dip it in
that tub of water.
                    I'm getting the chills,
turn up that whiskey, quick!
                            Go on, play
Come under, my honey, my love.
                            Well, it's
only for at the play party.
                            Boy, you sing
like the wind whistles.
                        Hey I'm getting ice
tags on my fingers, ain't we near done?

I look at the slow fire, fishing my hand
into the corn, and come up with, her hand:
all promise, in the off-and-on moon, joy
streams between skins, one simple touch:
I lead her out back, in weeds high as us.
what would Old Man
                        Before we do this, listen:
I'm one more morning star, oh I can't stay:
the mystery that lifted me into this world
will one day drag me back, I can't say when.
Only the blue mountains will still be here:
I won't be unfair.
                        her down eyes look up
in mine
            No way around?
                            No way: you choose.
only the wind sliding over Lonesome Ridge
Then love me now.
                        her lips: kiss paradise:

I hold her hand behind her and sway her in:
ah god, it was my love was under water

With my days to come mouth
I psalm your mouth, all its bygones,
oh your brown lips, backwater tongue,
you my possible eyes, I lay
love in the hollow of your neck,
my hand hallelujahs through
your backwoods hair,
you anthem my arms twining in yours,
out of my husk, your silk, with fingers,
I canticle your thin shoulders,

oh your brown nipples, you
with a moan, doves
homing, my open belly,
your backsliding hand
blesses my flank, I with my palm
your slow bare hip,
I kiss and hymn
your backcountry cunt, in mist, with my
hard cock, oh you and I, in
double surrender.

I blindfold her, and lead her in, our cabin,
Old Man not back
                    You just hold on.
                                        I lay
out the rare eggs, thick bacon, blackberries,
on the poor plates, undo the cloth
                                    What is
all this?
        I love you, and I been wantin to
It ain't our way.
                    Oh let it be, if only
in this house, and this morning.
                                    she lowers
her head: ah no
                    Why are you cryin?
                                        I thumb
tears from under her eye
                            I thought you'd like
this.
        she looks up, with all her soul
                                        Stay
on, stranger, yet awhile.

I rather go up a mountain than come down,
cause you caint hurry.
                              slow walking Joe
Where'll we stay, with no hotel?
                                        What, in
Deep Gap? Any old house.
                              Ain't we strangers?
We do like that.
                        In my world, we shy off.
In the lowlands?
                  Yeah.
                          I's green, and run
down off the mountain, and I nigh sultered.
All them folks, my la, ain't breath enough
to go around; and the water don't do a body
no good; with the noise, no sleep o nights.
They's money, and a lavish of things, but
why live through all of that bossin to get
at it? Daylong, I jest lay up dreamin of
the sting of the pines, and trout fishin.
Oh they needn't glory their old flat lands
to me: I high-tailed home.
                              I'm worried and
worn out, daddy.
                    little Judith
                                    Let's set
durin the while you get your wind; only
down off this laurel slick.
                              Rebecca hands
water to Sarah: I look in Rachel's eyes,
we steal back of an oak tree and kiss wild:
till Uncle Joe
                  See what we can.
                                        the venture
her idea, soon as the Grand Scientific and
Musical Theater was coming: only one tent;
no show: inside tall man in shirtsleeves

We're tearing down for all the holier than
thou around here.
                     Rachel, in hurt
                               But whar's
the science?
               he muses, and winks
                            All right,
for you, for free: hocus pocus.
                         he juggles
nothing, now a red ball, out of nowhere,
orange, yellow, through the rainbow, seven
balls, in the air, a dazzle, and down into
bare hands: she claps, and I
                        And where's
the music?
          Hey, bud,
                 he hollers
                       we got
a paper house.
                and this black shining man
steps in, deep breath, goes into
                      The first
white man in Cumberland Gap was Dr. Walker,
an English chap: oh lay down boys, and take
a little nap, 14 miles to Cumberland Gap. . .
he bows: I hear, outside
                    the air, the Lord
protects him; and the minstrel's hit songs
are all hallelujah in other words.
                      light
applause: men shove up for a handshake,
call him P. T. Barnum: he looks into me;
can he feel I'm from other days: and I
Don't let all this foofaraw get you down:
your name and pleasure will be intwined
all time to come.
                I thank you for the words,

but I can't lose: under this business suit,
I'm doing it for love. A fortune teller, eh?
I should pay you.

             he spins a silver dollar
into the air, and I catch it

For a country woman, time pours out of
the heavens, in circles, the sun differs
from hill to hill, lifting a shadow to
a mark, the moon rises to the almanac:
for us, it's all numbers, and the old

lights in the sky nothing but decorations;
we zone for business; electricity's washed
out morning and night; we ignore the dark,
the crack of spring, the waves of summer,
the chill of fall: she goes by what grows,

dies off, comes back, calls to plow, seed,
water, reap, then holiday, under the stars
and all their weathers, in a rhythm of need,
as day is lived, the month, known by a notch
on the mantle, the year, named after a baby.

miles south, on the cut trails, along the Blue
Ridge, and up a rise

                My body works, with you.
Oh it's just fine, maybe you was a thinkin
too much, and that got you afeared. You go
on lovin it the way I do.

              What is this rock?
They call it Wiseman's View. Times I wonder
if these hills are a book nobody can read.
grey snow: sundown: but that can't be: a ball
of fire, out of the slope

             What is it?

                  Brown
Mountain light.

       floats up: over the summit:
fades out

      Will o the wisp?

           No marsh.

              A kind
of lightning?

       No storm.

          Fox fire?

            Too pale.
Hunter's lantern?

       Into the sky?

             another
rising, at another place: we lay back and
watch the inexplicable lights: kiss her

The blue hills are islands in the cloud ocean,
and before dark, after goodbye, our kisses
hide out all night; on the thin snow, I pick
witch hazel, last blooms, mistletoe, for her
tomorrow, and sing bare songs under the stars

of Orion. She calls morning, the calm of day,
the Old Man makes himself scarce, saying he's
letting it happen, and she and I roll into
the bed. Where is his family, I see a loom
and hollow log cradle. She lifts a finger

to her lips, leads back over the Poor Fork
to Indian Gap, little graveyard, few rails,
falling in, no cross, no stone, low mounds,
or sunk in, stray cow, weeds, lone dead,
no ghosts, no shadows, in the winter sun.

Is it xmas, I hear gunfire, like a fool,
Old Man not here, bolt out the door, back
up hill: white crest, this man weaving,
slouch hat, long hair, porcupine quills
in a dirty hunting shirt

       Who on earth
are you on my hill?

     so drunk

       A stranger.
Well, I reckon you'll be goin.

       I'm stayin
with Tom Walker.

      I reckon you'll be goin
to hell, atter I'm done with you.

        breath
so foul

    Don't mean no harm.

       so calm: didn't
know I was brave.

      Oh, I got thunder heads
in my fists want to crack and rain down blows,
and in my brogans, kick all loose lightning!
poetry's everywhere

      Don't want no stranger
sweetheartin our gals. Take it stand up
knock down, or rough and tumble?

        he swings:
I lie down in the frost

      What in hell air you
doin?

   Not fightin.

      All right, I'll stomp your
skull in.

    I roll, he misses and slips, down
grovelling in the snow

       Ah, just for that
I'm goin to, why is this so hard?

Hold on,
Clay.
     Old Man, out of nowhere
                    Hey this here
man has the makins, and he can hep you out.
his eyes blue fire
           Ain't you swoonin over
that schoolma'am in Blowin Rock?
                  So what?
Well, he can write you out a letter to her.
Didn't nobody tell me. Pardon me.
                his hand
Yeah, sure.
     slap it: Old Man
              Let's go back
to yall afore we freeze in this here skiff.
to the south side: blind cabin, low chimney:
he nods
     Wild Bill.
         Old Man.
              he's all greasy,
log bed, hickory bark, sedge grass
             I brung
the stranger.
        Welcome, outlander. My boys
is out shootin up Christmas. They don't know
from nothin. Hey, Clay, what year is it?
18 and 37.
        Eighteen hundred and thirty-seven
years since what?
         Never heard tell.
             See?
He don't know beans when the bag is open.
On tother hand. One time, I's holdin up
this little razorback, this little shoat,
so he could graze on the simmons up hangin
in this old tree, stranger comes long, says,

You may get that hog fat, but it's a goin
to take a mighty long time. That may be so,
I says, but what's time to a damn hog?
                                        Old

Man, smiling
                    Wild Bill, wouldn't you say
this gap is narrow?
                            It's tolerable steep:
I got to look up the chimley to see if
the cows is comin home, and sow my corn
by firin it into the fur hill, and I tie
punkins to the stalks to stop em rollin
off of the slope; to harvest it I jest
shake it down over the rocks: it shucks
itself, it shells itself, all's I do is
rake up the kernels, and stack up the cobs.
This gap's so skinny we lie down to see
sky, and we have to pack the moonlight
out and daylight in, ever mornin.
                            I nod:
I got to get a goose quill, whatever,
pokeberry ink, and write this down.

Old haunts dissolve
under a question's finger;
in the true light
she rises and sets
a pitch pine fire, made vague
by the in and out sun;
the eaves are singing,
wren, redbird, pretty quick quick,
the wood thrush hymns,
and the apple tree answers.

Red ball, in the rising smoke,
breakfast out on the porch,
not much left from last fall,
in yet this spring,
nothing is happening, the grass
goes slow, bees shimmer, dog
lies down under the bed, creek runs
with kids hollering,
as she sings at the loom,
Oh don't you see that lonesome dove.

On the fireboard,
a box of seeds, a bottle
of whiskey, up from the spring house,
buttermilk, bucket of water, drifted
with corn silk, honeysuckle,
white oak chairs around
the crude table, maple bowls;
she sees the birch, shivering,
cloud shadows, blur at the horizon,
and fragments of the rainbow.

Under the easy rain
she brings out and puts away,
returns a kiss, the sun goes to roost
in the peach tree, now dark,

lantern with a busted chimney, light
on the supper, so good,
after the whippoorwill's grace,
talk, of the long gone, and all
that was crazy, get out the guitar
for a rocking chair song.

Oh nothing can annul
our time, once lived;
we were immortal
for this one day:
but we're ready for sleep,
crawl under the hand-me-down quilt
and the smell of the country
after rain; where all did we go,
and then come home; the stars pour in
our narrow window.

old laurels, little creeks
                              The air is sweet
and bitter this morning.
                              Like that story.
This Chickasaw girl was hauled up here by
her old daddy, get away from a white boy
a courtin her. One day dreamin, she seen
this Cherokee man off down in that flat
and shot an arrow, like a grouse will shake
tail feathers, to say Look at me. Not long
afore he's a singin his down below songs,
and they's in love. When the sky got red,
it's a sign to him his people was a hurtin,
she says don't go, and he's so torn till he
hurls off the clift, to nowhere: she prays
to the spirit, and a blast of crosswise
wind blows him up into her lovin arms.
That savin wind is all the time a blowin.
And that's Blowing Rock?
                              Go to the edge.
idea's dizzy
              Ah no.
                              Look over that boulder.
over the clouds and down to the thin ribbon
of a big river: she kisses me
                              Watch this.
handful of dust, over the side: oh look,
it's floating up

On the way back, to the blue mountains, only
white blooms and coral berries, is that fire,
red azaleas, she tags me, Race you acrost,
this clearing, and I love to run, hard when
I'm laughing, the sky is overcast, as I am,

so sudden, I can't turn to look at her,
am I sick, what is that buzzing, ah no,
airplane: I whirl, it's dusk, this world,
oh darling girl, can I walk back, no way,
this luminous world is empty as my arms.

I walked out to the highway, and this old
red pickup let me ride.
                              I look at Leah
Same day, same hour, I went into the wild:
I lived a year in one of your heartbeats.
The open notebook, the quilt, same page,
same folds, like I'd gone back in time.
Ah god, so young: I ever thank Old Man?
Because now words out of the gospel come
floating up like dust over Blowing Rock:
I was a stranger, and ye took me in.
You look up Godel?
                              Out of the country.
Next stop, Roanoke, two minutes.
                                        Oh: pale
already.
              the sun, lighting the sky over
the business center
                              All night: I was lost
in your local color: no train, no ghost
wheels ticking. Is it only hours we've
been shoulder to shoulder? It feels like
always. You're going back?
                              And if I fail,
will you and I, our talk go on, out west?
she smiles
              Down Ocean Blvd.

I make it back, and to the very milepost,
in hope, for talismans, the origin shoes
and a circus dollar; I walk up and down
in the sun without mercy; there's no back
road, and no lover up on Lonesome Ridge:

it gets used up. I smell white clover:
the past enduring; I see the branches of
two firs all twined together, and wish
for roots and a companion. Light shower,
I don't give up, go in to Blowing Rock:

bus station, speckled trout restaurant,
office, hickory furniture, cut off park,
hill cabins up for rent, and looking for?
In a sad cafe, one wall acts as museum,
relics, if anyone cares: in a glass case,

this early American pinhole photograph,
a scrap of paper that had come down all
the years, and not so blurred, so dark,
but I could look into her tender face,
her hair over one eye, oh one more time.

On purgatory mountain, in Canto 27, near
paradise, the morning star burning in love,
the poet met images of doing and not doing,
Leah and Rachel. That summer's allusions,
its twice-told tales, suggest a fiction:
and when it's over? We'll be language that
lasts, on the dark pages, out of the way
of deals and rages, in a mission of words,
where music is sacred, oh till it wells, at
the book's revival, that river, our voices.

Boats sag in toward the anchorage at dusk;
on this absurd wharf, what can I—The blue
mountains: I carry the wilderness inside,
in city, and sprawl, on the bleak streets,
and it's high country. The fair and tender,
who's over that hill, yesterday, yonder:
her southern way showed me how to loosen
into the joy, and if my only forget-me-not
is a crack in my heart, that's where love
leaks out, and in. Like the tide, sheering:
winds are blowing out there, the ocean is
invisibly urged, and the salt seance ended;
over the green revelation, white foam, lace
curtain, closes, a wave of water, nothing.

U. S. Rivers

Route 66

Sign
on the light standard, Lake Shore:
explorers, at the filling station,
river
to river, on
the Pontiac Trail: this way
to the nation of fire,
the unknown country,
Rooks Creek,
the dance pavilion, *the girl I left*

behind among the lilacs,
she was pretty,
tall Dreamland Park
road house *and handsome*: sky-
writing over
the Union Pacific rails
cross over the plains all
the way *she'll marry*
another man down the line,
Chicago to

      United reel
      headlines & song
      I hurry to
      by the strip mine,

      out to bio
      states of *my blue*
      & the corn field,
      eye America,

      Dos Passos, vag,
      thumb up, looking
      for a hitch, on
      the gloryroad.

Illinois, soil
too thick *by the Wabash,*
Ohio, and the Lakes
to plow *such land*:
it sticks to every. . .
get thirsty, suck
a weed, *was never known*
a crawfish hole:
so John Deere took
this old steel saw, and fit

on a bar iron
standard, and timber beam,
westward with sapling root
handles: ah corn,
take care: *your girls and boys*
seed this furrow,
and it's one hundred bushels
an acre: black dirt,
pronounce it Eden, and
the prairie opened.

> On the cold street,
> he has to get
> back to a boy
> walking the dark
>
> Miles on the road,
> memory, that
> gospel, that feel,
> it's in his blood,
>
> that kind of blues,
> and blow his horn,

open or mute:
he has to play

the stars, their flux,
and make, out of
their fire, and his
failing, music.

Between the headwaters:
the discovery
of the interior:
the Spirit of *St. Louis*
woman: and
the gulf: *Stackalee* shooting
at Jack O' Diamonds:
the confluence:
on the Mississippi flyway,
curlew and lark,

from under the hyperbolic
cosine,
over the museum
of westward, sternwheelers
under the bluff,
prairie schooners, *set forward*
by Brush Creek, crosses,
psalms facing east,
done left, the Osage Trail,
and by St. Clair,

100 gallons, 1 gal
at Rose's, white slaves,
in whoopee cabins, *cross*
the Old Wire Road,
lines cut on the gray poles,
weathered, tilting,

the wide bridges burning,
Lewis and Clark
in search *the wide Missouri*
of Sacagawea.

Out of St. Joe,
Johnny, on his
electron horse,
carries symbols,

and juice and his
encryption gun,
circuit riding
into the copper

wilderness, by
relay, switching
at that synapse,
the station, cross

country, in rain
and resistance,
into the speed
of light future.

Oh what is the fireball
on the back road
rolling by the first gunfight,
Springfield:
in the square, Wild Bill Hickok,
in sombrero,
and buckskin, and moccasins,
louder than
a horn a pair of .44
Colt Dragoon pistols

in his belt, backward:
the Missouri spook
light, first seen on
the Trail of Tears: *oh what is*
at the far end,
that rebel scout, looking
to kill him: *sharper than*
Susannah's arms,
the war between the States,
or some damn thing:

a thorn: in the slow July dusk:
not will
o' the wisp, not headlights,
not spirits: —Don't come
any closer, Davis: but he sideways
and draws:
It's one or the other: Wild Bill:
I come
to be perfect in the mountains,
dime mark:

he holes his heart
oh what is longer at
seventy-five yards, who hobbles
to the courthouse
colder: All over, what's the use:
as the fireball
passes *not God's*
he joins the Confederate
ghosts, still fighting for secession
at Wilson's Creek.

Can't help his frail,
quit whiskey, but

he can write it
on a shoe box:

Tennessee can
pen stars over
New Orleans, as
they fade, and look!

he can make that
country boy out
to be the dancing
bear, salvation.

They're driving longhorns
across Red River, on
the old Shawnee Trail:
the five of diamonds, on
the black oak tree:
Pony Johnny's shot
by Quantrill's raiders
Come a ki yi yippee:
up through Indian
Territory, into

the Kansas cow town,
Military Avenue:
Jesse James holds up the bank:
with the Whiz Kids,
Mickey Mantle switch-hits
into Spring River:
lovers, the healing waters,
and the silver horn
band, blowing in the pagoda
yippee yay.

Buffalo Bill's
wild west prairie
exhibition
Rocky Mountain

show. Overture.
Grand procession.
Sioux Indians.
Music. Vaqueros.

Music. The wing
and rifle shot,
Annie Oakley,
shooting double.

And next the tall
scout, avenging
Little Big Horn,
scalpsYellow Hair.

Cowboys, etc.
A last wave of
his hat, adios,
Mister Cody.

To this red dirt
where they death-walked Cherokee,
Chocktaw, Chickasaw,
Creek, and Cheyenne, out
from *the old Red River*
to the Cross Timbers,
where the white steed
that none can pace, with his
mane foam, and his tail fire,
streams *like a bird*,

at liberty, they've come
in tens of thousands:
Open them; they were booming it
for years,
to this run, on
the Unassigned Lands,
on the Cimarron:
the pukes in wagons and
jayhawks on horseback:
till the bugle is noon

and the blue cavalry
lets the frontier
dissolve: after the sooners,
the squatters go
over ditch and wallow,
ram the location stick
into the dust
the damnedest country storm:
centuries of shortgrass, gone
under the plow,

and the black rollers
carrying Oklahoma
back east, and sifting it
into the Atlantic:
the men and women
on the ghost road, refugees:
all they knowed was run.
At noon, wilderness,
sundown, tent city,
in the morning, red dirt.

     I, Sequoyah,
     lame by hunting,
     out looking for

the lost Cherokee

in the far west,
have invented
the alphabet,
to share with you

these syllables
that dance in sun
and that say that
paradise is green.

The pumpjack lifting
Where oh where is oil
in the slow hole:
where you find it: *Come on,*
boys: where lightning strikes:
let's go find the pool,
black gold
rush: under the capitol lawn:
the sucker poles
dipping, and the horse head

bobbing, on the walking beam,
as the bull wheel
turns, by the prime mover:
the automobile
out long 11th Street:
on top of hills:
he gives her gas: *oh where*:
way down under
the graveyard:
in the smoke over Tulsa.

Ford Lincoln

Mercury Chrysler
Plymouth Dodge
Pontiac Tempest

Firebird Vega
Ventura Eldorado
Cobra Torino
Capri Impala

Montego Barracuda
Mustang Maverick
Fury Stingray
Imperial Caprice

Colt Duster
Pinto Buick
Olds Chevrolet
on Route 66.

Coronado, *if*
I ever find
Cibola,
the seven cities of gold:
across the Llano Estacado,
only
pueblos, and that friar's lie,
Quivira,
across the Palo Duro,
only *the yellow*

rose of Pantex:
seventy-two hours
a week, he watches
that there's no breach
in the warheads,
pits, plutonium, over

692

the Ogallala aquifer,
Texas water,
under the prairies,
one thousand centuries.

　　　Amarillo Slim,
　　　that old rounder,
　　　says Open with
　　　anything, play

　　　no limit hold 'em
　　　hands tight only
　　　hard, in a fast
　　　game slow, losing,

　　　ready to quit,
　　　and winning, for
　　　the love of god,
　　　go on playing.

The superhighway *Oh god*
go on took all
the traffic, but not the pueblos:
—No water
in the ditches, bring out
the image *being*
above us of Jesus,
witness this dry,
do what you've done.
Over the Jemez, up

the Rio Grande,
storm banged, beating the corn
down: you lashed us,
for heresy, the hail killing,

hung us, for sorcery,
the fields. *for us*
Bring out the image
of Mary: see what
your boy has done.
Three Tewa shooting fire

out of their hands
told us undo one knot
a day *Bring us*
till the uprising. This
is no longer
San Juan, New Mexico,
it's Ohkay Owingeh,
and up Obsidian,
in a circle of stones,
that holy dirt,

in long lines, dancing,
green spruce, the lightning,
the rattle of seeds,
thunder, we bring *what's*
good down, gone back
to the smoke prayer, ah
Yellow Cloud man,
in love and mercy, rain
on the blacktop,
high weeds, the old motel.

> Billy the Kid,
> looking for meat,
> backing into
> the room: —Quien
>
> hay? in the dark:
> —Who's there? —Who is

it, Pete? —Who are
they, Pete? —That's him,

Pat. —Quien es?
Who's that? —Don't shoot
Maxwell! —Light that
candle, mother.

South, by
the badlands, into the Jornada
del Muerto:
minus twenty minutes: countdown:
the fugitives
from the pueblo revolt, no water,
no wood: the ten-
story tower: the bomb,
at Trinity: *faire is foule*
black lava,

dry lakes: ground zero,
five thirty a.m.
Mountain War Time:
the sky brighter than day-
light *and foule is faire*
as they look back
over the Oscura range,
the fireball, rising,
and the mushroom cloud *hover*
through the fogge

white sands, wavering
under the haze, fallout
and filthie aire: the shock
radius equals
five hundred sixty-four
times t plus the pillar

of fire, to the power,
luminous, red,
So faire and foule a day.
We are downwinders.

The truth, the Army
Air Force made me
lie: Roswell was
not a weather

balloon, cover
story, and not
surveillance, top
secret Mogul,

but a flying
saucer, spying
on A-bomb test,
in the thunder,

crash-landing at
the cliff: alien
bodies, and one
alive, violet

hieroglyphics,
and that strong foil
remembering
its shape: extra-

terrestrials;
read the archive,
Majestic 12,
the government. . .

He left no map: last words:
in search The key's
this paloverde tree,
stripped, arm pointing
away from the rose quartz,
ribbon *of gold*:
I left a number
of clues. Was he raving?
tied to the mesquite
for three days and nights,

Arizona flood:
out of the melted adobe,
five sacks,
in the candlebox, under his
sickbed. Go south
of the Salt River *when*
the truth is told on a line
between the Needle
and the Four Peaks,
behind the Superstitions,

to the lost Dutchman mine:
but vein or cache?
long years Aztecs, saving
silver and gold:
and his Apache *sweetheart vowed*
to show
the shrine, thunder:
the Mexican, rescued
in a brawl, gives him
map and title: to

this desolation:
pine stands on the slopes,
and dry arroyos:
slaves carry it out

of the garden, moons,
into the desert:
they're massacred:
she's killed *in thee my bones*
and he's wiped out:
it's hidden, under dirt,

and stones: Crawl through
a hole, and you can see
the military trail, the sun-
set *shining*,
under a juniper,
where no one looks:
north-sloping canyon,
the trail, the trick, but did
you hear it right? This game:
Chinese whispers.

> In soldier blue,
> she's scouting for
> General Custer,
> Indian campaign,
>
> drinking whiskey,
> cussing like any,
> daring rider,
> shooting like rain:
>
> she catches that
> captain reeling,
> and he calls her
> Calamity Jane.

Under a ridge
north of Tombstone, the slabs

of cedar, all those gone
into Boot Hill,
in an ambush *cold as*
the clay, and horse
bucking, and dynamite blast,
and knifed in back
of the old ice house, shot
through the body

behind the O. K. Corral,
and hanged: *now here*
Indian Charlie,
China Mary, Red River Tom,
the epitaphs fading
in the rain: low
mounds blowing away,
and the grass billowing:
Happy Jack, Dutch Annie,
the fife lowly

but the cowboys
come in across the flat,
read them, remember
Margarita, the dance
hall girl, the Kansas Kid,
in a stampede,
Six Shooter Jim, *the drum*
slowly and make
ballads for the trail, till
the lights go out.

   In skirmishes
   with me, the cold
   soldiers call on
   their saint and say

Geronimo.
At last, our few
against thousands,
worn out, I gave

up my silver
Winchester, my
ivory Colt,
my Bowie knife,

at Skeleton
Canyon. Ah son,
lean in, listen.
I should have never

Kit Carson, *a cowboy*, rides
through Cajon Pass
on the Spanish Trail,
too free, and pacing
by the Arrowhead Springs
hotel, burning,
Christ and the navy gone,
the forest fire,
over and over the Fourth
of July, arson

at the old Infirmary,
where the padre
goes for agua caliente,
catches a girl,
so long desired, *fair maid*
and consecrated,
in white, foretelling: That
you believe me,
the Spirit's sign's
in the heavens: sudden

light, the arrow in fire,
to the west
and California,
golden, beyond: thunder,
quiver, clouds into air:
all down the hill,
out of clear quartz, white sage,
the arrowhead:
good medicine
in *the wild rippling water.*

Los Angeles:
in the type-cast
sunlight, and fake
architecture,

American
Express, I hear
the radio
evangelist

and crazy, down
booming, modern
boulevards, with
sculptural ads,

driving, recite
the hurricane,
sunbathing at
Venice, swimming

to the tempest,
island, ideal.
I'm going grey
at twenty-eight,

in alcoholic
skin: oh all of
this make believe,
the stars behind

walls of mystery,
that silent screen
actress shakes her
tits, cries Apples,

how can I write
the windwrestlers?
My voyages
lover is off

the gangway, to
the speakeasy,
blue ruin all night,
and roughs beat us,

roll us, my blood,
San Pedro street;
I sleep it off
in a Salvation

Army hotel.
To live with Grace
is suicide.
This pink vacuum;

I love the salts,
the sea, its coils,
their enigmas.
As ever, Hart.

They're pitching this story
to the *Magic*
mirror yes-and-no man,
on Cahuenga:
Okay, it's like a cross
between The Big
Sleep and ah Lost Horizon,
what's that line,
going to follow the customs,
call it, In

Old California,
fade in on the outlaw:
. . . *wait for the sun*
to finish us off, dissolve,
and he's sailing, with *My,*
she was yare. . . from
the Cinerama Dome to *Doc,*
we're on the Moon!
This bit player:
Welcome to Shangri-La,

and the girls, *Both pretty,*
and both pretty—
wild: wow, Zorro's saying
to the blonde in
the bathtub, *One, who adores her,*
waits beneath
her window, but the starlet,
all legs, is up
on Sunset, stripping,
uh huh, cut to the chase,

that cartoon mouse,
with a submachine gun,
after the king of rock-
and-roll, *get paid for singin,*

and I mean
box office, *Play it, Sam,*
big finish, *Play*
As Time Goes By, catch it
at Hollywood and Vine,
the next music.

      Past the fan palms,
      the palisades,
      is the ocean
      and the long fetch,

      the wind in winter:
      in the swell, in
      the wave breaking
      in its own shape,

      out for, come to
      a high roller,
      she goes belly
      down on the board;

      as the top combs,
      at the one moment,
      she stands up, lithe
      and bare, sliding

      inside the curl,
      in the green hollow,
      ahead of that
      wild, and riding

      the surf, the surface,
      the absurd foam
      as if born there,
      in joy: I see:

as she touches
the shore, morning,
and from under
her feet, the highway.

.

Larry Beckett

Paul Bunyan	January 1970	December 1977
Chief Joseph	March 1982	March 1987
P. T. Barnum	July 1987	June 1992
Amelia Earhart	July 1993	December 1996
Blue Ridge	January 1998	October 2000
Old California	April 2001	December 2006
U. S. Rivers	January 2007	February 2010
Wyatt Earp	July 2010	December 2013
John Henry	January 2014	December 2016

Portland, Oregon

On the balcony, the moon

8va bassa

So - bre el bal - con, la lu - na, de las no -
bre la tie - rra, es - toy, para las fron -

On the bal - co - ny, the moon in - the
ea - rth, I stand, cut - by

ches blan - cas: a ell - a, le a - rro - jo mis besos, y al - zo u - na can -
tre - ras cor - ta - da; y la - ba - ta ho - la es - ta sin

whi - te nights: to he - r, I kiss my fing - ers, I - - raise a
bor - ders, whe - re the hur - ly bur - ly is - un - e - nd -

1 Am
cion. So -
fin.

song. On the
ing.

2 Am

LARRY BECKETT

Ballad of Mattie

Off of the farm, on- to the lights,
With her shadow hair and her shy way,

that six- teen run- a- way's in his sights.
she let him in; he lost a day.

He's on the trail of this out- law out of
He's on the trail of this out- law but she was

Dodge, east to Fort Scott: in a parlor house, girl of the
dear when she was bought: the stars laid out the common

night, and he was caught.
law, and he was caught.

Acknowledgments

Thanks are due to the audiences and editors who published *American Cycle*.

Readings

1978 *Paul Bunyan* Neighbors of Woodcraft, Portland, Oregon
1981 *Paul Bunyan* Northwest Film and Video Center, Portland
1984 *Paul Bunyan* Artist's studio, Portland
1987 *Chief Joseph* Cassidy's, Portland
1991 from *American Cycle* Wildsage, KZYX radio, Philo, California
1992 *P. T. Barnum* Bradley House, Portland
1993 from *American Cycle* Mendocino Arts Center, Mendocino, California
1997 *Amelia Earhart* Cassidy's, Portland
      Amelia Earhart Burning Rock Gallery, Willits, California
      from *American Cycle* Wildsage, KZYX radio, Philo, California
2000 *Blue Ridge* Contemporary Crafts Gallery, Portland
2009 *Old California* O'Connor's, Portland
2011 *U. S. Rivers* Mark Frethem studio, Portland
2014 *Wyatt Earp* O'Connor's, Portland
2015 *Paul Bunyan*, 4 View Two Gallery, Liverpool, England
      Paul Bunyan, 8 The Yorkshire House, Lancaster, England
      Paul Bunyan, 4 Five Leaves Bookshop, Nottingham, England
      Paul Bunyan, 8, 9 Ledbury Poetry Festival, Ledbury, England
      from *U. S. Rivers:* Ma Rainey Ledbury Poetry Festival
      from *Blue Ridge* SongCircle, KBOO radio, Portland
      U. S. Rivers: Highway 1: choral reading, Portland Actors Conservatory
2017 *Paul Bunyan*, 8, 9 Octopus Literary Salon, Oakland, California
      from *U. S. Rivers* SongCircle, KBOO radio, Portland
      U. S. Rivers: choral reading, Mission Theater, Portland
2019 *John Henry* Destination Universe, Portland

Publications

1989	from *Paul Bunyan*	Northwest Review
1990	from *Chief Joseph*	Galley Sail Review
2007	*Paul Bunyan*, 4	Margie
2015	*Paul Bunyan*	Smokestack Books
2017	from *U. S. Rivers*: Boston, Trenton, Harriet Tubman, Jornada del Muerto	The Recusant
	from *U. S. Rivers*: Amarillo	Militant Thistles
2018	from *Blue Ridge*: Grand Central	Empty Mirror
	Amelia Earhart	Finishing Line Press
2019	from *U. S. Rivers*: Long night	Beatdom Books
2020	*Wyatt Earp*	Alternating Current Press

Sources

U. S. Rivers

1

National Geographic Historical Atlas of the United States. Ron
       Fisher, 2004
Historical Map of the United States. The National Geographic
       Magazine, Cartographic Section, 1953
Our Fifty States. Mark Bockenhauer, Stephen Cunha, 2004
Eyewitness to America: 500 Years of America in the Words of Those
       Who Saw It Happen. Edited by David Colbert, 1997
Eyewitness to the American West: From the Aztec Empire to the
       Digital Frontier in the Words of Those Who Saw It Happen.
       Edited by David Colbert, 1998
A Treasury of American Folklore: Stories, Ballads, and Traditions of
       the People. Edited by B. A. Botkin, 1944
A Treasury of New England Folklore: Stories, Ballads, and
       Traditions of the People. Edited by B. A. Botkin, 1947
A Treasury of Southern Folklore: Stories, Ballads, Traditions, and
       Folkways of the People of the South. Edited by B. A. Botkin,
       1949 (autographed)
A Treasury of Western Folklore. Edited by B. A. Botkin, 1975
The Folk Songs of North America in the English Language. Alan
       Lomax, 1960
American Favorite Ballads: Tunes and Songs as Sung by Pete
       Seeger, edited by Irwin Silber, Ethel Raim, 1961

2

Explore America: America by the Sea. Edited by Alfred LeMaitre,
       1996
Explore America: Wild Kingdoms. Edited by Alfred LeMaitre,
       Elizabeth Lewis, 1996
Explore America: Places of Folklore and Legend. Edited by
       Elizabeth Lewis, 1997
Explore America: Historic Places. Edited by Elizabeth Cameron, 1993
Explore America: Our Living History. Edited by Elizabeth Lewis,
       1996
Explore America: Scenic Highways. Edited by Elizabeth Lewis, 1997

Explore America: Great American Journeys. Edited by Alfred
    LeMaitre, 1996
Explore America: Just Off the Interstate. Edited by Alfred LeMaitre,
    Elizabeth Lewis, 1996
Explore America: Man-made Wonders. Edited by Elizabeth Lewis,
    1997
Wikipedia, the free Encyclopedia. 2007-2010
Route 66: The Highway and Its People. Susan Kelly, 1988
Route 66: The Mother Road. Michael Wallis, 2001

Old California

1
Sketches of Early California: A Collection of Personal Adventures.
        Edited by Donald De Nevi, commentary by Oscar Lewis,
        illustrated, 1971
Life in California: During a Residence of Several Years in That
        Territory, with an Appendix. Alfred Robinson, 1846, 1891
Three Years in California. Walter Colton, 1850
Seventy-Five Years in California. William Davis, 1889, 1929
Monterey Peninsula. Edited by James Delkin, 1946

2
Eldorado or Adventures in the Path of Empire. Bayard Taylor, 1850
Bright Gem of the Western Seas. James Carson, 1852
The Shirley Letters. Dame Shirley, 1855
California Pastoral. Chapters VIII-XIII, Glossary. Hubert Bancroft,
        1888
The Splendid Idle Forties. Gertrude Atherton, 1902
Spanish Arcadia. Nellie Sanchez, 1929
On the Old West Coast. Horace Bell, 1930
Love Stories of Old California. Mrs. Fremont Older, 1940
Adobes in the Sun. Morley Baer, Augusta Fink, 1972
Ohlone Tribe. Mary Boule, 1992
In Few Words: En Pocas Palabras: A Compendium of Latino Folk
        Wit and Wisdom. Jose Burciaga, 1997
Contested Eden: California Before the Gold Rush. Edited by
        Ramon Gutierrez and Richard Orsi, 1998
Intimate Frontiers: Sex, Gender, and Culture in Old California.
        Albert Hurtado, 1999
Love Letters. Larry Beckett and Laura Fletcher, 2003
Consultation with Ignacio Mares. 2004
The Californio Page. Website, Songs Collected by Charles Lummis,
        2004

3
Romeo and Juliet. I, II.ii. William Shakespeare, 1599

Two Years Before the Mast. Richard Dana, 1840
The Old Pacific Capital. Robert Louis Stevenson, 1880
California: An Historical Poem. Alfred Robinson, 1889
American Humor: A Study of the National Character. Constance
        Rourke, 1931
Preface to Life in California. Doyce Nunis, 1969
Introduction to Life in California. Andrew Rolle, 1970
Old Monterey County: A Pictorial History. Robert Johnston, 1970
The Spanish West. Edited by George Daniels, 1976
The Spirit of the Monterey Coast. Frederic Hobbs, 1990
Historical Perspective on a Traditional Mexican Wedding. Cesar
        Plata, 1992
Land of Golden Dreams: California in the Gold Rush Decade, 1848-
        1858. Peter Blodgett, 1999
Items Actually Sold in Joseph Boston's Store in the 1850's. 2000
Panning; American Camp. Three miners, 2000
Cultural History. Point Lobos State Reserve website, 2001
Origins of the First American Cowboys. Chapter 9. Donald Chavez,
        2001

4

A Treasury of American Folklore. Edited by B. A. Botkin, 1944
A Treasury of New England Folklore. Edited by B. A. Botkin, 1947
Random House Spanish-English English-Spanish Dictionary.
        Margaret Raventos, David Gold, 1995
Sunset Western Garden Book. Edited by Kathleen Brenzel, 1995

Paul Bunyan

1
"The Round River Drive." James MacGillivray, Douglas Malloch, 1910, 1914
"Paul Bunyan in 1910." Edward Tabor and Stith Thompson, 1910, 1946
"Legends of Paul Bunyan, Lumberjack." Bernice Stewart and Homer Watt, 1916
Paul Bunyan. James Stevens, 1925
A Treasury of American Folklore. Edited by B. A. Botkin, 1944
Type and Motif-Index of the Folktales of England and North America. Ernest Baughman, 1966

2
Paul Bunyan and His Big Blue Ox. W. B. Laughead, 1914, 1922, 1934
Paul Bunyan. Esther Shepherd, 1924
The Saginaw Paul Bunyan. James Stevens, 1932
Ol' Paul. Glen Rounds, 1936
Paul Bunyan: The Work Giant. Ida Turney, 1941
The Wonderful Adventures of Paul Bunyan. Louis Untermeyer, 1946
Legends of Paul Bunyan. Edited by Harold Felton, 1947
They Knew Paul Bunyan. E. C. Beck, 1956
"The Making of a Myth." P. M. Clepper, 1971
(Paul Bunyan: Last of the Frontier Demigods. Daniel Hoffman, 1983)

3
Songs of the Michigan Lumberjacks. E. C. Beck, 1942
Woods Words: A Comprehensive Dictionary of Loggers' Terms. Walter McCulloch, 1958
Wisconsin Lore: Antics and Anecdotes of Wisconsin People and Places. Robert Gard and L. G. Sorden, 1962
Timber! Toil and Trouble in the Big Woods. Ralph Andrews, 1968

4
American Humor: A Study of the National Character. Constance Rourke, 1931

Holy Old Mackinaw: A Natural History of the American Lumberjack.
Stewart Holbrook, 1938

Davy Crockett: American Comic Legend. Anonymous, 1835-56,
edited by Richard Dorson, 1939

Down in the Holler: A Gallery of Ozark Folk Speech. Vance
Randolph and George Wilson, 1953

John Henry

1
"John Henry: Epic of the Negro Workingman." Negro Workaday
     Songs. Howard Odum and Guy Johnson, 1926
John Henry: Tracking Down A Negro Legend. Guy Johnson, 1929
Black Culture and Black Consciousness: Afro-American Folk Thought
     from Slavery to Freedom. Lawrence Levine, 1977
John Henry: A Bio-Bibliography. Brett Williams, 1983

2
John Henry: A Folk-Lore Study. Louis Chappell, 1933
"The Career of John Henry." Western Folklore. Richard Dorson, 1965
"The John Henry Epic." A Treasury of Afro-American Folklore.
     Harold Courlander, 1976
"If He Asks You Was I Running You Tell Him I Was Flying, If He
     Asks You Was I Laughing You Tell Him I Was Crying:
     Reading John Henry as American History 1870." Gale
     Jackson. Racing & (E) Racing Language: Living with the
     Color of Our Words. Edited by Ellen Goldner and Safiya
     Henderson-Holmes, 2001

3
Blacking Up: The Minstrel Show in Nineteenth-Century America.
     Robert Toll, 1974
The Emergence of Black English: Text and commentary. Edited by
     Guy Bailey, Natalie Maynor, Patricia Cukor-Avila, 1997.
     Recordings: The Library of Congress / American Memory /
     Voices from the Days of Slavery, website
Spoken Soul: The Story of Black English. John Rickford, 2000
I Freed Myself: African American Self-Emancipation in the Civil War
     Era. David Williams, 2014

4
This Old Hammer
"Nine Pound Hammer." Long Steel Rail: The Railroad in American
     Folksong. Norm Cohen, 1981

Shack Rouster
"Sinful Songs of the Southern Negro." Selected Writings: 1934-1997.
　　　Alan Lomax, 2003

Birth
"John Henry of the Cape Fear." Bundle of Troubles and Other Tarheel
　　　Tales. Glasgow McLeod, edited by W. C. Hendricks, 1943

Go Down, Moses
Jubilee and Plantation Songs: Characteristic Favorites. 1887

High John
Mules and Men. Zora Hurston, 1935
Manuscripts of the Federal Writers' Project of the Works Progress
　　　Administration for the State of Florida. Zora Hurston, 1938
"Riddles Wisely Expounded." The Singing Tradition of Child's
　　　Popular Ballads. Edited by Bertrand Bonson, 1976
"The Devil's Nine Questions." Songs and Tunes of the Wilderness
　　　Road. Ralph Smith, Madeline Mitchell, 1999
"Bow Down to the Bonny Broom." MainlyNorfolk.info/John.
　　　Kirkpatrick, 2007

Steam Drill
"Improved Tunneling; Drill." Scientific American, Volume 25 Number
　　　21, 1871
A Treatise on Explosive Compounds, Machine Rock Drills and
　　　Blasting. Henry Drinker, 1883

Daddy Mention
Manuscripts of the Federal Writers' Project of the Works Progress
　　　Administration for the State of Florida. Martin Richardson,
　　　1938

Long John
Afro-American Spirituals, Work Songs, and Ballads. Edited by John
　　　and Alan Lomax, 1941

Outlyers
River Runaways. www.ourstate.com, Philip Gerard, 2011
"Introduction." Slavery's Exiles: The Story of American Maroons.
        Sylviane Diouf, 2014

Signifying
"Tall Tales." Humorous Folk Tales of the South Carolina Negro.
        Edited by Mason Brewer, 1945
"More Tall Tales." American Negro Folklore. Edited by Mason
        Brewer, 1968

Steal Away
Jubilee and Plantation Songs

Breaking Iron
John Henry: A Folk-Lore Study

Cutting Tracks
Stoneman's Raid: 1st US Cavalry Official Report. Official Records,
        Volume 25. Richard Lord, 1863

Three Pigeons
"Meeting President Lincoln." Macmillan's Magazine. Goldwin Smith,
        1865

Colonization
"Address on Colonization to a Deputation of Negroes." Collected
        Works, Volume 5. Abraham Lincoln, 1862

Thirteenth Amendment
"Abraham Lincoln and the Corwin Amendment." Illinois Heritage.
        John Lupton, 2006

Questions
"5 Things You May Not Know About Lincoln, Slavery and
        Emancipation." www.history.com. Sarah Pruitt, 2012

Fremont
"John C. Fremont." wikipedia, 2012

Go Down, Old Hannah
www.worksongs.org 2012

Railroad Bill
The Hurricane's Children, Tales from Your Neck o' the Woods. Carl
        Carmer, 1937
Folk Song and Folk Poetry as Found in the Secular Songs of the
        Southern Negroes. Howard Odum 1911

Polly Ann Fletcher
Annals of Tazewell County, Virginia From 1800 to 1922. John
        Harman, 1922

Courting
"Old-Time Courtship Conversation." Southern Workman. Frank
        Banks and Portia Smiley, 1895

Swannanoa Tunnel
A Treasury of Southern Folklore: Stories, Ballads, Traditions, and
        Folkways of the People of the South. Edited by B. A. Botkin,
        1949 (autographed)

Green River Blues
Black Culture and Black Consciousness. Charley Patton, 1929

Minstrel Show
Essence of Old Kentucky. Containing a Choice Collection of New and
        Popular Songs, Interludes, Dialogues, Funny Speeches,
        Darkey Jokes, and Plantation Wit. George Christy, 1862
Original Pontoon Songster. Being a Collection of New and Original
        Ethiopian Comic and Sentimental Songs, Burlesque Orations,
        Witty Sayings and Conundrums. Johnny Cross, 1867

Zip Coon
Atwill's Music Saloon. Thomas Birch, 1834

John Henry
American Ballads and Folk Songs. Edited by John and Alan Lomax,
        1934
Folk Music of the United States, Album III. Edited by Alan Lomax,
        1942
Afro-American Spirituals, Work Songs, and Ballads
The Folk Songs of North America in the English Language. Alan
        Lomax, 1960

5
Dialogue in American Drama. Ruby Cohn, 1971
Reading Race: White American Poets and the Racial Discourse in the
        Twentieth Century. Aldon Nielsen, 1988
Sight Unseen: Beckett, Pinter, Stoppard, and Other Contemporary
        Dramatists on Radio. Elissa Guralnick, 1995
Theatre of Sound: Radio and the Dramatic Imagination. Dermot
        Rattigan, 2003

Chief Joseph

1

The Surrender Speech. Journal for the Protection of All Beings.
        Chief Joseph, 1877
An Indian's View of Indian Affairs. Chief Joseph, 1879
Hear Me, My Chiefs: Nez Perce Legend and History. Lucullus
        McWhorter, 1952
The Nez Perces. Frances Haines, 1955
The Flight of the Nez Perce. Mark Brown, 1967
Traditional American Indian Literatures: Texts and Interpretations.
        Jarold Ramsey, and others, 1981

2

Days with Chief Joseph. Erskine Wood, 1893, 1970
The Nez Perce Indians. Herbert Spinden, 1908
Yellow Wolf: His Own Story. Lucullus McWhorter, 1940
I Will Fight No More Forever. Merrill Beal, 1963
Saga of Chief Joseph. Helen Howard, 1965
Noon Nee-Me-Poo. Allen Slickpoo and Deward Walker, 1973

3

Sebastopol. Leo Tolstoy, 1855, translated by Frank Miller
Portraits from North American Indian Life. Edward Curtis, 1907-27
Black Elk Speaks. Black Elk and John Neihardt, 1932
Nez Perce Texts. Archie Phinney, 1934
The Earliest English Poems. 1966, translated by Michael Alexander
Nez Perce Grammar. Haruo Aoki, 1970

4

Shaking the Pumpkin: Traditional Poetry of the Indian North
        Americas. Edited by Jerome Rothenberg, 1972
"Indian Speeches." Translated by William Arrowsmith, 1973
A Rumor of War. Philip Caputo, 1977

Wyatt Earp

1
Testimony for the Defense—Statement by Wyatt Earp. 1881, in
    Stephens and Martin
How Wyatt Earp Routed a Gang of Arizona Outlaws. Wyatt Earp
    Tells Tales of the Shotgun-Messenger Service. Wyatt Earp's
    Tribute to Bat Masterson the Hero of 'Dobe Wells. 1896, in
    Stephens
Wyatt Earp. John Flood, 1926
Tombstone: An Iliad of the Southwest. Chapter II-XV. Walter Burns,
    1927
Wyatt Earp: Frontier Marshal. Stuart Lake, 1931

2
Dodge City. Michael Curtiz, director; Robert Buckner, writer, 1939
Frontier Marshal. All Duan, director; Sam Hellman, writer, 1939
Tombstone. William McGann, director; Albert LeVino, Edward
    Paramore, writers, 1942
My Darling Clementine. John Ford, director; Samuel Engel, Winston
    Miller, writers, 1946
Wichita. Jacques Tourneur, director; Daniel Ullman, writer, 1955
Gunfight at the O. K. Corral. John Sturges, director; Leon Uris, writer,
    1957
The Life and Legend of Wyatt Earp. 15 historical episodes. Lewis
    Foster, Frank McDonald, Roy Rowland, Paul Landres,
    directors; Frederick Brennan, writer, 1955-61
Hour of the Gun. John Sturges, director; Edward Anhalt, writer, 1967
Tombstone. George Cosmatos, director; Kevin Jarre, writer, 1993
The American Experience. Wyatt Earp. Rob Rapley, producer, 2010

3
Wyatt Earp Speaks. Edited by John Stephens, 1998
Tombstone's Epitaph. Douglas Martin, 1951 (autographed by the
    author and a relative of Holliday)
Inventing Wyatt Earp: His Life and Many Legends. Allen Barra, 1998
True West. Wyatt Earp: Without a Scratch. Bob Bell, 2001

The Illustrated Life & Times of Wyatt Earp. Bob Bell, 2008

Wyatt Earp. Philip Ketchum, 1956
Gunfight at the O. K. Corral. Nelson Nye, 1960
Wild, Wooly & Wicked: The History of Kansas Cow Towns and the
     Texas Cattle Trade. Harry Drago, 1960
A Treasury of Western Folklore. B. A. Botkin, 1975
Western Words: A Dictionary of the Old West. Ramon Adams, 1981
My Darling Clementine: John Ford, Director. Edited by Robert Lyons,
     1984
Explore America: Wild Kingdoms. Edited by Alfred Le Maitre,
     Elizabeth Leavis, 1996
Wyatt Earp: The Life Behind the Legend. Casey Tefertiller, 1997
Everyday Life in the Wild West. Candy Moulton, 1999
The Six-Gun Mystique Sequel. John Cawetti, 1999
Tombstone's Treasure: Silver Mines and Golden Saloons. Sherry
     Monahan, 2007
www.LegendsofAmerica.com, 2012

4

Revelation: 8. John of Patmos, 96
Lucrece. William Shakespeare, 1594
74, in Shakespeares Sonnets. William Shakespeare, 1609
The Design of Rimbaud's Poetry. John Houston, 1963
The Artistry of Shakespeare's Prose. Brian Vickers, 1968
Shakespeare's Use of Rhetoric, in A New Companion to Shakespeare
     Studies. Brian Vickers, 1971
The Lost Garden: A View of Shakespeare's English and Roman
     History Plays. John Wilders, 1978
Language in Literature. Roman Jakobson, 1987
The Development of Shakespeare's Rhetoric: A Study of Nine Plays.
     Stefan Keller, 2009

P. T. Barnum

1
Struggles and Triumphs: or, The Life of P. T. Barnum, Written by
        Himself. P. T. Barnum, 1855, 1869, 1889, edited by George
        Bryan, 1927
The Talking Machine, Volume 1. Talking Machine Record #TM-
        1887. P. T. Barnum, 1890
The Life of Barnum. P. T. Barnum, 1891
Selected Letters. P. T. Barnum, edited by A. H. Saxon, 1983
Trumpets of Jubilee. Constance Rourke, 1927
Humbug: The Art of P. T. Barnum. Neil Harris, 1973

2
Barnum. M. R. Werner, 1923
The Fabulous Showman: The Life and Times of P. T. Barnum.
        Irving Wallace, 1959
P. T. Barnum: The Legend and the Man. A. H. Saxon, 1989
Barnum's Big Top. Produced by Matthew Collins, 1992

3
The Select Letters of Major Jack Downing. Seba Smith, Charles
        Davis, 1834
Davy Crockett: American Comic Legend. Anonymous, 1835-56,
        edited by Richard Dorson, 1939
Authentic Anecdotes of "Old Zack," I-IV. Herman Melville, 1847
Walden; or, Life in the Woods. Henry Thoreau, 1854
"A Curious Pleasure Excursion." Sketches New and Old. Mark
        Twain, 1875
American Notes. Charles Dickens, 1885
A Treasury of American Folklore. Edited by B. A. Botkin, 1944
A Treasury of New England Folklore. Edited by B. A. Botkin, 1947
"Mathematical Recreations." Scientific American. A. K. Dewdney,
        November 1990

4
A Personal Record. Joseph Conrad, 1912

Remembering. Frederick Bartlett, 1932

Rabelais and His World. Mikhail Bakhtin, 1940, 1965, translated by Helene Iswolsky

Herman Melville: A Critical Study. Richard Chase, 1949

"The Witness," in Dreamtigers. Jorge Luis Borges, 1960, translated by Mildred Boyer and Harold Morland

Charles E. Ives: Memos. Charles Ives, edited by John Kirkpatrick, 1934, 1972

Washington: The Indispensable Man. James Flexner, 1974

The Structure of Human Memory. Edited by Charles Cofer, 1976

A Concise History of the American Republic. Samuel Morison, 1977

Memory Observed: Remembering in Natural Contexts. Edited by Ulric Neisser, 1982

Peterson First Guide to the Birds of North America. Roger Peterson, 1986

American Talk. Robert Hendrickson, 1986

Postmodernist Fiction. Brian McHale, 1987

Ringling Bros. and Barnum and Bailey Circus: 119th Edition Souvenir Program and Magazine. Penny Kar, 1989

Winslow Homer. Kate Jennings, 1990

Amelia Earhart

1
The Fun of It. Amelia Earhart, 1932
Last Flight. Amelia Earhart, 1937
Letters from Amelia. Amelia Earhart, edited by Jean Backus, 1982
Amelia: Pilot in Pearls. Edited by Shirley Dobson Gilroy, 1985
    (autographed)
Amelia, My Courageous Sister. Muriel Earhart Morrissey and Carol
    Osborne, 1987
Still Missing: Amelia Earhart and the Search for Modern Feminism.
    Susan Ware, 1993

2
20 Hrs. 40 Min. Amelia Earhart, 1928
Life. July, 1937
Soaring Wings. George Putnam, 1939
Daughter of the Sky. Paul Briand, 1960
The Search for Amelia Earhart. Fred Goerner, 1966
Winged Legend. John Burke, 1970
Amelia Earhart Lives. Joe Klaas, 1970
Women Aloft. Valerie Moolman, 1981
Amelia Earhart: The Final Story. Vincent Loomis and Jeffrey Ethell,
    1985
Eyewitness: The Amelia Earhart Incident. Thomas Devine, 1987
Lost Star. Patricia Lauber, 1988
Amelia Earhart: What Really Happened at Howland. George
    Carrington, 1989
The Sound of Wings. Mary Lovell, 1989
Amelia Earhart. Richard Tames, 1989
Amelia Earhart: Challenging the Skies. Susan Sloate, 1990
Amelia Earhart: Courage in the Sky. Mona Kerby, 1990
Life. April, 1992
Biography: Amelia Earhart. Produced by Jack Haley, 1992
The Search for Amelia Earhart. Produced by H. Thomas Jones,
    1992
The American Experience: Amelia Earhart. Produced by Nancy

Potter, 1993

"Love of Flying." The First Anthology. Gore Vidal, edited by Robert
     Silvers and others, 1993

3

Richard III. V.iii; Hamlet. IV. vii; A Midsummer Night's Dream. III.ii,
     II.i. William Shakespeare, 1623

Rubaiyat of Omar Khayyam of Naishapur, 44. Edward Fitzgerald,
     1879

The Wonderful Wizard of Oz. L. Frank Baum, 1900

"Zone." Alcools. Guillaume Apollinaire, 1913

"When My Dream Boat Comes Home." Cliff Friend and Dave
     Franklin, 1937

Wind, Sand and Stars. Antoine de Sainte-Exupery, 1939

The Student Pilot's Flight Manual. William Kershner, 1990

Asia/Pacific. Hong Kong Standard. www.hkstandard.com, 7/24/96

Weather Forecast for Local Aviation. Royal Observatory.
     www.info.gov.hk/ro, 7/24/96

4

The Complaint of Rosamond. Samuel Daniel, 1592

Folklore of Shakespeare. F. F. Dyer, 1883

The Second Sex. Simone de Beauvoir, 1949

"The Airplane." Jazz. Henri Matisse, 1947

Elizabethan Poetry. Hallet Smith, 1952

This Fabulous Century: 1930-1940. Edited by Ezra Bowen, 1969

Rhyme and Meaning in the Poetry of Yeats. Marjorie Perloff, 1970

Introduction to The Rape of Lucrece. The Riverside Shakespeare.
     Hallet Smith, 1974

Ghosts. Tim Appenzeller and David Thomson, 1984

Passport to World Band Radio. Edited by Lawrence Magne, 1990

Kids Discover Weather. Edited by Stephen Brewer, 1994

Blue Ridge

1
Appalachian Images in Folk and Popular Culture. 1860-1987,
    edited by W. K. McNeil, 1989
Sacred Formulas of the Cherokees. Myths of the Cherokee. James
    Mooney, 1891, 1900
The Spirit of the Mountains. Emma Miles, 1905
Our Southern Highlanders. Horace Kephart, 1922
An Adventure. Anne Moberly and Eleanor Jourdain, Fourth Edition,
    1931
Bangs, Crunches, Whimpers, and Shrieks: Singularities and
    Acausalities in Relativistic Spacetimes. John Earman, 1995

2
The Carolina Mountains. Margaret Morley, 1913
Cabins in the Laurel. Muriel Sheppard, 1935
The Great Smokies and the Blue Ridge. Edited by Roderick
    Peattie, 1943
"An Example of a New Type of Cosmological Solutions of
    Einstein's Field Equations of Gravitation." Reviews of
    Modern Physics. Kurt Godel, 1949
"A Remark about the Relationship between Relativity Theory and
    Idealistic Philosophy," with Einstein's reply. Albert Einstein:
    Philosopher-Scientist. Kurt Godel, Albert Einstein, edited by
    Philip Schilpp
"Lecture on Rotating Universes." Collected Works: Volume III. Kurt
    Godel, 1949, introduction by David Malament
The Devil's Tramping Ground. John Harden, 1949
Roaming the Mountains. John Parris, 1955
The Meaning of Relativity. Albert Einstein, 1955
The Cherokees. Grace Woodward, 1963
"Paths in universes having closed time-like lines." Journal of
    Physics A (Series 2). U. K. De, 1969
Look Back with Love. Alberta Hannum, 1969
"On the Paradoxical Time-Structures of Godel." Philosophy of
    Science. Howard Stein, 1970

North Carolina Folklore and Miscellany. Horton Cooper, 1972

"On the Contradictions of Time Travel." Scientific American. Martin Gardner, May 1974

The Southern Appalachians. Jerome Doolittle, 1975

Exact Solutions of Einstein's Field Equations. Edited by E. Schmutzer, 1980

Infinity and the Mind. Rudy Rucker, 1982

"Time Travel in the Godel Universe." PSA 1984, Vol. Two. David Malament, 1984

The Eastern Band of Cherokees. John Finger, 1984

Reflections on Kurt Godel. Hao Wang, 1987

Who Got Einstein's Office? Ed Regis, 1987

"A note about closed timelike curves in Godel space-time." Journal of Mathematical Physics. David Malament, 1987

Blue Ridge Range: The Gentle Mountains. Ron Fisher, 1992

Time Machines. Paul Nahin, 1993

"The Quantum Physics of Time Travel." Scientific American. David Deutsch and Michael Lockwood, March 1994

Tribes of the Southern Woodlands. David Thomson, 1994

"In Greenwich Village." New York Times. Mimi Sheraton, 1997

3

The Divine Comedy. Purgatorio, Canto XXX. Dante Alighieri, 1321, translated by Henry Longfellow, 1865

As You Like It. William Shakespeare, 1623, edited by Howard Furness, 1890

"The Vision of the Fountain." Twice-Told Tales. Nathaniel Hawthorne, 1835, edited by Roy Pearce

Lost Horizon. James Hilton, 1933

Grandfather Tales. Edited by Richard Chase, 1948

Holiday. January-May, 1966

Life. July 1, 1966

Appalachian Speech. Walt Wolfram and Donna Christian, 1976

The Birth of Photography. Brian Coe, 1976

Sunset Western Garden Book. Edited by Kathleen Brenzel, 1995

4

Tall Tales of the Southwest: An Anthology of Western and
    Southwestern Humor, 1830-1860. Edited by Franklin J.
    Meine, 1930 (autographed)
"Uncle Davy Lane." Fisher's River. H. E. Taliaferro, 1859, in A
    Treasury of American Folklore. Edited by B. A. Botkin, 1944
Sut Lovingood's Yarns. George W. Harris, 1867
In the Tennessee Mountains. Mary Murfree, 1887
The Time Machine / The Definitive Time Machine. H. G. Wells,
    1895, edited by Harry Geduld, 1987
Sister My Life. Boris Pasternak, 1922, translated by Philip
    Flayderman, 1967
Name This Child. Eric Partridge, 1942
The Jack Tales. Edited by Richard Chase, 1943
A Treasury of American Folklore. Edited by B. A. Botkin, 1944
A Treasury of Southern Folklore. Edited by B. A. Botkin, 1949
    (autographed)
The Lost Steps. Alejo Carpentier, translated by Harriet de Onis,
    1956
"As You Like It." More Talking of Shakespeare. Helen Gardner,
    edited by John Garrett, 1959
Future Perfect: American Science Fiction of the 19th Century.
    Edited by H. Bruce Franklin, 1966
The Heart's Forest: A Study of Shakespeare's Pastoral Plays.
    David Young, 1972
The Poetic Art of Robert Lowell. Marjorie Perloff, 1973
Pasternak. Nils Nilsson, Yury Lotman, Michel Aucouturier. 1959,
    1969, 1970, edited by Victor Erlich, 1978
"Two Aspects of Language and Two Types of Aphasic
    Disturbances," "Marginal Notes on the Prose of the Poet
    Pasternak." Language in Literature. Roman Jakobson, 1987
"An Interview." Collected Prose. Robert Lowell, 1987
Keeping Watch: A History of American Time. Michael O'Malley,
    1990
When We Were Young. Rita Kleinfelder, 1993

Reference

Hammond's New Supreme World Atlas. 1952

American Thesaurus of Slang. Second Edition, A Complete
Reference Book of Colloquial Speech, edited by Lester
Berrey and Melvin Van Den Bark, 1953

Hammond's Pictorial Travel Atlas of Scenic America. E. L. Jordan,
1955

The Folk Songs of North America. Edited by Alan Lomax, 1960

Roget's International Thesaurus. Third Edition, edited by Lester
Berrey and Gordon Carruth, 1962

The Concise Oxford Dictionary of Current English. Based on The
Oxford English Dictionary and Its Supplements. Sixth
Edition, edited by J. B. Sykes, 1976

The New Comprehensive American Rhyming Dictionary. Sue
Young, 1991

Notes

American Cycle

American Cycle, a sequence of long poems inspired by our folklore and past, was written over a period of forty-seven years. Its forms are invented out of the traditions of the language, as appropriate to its subjects. Its styles are deeply connected to American speech: Spanish words loaned from *Old California*, the rough colloquialisms of *Paul Bunyan*, the power of African-American vernacular English in *John Henry*, the bare oratory of *Chief Joseph*, the old west phrases in *Wyatt Earp*, the circus ballyhoo of *P. T. Barnum*, the aviation jargon in *Amelia Earhart*, the backwoods dialect of *Blue Ridge*, and *U. S. Rivers* braids eyewitness history, legends, and old folk songs. Plot, as a literary device, is replaced with life, in varying shapes, and character, with the universe inside. The *Cycle's* themes are love, local mythology, history, justice, memory, accomplishment, time. *I hear America singing, the varied carols. . .* These are texts for performance.

U. S. Rivers

U. S. Rivers is made of what I call braid odes and breath songs, in alternation. The odes are in a stanza of ten lines; each pair of lines is a blank verse line, broken anywhere. They flow, loose as water, and keep a rhythm. The songs are in stanzas of four lines, each line of four syllables. In so few syllables, meaning and music are clearer. The rivers are U. S. highways, and the poem follows Highway 1 from Key West, Florida, state by state, to northern Maine, and Route 66 from Lake Shore, Chicago, to the surf at Santa Monica.

Each ode is made from an American nexus: a place where history, legend, and song mysteriously cross, and all times coexist. For example, the first European to touch what is now the continental United States, Ponce de Leon, came ashore at Cape Canaveral. In the poem, he sees Apollo 11 lift off, as the old song Children Go Where I Send Thee counts down from 12 to 1. These are the three strands of this braid. It's followed by a characteristic song, Jack Kerouac, author of the road, at the end, listening to the wind talking in the Florida pines.

The primary sources for history were the eyewitness accounts compiled by David Colbert in *Eyewitness to America* and *Eyewitness to the American West*; for legend, B. A. Botkin's *A Treasury of American Folklore*, and his treasuries of New England, Southern, and Western folklore; for song, *The Folk Songs of North America*, by Alan Lomax, and the book and recordings, *American Favorite Ballads*, by Pete Seeger. Places were evoked by text and photography in *Just Off the Interstate*, edited by Elizabeth Cameron, with eight other volumes in the *Explore America* series. Details were found in Wikipedia and other internet sites.

The U. S. rivers are followed by a man in a Chevrolet Impala, looking for love, and witnessing the poetry. *American Cycle* opens with *Highway* 1, and closes with *Route 66*.

U. S. Rivers: Highway 1

Florida

Key West: *Oh the cuckoo*
The driver, looking for love, and setting out on the road
> *The Fourth Day of July;*
> *Crawdad*

Off the king's road,
James Audubon, bird watcher

Look, sandpipers: and a green rush,
Columbus discovers America;
Ponce de Leon steps ashore and looks for the fountain of youth;
Apollo 11 lifts off
> *Children, Go Where I Send Thee*

Long night, St. Pete,
Jack Kerouac, author of *On the Road*

Georgia

The sanctuary *Hushabye*
In the Civil War, Jefferson Davis, a northern commander ,
abandons the black refugees, who perish, at Ebenezer Creek;
legend of the lost island in Okefenokee Swamp
> *Hushabye;*
> *Many Thousands Gone*

Back from the late
Ma Rainey, first recorded blues singer
> *See See Rider*

South Carolina

Outside Columbia,

In the Revolutionary War,
with Light Horse Harry Lee, and the Swamp Fox, Francis Marion,
Rebecca Motte sacrifices her home to defeat the British
The Little Turtle Dove

At Snow's Island,

In the Revolutionary War, the American leader, Francis Marion,
the Swamp Fox, talks to a British prisoner

North Carolina

Governor White, gone for supplies,

Governor John White looks for the lost colony, Roanoke;
the Wright Brothers make the first flight;
the legend of Virginia Dare and the white doe
The Two Magicians

On a fire hunt

Daniel Boone, pioneer

Virginia

Six days upriver *Oh*

Pocahontas saves Captain John Smith from Powhatan;
Washington wins the Revolutionary War at Yorktown
Shenandoah

The winter slams

The driver sings a love song

District of Columbia

Grace walks out of

Calvin Coolidge's wife Grace sees Lincoln's ghost n the White House;
Lincoln sees two reflections in the glass and his wife predicts his death;
Lincoln accidentally tears the American flag in half
Marching Through Georgia;

The Star-Spangled Banner

Open fire, Tom
> Jefferson refuses to fight in the Revolutionary War

Maryland

Out at the Highway 17
> Traces of an attack are found by modern builders at Combahee
> Ferry;
> Harriet Tubman, who was enslaved, frees herself,
> founds the underground railroad to liberate other slaves,
> and leads an attack on southern plantations
>> *Michael, Row the Boat Ashore;*
>> *Go Down, Moses;*
>> *Follow the Drinking Gourd*

In Mobtown, with
> H. L. Mencken, journalist, author of *The American Language*

Pennsylvania

In the November frost,
> William Penn signs the first peace treaty with Tammanend
> and the native Americans;
> Jefferson writes the Declaration of Independence, but two southern
> colonies demand that phrases condemning slavery be taken out

Never, says Ben
> Benjamin Franklin invents the fire department

New Jersey

Washington crossing,
> Washington crosses the Delaware in the Revolutionary War;
> after King's assassination, people in Trenton riot;
> a bystander, Harlan Joseph, is killed by police by accident

Dance to the Music. Sly and the Family Stone

Impossible.
Thomas Edison invents the incandescent light

New York

***Come on and hear* The river**
Irving Berlin, actual name Israel Beilin, misspelled Baline, enters
America through Ellis Island, Gull Island to the Lenape tribe,
Oyster Island to the Dutch fishermen
Alexander's Ragtime Band

In your last days,
Stephen Foster, who wrote *Oh! Susanna,* the song of the century,
dies in obscurity
Oh! Susanna

Connecticut

The oldest municipal rose,
The poet Wallace Stevens and the composer Charles Ives were both
insurance men in Hartford
Sea Surface Full of Clouds (poem);
Central Park in the Dark (music)

—Come on in, to
Samuel Clemens' pen name is Mark Twain; his house is in Hartford;
in *Adventures of Huckleberry Finn* a boy escapes an abusive father
with a runaway slave, on a raft on the Mississippi

Rhode Island

After the *we left behind*
Anne Hutchinson believed in empowering women and treating the
native Americans fairly; for this she was banished from the colony
Cape Ann

Out of the grey
> In the slave trade, based in Rhode Island, they sent rum to Africa,
> in exchange for slaves taken to the New World, which sent sugar
> to New England; a pineapple was a sign of a safe return

Massachusetts

Old Solitaire,
> One gull stayed at Boston's wharf for many years;
> John Kennedy found a way out of the Cuban missile crisis;
> Paul Revere alerted the colonists in his midnight ride
> > *Riflemen of Bennington*

Ah, why leaf through
> Herman Melville, author of *Moby-Dick,* was tormented by
> the absence of God

New Hampshire

At the raising,
> A barn raising; Portsmouth ship builders put together John Paul Jones'
> sloop-of-war, The Ranger, first ship to fly the American flag
> > *Blow, Boys, Blow*

He, to windward,
> John Paul Jones engages a British ship in the Revolutionary war

Maine

***You get a line* the Chevy**
> The driver, at the end of the highway, still looking for love,
> heads south and west, to Chicago, and Route 66
> > *Crawdad;*
> > *The Maine Woods.* Chesumcook. 6. Henry Thoreau

Thoreau, floating,

Henry Thoreau, author of *Walden*, floats in a pond in the Maine woods
Walden. 9. The Ponds. Henry Thoreau

Old California

Old California opens with a song written in Spanish, and closes with its translation. Each of the five blank verse sections, Embarcadero, Pueblo, Presidio, Oro, Rancho, rolls through exuberant narrative, allusive dialogue, and variations on song, to an unrhymed sonnet. It's a comedy, less in laughing than in the old sense of leading to joy. Its inspiration was the culture of the Californios, before the Gold Rush, isolated from Mexico and the U.S., independent, centered not on work but dancing, living a paradise on earth.

Monterey as it was is evoked in detail, with the help of *Monterey Peninsula*, by WPA writers, edited by James Delkin for the American Guide Series. In research, preference was given to on the scene reports, in *Sketches of Early California*, edited by Oscar Lewis, with strong anonymous illustrations, *Life in California* by Alfred Robinson, *Three Years in California* by Walter Colton, and *Seventy-Five Years in California* by William Davis. This was extended by *Ohlone Tribe* by Mary Boule, classic histories, as *California Pastoral* by Hubert Bancroft, and *The Shirley Letters* by Dame Shirley, used by Harte and Twain, and contemporary studies, as *Contested Eden: California Before the Gold Rush*, edited by Ramon Gutierrez and Richard Ursi, and *Intimate Frontiers: Sex, Gender, and Culture in Old California*. There were literary models as well: the first act of Shakespeare's *Romeo and Juliet*, and the local color stories in *The Splendid Idle Forties* by Gertrude Atherton. I visited old Monterey during its living history festival, and the Martinez adobe; I heard oral history from three miners in American Camp.

The hero is first glimpsed in Richard Dana's *Two Years Before the Mast*, as a man working as a go-between for incoming merchant ships and the local indians. Like many early settlers, he's a runaway sailor, who long courts a girl of this strange to him place. After asking What is marriage, the poem walks through the worlds of politics, religion, gold digging, till it asks What is love. The language is starred with Spanish loan words, whether adapted, like vamoose from vamos, or adopted, like fiesta. The whole celebrates the culture of California, a country where you can start over among its beauties, and the vanished Californios, who, more than any, knew the art of living.

Paul Bunyan

Paul Bunyan is in a twelve-syllable line, where stress count and position are variable, which is a long-winded variation of the traditional blank verse line, with a sound that's loose and rough. My diction was drawn from American colloquial speech, with its natural poetry; the tall talk of the Davy Crockett almanacs, anonymous 19th-century comic prose pamphlets, was a primary influence, as well as its account in Constance Rourke's *American Humor*. Inside the narrative structure, taken from James Stevens' *Paul Bunyan*, I concentrated on the core tales from lumberjack folklore, rather than later popular elaborations, and I retold them episodically. They're studied in Daniel Hoffman's *Paul Bunyan: Last of the Frontier Demigods*. I loaded the text with American folk motifs from many sources, especially *A Treasury of American Folklore: Stories, Ballads, and Traditions of the People*, by B. A. Botkin.

The poem has no point, only pioneer spirit. It drifts westward, like the loggers, from Maine to Michigan to Oregon. Its flaws and extravagances are intentional violations of European values, in an attempt to work by an independent American aesthetic. By classical standards, the reader ought to look through the text to the idea, but in *Paul Bunyan* the words call attention to themselves, like those bragging backwoods men, or self-advertising Las Vegas neon architecture.

John Henry

John Henry is a play for voices. His life and death in Virginia are told in a four-beat line, in five acts, unfolding inside the steel-driving contest with the steam drill: growing up on an iron plantation; freeing himself, with the help of other runaways; meeting with Lincoln, in the White House, who proposed expatriating blacks to Central America; courting a Virginia girl in the hills above where he works; racing the steam drill at Big Bend Tunnel. Essentially all of the poem is written in African-American Vernacular English, which is not only not a substandard form of English, but a language with its own rules, and a syntax of power and immediacy.

Principal sources include, for the story, *John Henry: Tracking Down A Negro Legend*, by Guy Johnson, and *John Henry: A Bio-Bibliography*, by Brett Williams, and, for the language, *Voices from the Days of Slavery*, Library of Congress recordings, and *Spoken Soul: The Story of Black English*, by John Rickford. As for the history, how can there be a history of a people denied the alphabet? This was addressed in a book that revolutionized the writing of history, *Black Culture and Black Consciousness: Afro-American Folk Thought from Slavery to Freedom*, by Lawrence Levine. The answer was that much could be divined from oral tradition, including folk tales, like High John the Conquer, Daddy Mention, and Railroad Bill, and songs, like the jubilee, Go Down, Moses, gospel, Steal Away, work songs, This Old Hammer, and Long John, blues, Swannanoa Tunnel, and Green River Blues, and the ballad, John Henry, all of which appear in the text.

American racism is faced in a series of revelations. There were no slaves, only people called slaves. In the wilderness, there were communities of armed resisters, known as the maroons. Many people didn't wait for emancipation, but freed themselves. Abraham Lincoln supported a constitutional amendment that would make slavery "express and irrevocable," and the Emancipation Proclamation didn't actually free anyone. Love understands that our blood is irretrievably mixed. It's not so that business is business: business is hammer men, and shakers.

Chief Joseph

Chief Joseph is in a four-beat line, where syllable count is variable, which is a loose variation of the Old English stress meter, with a sound that's primitive and halting. The poem continues my fascination with pre-literate materials: its style is derived from studies of actual speech, which is paratactic rather than syntactic, that is, without coordination or subordination, and whose discourse is interrupted by qualification and digression. There is a kind of poetry in its repetitions and ellipses. This style at times tries to rise to the level of oratory: Chief Joseph's surrender speech, ending, "From where the sun now stands I will fight no more forever," is widely known. William Arrowsmith's translations of Native American speeches, especially that by Chief Seattle, were a primary influence.

I relied on Mark Brown's *The Flight of the Nez Perce*, and consulted many other sources, including L. V. McWhorter's indispensable transcriptions of native accounts, *Hear Me, My Chiefs! Nez Perce History and Legend*. Other texts include the overview *The Nez Perces: Tribesmen of the Columbia Plateau*, by Francis Haines, and the study of a myth in *Traditional American Indian Literatures: Texts and Interpretations*, by Jarold Ramsey and others.

The narrative structure is double: scenes from the war of 1877, the last Indian uprising, are told by an anonymous Nez Perce historian, from the point of view of Leapfrog, the brother of Chief Joseph, whose real name was Thunder Rolling in the Mountains. These alternate with scenes in a lodge on nights between battles, where the chief tries to hand down the stories of his life, his people's ways, their love of this world, and the war's beginnings, to his twelve-year-old daughter, Sound of Running Feet.

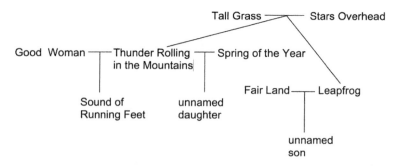

War sections are in the present tense, which is overwhelmed by sensation and action; talk sections are in the past tense, which imposes significance and order. The poem does not explain itself, and its consequent strangeness is only slowly dispelled: I wanted the reader to feel like a settler coming up against an unknown culture, so that the poem enacts its own subject.

Wyatt Earp

Wyatt Earp is his life in Tombstone, a natural five-act tragedy: the western zone, rise of the outlaws and hero, the showdown, fall of the outlaws and hero, the vendetta ride. The poem's style comes from love and study of William Shakespeare and William Faulkner. Analysis of Shakespeare's prose showed a way to replace the loss of the repetitions of meter in prose poetry with the repetitions of rhetoric: syntax, parison; words with words between, ploce; words at the beginnings of phrases, anaphora. Dialogue with description is without punctuation, as in memory passages in *The Sound and the Fury*, for immediacy and poetry. Coexisting spaces as in Arthur Rimbaud's "Villes I" are a setting for myth. Words and phrases from the old west turn to natural metaphors.

I told Wyatt Earp's story out of his own words, where possible: written testimony read at a preliminary hearing after the gunfight, in *Wyatt Earp Speaks*, edited by John Stephens, and original newspaper articles in *Tombstone's Epitaph*, by John Martin; articles years later for the San Francisco Examiner, in Stephens; interviews with biographers decades later, including Stuart Lake, who wrote the remarkable *Wyatt Earp: Frontier Marshal*. Out of that book, Hollywood generated the myth, in nine films and a tv series, inaccurate but cinematic, including "My Darling Clementine," directed by John Ford. I consulted the best modern biography, *Inventing Wyatt Earp: His Life and Many Legends*, by Allen Barra, the reconstruction of the O. K. Corral shootout in an issue of True West magazine, *Wyatt Earp: Without a Scratch*, edited by Bob Bell, and the accompanying *The Illustrated Life & Times of Wyatt Earp*, by the same author. Facts were checked in the definitive biography, *Wyatt Earp: The Man Behind the Legend*, by Casey Tefertiller.

Many accounts fail by leaving out the women: Urilla Sutherland, his first wife; Mattie Blaylock, his common law wife; Sadie Marcus, the love of his life. Other ways to fail are to indulge in the pleasures of iconoclasm, or rely on the slander of those he defeated or their descendants. Wyatt Earp was a man of his word, committed to the law, who faced his father, armed mobs, assassins, and, as I have his companion Doc Holliday say, he walked right in. At the same time, he believed in peace, and did all he could to avoid violence. His friend Bat Masterson said, "The story of Wyatt Earp is the story of the west."

P. T. Barnum

P. T. Barnum is in blank verse is loosely varied, and the text includes passages of prose, dialogue, free verse, and song; this variety is to entertain. Its diction is tart and plain New England speech, influenced by Barnum's extensive writings and the Jack Downing letters, originated by Seba Smith, which is interrupted by advertising hullabaloo, and invaded toward the end by circus hyperbole and slang. Subliterary material was an inspiration: broadsides, handbills, circus banners and posters, which Barnum called "home-made poetry," and which were the beginnings of modern advertising.

Based on Barnum's memoirs, it's a memory poem: cognitive science asserts that we take memory traces, and patch and square them, till they're more invention than recollection. It's a book of variations on recall: remembering only in fragments, remembering and then discovering it never happened, building a memory up, losing a memory, detail by detail.

My primary source was George Bryan's two-volume edition of *Struggles and Triumphs; or, The Life of P. T. Barnum, Written by Himself*, first published in 1854, and his letters and biographies were important, including Neil Harris' study *Humbug: The Art of P. T. Barnum*, and Constance Rourke's essay in *Trumpets of Jubilee*. The poem is infused with down east folklore, found in *A Treasury of New England Folklore: Stories, Ballads, and Traditions of Yankee Folk*, by B. A. Botkin. Our past is present to us in the mind, and so the narrative is not chronological, but spatial; notebook entries whirl around central themes, his passions: something for nothing, deals, love, hoaxes, acting, scrapes, ballyhoo, ads, writing. These are followed by a diary of bankruptcy, death to a business man, and an interior monologue resurrection as a circus manager. Barnum was a clerk, country store proprietor, newspaper editor, landlord, traveling circus manager, salesman, American Museum owner, impresario, farmer, real estate speculator, magazine editor, author, manufacturer, temperance advocate, lecturer, state representative, congressional candidate, mayor, philanthropist, and three-ring circus boss.

Postmodern techniques seemed to come naturally out of his many-world life: Bakhtin's carnivalized literature was appropriate, where alien genres—prose stories, dramatic scenes, folk songs, instructions, business contracts, puzzles, newspaper articles, speeches, handbills, letters, interviews, sales figures—all interrupt the primary blank verse text, and styles shift constantly without transitions. Structures I studied in Brian McHale's *Postmodernist Fiction* include Conrad's levels, Pynchon's demystifications, Joyce's lists, Beckett's negations, Marquez' magic, Simon's self-embedding, Nabokov's exhibitionism, Gass' space and simultaneity, and Borges' alternatives and authorial intrusion. These act to fuse the themes of memory, wheeling and dealing, and show biz, where appearances are deceiving. In this book, where everything is quantified, at the end, the poem splits into street pageant, side show, and big top, running in parallel across the page, creating three rings for the bewildered and I hope dazzled reader.

Amelia Earhart

Amelia Earhart is in the old complaint form, from Renaissance England, as in Samuel Daniel's *The Complaint of Rosamond*, and William Shakespeare's *Lucrece*. In it, the ghost of a woman appears and tells the story of her fall. The convention was the rhyme royal stanza, ababbcc: in my poem, the ghost condemns false approaches to her life in 7-line blank verse stanzas, and the inconclusive music of slant rhyme starts when she counters with the real story. The "iambic pentameter" line is continually varied, by dropping the first syllable, or transformed by dropping the first two.

AE, whose fall was literal, out of the skies, haunts the newspaper, as from year to year disappearance theories are laid out. In the poem, the ghost is in a rage because all the attention is on her death, and not her life. She thought that our culture's making such a big deal out of the death of a flyer when it was a woman was a sign of its all-pervading unfairness to women. Simone de Beauvoir's *The Second Sex* showed me how to stay clear of the male myths, which are tired images, no good for poetry, and concentrate on realities.

My primary sources were Amelia Earhart's own well-written books *The Fun of It* and *Last Flight*, and especially the evocative biography *My Courageous Sister*, by Muriel Earhart Morrissey, and Shirley Dobson Gilroy's charismatic anthology *Amelia: Pilot in Pearls*. The poem is studded with references to a generation of women flyers, as recounted in Valerie Moolman's *Women Aloft*. Amelia Earhart is a self-liberating woman; this is explored in the context of the Thirties in Susan Ware's contemporary study, *Still Missing: Amelia Earhart and the Search for Modern Feminism*.

The poem is a broadcast on the frequency of her last transmission: the Radio Hong Kong news is interrupted by the ghost. In the extended prologue, she recounts and rejects versions of her last flight—the Hollywood movie, in which she dies as a spy; the crackpot theory, in which she survives and comes back to America in disguise; the definitive biography, in which she drowns. Her own rendition is an interior monologue through the twenty hours of the last flight, punctuated by the actual radio traffic. Whenever necessary, she concentrates on the work of flying, then drifts into images of her life, in a rough chronology. She conjures her childhood on the banks of the Missouri, love of horses and the aeroplane, first flight and solo, first altitude record, celebrity and reluctant marriage, Atlantic and Pacific solos, Mexican flight, various crackups, and her 1937 round-the-world flight, up to the last moment. Memories are embedded in memories, and take different shapes— voice, letter, photograph, lecture, list, logbook. The current hit song When My Dreamboat Comes Home runs through her head, the lyrics misremembered in a way that shows her freedom of spirit. I hope the poetry of airplanes comes through everywhere.

Blue Ridge

Blue Ridge flows from songs and ten-line free verse lyrics, to five-line blank verse narrative stanzas, to blank verse dialogue. Its first impulse was in a forgotten year, north Oregon coast town, little museum, glass case, and a photograph on loan of a woman from the past, lovely, with a modern look, and seeing her I felt the mystery of living in time. I read about a novel where, as the hero goes into the interior, it gets more primitive, as though he were going back in time, and inspired by the southern Appalachians, that nexus of the Cherokees and American folk songs, in whose isolation time stands still, I devised the story.

The poem is a pastoral, best defined, in David Young's *The Heart's Forest: A Study of Shakespeare's Pastoral Plays*, by its "tensions and contrasts—between court and country, active and contemplative, fortune and nature, complex and simple," as well as our urban present and rural past. Pastoral, unlike history, comedy, and tragedy, has been submerged since Renaissance England, though science fiction can be seen as a contemporary version. In island fiction, a character goes to a place hard to get to and returns from it changed. If romance is added, courtship on that place's terms, then disparate genres may be seen to vary this one topos: fabulous voyage, in Odysseus and Nausikaa; classic pastoral romance in Longus' *Daphnis and Chloe*; pastoral romance, in Shakespeare's *As You Like It*; exotic romance in Pierre Loti's *Tahiti*; local color, in Mary Murfree's *In the Tennessee Mountains*; children's literature, in L. Frank Baum's *The Wonderful Wizard of Oz*; science fiction, in H. G. Wells' *The Time Machine*; lost world, in James Hilton's *Lost Horizon*; postmodern love, in Alejo Carpentier's *The Lost Steps*. This poem embodies this fusion of genres, avoiding facile exoticism by having the island be the familiar southern Appalachians.

The unnamed hero, an image of myself young, undergoes time travel, as he goes into the back country, where he stays with the old man, who may be an image of myself later, and the poem is a meditation on living in time. Many sources were consulted. The mathematical physics of time travel, which centers on Godel's solution of Einstein's field equation, is studied in John Earman's *Bangs, Crunches, Whimpers, and Shrieks:*

Singularities and Acausalities in Relativistic Spacetimes, its experience in *An Adventure*, by C. A. E. Moberly and E. F Jourdain. The great Cherokee love ode, as well as their language and culture, were found in James Mooney's *Myths of the Cherokee* and *Sacred Formulas of the Cherokees*. I discovered Blue Ridge life in *Appalachian Images in Folk and Popular Culture*, edited by W. K. McNeil, and the classic *The Spirit of the Mountains* by Emma Miles and *Our Southern Highlanders* by Horace Kephart. I tried to render the poetry of the Appalachian dialect with accuracy.

I chose the name Rachel, and alluded to Hawthorne's fantasy The Vision of the Fountain, from *Twice-Told Tales*, then found her name in it. After I'd come up with the name Leah, I found them both in Canto XXVII of Dante's *Purgatorio*. The story of the lover, who fails, who is redeemed, is mine.

U. S. Rivers: Route 66

Illinois

Sign
The driver
The Girl I Left Behind

United reel
John Dos Passos
My Blue Heaven

Illinois, soil
John Deere
El-a-noy

On the cold street,
Miles Davis
Kind of Blue

Missouri

Between the headwaters:
Stackalee, Meriwether Lewis, William Clark
Lewis and Clark Journals;
St. Louis Blues;
Stackalee;
Shenandoah

Out of St. Joe,
Johnny Fry

Oh what is the fireball
Wild Bill Hickok, Susannah Moore, Davis Tutt
The Devil's Nine Questions

Can't help his frail,
Tennessee Williams

Kansas

They're driving longhorns
Johnny Fry, Quantrill's raiders, Jesse James, Mickey Mantle
The Old Chisholm Trail

Buffalo Bill's
Buffalo Bill Cody, Annie Oakley, Yellow Hair

Oklahoma

To this red dirt
Trail of Tears, land rush, dust bowl
Ogallaly Song

I, Sequoyah,
Sequoyah

The pumpjack lifting
oil drillers
The Paw-Paw Patch

Ford Lincoln
drivers

Texas

Coronado, *if*
Francisco Coronado, Pantex plant
The Yellow Rose of Texas

Amarillo Slim,
Amarillo Slim: Thomas Preston

New Mexico

The superhighway *Oh god*

Tewa people
The Text of the Raingod Drama

Billy the Kid,
Billy the Kid: William Bonney, Pete Maxwell,
Pat Garrett, Carlita Maxwell

South, by
pueblo uprising, Trinity: atom bomb test
Macbeth. I. i, iii

The truth, the Army
witness, extraterrestrial crash, Majestic 12 committee

Arizona

He left no map: last words:
Jacob Waltz, Ken-tee
Lousy Miner

In soldier blue,
Calamity Jane: Jane Canary

Under a ridge
Boot Hill
Streets of Laredo

In skirmishes
Geronimo

California

Kit Carson, *a cowboy*, rides
Kit Carson, Arrowhead Springs, San Bernardino
The Wild Rippling Water

Los Angeles:

Hart Crane

They're pitching this story
movie makers
> *The Mark of Zorro;*
> *In Old California;*
> *The Outlaw,*
> *The Philadelphia Story;*
> *Destination Moon;*
> *Lost Horizon;*
> *The Big Sleep;*
> *Viva Zapata;*
> *Loving You;*
> *Casablanca*

Past the fan palms
The driver, a surfer

Past Titles
Running Wild Stories Anthology, Volume 1
Running Wild Anthology of Novellas, Volume 1
Jersey Diner by Lisa Diane Kastner
The Kidnapped by Dwight L. Wilson
Running Wild Stories Anthology, Volume 2
Running Wild Novella Anthology, Volume 2, Part 1 & 2
Running Wild Novella Anthology, Volume 3, Books 1, 2, 3
Running Wild Stories Anthology, Volume 3
Running Wild's Best of 2017, AWP Special Edition
Running Wild's Best of 2018
Build Your Music Career From Scratch, Second Edition by Andrae
Alexander
Writers Resist: Anthology 2018 with featured editors Sara Marchant
and Kit-Bacon Gressitt
Frontal Matter: Glue Gone Wild by Suzanne Samples
Mickey: The Giveaway Boy by Robert M. Shafer
Dark Corners by Reuben "Tihi" Hayslett
The Resistors by Dwight L. Wilson
Legendary by Amelia Kibbie
Christine, Released by E.a. Burke
Open My Eyes by T. E. Hahn
Turing's Graveyard by Terence Hawkins
Running Wild Anthology of Stories, Volume 4

Upcoming Titles
Running Wild Novella Anthology, Volume 4
Recon: The Anthology by Ben White
The Faith Machine by Tone Milazzo
Tough Love at Mystic Bay by Elizabeth Sowden
Gaijin by Sarah Sleeper
Magpie's Return by Curtis Smith

Running Wild Press publishes stories that cross genres with great stories and writing. Our team consists of:

Lisa Diane Kastner, Founder and Executive Editor
Barbara Lockwood, Editor
Cecile Sarruf, Editor
Peter Wright, Editor
Rebecca Dimyan, Editor
Benjamin White, Editor
Andrew DiPrinzio, Editor
Amrita Raman, Operations Manager
Lisa Montagne, Director of Education and Marketing

Learn more about us and our stories at www.runningwildpress.com

Loved this story and want more? Follow us at www.runningwildpress.com, www.facebook/runningwildpress, on Twitter @lisadkastner @RunWildBooks, Instagram at running.wild.press

CPSIA information can be obtained
at www.ICGtesting.com
Printed in the USA
JSHW030016060621
15611JS00002B/3